The Catholic Reformation

The Catholic Reformation provides a dynamic and original history of this crucial movement in early modern Europe. Starting from the late middle ages, it clearly traces the continuous transformation of Catholicism in its structures, bodies and doctrine. Charting the gain in momentum of Catholic renewal from the time of the Council of Trent, it also considers the ambiguous effect of the Protestant Reformation in accelerating the renovation of the Catholic Church.

This book explores how and why the Catholic Reformation occurred, stressing that many moves towards restoration were underway well before the Protestant Reformation. The huge impact the Catholic renewal had, not only on the papacy, Church leaders and religious ritual and practice, but also on the lives of ordinary people – their culture, arts, attitudes and relationships – is shown in colourful detail.

Ranging across the continent and beyond, *The Catholic Reformation* is an indispensable new survey which provides a wide-ranging overview of the religious, political and cultural history of the time.

Michael A. Mullett is Senior Lecturer in History at the University of Lancaster.

The Catholic Reformation

Michael A. Mullett

London and New York

First published 1999
by Routledge
11 New Fetter Lane, London EC4P 4EE

Simultaneously published in the USA and Canada
by Routledge
29 West 35th Street, New York, NY 10001

Routledge is an imprint of the Taylor & Francis Group

Typeset in Baskerville by Routledge
Printed and bound in Great Britain by Biddles Ltd,
Guildford and King's Lynn

British Library Cataloguing in Publication Data
A catalogue record for this book is available from the British Library

Library of Congress Cataloguing in Publication Data
A catalogue record for this book has been requested

ISBN 0–415–18915–2
ISBN 0–415–18914–4 (hbk)

For Austin Woolrych, who encouraged

Contents

Preface

This book offers a study in continuity of the transformation of Catholicism in early modern Europe. For much of the time I shall be emphasising an enduring tradition of reformism in the Catholic Church and stressing the way that aspirations towards religious reform found in late medieval Catholicism were strongly endorsed and affirmed in the Catholic Reformation that arose from the sixteenth century onwards. However, and while emphasising these continuities – stress on which has endowed this book with its title, *The Catholic Reformation* (rather than the perhaps more traditional *Counter-Reformation*) – I am also bound to acknowledge the extent to which my 'Catholic Reformation' was also a response to the Protestant one. The Protestant Reformation inaugurated by Martin Luther (1483–1546) was indeed such a titanic movement that its effect must be taken into full consideration in any account of the transformation of Catholicism in early modern Europe, a process that was largely set in motion by the Council of Trent (1545–63).

Luther's movement of protest and reform arose out of a widespread aspiration in favour of renovation within Western Christianity in the late middle ages. Though forced out of the Church he had initially – between about 1517 and 1520 – aimed to cleanse, Luther had a deep impact on its amelioration, in three areas: first, the inculcation of a sense of the urgency in Catholic minds of the need for reform, especially so as to avert what was seen as divine wrath in the form of the new schism in the Church that opened up from around 1521; second, an awareness, again amongst Catholics, of the need to give expression to reformist criticism of the abuses – especially the financial abuses – of the Catholic Church to which Luther drew attention in such works as *The Babylonian Captivity of the Church* (1520); and, third, responsiveness to the emphasis on the redemptive indispensability of divine grace which Luther himself inherited from the theological tradition of the early Church Father St Augustine (354–430) and, beyond him, from St Paul (d. AD 69).

George Yule writes: 'Catholics…[including] speakers at the Council of Trent, even if they did not offer positive assessments of Luther's teaching, could…see God chastizing the [Catholic] church through Luther'. He adds:

Luther has long been a theologian for Roman Catholics, though this has seldom been acknowledged. For example although some of the disciplinary reforms at the Council of Trent may have been thinkable apart from Luther – for example, the dissociation of almsgiving from indulgences, provision for proper education and discipline of the clergy, the crucial requirement that bishops be pastors of but one diocese and that they reside in it – it is quite unlikely that they would have been enacted without Luther's prophetic exposure of the harm done the church by the lack of such reforms. Luther's central doctrinal concern, the doctrine of justification by faith through grace, and its corollary, the unfreedom of the sinner to do anything for justification apart from the liberating grace of Christ was unquestionably heard and appropriated by Trent, to be sure in its own idiom.

Yule continues: 'One cannot say...that Luther was not a theologian for the Council of Trent....At Trent no less a person than the future Pope Urban VII [Giambattista Castagna, 1521–90] had to point out that Luther and Calvin taught many things that were true'.[1]

Thus, while much of the emphasis in this book is on the long-term continuities of the Catholic reform dynamic, which include the close reliance of the Council of Trent on fifteenth-century Church councils, as well as a discernible momentum towards papally directed reform going back to 1417, along with an emergence of episcopal and diocesan renewal traceable well back into the fifteenth century – I cannot but also be aware of the causal and stimulative link between, on the one hand, Luther's movement of protest and renewal and, on the other, the acceleration and intensification of a reformist upsurge within the Catholic Church in the sixteenth century and on into the early modern period.

There are features of early modern (not to say of modern) Catholicism that today's 'progressive' or 'liberal' Catholic might well deplore. The institution whose overhaul I attempt to describe in the pages that follow was heavily authoritarian in its structures, and male-dominated in its personnel and governance. These plain facts have two implications for the historian's approach to this subject. First, the authoritarianism of the early modern Catholic Church means that focus has to be directed heavily – whether we like it or not – on those in command of the institution and, indeed, on those with the power to bring about its transformation – popes, bishops, heads of religious orders, and so on. If such a focus creates a sense in this book of an old-fashioned historiography, dwelling on the role in history of 'great men' (and not, on the whole, 'great women'), that arises of necessity from the power structures of the institution I study. Despite much exciting recent research into topics such as the interaction of Catholic reform with popular culture, in the end the very topic I have chosen here to write about may have a great deal that is inherently 'old-fashioned' in its bedrock. This is certainly the case with regard to the absence, for much of the time and in key areas, of an active and positive role for women in reformed early modern Catholicism. The vital institutions – the Council of Trent, the papacy and its administration, most of the religious orders, including, of course, the

Jesuits, as well as the episcopate and the parish priesthood – were exclusively male in composition: a chapter about the Council of Trent is an essay on a male conference. That said, there is within the period and topic I endeavour to cover such an inherent greatness in the role of women of the like of the Spanish Teresa of Ávila (1515–82) and the English Mary Ward (1585–1645), such an unmistakable importance in the contributions of female religious orders, especially as they strove to combine male-imposed requirements of enclosure with the practicalities of active apostolate, such a prominence of the work of women in keeping alive the underground Catholic Church in the Dutch Republic, such a surpassing vigour and beauty in the spirituality of female religious authorship in the Spanish Netherlands – to warrant treatment of at least these features of a 'female Catholic Reformation'.

The research and writing of this book were made possible by the generous sabbatical leave provisions of the University of Lancaster and by the kindness and support of colleagues there, including successive heads of the History Department, Ruth Henig, Eric Evans and Steve Constantine, as well as our Director of Research, Gordon Phillips, my appraiser David Shotter and Ghil O'Neill. Jeremy Black and Richard Greaves have strongly encouraged all my efforts. I offer the dedication of this work to Austin Woolrych who has given me, and many other historians, inspiration and encouragement over many years.

I have benefited from conversations with, among others, Bishop Brian Foley, Christopher Black, Andrew Jotischky, Kurt Villads Jensen, Harro Höpfl, Paolo Rossi, Patrick Sherry, Deborah Sawyer, Emma Riley, Laurence Lux, Paula Bessa, and Anne Parkinson. Edward Vanhoutte very kindly provided research material from Belgium. Lancaster University Library staff have been, as always, a reservoir of swift and efficient courtesy and I am particularly grateful to Thelma Goodman and her most helpful staff in Inter Library Loans and to John Illingworth, David Barron, Lindsay Newman and Tim Hoare. This book could hardly have been attempted without the resources of the Talbot Library in Preston, recently founded by Bishop John Brewer. There I have spent many happy hours in study, assisted by the friendship, good humour, unfailing assistance and hot tea provided by Fr Robbie Canavan, Charles Miller and Judith Swarbrick.

In writing this book I have had the benefit of the expertise and the constant and cheerful encouragement of Heather McCallum and Kate Hopgood of Routledge. I should like also to thank a group of scholars who previewed my project and who carefully and positively encouraged my efforts.

I have gained enormously from discussing the ideas in this book with my wife Lorna who provided wise and helpful guidance, as well as indispensable computer assistance. Gerard, James and Rhiannon Mullett have given me steady support, as have my beloved family in South Wales. My brother may enjoy the dating of this book, on the feast of St Cornelius, 1998.

Michael Mullett
Lancaster

1 'Reform in head and members'

The medieval background of the Catholic Reformation

A traditional view of the reinvigoration of Catholicism that got under way from the 1540s onwards is that at that juncture the Church was shaken by the impact of the Protestant Reformation out of apparently almost total torpor to rid itself of chronic abuses: the phrase 'Counter-Reformation' sums up a view of a defensive, as well as aggressive, and somewhat delayed, reaction to Protestantism, without whose challenge the Catholic Church could hardly have revived itself out of its own depleted moral and spiritual resources. Such a view can be traced in a number of surveys. For instance, in his textbook, *Renaissance and Reformation*, V. H. H. Green wrote, 'Headed by non-reforming Popes, whose policy was dictated by family and secular interests, the Catholic Church might well have demanded a miracle if it was to be saved from…Protestant aggression'. Green went on to trace the origins of the Catholic response to Protestantism to a stimulus operating within the Church only from the time of Luther's protest – the Oratory of Divine Love, founded in around 1517. The author of another textbook, Harold J. Grimm, while acknowledging the medieval roots of the sixteenth-century Catholic renewal, nevertheless saw it as an 'amazing revival', triggered 'about the middle of the sixteenth century', in a 'defensive' Catholic Church that had so far 'showed few signs of spiritual vigor'. H. O. Evennett also pointed to the defensive nature of the Catholic revival as a reaction initiated within the sixteenth century to the Protestant challenge:

> By the Counter-Reformation is…meant the long and difficult process by which, after the unexpected shock of the Reformation, the old church underwent a spiritual revival and an administrative renovation, putting her own house into a better order and deploying her rejuvenated forces against her assailants.[1]

Against a view that the early modern revival in Catholicism had its genesis in a defensive reaction to Protestantism within the sixteenth century, mainly from its middle decades onwards, the argument of this chapter is that the renovation of the Catholic Church that gained momentum from the time of the Council of Trent (1545–63) represented an accelerated continuity of earlier reform trends and a number of realisations of earlier aspirations: by 'reform' in this context I refer to recurrent attempts to restore the Christian Church to its original state, ideally in the early centuries after Christ. Such campaigns for the renewal of the Church – for example, to sweep away superstition and financial exploitation of it, to improve the education and dedication of the parish clergy, to make bishops apostolic directors of renewal, to make the regular orders of monks, friars and nuns live up to their vows and rules, and so on – tended to look for leadership from the office of the papacy, the 'head' of the 'members' of the Church, without whose moral restoration the quality of the rest of the institution was thought likely to be parlous.

Attention is often drawn to the scandalous state of the Renaissance papacy under such popes as Alexander VI (1492–1503) and Julius II (1502–13) in the decades preceding Luther's protest against the Catholic Church, originating in 1517. Even so, it may be argued that the moral reputation of the papacy reached a particularly low point not in the early sixteenth century but during the fourteenth-century period when popes resided at Avignon in France (1309–77) and especially during the subsequent Great Schism of 1378 to 1417, Catholicism's 'Babylonian Captivity', when its papal leadership was divided between two and even three claimants. The Avignonese residence, though not lacking in achievements for the papacy, took it away from the base of its spiritual and institutional prestige, Rome, the city of St Peter, claimed to be the first pope, by Christ's appointment. The subsequent division in the papacy meant that there was discord in the very symbol of unity in the Church as the 'seamless garment' of Christ. The debased state of the papacy fostered the criticisms, which prefigured those of the Protestant Reformation, by the English heretic John Wyclif (*c*.1326–84) and the Czech critic John Hus (1369–1415). In the minds of more orthodox reformists, such as the Frenchmen Cardinal Pierre d'Ailly (1350–1420) and Jean Gerson (1364–1429) and the German Nicholas of Cusa (1401–64), representative councils of the Church, led by its bishops as successors to the Apostles, were the antidotes to the scandalous division of the papacy and the moral malaise of the Church. The prestige of such councils rose when a council, meeting in Constance between 1414 and 1418, achieved the cessation of the papal Schism with its deposition of rival claimants (three since 1409) and their replacement by Martin V (Odo Colonna, pope 1417–31), whose return to Rome made possible the papacy's full reclamation of its title to St Peter's leadership of the Church. Yet the rebuilding of the papacy was an uphill task, whereas the prestige of the council as an institution was at a high point as a result of the achievement of Constance in re-unifying the Church. The ideal of the council, says Delumeau, became 'in the minds of many Christians, inseparable from [the theme] of reform': 'medieval conciliar reform', writes O'Malley, 'climaxed in intensity at the Councils of Constance...and Basel'. At Constance, hopes of the council as the reforming parliament of the Church were set out in the constitutional blueprint, *Sacrosancta* (1415), which stated that councils, alongside the pope, derived their authority from Christ. The decree of Constance, *Frequens* (1417), made provision for regular meetings of councils. The aftermath was a period of frequent council sessions, at Basel between 1431 and 1437 and at Florence and Rome between 1438 and 1445. Claims that the authority of the council was equal or even superior to that of the pope – 'conciliarism' – posed an obvious threat to the still insecurely re-established papacy in the line of Martin V, himself put in place by a council. Conciliarism, then, was a recipe for a running conflict between popes and councils, thwarting the proceedings of the Council at Basel, leading eventually to a denunciation by Pope Pius II (1458–64) in the bull *Execrabilis* (1460) of the constitutional claims of councils and sowing seeds of the discord between the papal and conciliar principles that delayed the convening of the vital reforming council of Trent in the mid-sixteenth century. Even so, Trent had its precedents in the conciliar reforming proceedings of the fifteenth century and indeed may be seen as the fulfilment of those late medieval councils.[2]

Those councils, though, tended to be too much concerned with the constitutional questions of their authority to effect much actual reform, and Basel arguably was being unconstructively confrontational when it claimed that a council of the Church was superior in authority to the pope, that it took its authority direct from Christ and that the pope himself was bound to obey it. Nevertheless, Basel set out a clear programme of reform of the Church: it issued disciplinary regulations in areas where financial abuses were common, including rules on the conferment of ecclesiastical dignities, on elections to Church offices, on the award of ecclesiastical benefices in advance of their being taken up, on procedures over appeals and interdicts, as well as promulgating rules on the celebration of the Mass.[3]

In 1438 the Council, transferred to Florence under the control of Eugenius IV, made provisions for the worship and rites of the Church, focusing on the Sacraments. These were fixed at seven, an enumeration to be challenged by the Protestant Reformers but affirmed by the Council of Trent in an act of conscious continuity with its conciliar predecessor. It was especially important that, in asserting the creation of the seven Sacraments by Christ or the Apostles, Florence highlighted the sacramental ministry of bishops. This was particularly necessary in the fifteenth century when the process of converting bishops from pastors into politicians and administrators had reached a dangerous point of development. Even when, as was becoming increasingly rare, bishops concentrated on their dioceses, they tended to highlight their legal, administrative and disciplinary rather than their pastoral, priestly, evangelical and sacramental roles within their sees. Even more dangerously, bishops too often appeared not in the guises of fathers in God but were, rather, placed 'among the greatest territorial magnates of Europe....related to the most powerful families in their countries....primarily men of affairs'. A typical example of the breed was England's Cardinal Henry Beaufort (d. 1447), an illegitimate son of the royal family, made bishop of Lincoln in 1398 and of Winchester in 1404, Lord Chancellor of England and captain general of the army sent to crush the followers of Hus in Bohemia. In the context of the relentless politicisation of the episcopate, for the Council to reassert a bishop's primary sacramental capacity, requiring his presence in his diocese where he was the 'ordinary minister of holy confirmation', represented a reminder, pointing towards Trent, of what a bishop's reason for being actually was. Reform-minded bishops in the fifteenth century seized on this insistence that a bishop's duty was sacramental and his title apostolic.[4]

Trent took up that theme and in doing so magnified its fifteenth-century predecessor's statements on the apostolic nature of a bishop's sacramental and spiritual functions:

> the holy Synod [of Trent] declares that, bishops, who have succeeded to the place of the apostles...are placed...by the Holy Ghost, to rule the Church of God; that they are superior to priests, administer the Sacrament of Confirmation; ordain the ministers of the Church.

A hundred years in advance of Trent, the Council at Florence was heralding Trent's affirmations of the essential pastoral and sacramental roles of the bishops of the Church. It would be easy to be sceptical about the real achievements of this Council which was riven by conflict with the pope, and was transferred by him to Florence in 1438: at the sessions 'politics predominated throughout and the prelates from Italy attended at the will of their rulers, mostly to embarrass [Pope] Eugenius IV'. The Council's legislation was adopted in France and Germany but not in Italy. Yet it established, or rather reiterated from such writers on the episcopal office as St Gregory the Great (pope 590–604) an insistence that the bishop, in Gregory's words was 'a minister, not a master' and a pastor of the Church, not an officer of the state. This was the approach that was to be taken up in the Council of Trent's designation of the bishops as the implementers of the renewal of the Church in the dioceses of Catholic Europe.[5]

As we shall see in Chapter 2, the fifteenth-century councils heralded that of Trent in the enunciation of Catholic sacramental theology. The same would hold true if we were to take as a further example of continuity of doctrine from the fifteenth-century councils through to the Council of Trent, the setting out of beliefs with respect to Mary, in which the fifteenth century was a particularly creative period. Of particular interest in this field was the evolution, amidst much controversy, of a doctrine establishing the purity of Mary as a fitting vessel to bear the God-Man Christ, her 'Immaculate Conception', or freedom, when she was conceived in her mother's womb, from the 'original sin' with which, it was believed, all human beings save she and Christ were tainted in their very conceptions with an inherited sinfulness as a result of Adam's and Eve's first sin of disobedience. Perhaps because it was disputed even by some of those most devoted to Mary, especially St Bernard (1090–1153), the doctrine of the Immaculate Conception took a long time – until 1854 – to become established as a dogma, an essential or required belief of Catholics. Yet Basel made its own contribution to the development of the doctrine: Mary's

> immaculate conception is a pious opinion, consistent with the worship of the Church, to Catholic faith, to right reason and to Holy Scripture....[A]ll Catholics must assent to it;...no-one is allowed to teach, or preach to the

contrary....[T]he feast of the [Immaculate] Conception should be celebrated throughout the Church on the 8th December, according to the
custom of the Roman Church.[6]

The Council at Basel developed its position on the Immaculate Conception in
the process of setting it out: from a 'pious opinion', in a few lines the doctrine
had become an obligation of universal Catholic assent and observance marked
by a feast-day. The Council of Trent was, on the face of it, more cautious about
this doctrine and, as the authors of the *Histoire Écclésiastique* wrote, 'made no resolution on this issue'. That said, as Ashley and Sheingorn point out, what Trent
did was exempt Mary from its decree of 1546 on the universality of original sin,
resolving not 'to include in this decree, when it is dealing with original sin, the
blessed and immaculate Virgin Mary, mother of God'. In effect, this exemption
was tantamount to saying that Mary *was* immaculately conceived. The Council
of Trent also upheld a constitution in favour of the doctrine's adoption by a
pope who strongly approved the belief, Sixtus IV (1471–84). Trent, Ashley and
Sheingorn conclude, 'obviously favoured the Immaculate Conception'. The
Council of Trent, indeed, endorsed the whole sprit of late medieval special
reverence for the Blessed Virgin, known as 'hyperdulia'. Against a background in
which Reformation Christocentricity tended to downgrade Mary, Trent, in the
area of Marian doctrine as in the other topics to be considered, ratified the
conclusions of its fifteenth-century predecessors.[7]

A further feature of later medieval Catholic doctrinal evolution consolidated
by the mid-fifteenth-century councils and subsequently endorsed by Trent (also
in the face of Protestant objections) was the definition of the doctrine of
Purgatory, the place or state of punishment after death to exorcise the guilt still
accruing to sins forgiven in the Sacrament of Penance on earth. In this area of
doctrine the Council of Florence confirmed the doctrine that:

> if truly penitent people die in the love of God before they have made satis-
> faction for acts and omissions by worthy fruits of repentance, their souls are
> cleansed after death by cleansing pains, and the suffrages of the living
> faithful avail them in giving relief from such pains [by means of Masses,
> prayers and almsgiving].

Subsequently, Trent added its endorsement of the belief 'that there is a
Purgatory, and that the souls there detained are helped by the suffrages of the
faithful'. The Council of Trent's refusal to advance beyond that laconic formula-
tion and expand on the nature of Purgatory, along with its unwillingness to
countenance any further general discussion of the matter – 'let the more difficult
and subtle questions [about Purgatory] be excluded from popular discourses' –
were also well within the conciliar tradition of the fifteenth century in which it
had been established that 'the type of sufferings endured [by the souls in
Purgatory] is not a matter of importance'.[8]

Both the fifteenth-century Church councils and that of Trent made major contributions to a long-term campaign to 'purify' the worship of the Catholic Church, to make it more dignified, more carefully performed and purged of 'profane' or popular elements, especially in Church music. The Council of Basel's rulings in this regard are worth citing because they look forward to Trent's canons on liturgical propriety. In 1435 the Basel Council issued regulations on the 'Office', the cycle of prayers normally chanted daily in cathedrals and monasteries:

> that in all cathedral and collegiate churches, at suitable times and at the sound of a bell, the divine praises shall be reverently celebrated by everyone through all the hours, not hurriedly but gravely and slowly with reasonable pauses.…[Clerics] shall behave with such gravity as the place and the duty demand, not gossiping or talking among themselves or with others, nor reading letters or other writings. They…should sing to God eagerly in psalms, hymns and canticles.

There were denunciations of 'secular song', 'conversation and laughter' in choir, of wandering the premises, 'coming and going', strolling and chatting'; timetable boards were to be set up in churches where several clerics lived in common, listing the liturgical duties of the priests over the course of each week. The use of short-cuts and abbreviated forms of prayer in the Mass was condemned. Basel went on to attack inaudible and indecorous ways of saying Mass, for the Council's vision was of a clergy committed to an edifying level of liturgical performance. In association with this, Basel strove to purge from the liturgy its lay, popular and secular elements:

> Some people with mitre, crozier and pontifical vestments give blessings after the manner of bishops [,] called the feast of fools or innocents, or children. Some put on masked and theatrical comedies, others organize dances for men and women, attracting people to amusement and buffoonery. They prepare meals and banquets there. This holy synod detests these abuses.[9]

It could be argued that the rituals of inversion and saturnalia thus condemned helped integrate religious worship and popular culture in medieval Europe, especially through linking the Church's liturgy with vernacular culture's key themes of folly and clowning, but this interpenetration was seen by Catholic reformists in the fifteenth and sixteenth centuries as derogating from the dignity of the clergy, a status which Basel, in its ruling on the liturgy, was attempting to make priests themselves uphold. Delumeau connects the campaign conducted at Basel against the invasion of the rites of the Church by popular masquerades to a longer-term battle for liturgical solemnity evident in statutes of diocesan synods at Lyons in 1566 and 1577 and in constitutions of the archbishop of Cologne in 1617. Trent's measures formed a link in this long chain of purification of the liturgy. Bishops, Trent ordered, 'should keep out of their churches the kind of music in which a base and suggestive element is introduced into the organ playing or singing, and similarly all worldly activities, empty and secular conversation, walking about, noises and cries'.[10] Once more we observe Trent's continuities with its fifteenth-century predecessors, indicating that in key respects Trent concluded the series of late medieval general councils of the Catholic Church.

The traditions of conciliar reform of which Trent was to be the heir were resumed when, in the pontificate of Julius II, dissident cardinals, appealing to the reforming traditions of the fifteenth-century councils, met at Pisa in 1511. At loggerheads with Pope Julius, the Pisa Council achieved little of substance; however we should at least take note of the moral aspirations this Council adopted, since, whether or not these were devised as propaganda to challenge Pope Julius's immorality, they re-established targets of devotion, sobriety, self-restraint and piety for senior clerics which were the preconditions of the Tridentine achievement. For if the bench-mark of the decadence of the Renaissance papacy was the corruption and irreligion of which Julius was the leading practitioner, then the quest for renewal through austerity and religious observance pursued by the Council at Pisa reaffirmed standards for Catholic reform in terms of targets of personal holiness, and especially of asceticism, goals that were to be achieved as the sixteenth century unfolded in saintly popes, particularly Pius V (reigned 1566–72), and bishops, above all Carlo Borromeo (1538–84). Indeed, personal holiness was seen by the Council of Pisa as the precondition of institutional reform: it linked 'the need to reform oneself and the need to work for the reform of the church in its head and members'. The last phrase had by this time become a slogan, or even a cliché, of anti-papal conciliarism, while Pisa's reference to 'the reform of the church, whose irregularities are now so swollen' suggests a consciousness inherited from the middle ages that, in O'Malley's words, 'the Church as a whole might be subject to reform...[,] that moral and legal abuses were widespread, almost universal'. It was that awareness, the anxiety that corruption was omnipresent, the insistence that reform was always called for and that it operated in the first place from moral renewal, that fed the well-springs of reformist intention which surfaced at Trent. Pisa, then, may be considered an important council, though not in the political or legislative sense, from which point of view it can be disparaged, as Professor Dickens dismisses it, as a 'schismatic *conciliabulum* [mini-council]...unrecognized by the rest of Europe, consisting of little more than a knot of French bishops striving to appear impressive'. Yet Pisa was more than Delumeau's 'political comedy', for it voiced aspirations towards austerity and indeed puritanism otherwise largely buried in the worldliness of Julius II's court. The moral style of Pisa anticipated that of Trent and in particular its decrees concerning the conduct and manner of life to be expected from bishops: the fathers at Pisa bound themselves to celebrate the Mass of the Holy Spirit weekly (at which a collection for the poor would be taken), to conduct a weekly fast, to maintain the 'utmost sobriety' at meals (which were to be taken without female company), and to limit the size of entourages. Pisa helped to define the spirit of the Catholic Reformation.[11]

The Council which a war of propaganda against France impelled Julius II to convene in Rome's Lateran Basilica in July 1512 and which survived his death in 1513 to last until the year that Luther's protest exploded (1517), was, for all its relatively small attendance, a significant phase in the chain of conciliar reform that we have identified as connecting Constance to Trent. As A. G. Dickens writes, Lateran V 'may be regarded as a substantial link between fifteenth-century conciliarism and the Council of Trent', producing 'ambitious proposals which foreshadowed some of the Tridentine decrees'. Unlike Trent and its own fifteenth-century forebears, Lateran V was not productive in the field of theology: its decree on the immortality of the soul launched against 'certain philosophers' has about it something of the flavour of a platonic symposium of the High Renaissance rather than an authoritative restatement of classic Catholic doctrine. However, in its proposed educational reforms and its 'Rules for University Studies' the Lateran Council showed the way to Trent and towards its seminary provisions which we shall see were vital for the training of the clergy of the Catholic Reformation. In addition, Lateran V paved the way for Trent's exacting requirements for the scrutiny of candidates for the priest-hood and episcopate – 'worthy individuals, of good morals and sufficient age'. The Lateran Council also attacked the long-standing abuse of the *commendam* system by which incomes and privileges of monastic abbots were transferred to non-resident or titular heads. In 1515 Lateran V addressed the wider issue of monastic reform, anticipating Trent's provisions for episcopal oversight of reli-gious orders by legislating for bishops' annual visitations of convents of nuns. The Lateran Council also prefigured Trent's demand for a more elevated, less 'superstitious' Catholicism by requiring preachers to abandon their fabrications of bogus miracles and spurious traditions.[12]

Thus in a series of councils in the period before the outbreak of the Protestant Reformation the continuities of Catholic reform were established for Trent to take up and fulfil. Not all of these 'general' councils were of equal standing, and the Pisa gathering in particular contained elements of political opportunism and propaganda. Even so, we have seen in the 130 years before the convening of the Council of Trent the establishment by its predecessors of many of its main lines of work, in doctrine and reform.

A key feature of the Catholic Reformation gaining momentum in the sixteenth century was the restoration of the papacy and especially of its religious prestige, leadership and priorities. To set this restoration in context, we should appreciate that the century and more following Constance may be regarded as one of a slow, often hesitant and frequently interrupted rehabilitation of the papacy, a process, above all, of rebuilding the papacy's religious role and leader-ship that came to fruition in the following areas: the founding of the Jesuits (1540) and the convening of the Council of Trent (1545) by Paul III (1534–49); the direction of the Council, through their presiding legates, by Paul's successors and its successful conclusion by Pius IV (1559–65); the re-ordering of the Church's prayers and liturgy in the Breviary and Missal authorised by Pius V; the resumption of the papacy's own central liturgical role; the projection of its saintly charisma and mystique, especially with the canonised Pius V; and the involvement of a long line of popes with Rome's reconstruction and embellishment as the place from which the Holy Father derived his claim to be the heir of St Peter, as the spiritual capital of Catholicism, as a prime focus of pilgrimage and as the foremost new model dioceses of the Catholic Reformation. We shall look at the pontificates of most of the popes in the period between Constance and the Reformation to evaluate their roles in the rebuilding of the papacy's leadership of Catholicism.

Crucial to the long-term restoration of the papacy after the debasement of the Avignonese residence and the Schism was the recovery of the institution's Roman location and identity. Himself a Roman, of the local baronial family of Colonna, the first post-Schism pope, Martin V, secured the return of the papacy to its indispensable 'base'. He also freed the Papal States, the extensive lands in central Italy governed by the pope as their sovereign, 'from the chaos into which [they] had fallen during the Schism', an essential work of administrative rehabilitation. Beyond that, a 'good simple man, moderately well read, an enemy to intrigue, and loyal to his friends', Martin was not passionately devoted to Church reform, though in issuing concordats – treaties between the papacy and rulers – with four nation-states in 1418, he set up arrangements whereby local reform might be brought about in those kingdoms.[13]

Martin V's successor Eugenius IV (Gabriele Condulmero, pope 1431–47), though locked in conflict with the nobility and people of Rome and its hinterland and with the reconvened council of the Church, yet managed to promote reform. Indeed, Hay writes that 'Eugenius's interventions on the side of reform are far too many to list', including the reform of the friars, an attempt to provide a university in Rome and directives in favour of reform within Italian dioceses. Eugenius also furthered the cause of reform by maintaining the personal sanctity demanded by the strict Order of Canons Regular of St Augustine, of which he was a member and whose frugal lifestyle he maintained as pope, taking part in the recitation of the Office, and keeping a modest papal household of servants and dependants: he resembled his sixteenth-century successor Pius V in maintaining an austere monastic personal way of life amidst the public splendours of the papacy. Eugenius was also active in the overhaul of the papal Curia (the pope's court and administration) and in the purification of the lives of clerics, beginning in 1432 with the regulation of the morals of the Roman clergy. His 'zeal was directed to reform', which Gill says was one of the 'persistent aims of his life'. On his accession, Eugenius issued an 'almost savage' prohibition on priests keeping mistresses ['concubinage'], while measures were taken to end abuses in the award of church benefices to individuals and in the levels of fees paid to officials of the Curia, regulating the numbers of these functionaries in 1438 and 1444. Eugenius also aimed to promote reform by refusing demands from England and Portugal to confirm royal protégés as nominees for bishoprics when these were below the approved age; he also stoutly defended the clergy's rights in disputes with monarchs in Portugal and Scotland.[14]

Himself a member of a rigorous religious order, Eugenius favoured the elements in the religious orders, the 'Observants', that aimed at reform through the literal obedience of their rules. He was the 'avowed protector' of the Dominican Observants, aided the acceleration of the strict observance of their rule amongst the Franciscans, sanctioned the establishment of Observant houses, lent his support to reform measures requested by Observants and assisted with the foundation of the reformed Benedictine Congregation of Santa Giustina in Padua. Eugenius IV's encouragement of strict observance of their rules by the religious orders looked forward to the Council of Trent's insistence on strictness of life amongst the orders of the Church and also coincided with a golden age of the Observance, especially in Italy, the age of the saintly friars Bernardino of Siena (1380–1444) and Giovanni da Capistrano (1386–1456). Advocates of Church reform hailed this pope as the promoter of their cause: early in his pontificate, a cardinal wrote to him, 'if there is reformation still to be done of the Curia, let Your Holiness complete it as you have so praiseworthily began', while Antonino Pierozzi (1389–1459), bishop of Florence, a pioneer of diocesan renewal, acclaimed Eugenius as a reformist, 'most bountiful to the poor, generous in gifts for the repair of churches; he cherished God-fearing religious [members of regular orders] with an affection that was as practical as it was genuine'. A further area in which Eugenius anticipated Tridentine reform was in encouraging clerical education, as Trent was to do when it ordered the establishment of seminaries. In 1436 Eugenius set up in Florence 'a college of clerics with a master to instruct them in the music of the Church and in Latin'. In this, as in other respects, Eugenius IV should be regarded as a herald of the reform-minded popes of the Tridentine period – an educational and administrative reformer, setting a standard of personal holiness, and promoter of renewal in the religious orders.[15]

A different, but still essential, facet of the restoration of the papacy that was to be particularly intensified in the Catholic Reformation is evident in the pontificate of Eugenius IV's successor, Nicholas V (Tomasso Parentucelli, pope 1447–55). Despite being troubled by baronial faction in the Papal States, by conspiracy in Rome, disorder in Italy and the calamitous fall of the Greek Orthodox capital, Constantinople, to the Turks in 1453, Nicholas's pontificate saw important progress towards the reassertion of papal Rome's leadership of the Catholic world, part of a long-term recovery from the degradation of the Great Schism. The pope's primacy, though, was not that simply of a bishop, nor even of a patriarch, but that of Peter's heir as bishop of Rome, endowed by succession from Peter with Christ's commission of headship on earth over the whole Church. Alone in the world the papal see was the 'Apostolic See', the Petrine diocese. The pope wore a 'triple crown' of the governance that Christ had given to Peter over all branches of the Church. He alone wore the 'fisherman's ring', Peter's symbol. His emblem was formed of the keys that Christ had identified as the regalia of His lieutenant's authority: 'And I will give unto thee the keys of the kingdom of heaven' (Matt., 16:19). And, as the Avignonese residence and the Great Schism had shown, without Rome the pope was, to say the least, diminished, since he spoke 'to the world'…'from the city'. To express the relationship between the papacy and Rome as the city of Peter, an architecture was necessary, one that highlighted all that in Rome was associated with Peter and, in particular, the basilica, dilapidated or stylistically outmoded by the mid-fifteenth century, that covered, it was believed, the tomb of the 'prince of the Apostles', the proof of that link between Rome and Peter that was the essence of the pope's primatial claims in Christendom. It was Nicholas V who launched the rebuilding of St Peter's, as a vital ingredient in the reconstruction of the papacy. The scheme, massively protracted and expensive, may, from one point of view, be dismissed as a gigantic folly of grandiosity, a Tower of Babel of papal egoism, a project whose expense brought about the Reformation in Germany out of a protest against the levies of cash needed to carry forward the building programme. For all its expense, though, the rebuilding of St Peter's was in fact essential to the refurbishment of Rome as the popes' holy city, the focus and source of their most exalted spiritual claims. The re-edification of Rome, centring on the reconstruction of the basilica, was absolutely indispensable to the revival of the papacy.

This was why, as O' Malley shows, the reformer Egidio da Viterbo (Giles of Viterbo, 1469–1532), devoted as he was to the ideals of holy poverty and simplicity, strenuously encouraged the continuation of the basilica scheme, for he was 'convinced that the Church was localized in place, that it was by divine decree Roman', that 'the basilica dedicated to the Prince of the Apostles' must be raised ' "up to the very heavens" ', since it expressed 'Rome's claim to be the center of the religious world...the site to which Peter and Paul came...hallowed by their preaching and martyrdoms'. As Partner adds, the popes were 'the guardians of the pilgrimage, and custodians of the places sanctified by the blood of the martyrs'. In the course of the sixteenth century, affirmed by inter-national Catholic jubilees, Rome became more than ever the city of world Catholicism's primate. The strengthening of this role required an adjustment of the papacy's location within the city so as to emphasise Petrine leadership as well as, or rather than, an episcopal status as no more than bishop of Rome. Nicholas V, in the design of St Peter's as what was to be the world's vastest church, was also intimately involved in the relaunch of the papacy's global role expressed through a shift of the papacy's institutional presence within Rome's city-scape so as to focus the office on St Peter's. What was involved, Freiberg says, was a long-term

> grand scheme to rebuild St Peter's and the Vatican palace and restructure the entire Vatican area as an ideal city that centered on the person and cere-monial function of the pope. Not only would the Vatican at St Peter's replace the Lateran as the papal residence, but the honor of *Mater et Caput* [Mother and Head] that had adhered to Rome's [Lateran] Cathedral would be absorbed by St Peter's.

It is Nicholas V who can be credited with launching this programme, so vital to affirming the papacy's unique and global primacy, a role revived by the renewal of Rome's status as the world's most visited city, fount of ecclesiastical jurisprudence and the destination of suits and appeals from throughout Christendom, the mecca of ambassadors and clerics, and the focus of pilgrimages, especially in the great jubilees of 1450 and 1475, the predecessors of the magnificent repetitions in 1575 and 1600.[16]

The restatement of the papacy's Roman primacy through city planning and architecture was not, though, Pope Nicholas's sole contribution to restoring the papacy to the centre of Catholic life, for this pope also furthered the alignment of the papacy to current trends in popular piety. In promptly – within six years of the man's death – canonising the hugely popular Franciscan Observant Bernardino of Siena, Nicholas, as his predecessor Innocent III (1198–1216) had done in initially validating the Franciscans and as his successor Clement VII (1523–34) was to do in authorising the sixteenth-century Franciscan Observant revival of the Capuchins, made his contribution to closing the always potentially embarrassing gap between, on the one hand, the papacy's stature as an institution trammelled with wealth and power and, on the other, the Franciscan ideal of Christ-like poverty. A devotion whose currency Nicholas fostered, taking it, as did his successor Pius II, closely under papal auspices and helping to promote it as a universal devotion of the whole Church led by the papacy as its head on earth, was that of the Body of Christ in the Blessed Sacrament of the Eucharist. This cult of the consecrated host had attracted a strong following since the twelfth century as an international manifestation of piety. Its catholicity harmonised with the papacy's aspirations towards universality of command, for it did not depend, unlike so many pilgrimage devotions, on the limitations of a purely local shrine. It had in fact arisen under papal ratification and indeed developed as a special papal devotion, marked with particular attention by the entire Curia at the annual feast of Corpus Christi, the eucharistic body of Christ. Nicholas V's introduction of the custom of carrying the Host in procession from St Peter's to the Castel Sant'Angelo, within the city's newly emergent ritual centre of gravity around the Vatican, further attuned the papacy to the devotion of the Blessed Sacrament and its global feast, which, it was reported, 'is celebrated yearly in the Christian world with the greatest devotion and profound worship by all nations'. The Council of Trent was also to recommend with great enthusiasm the devotion of the Blessed Sacrament.[17]

While Nicholas V thus contributed substantially to the restitution of the role of the pope as Catholicism's chief priest, launching Rome's return to its place as Catholicism's primary pilgrimage centre, and giving papal direction to the cult of the eucharistic host as a magnet of adoration, under two of his successors Calixtus III (Alfonso Borgia or Alonso de Borja, pope, 1455–8) and Sixtus IV (Francesco della Rovere) the emphasis in papal devotional leadership shifted towards the expanding cult of Mary. The historian Artaud de Montor gave Pope Calixtus the credit for promulgating the Marian prayer the *Angelus*, a brief set of invocations said normally at fixed times of day and forming a meditation on the Annunciation that Mary was to be the mother of God. A Franciscan – that is to say, from a preaching order with a traditionally close involvement in both the shaping of popular piety and in producing responses to its aspirations – Pope

Sixtus (as well as urging Curial officials and cardinals to join a pious confraternity, the Hospital of the Holy Spirit) stepped up the relationship between devotion to Mary and papal patronage of it by authorising, in 1476, the celebration of the feast of the Immaculate Conception in Rome. In ratifying this cult, Sixtus was adding to the development of an aspect of Marian piety that Trent, as we saw, was to endorse.[18]

The fifteenth-century papacy's association with the reform of the Church was evident in the pontificate following that of Calixtus III, that of Pius II (Enea Silvio Piccolomini) especially in the pope's relationship with the German reformer Nicholas of Cusa, who submitted memoranda to Pius on the renewal of the Church, and in his endorsement of the work as a diocesan and civic leader of reform of Bishop Antonino Pierozzi who, in Pius's assessment 'reformed the morals of both the clergy and the laity' of Florence. One of Pius's first actions on becoming pope was the establishment of a reform commission; the Venetian philosophy professor Domenico de' Domenichi (1416–78) set out reform proposals calling candidly for the end of papal nepotism and extravagance, a simpler life-style for the cardinals and residence by bishops in their dioceses. Pius also renewed Nicholas V's close involvement in devotion to what the pope called 'the most divine Sacrament of the Body and Blood of Our Lord Jesus Christ'.[19]

The restoration of the papacy's role, not so much as the head of the Church's government or its financial bureaucracy but as the chief celebrant of its rites, with 'the mystical powers of a holy leader' (Partner), took a step forward in the next pontificate, that of Innocent VIII (Giovanni Battista Cibo or Cybo, pope 1484–92), with the publication of a work lavishly describing the liturgical functions of the pope and his entourage, *Commentarii Rerum Urbanarum sub Pontifice Innocentii VIII Papae* (*Commentaries on Proceedings in Rome under Pope Innocent VIII*) by the German papal master of ceremonies Bishop Johannes Burchard (or Burkhard, 1450–1506). At the same time, while what Lee calls the papacy's 'liturgical…competence' was thus stressed, even under the nepotist Innocent VIII, the Holy See's role in furthering the religious teaching of the Church was re-emphasised, and the Curia presided over by this pope 'was less exclusively wrapped up in purely secular concerns, less subject to paganising humanist influences, and more critical [of abuses] than a long line of historians has led us to believe'.[20]

The long-term 'restoration of the papacy' that was in train between Constance and Trent was, to say the least, not advanced during the scandalous pontificates of Alexander VI (Rodrigo Borgia or de Borja) and Julius II (Guliano della Rovere). These pontificates formed, in fact, a two-decade period in which the papacy, losing sight of its purpose, of moral and religious leadership in Christendom, of liturgical and doctrinal direction, dropped its sights, to become immersed in power politics, in the Italian Wars (1494–1559), in dynastic promotion and in an expensive aestheticism designed, not to restore Rome as a holy and ideal city but to put a gloss of splendour on the naked exercise of power: the papacy was in danger of becoming no more than a minor secular state. The role of Girolamo Savonarola (1452–98), the puritan reformer of Florence in power between 1494 and 1498, was to point out the dangers of that drift into dynastic politics under Alexander VI. The sharpness of the contrast between the austerity of the Dominican Observant Savonarola and the corruption of Alexander VI showed up the decadence of the papal office in the 1490s. It was, however, the pope, not the papacy, that Savonarola attacked, on the grounds of Alexander's corruptly bought papal election, his favours to his family and his scandalous personal life. Seen from one point of view, Savonarola might, in the dark days of Alexander VI, be viewed as one voice in favour of the papal restoration which we have been considering and the herald of the Catholic reform of the next century – including the reform of the religious orders and the moral and social renewal of Italian cities. His loyalty to the Church and the papacy was strong: 'the bishops of Rome', he wrote, 'are successors of Peter, so that the Roman Church is leader and mistress of all other churches, and all faithful Christians must be united with the Roman Pontiff, as to their head'. In attacking Alexander VI Savonarola castigated him on a platform of moral rectitude from which this pope was seen as an aberration. De la Bedoyere, in his study of the conflict between the friar and the pope, compared Savonarola with the sixteenth-century agents of renewal Ignatius Loyola (1491–1556), the founder of the Jesuits, and with Filippo Neri (1515–95), the Florentine-born 'apostle of Rome' in the sixteenth century. The intellectual and spiritual legacy from Savonarola to Neri, who greatly admired Savonarola's treatise *Il Trionfo della Croce* ('The Triumph of the Cross'), formed a lineage of renewal linking the Florentine reformism of the fifteenth century with that taking place of Rome in the sixteenth.[21]

The kind of distinction on the basis of which Savonarola operated, as critic and reformer, between the office of pope and the character of its holder was crucial to the eventual resumption and ultimate success of the longer term restoration of the papacy, for, as Muldoon writes:

> Even though [Alexander VI] may have been a disgrace to the office which he held, nevertheless the papacy was an institution that did not depend on the vagaries of personality to function. The distinction between person and office was long understood so that even the poorest of popes was limited in the harm he could do because of the institutional structures which bounded him on all sides.

In fact, the 'institutional structures' of the papacy, the Curia, the financial offices, such as the *Dataria* and the College of Cardinals, themselves urgently needed renewal inasmuch as, through the system of personal papal appointments, they had a tendency to regress in quality to the level of the 'poorest of popes'. Even so, there may have been some corrective mechanisms within the papal system as an ongoing institution characterised, generally speaking, by the short reigns of elderly occupants, by a responsibility accruing to the 'permanent staff' to maintain equilibrium, especially during the interregna of often protracted elections, and by a papal voting system that created alternative poles of party affiliation and a constant culture of looking to the next regime, its prospects and policies.[22]

Indeed, occupants not always of the most sterling quality sometimes showed a capacity for positive response to altering circumstances. For example, Pope Alexander's reaction to the murder of one of his sons in 1497 was the setting up of a 'very powerful' reform commission. His response to a challenge of a different order – that of the implications of Columbus's discoveries in the first year of his pontificate – was set out in his bull of 1493 *Inter Caetera*, a 'carefully worded statement which balanced the rights of the individual, the papal responsibility for preaching the Gospel and the political realities of aggressive expansionism'. The bull upheld papal protection of indigenous peoples under the 'vicariate of Christ' and anticipated the unfolding assumption during the Catholic Reformation of papal responsibility for world missions – as, for example, when Pope Paul III sent Francis Xavier to Goa and the far east in 1541.[23]

If Alexander VI's moves in the direction of Church reform can be described as 'surprising', those of Julius II, given his reputation for monomania and aggression, might fairly be described as astonishing. The oppositionist Council convened at Pisa induced Julius to summons the Lateran Council, whose measures, anticipating those of Trent, we have already considered. It is note-worthy, though, that in summoning his Council to Rome, the last to be held there, as Partner points out, until 1870, Julius was playing his own part in the revindication of the city's special identity as, once more, the ark of Catholicism's covenant. Arthos, analysing the contents of sermons delivered in Pope Julius's presence, comments on 'a certain simplicity and decency in honor at the Papal Court, with something of the purity the reformers of the time were calling for', and he goes on to instance Egidio da Viterbo's clarion call for reform voiced in the opening session of the Lateran Council. Even Pope Julius II maintained some of the momentum of papal devotional leadership, especially in veneration of the Blessed Sacrament, encouraging a group of Curial officials to join a confraternity set up in its honour.[24]

The Lateran Council was spread over two pontificates, and in that of Julius's successor, Leo X (Giovanni de' Medici, pope 1513–22), the passage, if not the implementation, of reform legislation need not have disappointed those crying out for renewal. In submitting their extensive programme of Church renewal, *Libellus ad Leonem Decem* (*A Little Book for Pope Leo X*) – including proposals for the creation of a holy episcopate and a pastoral clergy, along with stress on the Scriptures and attacks on superstition, two monks of the strict Camaldolese Order, Tomasso Giustiniani (1476–1528) and Vincenzo Quirini (1479–1514), expressed the assumption that the pope was the 'sole hope of reform', magnifying his office. Reforms of the religious orders, anticipating Trent, came in 1516. They featured the disciplinary subjugation, which Trent was also to instigate, of the orders and their houses to the bishops, whose authority to carry out reforms was further bolstered through giving them the right to conduct visitations of parish churches within their dioceses which lay in the hands of religious orders. The relentless attention to be paid by the Council of Trent to the bishops as the directors of the reform of the Church in the regions of Christendom, in particular by entrusting them with the regulative discipline of the regular orders, was heralded by such legislation under Leo as that requiring heads of regular houses to submit to episcopal approval members of their orders whom they wished to employ as preachers and confessors; bishops were empowered to examine these for the orthodoxy of their doctrine and the soundness of their sacramental practice. Insofar as the indiscipline of unreformed orders and houses of monks, canons, nuns and friars was a source of corruption and scandal in the Church, requiring close control by reform-minded bishops to amend it, the legislation under Leo X and that of Trent addressed the perceived problem in remarkably similar ways. Thus Pope Leo imposed on regular orders permanent binding force to all agreements they had entered into with bishops, restricted entry of regulars into parish churches which came under the ultimate authority of bishops, required episcopal examination of regulars raised to priests' orders, demanded that the churches belonging to regular orders be consecrated by bishops whenever possible, restricted the scope for competition in offering religious services between the regulars' churches and cathedrals under the jurisdiction of bishops, insisted on the direct payment of parish tithes to the bishop's diocesan clergy, and tried to encourage the reception of the Sacraments by the laity in the diocesan churches. In parallel fashion, and in the same vein of suspicion of the regular orders and a demand that the bishops control them, Trent was to forbid regulars from preaching in diocesan churches without episcopal inspection of their licences to do so, order episcopal examination of regulars proposing to hear Confessions and, in general, place the 'cure of souls' exercised by regulars under the control of the bishop of the place in question. Clearly, the second decade of the sixteenth century, and before Luther's protest first exploded, saw important initiatives in the direction of institutional reform of the Church, prefiguring Trent in important respects.[25]

During the brief pontificate of Leo X's successor, the devout and ascetic Adrian VI (Adriaan Florenszoon or Floriszoon, pope 1522–3), the papacy underwent a return to the personal sanctity of Eugenius IV. While Adrian brought to Rome the currents of spirituality from his native Netherlands in the form of the late medieval 'new piety' (*devotio moderna*) of the Brethren of the Common Life, who had educated this pope, he also invited to the city his fellow Netherlander, and fellow product of the Brethren's schools, the leading Catholic reformist of the age, Desiderius Erasmus (1469?–1536). At the same time, though, this Dutch pope nourished the Italian sources of renewal that were to provide the main inspiration for Catholic reform from the mid-century onwards. He selected as advisers two leading Italian worker for reform, Gaetano di Thiene (*c.* 1480–1547) and Gian Pietro Carafa (1476–1559). Adrian also tackled the financial abuses of Indulgences, hacked away at the cardinals' spoils system and aligned the papacy to the episcopal reform movement that had got under way in the previous century by canonising in 1523 its leading representative, Antonino

Pierozzi of Florence. Perhaps, though, in his short and careworn pontificate, Adrian's more important contribution to the reform programme was the accomplishment of the simple yet forbidding task of admitting the responsibility of the whole ecclesiastical establishment for the defects of the Church that had by now provoked the Lutheran schism. Adrian's assumption of blame 'on account of the sins of men, and especially those of priests and prelates of the Church' was a necessary precondition of renewal, and this pope represents, says Kelly, 'the first step towards the Counter-Reformation'.[26]

With Adrian VI's successor Clement VII (Giulio de' Medici), we can no longer speak of pre-Reformation Catholic reform, for the Protestant Reformation assumed real momentum within this pontificate as large parts of Germany and Switzerland, as well as the Scandinavian kingdoms and England, left the Roman allegiance, and Protestantism became embedded in France. Yet Catholic reform under papal auspices continued under Clement with his recognition of da Thiene's and Carafa's new Order of Theatines. In the next pontificate, that of Paul III (Alessandro Farnese), the association between the papacy and Church reform, traceable over the course of the previous century and more, was firmly renewed with the papal foundation of the Jesuits and the summoning of the Council.

The papacy's centrality to long-term Catholic revival should not conceal the fact that an indispensable feature of Catholic reform in early modern Europe was the return of bishops to their essential duties, which were diocesan, spiritual, pastoral, disciplinary and didactic, drawing them away from the political responsibilities that had involved too many of them, too much, in royal systems of government. The Council of Trent was especially determined to reinstate the spiritual, sacramental and disciplinary dimensions of the bishop's office, entrusting bishops in the hundreds of dioceses of Europe and the Catholic world with the tasks of carrying out the reform measures it decreed. These Tridentine episcopal reforms were also anticipated in the fifteenth century, by such figures of Antonino Pierozzi in Florence.

Before embarking on his work of diocesan reform Pierozzi was associated with the renewal of the spiritual life of the religious orders, a key feature of fifteenth-century Catholic reformism, especially in Italy. In 1404 he entered the Observant Dominican house of Santa Maria Novella in Florence, a convent directed by Giovanni Dominici (1355/6–1419), a renowned preacher and leader of the Italian Dominican Obervance. Subsequently, Pierozzi was to carve out his own reputation as a campaigner for the Dominican Observance, and in 1436 established the Florentine convent of San Marco that was later in the century to be Savonarola's centre of operations in the city. It was on the basis of Pierozzi's's reputation as a rebuilder of the strict Dominican way of life that Eugenius IV in 1444 designated him archbishop of Florence. As the entry on him in the *Catholic Encyclopedia* says, 'As he had laboured in the past for the upbuilding of the religious life throughout his Order, so he henceforth laboured for it in his diocese'. He undertook the regular visitation of the parishes and convents in an annual circuit of inspection carried out on foot; preaching and poor relief were the archbishop's personal concerns. Perhaps even more dramatic in its impact, though by us taken largely for granted, was Pierozzi's actual residence in his see, breaking with a recent custom of absenteeism, but affirming in his uninterrupted presence what was to be a fixed point of Trent's regulations on the episcopate. Resident as he was, Pierozzi became a civic personality and urban hero in Florence, the friar in the archiepiscopal palace, honouring total Dominican simplicity when surrounded by the splendour of his circumstances: Borromeo as archbishop of Milan was to live out the same (well-publicised) kind of drama of contrast between external magnificence and a self-denying way of life.[27]

Pierozzi may indeed be regarded as a late medieval precursor of Borromeo's Tridentine episcopal reforms and came to be regarded before the end of the sixteenth century as belonging in a tradition of episcopal sanctity that led up to Borromeo.

Both men conformed to, and Pierozzi wrote on, what may be described as the 'episcopal ideal', a prescription of what the model bishop should be like in his character and actions, a formula in part based on a Scripture (I Tim., 3). However, if the 'episcopal ideal' represented a fixed standard, for its success in implementation it depended on its application to the requirements of individual dioceses. Pierozzi's success in implementing a programme of episcopal reform in Florence arose largely from his effectiveness in applying solutions to the particular issues confronting the Tuscan city, a place of commerce, banking and enterprise in which, when businesses failed, the archbishop's charity was on hand to provide financial assistance, while much of Pierozzi's extensive writing on economics was concerned with modernising the Church's teaching to take account of a rising proto-capitalist urban economy of which Florentines were leading exponents. The prevalence of a money economy in Florence was reflected in the city's notorious proneness to gambling, and Pierozzi, like Savonarola in the 1490s, addressed himself to the social problems arising from this. Anticipating Carlo Borromeo in Milan, Pierozzi was concerned with the urban politics of his day, and, again like Borromeo, 'did not flinch from opposing the magistrates and the secular authorities on those occasions when they exceeded the limits of their powers by trespassing on the rights and privileges of the Church'. Normally, though, and again like Borromeo, Pierozzi worked harmoniously with government, in his case that of Cosimo de' Medici (1389–1464), a politician keen to harness the support of religion for political stability. Pierozzi, indeed, involved the Church in every aspect of Florentine public life, including plague relief, and 'gave audience every day to all that addressed themselves to him, but particularly declared himself the father and protector of the poor'. When death came to the archbishop, the funeral, 'already like a canonisation procession', of this Florentine hero provided an opportunity to proclaim his sanctification in the eyes of his fellow citizens in advance of his formal canonisation by Adrian VI. The discovery of Pierozzi's uncorrupted body in 1589 drew fresh attention to him as the leading pre-Reformation exemplar of the diocesan renewal that reached a high point in Borromeo's career in Milan.[28]

Some of the clearest examples of late medieval anticipations of the diocesan reforms that were legislated for by the Council of Trent and subsequently implemented throughout Catholic Europe came from England in the fourteenth and fifteenth centuries. Simon Langham (d. 1376), bishop of Ely and archbishop of Canterbury, spearheaded reform by imposing stringent regulations of priests' fees and forbade priests from levying charges for hearing Confessions, while the 1391 Constitutions of Archbishop William Courtenay (1342–96) of Canterbury controlled the conditions for priests hearing Confessions, required their consistent attention to Mass and the Office, and banned them from taverns and plays – just as the Council of Trent was to direct bishops to penalise priests' involvement in 'loose living, feasting, dances, gambling, gaming and offences of all kinds'. In 1342 Bishop John Grandison of Exeter (1262–1369) anticipated the Council of Trent by insisting on a clear demarcation between clergy and laity, demanding that in their costumes and hairstyles priests be clearly known and distinguished from laymen – just as Trent was to rule 'that by dress, gesture, gait, speech, and in every other way [priests] express only what is serious, moderate and wholly devout'. Again, just as the Council of Trent was to commission bishops to inspect priests' 'birth, age, conduct, life-style and other factors required by the holy canons', so the Constitutions (1342, 1343) of Archbishop John de Stratford (d. 1348) of Canterbury, demanded that a priest appointed to a rectory have all the qualities of a teacher, evident 'by his holy life, his learning'.[29]

Frankfurter concludes:

> Late-medieval England has plentiful evidence of episcopal renewal and bishops' registers do suggest that the Church was far from moribund. Canonical requirements for holding parish livings were closer to realisation than at any other time in the middle ages and the parish clergy were consequently better prepared to care for their people than they had ever been before. Episcopal administration had increased in efficiency and professionalism to the degree that a bishop could truly take an effective hand in the direction of parish life.

This analysis suggests that long before the Reformation the sort of targets of quality envisaged by the Council of Trent for the dioceses and the parishes were being realised in late medieval England.[30]

While Frankfurter is absolutely right to place emphasis on legislation and administrative efficiency, there was more to diocesan renewal than executive competence, for what was also required for a successful programme of episcopal reform was example, inspiration and the encapsulation of the 'episcopal ideal' in a focal figure. Such a one was present in pre-Reformation England in the person of John Fisher (1469–1535), bishop of the impoverished diocese of Rochester for three decades from 1504 until his execution by Henry VIII, for refusing the oath under the Act of Succession, in 1535. Fisher has been described as 'a truly pastoral bishop, encouraging his priests by his manner of life and by his interest in their welfare....[A] noted and assiduous preacher...he did all he could to provide well-instructed priests who could preach to the people'. It is, in short, possible to describe Fisher as a further example of a 'Tridentine' before Trent. Like Pierozzi and, later, Borromeo, he provided the indispensable spurt of personal example in sanctity that was needed to ignite otherwise inert administrative orders into genuine renewal. Trent was particularly aware that bishops must set an example of personal frugality, even, or especially, amidst the dignity of their office, and 'be content with…a frugal table and diet', living out 'a kind of perpetual sermon' on the text of moderation. One of Fisher's early biographers showed how his hero lived out such principles: 'His diet at table, was…for himself very mean…with such temperance, that commonly he was wont to eat and drink by weight and measure'. It was on the basis of his own self-denial that Fisher could claim the moral authority to restrain others, which he did, for 'where any fault was tried, he caused it to be amended.…[S]equestering [ejecting] all such as he found unworthy to occupy that high office [of priest], he placed others in their room'. In the same way, Trent was to order that bishops deprive immoral priests of their benefices. Such discipline was to be implemented through personal contact in visitations, like the one Fisher undertook at the beginning of his episcopate, when he 'carefully visited the…parish churches within his diocese in his own person'. Trent, likewise, was to order 'Local ordinaries will be obliged to visit each year churches, no matter how exempt'. Besides the parish churches, Fisher's disciplinary pastoral care extended – just as Trent would order bishops to undertake it – to the investigation of monasteries within his diocese, and he demanded that they observe 'obedience, chastity and true observance of their monastic vows'. Yet discipline and admonition were only part of Fisher's exercise of pastoral care, uppermost in which was his attention to his teaching and sacramental responsibilities: 'he omitted neither preaching to the people nor confirming of children': his efforts pointed in the direction of Trent's decree to the effect that 'the office of preaching, which particularly belongs to bishops, should be exercised as often as possible for the salvation of the people.…[T]he ordinary minister of holy confirmation is a bishop only'. Fisher's pastoral approach to his diocese was characterised by attention to its needs over a lengthy period and by as much residence and work within the diocese as his other responsibilities would permit. As far as the long-term care of his see was concerned, Fisher stayed in his original appointment to England's least remunerative diocese, worth a mere £411 a year, and eschewed the pattern of his six predecessors at Rochester who had all moved on to richer sees. As for his full-time oversight of his diocese, Fisher made every effort to avoid the character of the kind of diocesans condemned by Trent who lost their episcopal identities to the demands of political service. Fisher was, however, undoubtedly side-tracked by political responsibilities on behalf of the king. Indeed, state service by English bishops was an expectation built into the very process of their appointment, in effect by the sovereign, on the understanding that each spend at least some part of his time on government affairs. In this position, Fisher could only bewail what Trent legislated against – the constant call of bishops 'to other business' than the pastoral, by 'higher authority' – the crown – and away from a bishop's 'care of my flock committed unto me, to visit my diocese, to govern my church, and to answer the enemies of Christ'. As a would-be full-time parochial bishop, Fisher faced in an acute form a tension between the demands set up by a political mode of appointment to the office and the 'ideal of the bishop' as a single-minded father in God.[31]

Some of Fisher's episcopal colleagues were also precursors of Trent in their attention to the kinds of business, in particular the reform of monasteries, which the Council was to direct bishops to undertake. Two bishops of Lincoln, William Atwater (bishop 1514–21) and John Longland (bishop 1521–47) were particularly vigorous in this area, Longland in 1525 threatening the corrupt abbey of Thame in Oxfordshire, where the monks used to give banquets in local taverns, that he would 'apply the possessions of the monastery to some use more acceptable to God' – in other words, dissolve it for its own good. Fisher was also a monastic reformer of this kind, closing down the nunnery of Higham, an alleged nest of lechery within his diocese, and diverting its income to support the new royal foundation, St John's College, Cambridge. In the ranks of these English episcopal reformers it may occasion surprise to find Cardinal Thomas Wolsey (*c.* 1475–1530), usually identified as the source and epitome of the problem of ecclesiastical corruption in pre-Reformation England. Yet Wolsey undertook the reform of monasteries, using, like Longland and Fisher, the weapon of selective closures. Indeed, in this area he was fully supported by Fisher, because:

> Whatever reservations the future saint may have had about Wolsey as a man of God, he must have realized…that Wolsey's [papal] legatine powers, his closeness to the king, and his proven administrative and political ability offered a unique opportunity for reform.

In 1518 Wolsey obtained powers jointly with the papal legate Cardinal Lorenzo Campeggio (or Campeggi, 1474–1539) to make visitations to all religious houses in England; Wolsey's selective dissolution of monasteries can be seen in the light of Catholic reformism, and, writes Gwyn, 'it rather looks as if Wolsey's often-declared concern for reform was not the mere window-dressing that it is commonly taken to be'.[32]

If pre-Reformation England, even in the case of Wolsey, presents examples of the kind of diocesan reformism that Trent would later order, the same is true of France, the scene of some of the best-known undertakings in pre-Tridentine diocesan reforms. In the year of Luther's denunciation of Indulgences, 1517, the bishop of St Malo began to tackle the 'crudity, ignorance and inadequacy' of the clergy as teachers in his diocese, promoted an 'evangelical' programme of prayer and the recitation of the Ten Commandments and republished a standard textbook on lay and priestly education by the conciliarist reformer Gerson. At around the same time, the diocese of Meaux under its bishop Guillaume Briçonnet (1472–1534), appointed in 1518, saw the beginning of a drive to 'set the entire Church of France the example of a purification and a return to the Gospel backed by royal authority'. The central ingredients in this programme were the moral discipline of the clergy and preaching to the laity. The preaching was co-ordinated by France's leading Christian humanist, Guillaume Lefèvre d'Étaples (1455–1536) who was largely responsible for a work designed to foster preaching by the parish clergy, *Les Epistres et Évangiles des cinquantes et deux dimanches de l'An avecques briefves et très utiles expositions d'ycelles* (*The Epistles and Gospels for the Fifty-two Sundays of the Year, with Short and Very Useful Explanations of Them*) (1512). Lefèvre belonged to the 'evangelical' wing of French Christian humanism and was determined to restore the simplicity of belief and worship, the central concern with Christ as Redeemer, that he encountered in his studies of St Paul and the early Church. In line with that evangelical programme, the group of reformers in Meaux eliminated from the churches all images save those of Christ and replaced the popular prayer to Mary, the 'Ave Maria' ('Hail Mary') with the petition to God, the 'Pater Noster' ('Our Father') said in French, as the Gospels were available also in the vernacular in the form of *Les Epistres et Evangiles*. Certain features of the Meaux reforms, then, might seem to have had tendencies that were to characterise Protestantism – the use of the vernacular, the pruning of images and the apparent downgrading of Mary. Nevertheless, the Meaux experiment, which featured the regulation of public and clerical morals, regular diocesan synods, the promotion of learning and controls on religious orders, looked forward unmistakably to the Catholic reforms of Trent. Indeed, the *Dictionnaire de Théologie Catholique* viewed the Meaux renewal as the direct proto-type of the Tridentine reforms and Briçonnet as 'undertaking the reform of his diocese with the zeal of a...Carlo Borromeo'.[33]

Spain was another centre of pre-Tridentine diocesan reform under the leadership of Cardinal Francisco Ximénez de Cisneros (1436–1517), like Pierozzo an Observant friar made bishop, strict with himself and open-handed in charity. As archbishop of Spain's primatial see, Toledo, from 1495 Cisneros conducted visitations of the monasteries of Castile and 'strove to fashion the priests of his diocese into a model clergy'. Cisneros was also a herald of Trent in his care for education, setting up the University of Alcalá as a centre of Catholic scholarship and biblical studies. He also provided a model of action for fellow Spanish bishops such as Thomas of Villanueva (1488–1555), archbishop of Valencia, creating a legacy of Spanish episcopal reformism that was strongly influential at Trent.[34]

As we approach the figure of the Italian reforming bishop of Verona, Gian Matteo Giberti (1495–1543) we are leaving the area of pre-Reformation diocesan reformism and nearing the period of the Council of Trent. Borromeo, who studied the Giberti model – the *Gibertalis disciplina* – implemented the kind of diocesan reforms taken up by Pietro Lippomano (or Lippomani, d. 1548), Giberti's successor in his Verona diocese, along with those of other episcopal reformers, especially in northern Italy – in Brescia, Vicenza, Mantua, Belluno, Alba (in Lombardy), Padua, Brindisi, Genoa and in Trent itself. Our overall impression now is of a composite diocesan renewal, along the lines that the Council of Trent was to set out, put into effect by considerable numbers of bishops in Italy, England, France and Spain since the lifetime of Antonino Pierozzi.[35]

Having now examined the late-medieval sources of three categories of Catholic reformism of the sixteenth century – the conciliar, the papal and the episcopal – we turn next, in our pursuit of the medieval roots of the Catholic Reformation, to consider the possible medieval precedents of the new religious orders founded to deal with the special circumstances of the age of the Reformation. Historians have emphasised the modernity of the orders known as 'Clerks Regular', and especially the Jesuits. In the view of Dickens, the success of the Jesuits was due to their adaptation to the new challenges of the age in which they were born, and, in particular, their ability to counter the Protestant Reformation: 'the work of Loyola' [the Jesuits' founder], writes Dickens, 'cannot be assessed save in the context of a world shaken to its foundations by Luther and Calvin'. Brinton adds 'the Jesuits…were…one manifestation of a…new spirituality which was springing up in the Catholic Church…sharply divergent from similar-sounding organisations of the Middle Ages'. Grimm comments that Loyola was responsible for 'creating a new conception of holiness which found the fullest expression in a practical activity on behalf of God'. We need, though, to consider whether the 'new orders', including the Jesuits founded in the sixteenth century, were in fact quite as revolutionary in their values and aspiration as some commentators have taken them to have been. Focusing particularly on the Jesuits, we might ask if their aim was indeed expressive of a 'new spirituality', if it was 'sharply divergent' from medieval forms of organisation of religious life in 'a new conception of holiness' and if their concern with 'practical activity on behalf of God' was quite as novel as it has appeared to some.[36]

The belief that the aims of the new Orders, and of the Jesuits in particular, amounted to an essentially 'new conception of holiness', grounded for the first time in practical effort in the world, may in fact be based on certain stereotypical assumptions about the nature of the life and purpose of the medieval religious orders, as if the sole and unvarying concern of their spirituality was, in Brinton's words 'associated with withdrawal from the world', so that it was only in the 'new age' of the sixteenth century that 'men found the service of God among their fellow men'. In fact, we shall find that dedication to work in the world, especially in towns and cities, a common feature of such new orders of the sixteenth century as the Theatines, the Barnabites, the Somaschi and the Jesuits, was already strongly marked in the life of the religious orders of the middle ages. Indeed, through his religious reading, Loyola came to admire two founders of medieval religious Orders, Francis of Assisi (c. 1181–1226) and Dominic de Guzmán (1170–1221), who had preceded him in devising regular orders concerned primarily with an apostolate to the laity. Francis and Dominic were themselves, in turn, part of a long-range evolution in the life of the religious orders of the Catholic Church in the middle ages which we might describe as a shift in emphasis away from personal sanctification through monastic contemplation, prayer and asceticism towards active evangelism in the world.

It is indeed true that the great monastic religious orders of the early and high middle ages, from the establishment of Benedictine monasticism in the sixth century through to the foundation of the Benedictine tree's branches, the Cluniac and Cistercian Orders in the early tenth and late eleventh centuries respectively, had been chiefly concerned, as Knowles wrote, to lead 'men away from the world and set before them life in a monastery as the norm'. In fact, though, the 'contemplative' Benedictines also played a leading role in the conversion of much of northern Europe, and their engagement with the world, their sense of apostolate, were taken up and developed, from the twelfth century, with the rise of the missionary orders of Canons Regular. There are indications that these emerged partially as a response to the challenges of urbanisation during the economic expansion of the high middle ages. The Premonstratensian Canons Regular, founded by the German Norbert of Xanten (1080–1134), for example, provided in their preaching an antidote to a heresy that had arisen in the expanding port of Antwerp. The Order's organisation, based on provinces which looked to the abbot of the founding house, Prémontré, was, like that of the Jesuits, designed for effectiveness in the pastoral field.[37]

If we regard preaching as the hallmark of apostolate, it was in the forefront of the purposes of a founder strongly influenced by Norbert: Dominic. And as we approach the Dominicans, the 'Order of Preachers', we move ever closer to the preoccupation with evangelism through preaching and teaching that was to characterise the Jesuits. Because of those demands of preaching, the Dominican Order was prepared to downplay the time-consuming collective prayer that was the hallmark of the monk, a lessening of emphasis which reached its conclusion in the Jesuits' abandonment of this practice: the Dominicans would dispense with the choral recitation of the Office when, as Jarrett wrote, it 'proved a hindrance to the apostolical life which was the central work of the Order'. Services were shortened, and fasting could be relaxed in favour of study and preparation to fashion expert preachers. All in all, then, with a system of priorities emphasising evangelical work to the wider community, the Dominicans represent a key medieval stage in a long evolution of the religious orders – 'the de-monachization of the religious life' – away from the pure contemplative and prayerful ideal of the monks towards the missionary and activist aims that were enshrined in the Clerks Regular founded in the sixteenth century. We should not exaggerate the closeness of the Dominicans to the Clerks Regular nor forget the extent to which the Order of Preachers remained attached in their monastic evolutionary antecedents, especially in the primacy of prayer, contemplation and self-denial. Nevertheless, in the Dominicans, with their 'centralization and firm rule', the Jesuits had their closest medieval progenitors: the order often regarded as being in the advance post of Catholic modernisation in the sixteenth century, the Society of Jesus, was firmly anchored, as were other aspects of the early modern Catholic Reformation we have so far considered, within the medieval past. (As we shall see, the Carthusian Order combined the contemplative and evangelistic ideals through their work in religious publishing.)[38]

One of the ways, though, in which the new orders of the sixteenth century might be seen as innovative is in their use of mass media and techniques of salesmanship and publicity which we associate with modernity, the media and mass culture. For example, Jesuits in Germany, led by Peter Canisius (1521–97), were phenomenally successful in promoting their message and in winning over opinion in large tracts of the German lands: they composed catechisms for the use of schoolmasters, published plays, poems and hymns, tracts and brochures conveying the themes they wanted to put across, set up and directed sodalities, organised pilgrimages, and carried out missions deep into Protestant territory. Likewise, few could excel the Oratorian founder Filippo Neri in mastery of the techniques of publicity. Neri's mission was largely directed at the ordinary people of Rome, apprentices, students, craftsmen, textile and leather workers. For these people Neri devised prayer cycles and rosaries, gave them social work to do, but also enthusiastically used the resources of popular theatre, including the clowning of the Italian *commedia dell'arte*, to promote his message. Neri, quite simply and brilliantly, took his apostolate to the streets of Rome, trundling out his Confessional box like a merchant's market stall, 'ready for all comers'. He employed the composer Giovanni Animuccia's (1505–71) *Laudi Spirituali* (*Songs of Spiritual Praise*, 1563, 1570), adapted from a popular Florentine medium, to accompany his well-attended tours around Rome's basilicas. The flavour of his ballads was unmistakably that of mass culture and advertising, using catch-phrases and jingles, such as '*Giesù, Giesù, ogni chiama Giesù* ('Jesus, Jesus, everyone's calling Jesus!').[39]

If, though, Neri in Rome and the Jesuits in Germany used recognisably 'modern' techniques of promotion and religious advertising, such methods were already well developed by the most popular of the medieval preachers, and above all by the Franciscan Observant Bernardino of Siena, called by Hay, 'the greatest preacher of his day'. Bernardino delivered 'racy vernacular sermons, preached at Siena in the great *piazza* before the Palazzo Pubblico on which is still painted the Holy name, surrounded by radiant beams of light, which was his symbol'.

If Bernardino's modern-seeming use of a 'logo' for recognition and publicity puts us in mind of Neri's deployment of popular song for the same purposes, Bernardino, like Neri, added street humour to his repertoire of crowd-pulling, including black comedy, as in his story of the woman who had been having sex with the devil over the course of some months, only to find (somewhat belatedly, one might think) that her lover had a suspiciously scaly belly. The popular outreach of Catholic Reformation preaching, its uninhibited use of techniques of entertainment, drama, spectacle and publicity, as on display in dramatic preaching by various orders in Europe between the sixteenth and eighteenth centuries, was fully anticipated in late medieval methods of evangelism.[40]

As far as the popular piety of the Catholic Reformation is concerned, we are, once again, aware of continuities rather than innovations between the late medieval and early modern periods. The Rosary, for example, whose vogue as a meditative prayer was fostered in the fifteenth century by Alain de la Roche (Alanus de Rupe, *c.* 1428–75) increased in popularity, as Winston-Allen writes, 'in the Counter-Reformation period following the reforms of the Council of Trent'.

As Herlihy says, 'The Tridentine reformation of Catholic piety had deep medieval roots', the devotional styles of 'the new Catholic world' of the sixteenth century, being, as Dickens writes 'deep-rooted in tradition' and in 'medieval instruments of devotion'. Many of these roots went back to late-medieval Florence, whose revivalism Neri brought to Rome. A particular feature of the late-medieval Florentine Christian Renaissance, anticipating the vigorous apostolate to the laity in the Catholic Reformation, was what Becker terms the 'democratization of spiritual life', in which the pursuit of holiness was viewed 'not as the special preserve of orders and individuals' but as a civic and communal goal, absorbing the 'collected good works of the community', giving Florence 'a new direction in Christian piety' and involving 'virtually all Florentines above the poverty level' in membership in one or another of the city's confraternities, with their focus on charity. Late medieval Florence was a leading laboratory in devising what were to emerge as the civic and social programme of the Catholic Reformation, aimed at, and fully involving, the laity, especially through their enrolment in pious confraternities.[41]

The civic and social programme of Catholic renewal in late-medieval Florence, pursued by Antonino Pierozzi, was taken up by Savonarola in the 1490s in his puritan crusade to reform Florence. Yet there was a further way in which Savonarola prepared the way for the Catholic Reformation and that was in the field of the doctrine of salvation ('soteriology'). Savonarola's prison meditations of 1498 'exhibit his confidence in the grace and mercy of God, and the certainty that salvation is to be found in the merits of Christ alone': 'Yes, I have Faith', Savonarola exclaimed: 'Then know that it is a great gift of God, for Faith is God's gift, nor is it to be obtained by our works lest anyone should take glory to himself'. This was not a case, as Luther claimed, of Savonarola's having taught Luther's doctrine of justification (or salvation) by faith alone. It was, though, typical of a late-medieval and early sixteenth-century resumption of St Paul's (d. *c*. 69) and St Augustine's insistences on the centrality of grace and faith in redemption. For example, Richard Fox, bishop of Winchester from 1501 to 1528, recommended Religious to concentrate their 'thoughts and remembrances upon Christ and his passion, merit and benefit', while a series of papal preachers in Renaissance Rome dwelt on the 'absolute necessity of grace' and the insufficiency of man's works under the law to win justification. The culmination of this tradition, which ran through Savonarola, was Trent's declaration of Christians' reliance on the saving merits of Christ: 'all our glorying is in Christ; in whom we live, in whom we merit; in whom we satisfy; *bringing forth fruits worthy of penance*, which from him [Christ] have their efficacy'.[42]

As well as a civic reformer and a pioneer of the soteriological insights of the Catholic Reformation, Savonarola should also be seen as a vital factor in the reform of the regular orders that was taking place between the fourteenth and sixteenth centuries, and his vigorous attempts to restore the Dominican Observance in Tuscany may be seen as a microcosm of his commitment to the purification of the Church as a whole. Monastic reform was an essential part of the Tridentine Reformation and was, again, anticipated in late-medieval developments. The monastic Carthusian Order, founded by St Bruno in 1084, dedicated to silence, study, solitude and prayer, and according to its own claim 'never reformed because never deformed', acted as a bench-mark of moral quality by which the other orders and, indeed, the Church at large might be assessed. In 1368, when faced with a papal invitation to relax their pristine austerity, the Carthusian Order, in its *Nova Statuta* (*New Regulations*), firmly restated its fundamental principles of asceticism. In England, when monasticism faced a double crisis, of numbers and of morale, following the Black Death of the mid-fourteenth century, a new Carthusian foundation was established at Mount Grace in Yorkshire in 1398. Today, the largely extant site at Mount Grace conveys the Carthusian ethos and purpose graphically, for the lay-out of separate apartment-like cells provided the physical framework for a 'private, self-conscious' contemplative spirituality on the basis of which Carthusian authors such as Adolf of Essen (d. 1439) and Dominic of Prussia wrote with pious lay folk in mind to convey methods and themes of meditation. The English Carthusians were particularly to the fore in transmitting the approaches of the Continental *devotio moderna* to pious lay people as well as priests in England. The largest of the English Charterhouses was founded by Henry V at Sheen (later Richmond) in 1414; its links with Catholic reform in mid-sixteenth-century England are evident in the influence Sheen had on Queen Mary's Archbishop of Canterbury between 1556 and 1558, Cardinal Reginald Pole (1500–58), who spent two of his formative years at Sheen, in retreat and study. In London, the Carthusians' ability to bring the world of meditation to bear on the mundane concerns of the bustling city was encapsulated in the placing of the Charterhouse (founded in 1471) under the very walls. And just as Sheen influenced Pole, the London Charterhouse contributed to the religious development of another major Tudor Catholic reformist, Thomas More (1478–1535).[43]

If, in pre-Reformation England, the Charterhouses provided models of monastic observance, influencing lay people both by their example and by their literary productions, at the original centre of the Order, the Grande Chartreuse near Grenoble in France, a succession of abbots maintained strict observance in the decades before the Reformation. New houses were established in Aragon and Granada, as well as in France, and the Jesuit founder Ignatius Loyola was strongly drawn to enter the famous Carthusian house in Seville. In the year of Luther's appearance at the Diet of Worms, 1521, the Carthusian Order in Europe had never, Mathew and Mathew write, 'been more flourishing'.[44]

As a monk and Catholic reformer, Martin Luther (1483–1546) took his inspiration from the monastic renewal of the late middle ages where, in Germany, the influence of the reforms implemented in the Dutch Windesheim congregation of Augustinian Canons Regular were helping to reinvigorate conventual life. Luther himself first rose to prominence as a monastic reformer. Under the inspiration of his superior Johann von Staupitz (*c.* 1460–1524), the vicar in Germany of Luther's Order and leader of the Observant wing within it, the young monk Martin Luther, from his entry into an Augustinian Eremite monastery in 1505, was indeed a prime example of the moral perfectionism of the monastic ideal in one of its more austere variants. In fact, Luther's entry into the monastery occurred near the time of the restatement in 1504 of his Order's goals of personal sanctification to be achieved through prayer, austerity and unrelenting effort. These Constitutions of the Reformed Congregation of the German Augustinian Order of 1504 laid special stress on the most searching confession of sin within the Sacrament of Penance. Luther recalled how compulsively he had pursued that goal: 'I was accustomed, once I was contrite, to confess and enumerate every one of my sins. Frequently I repeated my confession and I assiduously performed the penance laid upon me'. The moral perfectionism of reformed monasticism provided the framework for Luther's extremely conscientious pursuit of forgiveness won by himself, for himself, through his penitential exercises. However, Luther was not simply a recipient of the reformed Augustinian discipline but became himself an active campaigner for monastic renewal, along lines set out by Staupitz. He was, indeed, Staupitz's protégé, sent by his superior to lecture at the University of Wittenberg in 1508 and succeeding him there as Professor of Sacred Scripture: when Luther travelled to Rome in 1510 to protest on behalf of his Erfurt house against Staupitz's proposed unified Augustinian rule, the protest was made on the grounds that the house in Erfurt, like that in Nuremberg and other places, had already reformed itself on Staupitz's model. By 1515, as Staupitz's disciple, Luther had become regional vicar of eleven Augustinian houses. He was a monastic martinet who, in the very year before his breach with Rome was first opened in 1517, was writing in the most severe disciplinarian fashion to various negligent priors of houses to encourage them to keep their communities up to the Staupitz programme. The Catholic monastic reformer Luther, then, extending his range in 1517 to take in the renewal of the Church, displayed, up to and somewhat beyond the year of the genesis of his reform critique of the Church, the roots of sixteenth-century Church reform in the monastic revival of the late middle ages.[45]

2 The Council of Trent and the Catholic Reformation

Coming to prominence first as a monastic reformer, Luther extended his range to take in the wider issue of the reform of the Church at large, to restore it, as Atkinson writes, to 'its original character and message, to offer *re-formatio* to that which had suffered *de-formatio*....Luther protested as a Catholic within the Catholic Church....He wanted his Church to be truly and fully Catholic and to take within itself the pure Gospel'. Hendrix adds that for Luther during the second decade of the sixteenth century the Roman Church was the 'chief part' of the Church whose faith would not fail. He castigated laxity in the Church, as he did in his own order, but 'none of Luther's criticism impugned the authority of the Roman hierarchy or the authority of the pope himself. Luther's criticism was not revolutionary'. Nevertheless, between 1505 and 1518 Luther discovered in Scripture, in the Epistles of St Paul and above all in Romans, Chapter 8, that Christians were made acceptable to God, forgiven and made just – 'justified' – not by their own pious practices and good works but solely through the merits won by Christ's saving death on the cross. Therefore, with increasing urgency Luther demanded a theological *reformatio* by which the Church, eliminating its trust in what Luther saw as human devices, including indulgences, would affirm with Luther the truths he had found in St Paul. The 95 Theses of October 1517 should be seen as Luther's call to the Church to reaffirm a Pauline soteriology of justification by the merits of Christ, received in faith. Seeking to bring the entire Church round to this position, Luther sent his supplement to the 95 Theses to Pope Leo X. However, since it was difficult, if not impossible, to reconcile Luther's Pauline soteriology of justification by faith alone with the Catholic Church's routines which rested on assumptions that men and women were saved in part by their own efforts supported by the Sacraments and other procedures of the Church, Luther's severance from Catholicism was basically unavoidable. Certain circumstances leading to the separation of Luther and the Catholic Church could, perhaps, have worked out otherwise than they did: Luther's orthodox polemical foes, Johann Tetzel (1465–1519) and Johannes Maier von Eck (1486–1543), were determined to arraign him; the primate of Germany, Albrecht von Hohenzollern (1490–1545), dealt extensively in indulgences and had a vested interest in suppressing Luther's protest against them. The theological concerns, though, were those of fundamentals rather than of circumstances and turned on the means of grace and forgiveness of sinners. The deep rift led to the excommunication of Luther by Leo X in 1520 and his condemnation by the Diet of Worms in 1521. When the Catholic Church turned to these all-important soteriological issues in the course of the Council of Trent, it restated the position that the just were saved by faith but stopped well short of agreeing with Luther's belief, based on Paul, to the effect that they were saved by faith alone.[1]

Calling the council that was to set out that position was subject to protracted delay, in the first place because the papacy had an institutionally inbuilt distrust of councils, for fifteenth-century councils had challenged papal powers, while Savonarola had appealed to a council against the papacy of Alexander VI, and opportunist rulers such as Ferdinand (1452–1516) and Isabella (1451–1504) of Spain had used the threat of calling a council as a tactical weapon against popes. The historian of the Council of Trent, Hubert Jedin, recounted the delay in convening a council. Calls for it rose in volume in Germany in the 1520s, focusing on 'a free Christian Council in German lands'. Jedin went on to specu-late that if such a council had met in that decade – in 1525, say, rather than twenty years later:

> it would only have been faced with a heresy and a popular movement insti-gated by it....Lutheran churches were not yet organised, the princes and towns who had embraced the new faith did not as yet constitute a political power, the mass of the people were still moulded by Catholic teaching and piety. A conciliar condemnation of Luther's teaching would probably have been accepted by the great majority of the German people and a reform decreed by the Council might yet have prevailed over the Lutheran one.[2]

It is indeed true that determined efforts were being made within Germany to summon a council, at about the time that Jedin believed that such a body might have suppressed the Lutherans. The German national assembly, representing the princely states and self-governing cities into which the country was divided, the *Reichstag*, or Diet, meeting in Nuremberg in 1524, published a decree in April pointing towards a council to be held in some convenient place within Germany. At that juncture, as Jedin wrote, religious conservatism still characterised most ruling German circles, as the *Reichstag*'s proceedings show: the country's rulers were instructed by their own representative body to take measures to have the Gospel preached according to the doctrines of theologians approved by the Catholic Church; those in authority were to suppress all defamatory publications attacking the Roman Curia, as well as the satirical cartoons ridiculing the pope and bishops. The same impression of Catholic resolve was given at around this time when the Archduke Ferdinand of Habsburg (1503–64), brother of the Holy Roman Emperor Charles V (1500–58), along with other German Catholic secular and ecclesiastical leaders, met with the papal legate Cardinal Lorenzo Campeggio in Regensburg in July 1524 to demand the enforcement of the1521 Edict of Worms against Luther and his supporters. These rulers and prelates also insisted on the retention of the existing rites of the Mass and sacraments and demanded that priests and nuns who had abandoned their vows, as well as priests who married (as Luther did, in 1525) and all those who had presumed to receive Holy Communion without first going to Confession should be punished.[3]

Might such Catholic determination in Germany in these early years of the Lutheran Reformation, combined with a desire to convene a council, have been able to stifle Protestantism in its infancy in Germany, twenty years before the much-delayed council finally met in Trent? In other words, were the two decades that lay between the Reichstag of Nuremberg and the convening of Trent years of wasted opportunity for the Catholic Church, decades in which Lutheranism, vulnerable in 1524, became irremovable from the scene by 1545? One possible answer to those questions is that the council that was envisaged at Nuremberg – *ain sinodum teutscher nacion* (a synod of the German nation), a *nacional Consilium* (national Council), essentially concerned with German issues – was not of the kind that eventually met at Trent to reform the whole Catholic Church. It was on convening a *general* council that Rome's legate Campeggio insisted in the 1520s. However, to bring together that kind of assembly would take time – decades, in fact, during which, it is true, much of Germany and of northern Europe were to be lost to Rome. In 1524 Campeggio warned of a possible delay of two to three years in calling a council of Christendom, 'since the pope would have to summon six different nations and he would also have to come to an understanding on the subject [of a council] with the princes'. The two years turned into two decades, but the council that eventually sat was able to address the problems of the Church as a whole and, indeed, constructed measures which resulted in Catholic recoveries in the German lands themselves.[4]

While Campeggio emphasised the diplomatic obstacles to calling a council, the most formidable barrier was what Jedin called the papacy's 'notorious aversion from a Council'. This distaste would have to be overcome rather than over-ridden, for to proceed with a non-papal or rebel council would have crippled the Catholic Church in its anti-Lutheran counter-offensive. Papal antipathy arose from the memory of antagonism between popes and council in the fifteenth century, especially the tussle between Eugenius IV and the Council of Basel in 1431 over the pope's powers to dissolve the Council, and the Council's purported deposition of Eugenius in 1439. Further, the revival of proposals for a council in the wake of Luther's protest came at an unfortunate juncture in the long-term construction of the papal monarchy following the Great Schism. Anthony Black writes of a conciliar ideology grounded in the political 'idea of communal government' and the 'corporational notion of popular sovereignty' which are traceable to the late medieval 'idea of the commune' and posited 'a kind of constitutional monarchy' in the Church. Not until the sixteenth-century papal monarchical system's inherited fears of the constitutional threats from councils could be appeased would it have been realistic to expect the papal administration – the Curia – to accede to summoning such a body. Assurances of the papacy's ability to control a council were constantly sought in advance of a convocation and were particularly expressed in delay-inducing attempts to site a gathering in a place within Rome's oversight. In 1537, for example, Paul III was favouring as locations Piacenza or Bologna, 'places belonging to the church, the common mother of all'. It was also the case that institutional anti-conciliarism in Rome arose from the fear of curial administrators who surrounded and advised the pope of the threat to their spoils system from a critical, reformist, anti-curial council. A considerable period of time could be expected to elapse before the papacy's historic fears, inherited from the fifteenth century and boosted by self-interest in the pope's entourage, could be sufficiently assuaged to make a summons possible.[5]

A period of great difficulty for the Catholic Church, when a council summons might have been expected, was that of the long pontificate of Clement VII. Clement became pope at roughly the point in time at which Jedin calculated a council would have been opportune for resolving Germany's religious problems. On his election Clement showed promise as a reforming pope. He was, wrote Jedin, 'intellectually wide-awake, earnest and free from moral taint', and the Venetian ambassador Foscari described him as 'a just man and a man of God'. While archbishop of Florence, he had shown awareness of the need for diocesan reform and following his election he set up a commission of cardinals to enforce the decrees of the Fifth Lateran Council. A leading reform-minded cardinal, Gasparo Contarini (1483–1542), acknowledged Clement's good intentions: 'He is certainly desirous of relieving those evils by which the church is oppressed'. Clement was particularly keen to address Germany's religious problems by focusing on the quality of the country's bishops, their officials, the parish priests and other clergy, and he sent Campeggio to the *Reichstag* at Nuremberg to negotiate. However, as the hostile historian of the Council of Trent, Paolo Sarpi (1552–1623), suggested, Clement was primarily a political operator: it seems significant that virtually all the entries concerning him in the index to the relevant volume of the *Histoire Ecclésiastique* are taken up with his political manoeuvres and above all with his aim of restoring his Medici family to rule Florence. Clement's concerns with politics meant that he was unlikely to give priority to Church reform by means of summoning a council. The effects of Clement's preoccupation with politics and diplomacy in delaying reforms were compounded by his indecisiveness. He 'talked well but decided weakly', a contemporary said of him, and Foscari added that he was 'slow to resolve…irresolute and changeable in his proceedings…very timid'. Clement's inherent timidity and lack of resolution were probably intensified by the disastrous outcome of his anti-Habsburg foreign policy, when, in 1527, Rome was ransacked by Charles V's mutinous soldiers and the Pope was taken prisoner. Calling a council, reforming the Church, were ventures full of risk. It is true that in his reconciliation with Charles V at the Imperial coronation of 1530 Clement formally committed himself to a summons. Nevertheless, towards the end of his pontificate, in 1533, Clement was still using delaying tactics to stall the summoning of a council. Contarini's summary of Clement's incapacity for reform – he 'does not adopt any effectual measures for that purpose' – sums up a pontificate barren of efforts to convene a reforming council.[6]

That is not true of the following pontificate, that of Paul III. Personally, Paul epitomised much of the decadence of papal Rome in the High Renaissance period – he had been appointed cardinal by the corrupt Alexander VI and was passionately devoted to the interests of his Farnese family, using the *Dataria* as a source for what Hallman calls his 'lavish and colourful expenditures' on them. Even so, Paul engineered a revolution in papal policy towards councils and indeed came to the papacy on a kind of electoral pledge to issue a summons. As early as October 1534 Paul addressed the cardinals on the need for a council. Yet Paul's enthusiasm had to defer to the hold-up caused by a fresh outbreak of Habsburg–Valois war between 1536 and 1538, putting a peaceful and well-attended council out of the question. Delays were also caused by disagreement, featuring in talks between Paul and Charles V in 1536, over location. Was the proposed council to be called to an Italian city such as Verona, Vicenza, Turin, Piacenza, Bologna or Mantua (announced in consistory June 1536 as the meeting place for 23 May of the following year), or to a German venue? Strasbourg, Cologne, Mainz and Metz had all been mentioned. These skirmishings arose from the issue of what kind of council was envisaged, whether this was to be an essentially reaffirmative Catholic body under papal control or an open forum to accommodate Lutherans and deal, in Germany, with German grievances against the Church. However, Paul's delays were, unlike Clement's, hesitations in reaching a goal that the pope genuinely desired. That Paul was pledged to a programme of reform which it was hoped a council would implement was evident in his appointments to the Sacred College of Cardinals. His promotion of John Fisher was of a leading exemplar of diocesan renewal. Indeed, Paul can be said to have drafted into the Sacred College an identifiable party of reformists, including Reginald Pole (1500–58) and Gasparo Contarini, two leading proponents of a mediating soteriology of grace thought to be capable of conciliating Lutherans. Other new cardinalatial appointments from the reform group included those of Giacomo Sadoleto (1477–1547), a devout scholar and the reforming bishop of Carpentras, and Gian Pietro Carafa, joint founder of the new order of Theatines and future pope, as Paul IV (1555–9).[7]

The year when Paul issued his bull summoning the council was a momentous one for reform in Germany and in Rome. In Germany what may be regarded as a prototype for Trent was assembled in the Archbishopric of Cologne by its prelate Hermann von Wied (1515–47) supported by its reform-minded chancellor Johannes Gropper (1503–59). Von Wied was inclined to Protestantism and was deposed in 1546. However, his council, under the guidance of Gropper, the leading spokesman of Catholic reform in the Rhineland and made a cardinal by the ultra-orthodox Pope Paul IV, may be seen as a pointer towards the proceedings of the Council of Trent in practical questions, if not entirely over doctrinal issues. The parallels between Cologne and Trent are above all evident in the attention that the Cologne assembly gave in thirty-six chapters to the office and duties of bishops, emphasising a bishop's duty to exercise meticulous discernment of candidates for ordination and prefiguring Trent's rulings that bishops should 'carefully investigate and examine the...person, age, education, morals, learning and faith of those who are to be ordained'. Again, the Cologne council's strictures against pluralism point towards Trent's order that 'those who now hold several churches' should retain one only. Of course, such rulings were to be found in the aspirations to reform of many medieval Church councils and synods. Nevertheless, the concentrated attention that both Cologne and Trent gave to the parochial priesthood – the elimination of lay recreations, dress and behaviour from priests' lives, the insistence that priests preach in discourses suit-able to the capacities of their congregations – and to the duties of the episcopate in upholding standards – indicate how prominent these priorities had become in Catholic reformist circles by the middle decades of the sixteenth century. In their shared aspirations, Cologne and Trent literally spoke a common language, so that, where Cologne condemned priests who 'approached the altar with corrupt hearts', Trent insisted that Mass be celebrated 'with the greatest possible interior cleanness and purity of hearts'. Both councils called for reforms of the Missal and Breviary, and Cologne prefigured Trent in condemning the subordination of the liturgy to the 'purely secular pleasure' of music – where Trent ruled against 'all such music which, whether by the organ or in singing, contains things that are lascivious or impure'. Von Wied's Cologne synod allows us, then, to identify the dominant concerns of Catholic reform in the decades up to and including the Council of Trent.[8]

In Rome, too, the year 1536 saw a rapid acceleration in the momentum of reform in the shape of an outline agenda for what were to be principal concerns of the general council that lay in the future. In the summer of 1536 Paul III set up a nine-man select committee including his newly appointed reform-minded cardinals, Carafa, Contarini, Pole and Sadoleto. This committee submitted its report to the pope early in 1537: *Consilium Delectorum Cardinalium et Aliorum Praelatorum de Emendanda Ecclesia – Recommendations of the Select Committee of Cardinals and Other Prelates on the Reform of the Church.*[9]

One of the most striking features of this report, linking it with the Cologne council and pointing forward to Trent, is its insistent concern with the priest-hood, its training and selection, in which, the report observed, at the time of writing 'neither care nor diligence is used. Candidates may be anyone from anywhere, ignorant in the highest degree...of bad morals...mere youths'. The authors of the report offered as a solution to this state of affairs a sketch of the educational system for the clergy that Trent was to adopt:

> we think it would be best for the future, if your Holiness would first of all in this city [of Rome] assign two or three learned and virtuous prelates who will take charge of the ordination of clerics. You should also enjoin all bishops, even threatening the penalties of censure, that they do the same in their dioceses....Moreover, each bishop should have in his churches a master to instruct the minor clerics in both letters and morals.[10]

We should note that the authors of the report, even though their brief was the reform of the whole Church, introduced their educational proposals, as they prefaced their survey of the parlous moral state of the Church, with the situation in Rome, where the authors noted the scandal of prostitutes consorting with the associates of cardinals. In focusing their attention on Rome, the committee members who were cardinals may have been alluding to the origin of their offices as priests of the city, with responsibilities for its churches. However, the authors were also aware that Rome was the head and mother of the Catholic Church so that the city's moral and spiritual state, for good or ill, must inspire that of the Church at large, and renewal had to begin there and with the pope, spreading out from the head to the limbs of the body of Christ, the Church. The pope, 'director of the mother church and teacher of all other churches', was to direct the bishops to undertake clerical education, confer benefices on worthy recipients, avoid mercenary motives in making appointments, impose clerical residence, discipline the clergy, oversee preachers from the religious orders and ensure that members of orders wore their habits, supervised the orthodoxy of school teaching and reconciled quarrelling neighbours. As Trent was to do, the authors of the 1537 report charged the bishops, under the authority of the pope, though with extensive powers of their own, with responsibility for the transformation of the Catholic Church.[11]

Did the *Consilium* imply any criticism of Paul III, with his nepotism and financial corruption? The authors of the report in fact pointed the finger at curial officials for breeding abuses through 'the cunning of some skilled persons' – courtiers, bureaucrats and hangers-on. In adopting this approach, the report's authors were borrowing from the language of contemporaneous secular politics in the shape of appeals to kings to put an end to the oppressions carried out in their name by their servants and ministers, especially those who flattered the ruler that his power was limitless. Something of this tone was present in the request made in the *Consilium* that the pope discover 'whence comes the craven doctrine by which it has finally been effected that what is desirable is permissible'. This approach presented Paul not as the source of the ills of the Church but as the sole hope of its renewal:

> under your leadership, may we see the Church of God purged, beautiful as a dove…to restore to our hearts and chosen undertakings the name of Christ among the people and us clergymen. May you heal infirmities, return the sheep of Christ to our fold.

Far from threatening the papacy as an institution, as conciliar reformists in the past had sometimes appeared to do, the *Consilium* paved the way for papal direction of Catholic reform in the sixteenth century by putting its confidence in the Holy See to renew the Church, affirming its confidence in what St Bernard called 'the sacred duties of the pope's office to watch over the universal Church'.[12]

Paul's response to such expectations of his taking the leadership in reform was encapsulated in his summons of the council to Mantua, a tactical decision, though, that evoked an angry reaction from Charles V, whose goal was to find a site within the Holy Roman Empire which would give out, in a divided Germany menaced by the Turks, messages about a reconciling council. May 1537 came and went without a council meeting in Mantua. While German Lutherans insisted on a kind of council that the papacy would not tolerate, including lay members and with its deliberations based on Scripture alone, bickering over an armed guard for the assembly caused further delays in activating the council at what would have been an inopportune time, when the French were unlikely to attend. When Paul, in November 1537, called the council to Vicenza, in Venetian territory, Henry VIII of England lodged a protest against the summons, though the pope travelled to Nice to encourage the reconciliation of Charles V and Francis I of France (1494–1547) so as to make way for a gathering attended by the indispensable emissaries from the two leading Catholic state systems, France and the Habsburg territories. In the new year, however, the pope's legates reported from Vicenza that the Emperor and King Francis had failed to send any bishops from their realms. Francis was reluctant to forfeit his alliance with German Lutheran princes against Charles V in favour of full support for the council project, while on the domestic front he was concerned at a reforming council's potential threat to the royal control of the Church in France. Political stalemate ensured that in spring 1538 the pope further suspended the coming together of the assembly. Then in June 1539, with several cardinals arguing that continued war between the leading Catholic rulers would make a council unproductive, Paul formally suspended the project of the council 'at the pleasure of the pope and the apostolic see'. This suspension *sine die* was in fact to last for a further three years, a period of what Jedin called 'Reform without a Council', which was also one of a search for agreement with the Protestants.[13]

In his search for supporters of reform, Paul advanced some individuals who sympathised with the view which the Lutherans had appropriated that the just were saved by faith. In 1542, for example, he appointed to the College of Cardinals Giovanni Morone (1509–80), who, in 1537, wrote to another reconciling theologian, Sadoleto, to condemn those 'reputed defenders of the Catholic faith who think that our religion consists in nothing but hatred of the Lutherans...they take in bad part...all negotiations with the Lutherans'. In fact, such negotiations were brought to centre stage in the period 1539–42 during which the council project was suspended in favour of 'conferences' and in which members of what Daniel-Rops calls the 'modernists' – with Contarini and Pole alongside Morone and Sadoleto – were given their head against the conservative 'integrists' led by Carafa. The most important opportunity the reconcilers had to justify their policies and make them succeed came at the conference held alongside the *Reichstag*, held in Regensburg (or Ratisbon) in southern Germany in 1541.[14]

The Regensburg talks had their origin in projects for reunification put forward within the period of the German Reformation, for example when the

Reichstag at Frankfurt in 1539 supported Charles V's plan for a conference of national religious reconciliation rather than a unilateral Catholic assembly thought likely to intensify discord with Protestants. However, the scope for collision between Catholicism and Lutheranism was wider than the issue of justification, on which, as we have seen, some Catholic leaders, especially the pope's representative at Regensburg, Contarini, were close to the views on salvation that the Lutherans had made their own. Though an extensive measure of agreement was produced on justification, thanks to some concurrence of views between the 'evangelical' Contarini and the moderate Lutheran negotiator, Philipp Melanchthon (1497–1560), other issues, and especially that of the Eucharist and Christ's presence within it, opened up a second front of conflict at Regensburg, so disastrously that Matheson writes: 'The dialogue between Protestantism and Catholicism at…Regensburg…did not fail. It never took place'. The failure of the Regensburg talks, for which Jedin ascribes the blame to Contarini, re-opened the avenue for a more exclusively Catholic settlement, in a council of the Church. As Jedin writes, 'Only the failure of the Ratisbon attempt at re-union could justify the drawing of the Tridentine line of demarcation'. Indeed, the reforms in the Curia and the Church that Paul III introduced in the late 1530s and early 1540s, including a bull in 1542 encouraging episcopal residence, renewed the stress on disciplinary injunctions that was to characterise Trent. Paul resumed the project of the council in an offer to the Germans in the summer of 1541; a formal summons was issued in May 1542. In the July of the same year the establishment of the Roman Inquisition under Carafa, designed to root out heterodoxy and, specifically, views on justification deemed akin to Lutheranism, could be read as a signal that the 'modernists', though far from crushed, must now cede the 'integrists' their turn.[15]

The period between the collapse of the Regensburg talks and the realisation of the council saw a clearing away of obstacles to a council gathering. The choice of location having acted as a barrier to a meeting, Ferdinand of Habsburg's suggestion of Trent, a small Italian-speaking city within Imperial territory, reconciled the papacy's desire for an Italian venue with the Germans' insistence on a meeting upon the soil of the Holy Roman Empire. A greater obstacle to a council, though, was what Paul III called, in his bull of convocation, the 'hatreds and dissensions' of 'those princes to whom God has entrusted almost the entire direction of affairs', Charles V and Francis I, between whom war once more broke out in the year, 1542, of the summons. Apart from the practical problem of the attendance at a council of delegates from belligerent powers, the possibility of the vital presence of the French was over-shadowed by their king's support of any ally, including the German Lutherans of the Schmalkaldic League and even the Turks, against Charles V. However, the peace signed by Charles and Francis in 1544 at Crépy, ending their last war, formally bound these sovereigns to join together to put pressure on the pope to call the council.[16]

If Habsburg-Valois peace removed the major obstacle in the field of international relations to the realisation of the council, further diplomatic work still

needed to be done before it could be brought together, at Trent, by postponement from March to December 1545. Indeed, that the Council of Trent
assembled at all, with a meagre initial attendance of four cardinals, four archbishops, twenty-one bishops, five heads of religious orders, plus experts in
theology and canon law, was a tribute to the indomitable persistence of Paul III
in bringing it to birth. The papacy was also to provide leadership of the Council
once it was assembled through its legates who were, in the first sessions,
Cardinals Giovanni Maria Ciocchi del Monte (1487–1555), Marcello Cervini
(1501–55) and Reginald Pole. No sooner had the Council gathered, however,
than, Christmas intervening, it resolved on its adjournment to 7 January 1546.
Upon its resumption, the Council was immediately confronted with the issue of
the order of its business, whether doctrinal definition would precede reform of
abuses or vice-versa. Pressure for a restatement of traditional doctrine, to be
derived principally from the medieval councils and theologians, would run
counter to the Habsburgs' desire to avoid stirring up further doctrinal discord
with the Lutherans in Germany and to Charles V's wish that the Council deal
with non-controversial practical reforms, especially in areas of abuse that had
boosted Lutheranism's popularity. In the event, a proposal from Bishop
Tommaso Campeggio (*c.* 1482–1564) that reform and doctrine be taken in alternation, was adopted. The programme of reform was along a familiar track of
desiderata for restoring the Church to what was seen as an earlier, purer condition. The agenda of doctrine would be largely a matter of focus on issues that
Luther had raised – Scripture, justification and grace, and the Sacraments.[17]

Before proceeding further, the Council fathers committed themselves in the
Decree Concerning the Manner of Living during the Council, of January 1547, to a frugal,
pious and sober way of life at Trent, recalling to us similar resolutions at Pisa in
1511, and anticipating Trent's delineation of the ideal and scriptural manner of
life of a bishop. At the same time, a resolution denounced 'all false vain and
obstinate disputations', though in point of fact debates in the Council were
sometimes to be heated and even violent, because of the vehemence of opposing
schools of doctrine present. A discordant issue that would haunt the Council, the
balance of power between the pope and the bishops, arose in what Jedin calls
'early stirrings of episcopalism' over the implications for the independent
standing of bishops of accepting financial concessions from the pope.[18]

The Council, which could call on a bank of theological and legal experts,
deputed much of its work to committees. Plenary sessions were made up of the
diffinitores, the Council fathers proper, dominated numerically by bishops, while
in the committees *consultores*, the specialists in theology and Church law, played a
vital role. At whatever point in time resolutions were adopted, they were not
formally endorsed until the concluding session in December 1563. The course of
some of the debates was to be conditioned by national orientations. Though
there were recognisable national groupings, with priorities of their own, especially the Spanish, in the early sessions there was only a token northern
European presence – two Frenchmen and one German – and throughout its
history the Council had an in-built Italian preponderance: Italy being awash

with small dioceses, 187 bishops present at one time or another were Italians. The dominance of bishops in the ranks of the *diffinitores* had the effect of emphasising the Italian hegemony. Many of these Italian bishops ran impoverished dioceses and their financial necessities may have made them amenable to accept the Holy See's line on various issues. However, the idea that the 'Italians' formed a solid papalist bloc in the Council is groundless, because the 'Italy' from which so many of the Council fathers came was not a papal state but a myriad principalities and republics, each one with its own interests, not necessarily tied to Rome's. That said, the legates, and especially del Monte, were skilled in presenting papal viewpoints, though the Spanish could be expected to manifest episcopal independence; the Council was 'no pliant tool of the pope', as Jedin wrote.[19]

Despite its important political dimensions, the Council of Trent, was, of course, primarily an ecclesiastical body, a synod 'lawfully assembled in the Holy Ghost', held in a cathedral and opened with del Monte's celebration of the Mass of the Holy Spirit. It was in the character of a congregation that in February 1546 the Council accepted 'in pious solicitude' the Creed of Nicaea-Constantinople which it enrolled as a kind of opening invocation, for this creed was more than a profession of faith but was also a prayer and what Cardinal Newman was later to call a 'devotion'. The ancient Nicaeno-Constantinopolitan Creed, long accepted as a prayer setting out the basics of Christian belief, certainly created no disagreements within the Council and posed few obstacles to Christian unity beyond the Council and the Catholic Church. Although Luther condemned Paul's papacy in his 'most vehement' (Hendrix) attack on the institution, his *Against the Roman Papacy, An Institution of the Devil* (1545), he stood firmly by the Council of Nicaea, the accepted initiator of the Creed the Council of Trent adopted: it was 'the holiest of all councils', he wrote, and he placed that council's authority against the pope's.[20]

If the Council's acceptance of the Nicene Creed contained some potential for Christian consensus, the same was not true of its determinations, in the fourth session, in April 1546, on *The Canon and Authority of Scripture*. With the membership filling up by that month to double its initial volume, the discussion on Scripture occasioned discord within the assembly, and the resolutions eventually agreed on the subject formed the first of a series of positions adopted which put clear water between Trent and Wittenberg, along with the growing Protestant movement outside Germany. The Council in fact arrived at three sets of determinations on the Bible: on the extent and sufficiency of its authority; on the schedule of authenticated books of Scripture, the 'canon'; and on the translation of the original Hebrew and Greek of the text that was to be accepted. The positions arrived at on the place of Scripture alongside other forms of authority for Christians were the most disruptive of its observations on Scripture in terms of Catholic–Protestant relations, for they gave the 'traditions' of the Catholic Church, its accumulated corpus of teaching, parity of authority alongside the Bible, which Protestants regarded as the uniquely authoritative word of God. The Council laid down that the 'truths and rules of faith' 'contained in the written books and in the unwritten traditions which, received by the Apostles from the mouth of Christ Himself, or from the Apostles themselves, the Holy Ghost dictating, have come down to us, transmitted as it were from hand to hand'. A key phrase authenticating the traditions of the Church was that they were established with 'the Holy Ghost dictating' (*'Spiritu Sancto dictante'*), for, just as Calvin saw the Holy Spirit as the actual author of Scripture, its human writers being the Spirit's 'amanuenses', or secretaries, so the Council was endowing the Catholic Church's traditions with divine authorship, on a par with Scripture: 'one God is the author of both [the Old and New Testaments]; also the traditions...as having been dictated by the Holy Ghost, and preserved in the Catholic Church in unbroken succession'.[21]

What exactly these traditions, having Scriptural equivalence, were was left unstated, though in the previous December an amateur lay theologian had drawn up a list of thirty-four of them, including the Apostles' Creed, the sign of the cross, Sunday observance, infant Baptism, and Confession to priests. But whatever the traditions were – and it might have restricted the useful flexibility of the concept to itemise them – their existence and authority were vital to the Catholic Church which claimed, on the basis of Matt., 16: 13–20, a teaching mandate unfolding over time. Precisely because the concept of tradition (from the Latin *traditio*, a handing on) reserved so much scope to the teaching authority of the pope and councils, and because it ran counter to the exclusive reliance on Scripture that Luther had proclaimed at the Diet of Worms in 1521, when he had declared himself to be 'captive to the Word of God', the notion of tradition as a source of truth was attacked by the German Lutheran commentator, the pastor of Braunschweig, Martin Chemnitz (1522–86). In his vast *Examen Concilii Tridentini* (*Analysis of the Council of Trent*) (1565–73) Chemnitz wrote that Trent's doctrine of tradition:

> is very far-reaching, embracing in its bosom whatever the papalist church transmits and preserves of things which cannot be taught and proved with testimonies of Scripture. It is truly a Pandora's box, under whose cover every kind of corruption, abuse and superstition has been brought into the church.

Amidst Lutheran charges that the notion of tradition conferred arbitrary authority on the papacy, the Council's equalisation of tradition with the Bible drove a deep wedge between Trent on the one hand and, on the other, the whole Reformation movement based on Scripture, its all-sufficiency and inerrancy.[22]

Trent followed its predecessor Florence in establishing the canon of approved books of the Bible. Where Luther followed St Jerome (340–420) in classifying certain books, such as *Ecclesiasticus* and *Maccabees*, as apocryphal – beneficial and edifying but not of divine inspiration – the Council accepted these as being of the canon. Finally, the Council pronounced its verdict on the preferred text of Scripture. The Council's insistence that 'of all the Latin editions of the sacred books now in circulation, the old Latin Vulgate', version of St Jerome – even though this version did not incorporate the fruits of the Christian humanist scholarship by Erasmus and others into the Greek original of the New Testament – was entirely in line with Trent's strong sense of the value of tradition, for Jerome's Latin Vulgate had been in 'long use' in the Catholic Church.[23]

Its work on Scripture completed, the Council turned, in its fifth session, on 17 June 1546, to the doctrinal question of original sin. Since this issue was closely related to those of free will and justification, we shall postpone our consideration of those connected topics. Meanwhile, in the fifth session the discussion of Scripture led into practical matters of what Jedin calls 'Proclaiming the Faith', the teaching of the Church, grounded in the Scripture which parish priests were supposed 'to expound and interpret'. The problem throughout the middle ages had been what a decree of the Province of Canterbury in 1281 had called '*ignorantia sacerdotum*' – clerical ignorance – had impeded the teaching of the laity in even such basics as 'some simple understanding of the sacraments...a simple understanding of the faith'. Medieval bishops such as Robert Grosseteste of Lincoln (1175–1253) anticipated their Tridentine successors in their attention to preparing parish priests to teach the faith through preaching, and Grosseteste pioneered the issue of manuals to assist parish priests in this duty. Obviously, though, even these were of little use to the large numbers of illiterate parish priests. The friars, of whom Grosseteste was the foremost English sponsor, arose from the early thirteenth century largely as providers of the instructional sermons that too many parish priests simply could not deliver – 'a failure', writes Lawrence, 'of the *ecclesia docens* [teaching Church] at ground level'.[24]

What the friars provided was not simply plain instruction but what Lawrence calls a 'new art of preaching', replete with legendary and fictional material especially concerning miracles and saints' lives. St Francis, who himself preached in a 'rousing fashion', was a pioneer of the evolving '*artes praedicandi* ', the special craft of sacred rhetoric whose ingredients included responsiveness to popular culture, eloquence of diction and gesture, and command of drama and humour. Two of the foremost practitioners of these 'arts' in the fifteenth century were the Franciscan Bernardino of Siena, whose phenomenally popular preaching wove comedy and horror in equal parts, and the Dominican Savonarola, who commanded a powerful repertoire of apocalyptic terror and messianic hope. Many of the friars' rhetorical techniques amounted to salesmanship and promotion, as with the by-line that the sight of a corpse clad in the habit of a friar deterred the devil more effectively than even a view of the crucifix. The Dominican Johann Tetzel, who in 1517 was said to back up his promotion of the Indulgence that aroused Luther's ire with the claim that it was sufficient to expiate a sexual assault on the Virgin Mary, was a prime example of commercial vulgarity in friars' preaching. A further feature of this homiletic tradition was that it tended to leave Scripture far behind, in favour of sensational stories, *exempla*. It was the alleged meretriciousness of their sales-pitch approach that induced Erasmus to accuse the friars, 'excessively hungry for notoriety', of allowing their preaching to be conditioned by an 'extraordinary lust for money'. The voice of Erasmus's disciples could be heard at Trent in fastidious denunciations of the friars and other members of the regular orders as 'wolves' gaining

'access to the sheepfold' that was properly tended by the parish priesthood –
though the friars also had their defenders in the Council who pointed out that
they had made good the deficiencies of the parish clergy: 'What would have
become of the Church of Christ if the regulars had not made good the omission
in the cure of souls?', one asked. The solution, though, surely was for bishops to
amend the shortcomings in their parish priests which had necessitated the friars'
services because parish priests were not trained to teach others. According to the
Council's decree, *Super Lectione et Praedicatione Sacrae Scripturae* (*Concerning the Study
and Preaching of Holy Scripture*) of 17 June 1546, and reiterating similar legislation
of the Fourth Lateran Council, the bishops were to repair the 'slender theological formation' of most parish priests by introducing 'instructions in the Holy
Scripture' for clergy already in post with a view to their preaching on Sundays
and feast-days, spurred on by the example of the bishops themselves. Regulars
might still be used as a supplement, but only with episcopal approval – even in
the churches of their own orders.[25]

Trent's later seminary scheme was already present in embryo in this measure.
In particular, as O'Donohoe shows, the project for what would eventually
emerge as seminaries was given currency in remarks by the Jesuit Claude Le Jay
(*c.* 1500–52) to the effect that the establishment, as envisaged, of professors of
Scripture in each cathedral, would be all very well – if they ever had any suitable
students to teach. Le Jay went on to make the suggestion, enthusiastically
endorsed by Council fathers as a revival of the 'ancient practice' of the Church
and taken up by the legates, that diocesan 'colleges should be erected in which
young men could be properly formed for the ecclesiastical ministry'.[26]

Some of the most important doctrinal resolutions of the Council emerged out
of two separate sessions, the fifth, 17 June 1546 and the sixth, 13 January 1547,
which we shall consider together because they concerned the mechanics of
human redemption. The subjects under this heading were original sin and justification, along with the connected themes of free will and predestination, the
central issue being justification.[27]

A Christian doctrine of the fall of man holds that, as a consequence of
Adam's and Eve's original sin in Eden, the will and capacity of the descendants
of Adam and Eve to choose virtuous courses of action ('free will') to placate the
Almighty were, at the very least, severely handicapped. Contending against the
heretical theologian Pelagius (flourished *c.* 400), who taught that human beings
had a capacity to will and achieve good works which contributed to their forgiveness and redemption, Augustine eliminated free will from his soteriological
scheme and placed all his stress on God's saving of His elect people, a salvation
effected by Christ crucified. God's free grace, unmerited by men and women,
though apprehended by them in faith, was the source of forgiveness:

> When man tries to live justly by his own strength without the help of the
> liberating grace of God, he is then conquered by sins....We conclude that a
> man is not justified by the precepts of a holy life but by faith in Jesus Christ.
> That is to say, not by the law of works, but by that of faith.[28]

Augustine, *'doctor gratiae'*, 'the teacher who taught grace', enjoyed high repute in medieval theological circles, and renewed attention was directed at him by Petrarch (1304–78), the pioneer of humanism who in 1342 devised an imaginary dialogue between himself and Augustine. Some members of the Augustinian family of regular orders which claimed the saint as their founder directed particular attention to his theology, creating what has been described as a 'school tradition' amongst the Augustinian orders. Representative figures included Gregory of Rimini (d. 1358) and, at the time of Trent, Cardinal Girolamo Seripando (1493–1563), the Augustinian general.[29]

Luther was an Augustinian 'eremite' whose superior in his order, Johann von Staupitz (*c.* 1460–1524), advised him to read Augustine, sowing the seeds of Luther's 'passion' for this theologian, whose works he 'devoured' and memorised. From Augustine, Luther's reading and preparation for his lectures on Scripture moved, as it were, backward in time, to a 'direct appeal to Biblical testimony', in St Paul, in the Epistle to the Romans, especially in Rom., 3: 28, where Luther found the New Testament source for Augustine's version that 'a man is not justified by the precepts of a holy life but by faith in Jesus Christ'. Luther derived the sense he gave to Paul's words in Rom., 3: 28, 'The just are saved by faith' from Augustine, and claimed Augustine's authority for adding to Paul's text the crucial 'alone': 'The just are saved by faith alone'. The necessary accompaniments to this viewpoint were a denial of free will and an acceptance of predestination. Erasmus stood out for the role of human free will and meritorious action in the attainment of God's favour: 'We should strive with all our might, resort to the healing balm of penitence, and try by all means to compass the mercy of God'. Against this, Luther insisted, in *The Bondage of the Will* (1525), that 'It is fundamentally necessary and wholesome for Christians to know that God foresees, purposes, and does all things according to his own immutable, eternal and infallible will. This bomb-shell knocks "free-will" flat and utterly shatters it.' 'False and blasphemous against Christ' was the belief 'that a man...obtaineth remission of sins and justification'.[30]

Erasmus inherited from the middle ages a neo-Pelagian voice that had been heard in such theologians as Gabriel Biel (*c.* 1418–95), who taught that God in His mercy credited the efforts of individuals to win grace. We should be aware, though, of how influential the opposed Augustinian or 'evangelical' soteriology was, not just in Luther's discipleship but in the heart of the Catholic Church which, especially in the 1540s, was confronted with a choice of opposing soteriologies. An 'evangelical' theology of reliance on the cross of Christ rather than one's own efforts for redemption was particularly attractive to some pious Italian Catholics in the 1530s and 1540s. These included the artist Michelangelo Buonarroti (1475–1564), the noblewoman Vittoria Colonna (1490–1547), the priest Marc'Antonio Flaminio (d. 1550), Cardinal Contarini and Abbot Gregorio Cortese (*c.* 1482–1548), along with the English Cardinal Pole. The group looked to the religious inspiration of the Naples-based Spaniard Juan de Valdés (1500–41). Its Augustinian soteriology, emphasising the redemptive 'benefits' of Christ crucified (and, in the case of a community of Benedictines in

Padua, of Christ risen) produced, in 1542–3 the work, primarily of the monk Benedetto da Mantova (d. *c.* 1546), known as *Il Beneficio di Giesù Christo Crocifisso*. The most powerful member of this evangelical circle was Contarini, who had negotiated a doctrinal truce over justification with the Lutherans at Regensburg in 1541 and whose intellectual legacy, after his death in 1542, was carried into the Council of Trent by no less a figure than the legate Pole.[31]

Against this background, views expressed in the Council by the Franciscan Asart, who spoke the language of justification by faith, or the attribution by a Council father of 'every stage in the process of justification' to Christ, could not be dismissed as alien to Catholic thinking. Nor would it suffice to dismiss the views of Contarini, Pole and much of the Augustinian order led by Seripando as being 'infected with the teaching of…Luther', for the Augustine who so profoundly affected Luther also had the deepest impact on theologians in the Catholic mainstream, including the most authoritative theologian of the middle ages, Thomas Aquinas (1225–74). This deep embedding in Catholic theology of an Augustinian view of justification ensured that the debates in the Council on this question were protracted, that they included an attempt by Pole to secure assent for a compromise formula according to which those justified outside of themselves would gradually acquire a capacity for good works, and that the final resolutions on the subject would incorporate a strong anti-Pelagian line. The Council, in the *Decree Concerning Justification* of the sixth session on 13 January 1547, in fact came down on the side of Paul, Augustine and Aquinas in asserting man's reliance for salvation on God's grace sealed by Christ's saving death:

> The causes of…justification are: the final cause is the glory of God and of Christ and life everlasting; the efficient cause is the merciful God who *washes and sanctifies*…the meritorious cause is His most beloved only begotten, our Lord Jesus Christ, who, *when we were enemies* merited for us justification by His most holy passion…and made satisfaction for us to God the Father….[W]hen the Apostle [St Paul] says that man is justified by faith and freely, these words are to be understood in the sense that we are said to be justified by faith because faith is the beginning of human salvation, the foundation and root of all justification….[W]e are therefore said to be justified gratuitously, because none of those things that precede justification, whether by faith or works, merit the grace of justification.

The summary canon, free of the theologising language of 'efficient cause' and the rest, made it even plainer that sinners were made just through the merits of Christ, won for them outside of themselves and conferred on them freely:

> If anyone says that man can be justified before God by his own works, whether done by his own natural powers or through the teaching of the law, without divine grace through Jesus Christ, let him be anathema [cursed].[32]

Trent, then, resolved its doctrine of salvation not in a spirit of confidence in human capacity to achieve salvation by free will through good works but rather with a trust in saving grace apprehended in faith. Its firm statement 'that we are...justified by faith' appeared to Chemnitz so close to the Lutheran position that he suspected that the Council had cunningly established a spurious proximity to Lutheran doctrine. In fact, though, the Council's Augustinian soteriology was balanced by an acceptance of the contribution of men and women in their justification. Trent would not accept the little word, vast with significance, 'alone' – 'by faith alone' – that Luther had placed in Rom., 3:28 so as, he believed, to shore up the verse's unmistakable meaning. The Council ruled:

> If anyone says that the sinner is justified by faith alone, meaning that nothing else is required in order to obtain the grace of justification, and that it is not in any way necessary that he be prepared and disposed by the action of his own will, let him be anathema.

Though damaged by the consequences of Adam's and Eve's sin, man's will was not fatally flawed but retained a capacity to choose the good. The effects of the justification secured by Christ's sacrifice and credited – 'imputed' – to the sinner were to enhance that capacity 'through the voluntary reception of the grace and gifts whereby an unjust man becomes just': 'not only are we reputed [just, righteous] but we are truly called and *are* just' [my emphasis]. Trent achieved a compromise between Augustinian and Pelagian views of justification, but within that formula envisaged the sanctification of Christians, aided by the ministrations of the Church. For those provisions to function at their most effective required the reform of the institution, the topic to which, by the previously agreed alternation of its agenda, the Council next turned, concerning itself with the responsibilities of bishops and in particular with what Jedin calls 'The Pivot of Church Reform', episcopal residence, the indispensable presence of the bishop as pastor in his diocese.[33]

Apart from the preferences of individual bishops for living in glittering cities such as Venice and Rome over and above the squalid conditions prevailing in many dioceses, a serious obstacle to residence was the political pressure on diocesans to continue functioning as civil servants in various kingdoms. In fact, though, probably the worst culprit in keeping bishops away from their sees was the papacy, which commonly used the revenues of bishoprics in the various states of Europe to pay the salaries of its diplomats in those states, while the incomes of bishoprics throughout Europe paid curial salaries. There were, for example, ten bishops who were absentees from their titular dioceses among twenty-four papal secretaries under Innocent VIII (1484–92), while one third of curial officials starting their careers between 1528 and 1548 were, officially at least, bishops. To insist, as some reformers in the Council did, that the duties of bishops to be resident in their dioceses was an absolute divine mandate undermined the pope's power to dispense from residence men in his employment who drew their incomes from bishoprics. Despite these 'barriers to the principle of residence' (*Impedimenta residentiae*), the adoption of the principle in the sixth session in January 1547 indicates the seriousness with which the Council viewed the need to restore episcopal residence so as to repair the 'very much collapsed ecclesiastical discipline'.[34]

The Council turned next, under the heading of doctrine, in the seventh session on 3 March 1547, to another issue of controversy between the Catholic and Protestant Churches, the Sacraments – the Church's channels of divine grace – and considered their number and their nature. Thematically, this topic arose directly out of the previous doctrinal discourse, on justification, in fact rounding off the Council's treatment of the previous subject:

> For the completion of the salutary doctrine on justification, which was...promulgated in the last session, it has seemed proper to deal with the most holy sacraments of the church, through which all true justice [*iustitia* = righteousness] either begins, or...is increased, or...is restored.

The resolutions on justification had already depicted a continuous and, usually, interrupted process involving the individual Christian in the restoration of his or her justification following lapses, so that 'he [who] has fallen [into sin] after baptism' could 'by the grace of God rise again'. The Sacraments, above all Penance and Holy Communion, received over the course of a Christian's lifetime, were the vital media of restoration to grace and without them it was not the case that 'men obtain from God through faith alone the grace of justification'.[35]

Having established their role in conferring grace within its doctrine of justification, the Council went on to determine the number of the Sacraments defined as having been established by Christ or the Apostles – no more, and no fewer, than seven: Baptism, Confirmation, Holy Communion (the Eucharist, the Lord's Supper), Penance (Confession), Extreme Unction, Holy Orders, and Matrimony. In assembling this schedule, the Council was doing no more than reaffirming established Catholic, theological, papal and conciliar pronouncements going back as far as the mid-twelfth century and forming an 'extraordinarily differentiated sacramental theology', as Jedin describes it, endorsed by the Council of Florence which, in turn, largely derived its summary from Aquinas. Trent followed Florence's listing, using the identical language of 'seven sacraments of the New Law'. However, if the 'septenary number' of the Sacraments had become a fixed point of Catholic teaching before the end of the middle ages, from the first years of the Reformation the enumeration became a readily identifiable controverted point between Catholic orthodoxy and its new rivals. Thus England's Henry VIII (1491–1547), anxious at that stage of his career to proclaim his Catholicity, published his *Assertio Septem Sacramentorum* (*Defence of the Seven Sacraments*) in 1521. Henry's 'defence' was of the number of Sacraments questioned by Luther in the 1520 *Babylonian Captivity of the Church*: 'I deny that they can be proved from the Scripture', Luther wrote. In further works, such as

Confession Concerning Christ's Supper (1528) Luther set out his drastically reduced number of Sacraments which he believed could be validated scripturally as having been established by Christ or the Apostles. Pastorally useful, Confession was not a Sacrament and only 'two Sacraments remain, baptism and the Lord's Supper'. Rites such as matrimony were 'sufficiently holy in themselves' not to need to be ranked as Sacraments. Chemnitz joined his voice to Luther's with the accusation that the five Sacraments that Luther invalidated were the post-Scriptural additions of medieval theologians – 'brought into the church by scholastics'. In contrast to the issue of justification, where there were different Catholic views, over the Sacraments there was a solid Catholic consensus and it opposed a sacramental theology associated since 1520 with Luther in person. (The full title of Henry VIII's *Assertio* reads 'Defence of the Seven Sacraments against Martin Luther' and the work directs personal insults against the Wittenberg reformer as the 'worst wolf of hell'.) Trent also had Luther in person in its sights when it ruled on the Sacraments, citing from the 1520 *Babylonian Captivity*. Trent's affirmation of the seven Sacraments once more put a high fence between Rome and Wittenberg.[36]

The Council turned in the same seventh session, on 3 March 1547, to promulgate a series of decrees concerning reform on such matters as the holding of cathedral churches, the conferment of benefices (with strict rules to prevent pluralism), the repair of churches, the examination of candidates for ordination, and diocesan hospital management. Once more the rulings underlined the responsibilities of bishops.[37]

The Council of Trent conducted its often intricate deliberation against a background of the recurrent threat of disruption. Chosen on political grounds for its location within the Empire, the small Italian city was near enough to Germany proper to be exposed to Lutheran military assault. In 1547 a different foe threatened, epidemic, in the form of a dangerous strain of influenza. The Council was transferred south to Bologna, within the Papal States, to the fury of Charles V, who published a protest which Jedin describes as 'tantamount to a declaration of war upon the papacy', commanding all his subjects who were members of the Council to remain at Trent. The Emperor went on to win a sensational victory over the German Lutheran Schmalkaldic League in 1547, and in 1548 implemented an imposed religious settlement in Germany known as the Interim of Augsburg. Meanwhile, the Bologna sessions of the Council proved fruitless, were prorogued twice and wound up in 1549 as the last act *vis-à-vis* the Council of the pope who had called it into existence. In its sessions from 1547 to 1549, though, the Council had drafted essential reform through the restoration of episcopal authority and had made a start in tackling the education of priests. In the field of faith, the Council had pronounced on the authority and composition of Scripture, had produced a position on justification which partly accommodated two viewpoints and had reaffirmed the Catholic Church's sacramental theology. Following Paul III's death in 1549 his elected successor as pope was the Council legate Giovanni Maria Ciocchi del Monte, Julius III (1550–55). A false start in reconvening the Council in May 1551 made way for the thirteenth working session, on 11 October 1551, when the Council resumed its deliberations on the Sacraments.[38]

This session produced the Council's resolutions on the 'Real Presence of Our Lord Jesus Christ in the Most Holy Sacrament of the Eucharist':

> by the consecration of the bread and wine a change is brought about of the whole substance of the bread into the substance of the body of Christ…and of the whole substance of the wine into the substance of His blood…[,] transubstantiation.

In this resolution Trent's foundation was the Fourth Lateran Council, 1215. Trent reiterated Lateran IV's requirement that the faithful communicate at least annually and also restated the Lateran Council's basic eucharistic theology. Lateran IV established that in the Mass, despite the continued appearance of bread and wine on the altar following the words of consecration, Christ's 'body and blood are truly contained in the sacrament of the altar under the forms of bread and wine, the bread and wine having been changed in substance by God's power into his body and blood'. Following Lateran IV, Aquinas developed the Council's distinction between unaltered appearances of bread and wine – 'accidents' – and an altered underlying reality, 'substance':

> The true body of Christ begins to be in this sacrament by the fact that the substance of the bread is converted into the substance of the body of Christ and the substance of the wine into the substance of His blood.

Aquinas further argued that unless the total transformation of the substance of the bread and wine into the substance of the body and blood of Christ were accepted, the logical alternative would be that in the Eucharist, Christ's body and blood co-existed simultaneously with bread and wine. Wyclif, condemning Aquinas's eucharistic doctrine as 'rash', proposed just that – that bread and wine remained in their substance, albeit alongside the eucharistic presence of Christ, after the words of consecration. A variant of the eucharistic theology associated with Wyclif and known as 'remanence' from the Latin *remanere*, 'to remain', characterised Luther, who maintained with Wyclif that the bread remains, alongside the presence of Christ in the Eucharist.[39]

Trent derived its eucharistic theology from a medieval conciliar tradition which went back to Lateran IV, and which ran through Constance in the repudiation of Wyclif's doctrine of remanence with which the Council of the early fifteenth century was confronted. Constance denounced the belief attributed to the 'pseudo-Christian' Wyclif that 'The material substance of bread, and…the material substance of wine remain in the sacrament of the altar'. Trent took this up to anathematise the view 'that in the…Eucharist the substance of the bread and wine remains conjointly with the body and blood of our Lord Jesus Christ'. Thus Trent stood by Constance, as Luther stood by Wyclif, and the outcome was two conflicting versions of the nature of Christ's presence in the Eucharist.

Given, though, that as the legatee of Wyclifian remanence (or 'consubstantiation') Luther also insisted strongly on the actual presence of Christ in the Eucharist, did it matter very much that Trent differed from Wyclifian-Lutheran eucharistic metaphysics over whether Christ was present in the Eucharist alongside bread and wine, or totally replaced those 'species' in 'substance'? After all, these relatively minor variations in a basic acceptance of the objective presence of Christ in the Eucharist were now being challenged by much more radical interpretations of the Sacrament which viewed it as a congregational and memorial meal. Such interpretations Luther decisively rejected with his insistence on the literal truth of Christ's words in the Last Supper, 'This is My body', in his meeting in 1529 with the Swiss reformer Huldreich Zwingli (1484–1531) who saw the Eucharist as a commemoration of Christ without His bodily presence. In point of fact, though, the difference between consubstantiation or remanence in the tradition from Wyclif to Luther and transubstantiation in the lineage of Lateran IV, Constance and Trent was also essential, for the formula of transubstantiation that Trent adopted implied a much more complete and miraculous transformation of the bread and wine than the rival Wyclifian–Lutheran line. And acceptance of the exclusive totality of Christ's presence in the Eucharist made the host a fitting object for eucharistic adoration, especially the 'special veneration and solemnity' shown annually in the feast of the 'Blessed Sacrament', *Corpus Christi*. The maintenance of this observance and the range of novel eucharistic devotions emerging in the Catholic Reformation period, especially the exposition over forty hours of the host, *Quarant' Ore*, were intellectually validated by Trent's acceptance of transubstantiation. On the other hand, Protestant understandings of Christ's presence in the Eucharist – the Confession of Württemberg (*Confessio Virtembergica*, 1551) denied eucharistic 'transformation' and described Christ present in the Sacrament as 'close to the bread' – had the effect of eliminating processions and adoration of the eucharistic host from Lutheran worship: if the host was God, it was also bread.[40]

The use of the intellectual method, 'Scholasticism', in which formulae such as transubstantiation were grounded, a set of techniques whose origin lay in the twelfth and thirteenth centuries, did not go unchallenged in the Council. The opinion was voiced of the anti-Scholastic Christian humanist school of disciples of Erasmus that Scholastic terms such as 'substance' and 'accident' were not found in the early Church, but were 'novel, or, as we might say, 'medieval'. Nevertheless, the Council witnessed what Dickens calls 'the victory of scholasticism over biblical humanism'. In particular, the interventions of the Spanish Dominican theologian Melchior Cano (1509–60), a leader of the revival of the Scholastic teachings of Aquinas ('Thomism') spreading out from the University of Salamanca, were crucial for the adoption by Trent of an eucharistic theology derived from Lateran IV by way of Aquinas. Other Spanish theological consultants, including the Jesuits Alfonso Salmerón (1515–85) and Diego Laínez (or Laynez, 1512–65), helped ensure the ascendancy of the traditional Scholastic theological method at Trent.[41]

Arguably, the affirmation of conservative doctrinal views of the Eucharist came at an unfortunate time in the history of the Council of Trent, when, in its middle period, hopes were running high of concord with the German Lutherans, who had delegates present from their states and cities, from October 1551 to March 1552. As Church writes, the 'question of the Eucharist' 'proved insuperable' as a barrier to unity. However, that barrier had already been put in place by the failure, even on the part of such a 'liberal' Churchman as Contarini, to reach accord at Regensburg over what a contemporary called 'one word concerning the eucharist, namely transubstantiation'. Contarini had realised that his own room for negotiation at Regensburg was circumscribed, as he said, by previous resolutions made and 'settled centuries before by a council [Lateran IV] with the authority to do so'. The same sense of being tied to past decisions seems also to have prevailed at Trent, which was committed to the history and traditions of the councils from which it derived its own status.[42]

In the decrees of the October 1551 thirteenth session concerning reform, the Council returned to its powerful insistence on the jurisdiction of bishops and their particular duty to raise and maintain the quality of their priests, through a mixture of severity and kindness. Also in this session, as one gesture, on a relatively superficial level, of conciliation to the Protestants, the Council adjourned the issue of the reception of Holy Communion in the forms of both bread and wine (on which Protestants insisted). It turned, in session fourteen, in November 1551, to the subject of the Sacrament of Penance, guided in a series of three-hour classes led by Laínez and Cano and linking its treatment 'by the affinity of the subjects' to its earlier consideration of justification. Penance was the mechanism of the absolution of sins by which God's forgiveness was channelled sacramentally through a priest as auditor of the penitent's full and contrite confession of sins, the confessor reciting the words of absolution and setting a penance as a condition of complete forgiveness. Out of an adjunct of this Sacrament, indulgences, which were dispensations to discharge penances and were also applicable to the dead, Luther's Reformation had first arisen in a protest against these devices viewed by Luther as false man-made attempts to secure salvation.[43]

The thirteenth century was a particularly creative period in the evolution of the Sacrament of Penance. The Fourth Lateran Council instructed the faithful to confess to their parish priests at least annually, envisaging the Sacrament as a regular part of parochial pastoral care. However, in 1227 Gregory IX gave the Dominican Order a universal mandate of hearing Confessions (a privilege later extended to other orders of friars) and it was the Dominican Aquinas who provided much of the Church's understanding of this Sacrament through which 'spiritual healing' took place. In particular, Aquinas emphasised the operative contribution that the penitent's remorse, or contrition – even though this varied in power according to the spiritual capacity of the individual – made to the efficacy of the Sacrament. By virtue of contrition 'the offence to God is removed'; personal satisfaction by means of acts of repentance for sins was also essential. Aquinas's emphasis on the necessity for contrition to make this Sacrament 'work' was carried forward by medieval commentators, including Biel, who propounded the view that God would reward with forgiveness the efforts of the individual who did his or her best, according to his or her capacity, to acquire forgiveness and grace. For some, though, this placing on their own shoulders of the onus of responsibility for their forgiveness created, says Tentler, 'tensions that remained until the time of Luther'. Indeed, Luther the monk was a case-book example of these tensions and anxieties, for, as he recalled, 'my conscience would not give me certainty' and it constantly nagged him that 'You left that out of your confession'. It was Luther's discovery that the just were saved by faith alone, lifting from them the task of securing their forgiveness, that relieved those terrible anxieties. Luther came to see that the struggle to muster individual contrition so as to make Penance efficacious, was a kind of psychological 'good work'. But 'The diligence with which we have recollected and enumerated our sins' was made redundant by God's 'fidelity' in taking charge of the forgiveness of men and women (he subsequently developed an appreciation of the pastoral value of Confession as 'a singular medicine for afflicted consciences'). Trent, in contrast, restated insistence on the necessity for the individual's summoning up his or her capacity for contrition: 'Contrition…holds the first place among the acts of the penitent…at all times necessary for obtaining the forgiveness of sins'. This disagreement over the role of contrition in winning forgiveness of sins was an aspect of the gulf between the Catholic and Protestant Reformations over the part played by individuals in securing redemption. One more, we may see that Trent's role was that of setting out the frontier between the Protestant and Catholic Reformations.[44]

In late October the Council turned its attention to the final Sacrament in a person's life, Extreme Unction, the anointing of the sick, 'the completion not only of penance but of the whole Christian life', which the Council of Florence had included in the list of seven Sacraments. There were two Lutheran challenges to the claims made for Extreme Unction to be a Sacrament originating with Christ or the Apostles. The first was on the grounds of its scriptural warrant. Florence had identified the scriptural source of Extreme Unction in a passage in the Epistle of James, 5: 14–15 (Jerusalem version): 'If one of you is ill, he should send for the elders of the church, and they must anoint him with oil in the name of the Lord and pray over him'. Luther questioned the canonical status of this Epistle of James which, in James, 2: 17 ('Faith is like that: if good works do not go with it, it is dead'), ran counter to the proof text of justification by faith alone (Rom., 3: 28). However, and since there was another New Testament source for the rite of anointing (Mark, 6: 13), the primary disagreement between Trent and Wittenberg over Extreme Unction arose not so much from divergent interpretations of scriptural validation but, and once again, from a fundamental dissension over the role of Sacraments as the Church's aids to human striving within the entire economy of salvation. For the Catholic Church, Extreme Unction was the final stage in the lifelong process whereby Sacraments enabled sinners to secure reconciliation with God. They were dispensed to those 'who by sin had been cut off from God, [who might] be disposed through his quickening and helping grace *to convert themselves to their own justification by freely assenting to and co-operating with that grace'* (my emphasis). The decree's words reveal the extent of the gulf between Trent and Luther, who denied any human participation in redemption which involved free will, except for the passive response of divinely implanted faith. The centrality of justifying faith in Luther's mind is caught in his comment on Extreme Unction that its sole effect in inducing forgiveness was that of persuading people that they were forgiven, and if they believed they were forgiven, they were.[45]

In the fourteenth session in November 1551 the Council returned to the programme of reform, highlighting once more the disciplinary functions of the bishops, including the suspension of refractory priests. However, parish priests (usually not members of religious orders but 'secular' clerics) themselves had corrective functions, in order to perform which they must be above reproach, for 'with what freedom shall priests be able to correct laics when they must answer silently to themselves that they have committed the same things that they censure?' The demand for a worthy parish clergy, which has culminated in Vatican II's insistence that priests 'carry out their ministry with holiness and zeal', can be traced at least as far back as the 'Hildebrandine' moral reforms of the priesthood initiated under Pope Gregory VII (Hildebrand, pope 1073–85). That movement to improve the secular clergy, educationally as well as morally, produced the decrees of the Third Lateran council (1179) to the effect that from those 'in holy orders...a serious character and knowledge of letters should be required'. Lateran IV in 1215 followed this up in condemning the absurdity of promoting to benefices men without 'learning and honesty of behaviour...who follow the urgings of the flesh rather than the judgement of reason'. This Lateran Council also went into considerable detail on how the parish clergy must be different from the laity. The differences were a way of life especially as regards pleasure and its avoidance – plays, taverns, gambling – but distinctness was crucially a matter of dress, since in medieval and early modern European society people were recognised for what they were by the colour and style of what they wore – prostitutes with ear-rings, friars and monks in the variously coloured habits of their orders, academics in gowns, Jews wearing yellow discs, and so on. Lateran IV ordered priests not to wear the clothing of those they were not, or were not supposed to be – the fashionable and brightly coloured fabrics of young men of fashion, the 'bridles, saddles, breast-plates and spurs' of knights, for they were not knights or men-about-town but an order apart, the 'order of Melchisedech', and, as Trent reaffirmed must 'wear a becoming clerical dress, conformable to their order and dignity'. If priests were not to wear the garb appropriate to other orders of society, pressure was to mount in favour of their being all clothed in the standard vesture of a 'uniform corps' (Tackett), their own 'order' of parish priests, in the shape of the black cassock.[46]

From the autumn of 1551 debates occupied the Council on the Sacrament by which the priestly order was constituted, Holy Orders, while the assembly was thrown into disarray over the nature of the sacrifice, the Mass, that priests offered, an issue that had already arisen at Bologna and which was to be settled before the conclusion of the Council. In January 1552 it was decided to defer the questions under discussion until the following March, in a fifteenth session when, albeit given out in courteous language 'those who call themselves Protestants' were expected to be present to 'acquiesce in the decrees'. That session was in fact taken up with the procedural issues of a prorogation and of a safe conduct for the Protestants. However, a threatening situation in Italy and in the vicinity of Trent now endangered the continuance of the Council. Paul III's grandson, Ottavio Farnese (1524–86), had been placed by Julius III in possession of the principality of Parma, whence Charles V wanted him evicted, bringing the emperor's rival, Henry II of France (1519–59) into Italy on Farnese's side. While central Italy lapsed into chaos, the Council heard that a leading Lutheran prince, Maurice of Saxony (1521–53), who had narrowly missed capturing Charles V, was advancing on Trent. Amidst such threats – as the pope put it, 'such tumults and wars…Germany…ablaze with arms and discords' – on 28 April 1552 the Council reconvened to be adjourned for two years.[47]

The intended two-year adjournment was to turn into the longest suspension, one of a decade, in the Council's history. During that long interruption there was some evident disillusionment with the project of the Council, voiced by a highly active participant, Seripando, who in 1555 wrote to the pope, 'There is nothing in the council, it has had no effect whatsoever'. Heated debates on the Mass had exposed the inherent divisive potential in such large and heterogeneous assemblies, likely, as Daniel-Rops writes, 'to produce an overdose of controversy'. Despite cordial language inviting Lutherans to 'confer charitably and respectfully and without hindrance…reproachful, vexatious and offensive language being absolutely put aside', and promising to 'receive them kindly and listen to them favourably', the Council had had no success in reconciling Protestants, whom it had tended to treat as lapsed Catholics 'who call themselves Protestants' and who were to 'acquiesce' in the proceedings. Even so, Protestants *had* been in attendance, in itself an achievement, and the middle sessions of the Council had not been bereft of others, for example in consolidating the Church's sacramental theology and in defining the status of the priesthood. Julius III expressed himself as pleased with the successes of the sessions, in which 'the business progressed earnestly and happily in the midst of a great concourse of the faithful.[48]

In fact, it was Julius, even though as a cardinal his career had been so closely involved with the Council, and who had come in as pope in 1550 on a platform of reconvening it, who kept it in abeyance for the remainder of his pontificate, down to 1555. Julius ('Naturally indolent', 'Essentially weak', 'an irascible hedonist') has not had a good press, and it is true that his mode of life recalled the pleasure-loving aura of the pope whose name he took, his early patron Julius II. Nevertheless, though the Council was suspended in Julius's pontificate, the project of reform was not, but was, rather, taken under the pope's wing in what Jedin calls a plan 'to reform the entire church…by means of a great papal reforming constitution'. The intended bull, *Varietas temporum*, in 150 clauses adopted conciliar measures such as the prohibition of episcopal pluralism and the commandment of residence and can be seen as 'sustaining and amplifying the work of Tridentine reform' by taking it under papal direction. Even so, hopes of the production of the 'great papal reforming constitution' were not met before the pope's death in March 1555. Meanwhile, though, the fact that the impetus of conciliar reform was far from lost was evident in the adoption in Portugal in 1553, with royal approval, of reforms so far submitted at Trent, supplemented by rulings of Lateran V.[49]

The election in 1555 of the committed supporter of the Council, the legate Marcello Cervini as Marcellus II, may, as Jedin says, have been a 'clear victory for the reform party' but it did not interrupt the decade-long suspension of the Council. Following the death as a result of overwork of Marcellus II after three weeks as pope, Gian Pietro Carafa was elected as Paul IV. The new pope, member of the Oratory of Divine Love, joint-founder of the Theatines, member of Paul III's reform commission, was, while he showed too much favour to his Carafa relatives, unmistakably a reformer, though not a conciliar one. Paul IV was by nature an autocrat and was suspicious of Trent. He replaced conciliar with papal reform and set up a commission of reform, made up of sixty prelates, which was seen as an alternative to the Council. However, most of Carafa's career had been involved with the Curia, Rome and Italy. For this reason, his reforms, though valuable and involving the questions of dispensations from the *Dataria*, reductions in cardinalatial and papal expenditure, and social and moral reform in Rome, were restricted in their scope, tended to go over the same ground as the Consilium of 1537–8 of which Carafa had been a member and were concerned with the Papal States and city and the papal administration. It is true that the renewal of Rome was the starting point of the Catholic restoration elsewhere, but what the Council had done, as a body aspiring to represent Catholic Christendom, was to undertake the reform of the Church at large. Of course, Paul too took in hand reform beyond Rome and Italy, for example directing heads of religious orders to control convents within their jurisdiction. His instructions reminding bishops of their duty of residence and insisting on minimum age at appointments were, in terms of their content, valuable. But in tone these measures were centralist, autocratic orders from on high, typified by Paul's appointment of cardinals in each Catholic country to convey papal orders. Apart from lacking tact in a period when many bishops, and not only in Spain, were more conscious than hitherto of the divine creation of their office, Paul's 'peremptory decrees' were imposed *on* the pastors of the Church rather than, as with the Council's rulings, arising from the consensus of bishops of what was necessary and practicable to be implemented in the dioceses. When the experiment in unilateral papal reformism was over with Paul's death in 1559, there was every prospect that the project of the council would be revived.[50]

Apart from a reaction away from Paul's extremism – his contempt for 'gentleness', his prosecution of Cardinal Morone for doctrinal deviance – the renewal of the Council was given added urgency by the new down-turn in the fortunes of Catholicism in Europe in 1559. England, restored to the faith by Mary (1516–58) under Julius III, was once more lost following the accession of Elizabeth (1553–1603), while a national assembly of the burgeoning Calvinist church in France was held in 1559. The new pope, said to be elected with the support of Philip II of Spain (1527–98), with whom Paul IV had been at war, Giovanni Angelo Medici, taking the title Pius IV (1559–65), announced the resumption of the Council in June 1560 and in the bull *Ad ecclesiae regimen* of November called it to Trent for Easter 1561 (it was in fact to meet in January 1562). The pope specifically referred to the expansion of Protestantism as a good reason for reconvening the Council: 'far and wide the pest of heresy and schism have penetrated'.[51]

There was an unmistakable sense of optimism, alongside urgency, surrounding the resumption of the Council. Pius himself expressed an almost apocalyptic mood, anticipating from the Council 'the recovery and salvation of the scattered sheep, and the lasting peace and tranquillity of the Christian commonwealth'. When the assembly met, the vastly improved attendance figures – rising in 1562–3 to over 250, compared with, at most, eighty, in the early session of the 1540s – inspired enthusiasm in place of the scepticism shown in 1555 by Cardinal Seripando. He now served as one of the four working legates alongside Cardinals Ercole Gonzaga (1505–63), Stanislaus Hosius (1504–79) and Luigi Simonetta (d. 1568).[52]

Given that the council had been in abeyance for so long, there was some plausibility in the reasoning that a *new* council was being gathered, as was argued by the new Emperor, Ferdinand I (reigned 1558–64), who wished to avoid the further discord that might arise in Germany as a result of the confirmation of earlier statements, on justification, which were unacceptable to the Lutherans. However, Ferdinand's Habsburg nephew Philip of Spain (reigned 1555–98) favoured the line that the Council was simply being resumed. Pius was determined to work with, not against, the Catholic sovereigns, and a diplomatic offensive through Morone won Ferdinand over, to the extent that he sent three distinguished representatives to the Council. The continuity of location favoured the view, which was implicitly accepted, that the new sessions took up, 'with every kind of suspension removed' where the earlier ones had left off, the earlier enumeration of sessions being extended.[53]

Though the Council in the eighteenth session, on 26 February 1562, was in effect in sequence with its predecessors, it did not take up the divisive subject deferred in the fifteenth session of January 1552, the sacrifice of the Mass (sessions sixteen, April 1552, and seventeen, January 1562, concerned the suspension and holding of the Council). Instead, the February 1562 eighteenth session turned to the work that Seripando had already begun on the revision of the Index of Prohibited Books promulgated by Paul IV. The aim of this revision was to moderate the intolerance that had proscribed all the works of Erasmus and which had produced what the Jesuit Canisius called a 'stumbling block' of whose 'extreme severity', said Laínez, even the 'best Catholic disapproved'. On the subject of the Index, the new session offered a courteous hearing to all those who considered themselves affected by censorship and used a more tactful language in inviting not 'those who call themselves Protestants' but 'those of the [Lutheran] Confession of Augsburg' to 'confer charitably and respectfully'.[54]

The issue of episcopal residence returned to divide these sessions, as it had rocked the sixth, in January 1547, when an attempt had been made to defend the obligation of residence in terms of fundamental divine law, from which papal dispensations would not normally be given. The venerable tradition of seeing the bishop's residence as commanded by God, and therefore not usually to be relaxed by dispensation, had been restated in the earlier sixteenth century by the influential Cardinal Cajetan (Tommaso di Vio, 1468–1534). In 1562 the issue split the Council into two factions in what Jedin calls a combat – '*Kampf*' – over episcopal residence – though it should be emphasised that no one called into question the pope's essential dispensing power over all branches of the Church: one observer noted, 'all admitted the superiority of the pope, his authority over all bishops and his power of suspending them and of depriving them of the exercise of their jurisdictions'. Even so, a vote on 20 April 1562, on whether residence was an obligation of God's command, grounded the Council in discord, for a simple majority was for the proposition while a larger group combined those against and those who favoured referring the matter to the holy father. The minute of session nineteen postponing the publication of a decree specially invoked God as 'the author of all peace'. On 3 June the Council accepted an adjournment decree and the Spanish members, the most ardent for the divine-law proposition, retreated. The Council was prorogued in June 1562, the matter of residence by divine law shelved not settled.[55]

Following the postponement session, the twentieth, of 4 June 1562, the Council's next business session, the twenty-first, on 16 July, took up the question of reception of the Eucharist either in the two forms of bread and wine or in the form of bread alone. This was a 'political question' (Jedin) – one both of ecclesiastical and secular politics – and also an issue of the doctrine of the Eucharist. Equal access, with the clergy, of the laity to the chalice had arisen as the eucharistic practice and symbol of the dissident evangelical Hussite movement in Bohemia in the early fifteenth century, though it was endorsed by the founder of the movement, John Hus rather than being initiated by him. It evoked the issue of ecclesiastical politics concerning the equal rights of the laity in the Church because it was, wrote Lutz (quoted in Jedin), 'the symbol of militant revolt against the priestly church of Rome and the essence of the mature status of the laity and the freedom of all Christians which had to be secured by force'. The availability of the chalice to the laity in Bohemia also implied the local autonomy and variety of branches of the Church as opposed to Roman uniformity. The Council of Constance condemned and executed Hus and refused the use of the chalice, denouncing 'Communion under both kinds, recently revived among the Bohemians' and attacking those who 'dared to assert that the Christian people ought to receive the holy sacrament of the eucharist under the forms of both bread and wine'. Constance insisted 'that the whole body of and blood of Christ are truly contained under both the form of bread and the form of wine', rendering lay access to the chalice unnecessary.[56]

If that was the doctrinal position, the political situation was that by the time of the Council of Basel, the Hussite movement in Bohemia had proved itself to be such an effective military force that it had to be negotiated with, and the use of the chalice was conceded to the Bohemians by the Council of Basel, which, however, reserved the doctrinal position of Constance 'that the whole Christ both under the form of bread and the form of wine' was present. Luther took up the parity of the laity in access to the chalice so as to promote the eucharistic symbolism of unity between Christ and the Church. The value he placed upon lay reception of the chalice linked him with Hus, and a print showed him and Hus administering the chalice to members of the pious Lutheran ruling House of Saxony, a reminder that the Lutheran Reformation revived the issue as Jedin's 'political question'. As a practice that did not *seem* to go to the heart of the matter of the faith, it was be adopted, like clerical celibacy – another 'bye-law' of the Church – as a concession to win compromise in religiously polarised Germany. It was a key feature of Charles V's attempt at reconciliation in the 1548 Interim, and in 1563 a *Landtag* (or territorial diet) in Bavaria approved the sharing of the chalice by the laity as part of a raft of reconciling offers. The Catholic Duke Albrecht V (1528–79) of Bavaria told the Council that the concession was necessary to keep his duchy within the Catholic fold, while Emperor Ferdinand led the demands from Germany for this franchise. In 1564 Pius IV himself empowered bishops in five German provinces to grant the chalice to lay people who desired it.[57]

If the pressure for this pacifying concession – which many theologians favoured – was so powerful, reasonable and persuasive, why, in the event, did the Council of Trent opt for the inflexible line it took when it passed its 'stringent' ruling in the twenty- first session to the effect:

> that laymen…are bound by no divine precept to receive the sacrament of the Eucharist under both forms.…For though Christ…at the last supper instituted and delivered to the Apostles this…sacrament under the forms of bread and wine, yet that institution and administration do not signify that all the faithful are by an enactment of the Lord to receive under both forms. [The] Church…has…approved this custom of communicating under either species and has decreed that it be considered the law.

It is true that, on the practical level, the Council authorised the pope to award the concession of the chalice, but its theoretical line was much more inflexible, and again we must ask why. Was it the case, for example, that the Council, made up of clerics, was evincing the obverse of anti-clericalism in putting the trouble-some laity in their place over the chalice? Or, now that the Catholic recovery in Germany was getting under way, there may have been a pressure to do away with half-way-house compromises and what Po-Chia calls the 'fuzziness in liturgy and religious practice' which muddled separate identities of church membership and made it difficult to draw the frontiers of 'confessionalisation': it was revealing that, as Catholic recovery was accelerated from the second half of the sixteenth century, the lay chalice was withdrawn in Bavaria, and Gregory XIII (1572–85) retracted Pius IV's concession. Further, Trent's instinct was always to side with its predecessors, and we have seen that Constance rejected the lay use of the chalice. Finally, the Tridentine Church inclined towards standardisation and romanisation of worship, and lay reception of the chalice was a variation from the Roman norm, maybe seen as untidy. Perhaps some or all of these thoughts were present at the Council, yet none will sufficiently explain Trent's obdurate line on the chalice, and to understand the deeper dimensions of that refusal we need to focus on the sense in which the Council envisaged the Eucharist (or the Mass) as a reprise of Christ's Last Supper. Though Luther was convinced that Christ was really present in the Eucharist, he conceived of it as a congregational meal imitating the Last Supper, and so to be enacted with authenticity as to the drinking of the chalice as well as the eating of the bread. The disciples, he wrote, first took up this imitation of Christ in the Supper: 'by Christ's giving his own cup and commanding all to drink of it he must surely have moved [the disciples] also, because he had never done such a thing, with any other cup, saying that it was his blood'. The Council, in contrast, seems to have considered that the exact details of what was done in the Upper Room did not need to be replayed: for, '*though* [my emphasis] Christ...instituted...this sacrament under the forms of bread and wine', the Last Supper should be viewed not so much as a meal to be re-enacted as the commencement of the sacrifice, unique to Christ, of the following day ,and Christ began at that meal to institute 'a new Passover, namely Himself, to be immolated under visible signs by the Church'. The Last Supper was the first Mass, and the Mass, as the Council was soon to decide, was the sacrifice of Calvary. Faithfully imitating the exact components of the Supper as a meal with bread and wine was perhaps seen as a lesser priority.[58]

There was one other possible undertone to Trent's effective exclusion of the Catholic laity from the reception of the chalice, arising from the formula of transubstantiation discussed above. In medieval devotion, the eucharistic host rather than the chalice was the focus of adoration of 'this sublime and venerable sacrament', as Trent's thirteenth session expressed it. Veneration of the host, especially when it was elevated by the priest at the consecration or when it was exposed for devotion in processions and rites of exposition, was a more usual congregational activity than reception of the chalice could be. Visible in ways that the 'precious blood' contained within the chalice could not be, the host, a pure white unleavened wheaten bread disc, contained within 'monstrances' (rayed showcases designed for spectacular exhibition) and carried in countless processions, came ineluctably to be regarded as the prime form of the transubstantiated eucharistic body of Christ. For example, in the numerous desecration stories that filled late medieval Europe, it was the host that was believed to suffer – to bleed – when stabbed, proving that *it* was the 'body of Christ'. Special devotion to the host was attributed to the Habsburgs in Counter-Reformation historical writing. The chalice by no means faded from attention and was the focus of a rich Catholic iconography both before and after Trent. Yet one cannot escape the conclusion that it was the host, held in fact to contain both the body and blood of Christ, that was viewed as the essential Eucharist and therefore sufficient for the laity to receive as Holy Communion. The celebrant priest received the chalice as, perhaps, the heir of the Apostles, the first priests, to whom Christ had proffered the cup in the Supper.[59]

In the twenty-second session, on 17 September 1562, the Council took up the subject of the Mass, which had already occupied it at Bologna in 1547 and at Trent in 1551–2. The issue at stake was the nature of the Mass as a sacrifice. No one at Trent or Bologna denied that the Mass was a sacrifice: '*hoc sacrificium laudis*', 'this sacrifice of praise'. The question at issue was whether or not it was *Christ's* sacrifice, of Calvary. As early as 431 the Council of Ephesus had indicated a conception of the Mass as Calvary when it established that 'proclaiming the death...of...Jesus Christ...we offer the unbloody worship in the churches'. However, Jedin speaks of a long-standing 'inadequacy', meaning confusion, in the Church's doctrine of the Mass up to the time of the Reformation. For instance, Luther's orthodox antagonist Johannes Eck did not teach that the Mass was Calvary but rather 'a memorial and a representation of the Passion and Death of Christ'. Cajetan, on the other hand, in his 'The Celebration of the Mass' (1510) wrote that 'The efficacy [of the Mass] in itself is the immolation of Jesus Christ, so that that which is offered up is Jesus Christ....The effect of Christ crucified is of infinite sufficiency'. This certainly approached the position that was to be adopted at Trent, where Laínez in 1551–2 restated an interpretation already voiced at Bologna: each Mass was the same sacrifice, 'offered by the very same High Priest', Christ, as was made on the Cross, 'the oblation made on Calvary bloodily, on the altar of the mass bloodlessly'. Each Mass applied the fruits, which were forgiveness of sins and grace, of the sacrifice of the Cross. Since such views threatened, in the minds of some, to undermine the unique redemptive value of the sacrifice of Calvary, lengthy and complex debate took place in the Council, running into the political storms which the sessions of 1551–2 encountered. In January 1552 it was decided that the issues relating 'to the most holy sacrifice of the mass' (along with Holy Orders) would be held over to a fifteenth session on 19 March, a session which, in the event, was taken up with the procedural matters of a prorogation and of a safe conduct for Protestants. When the sessions of 1551–2 were concluded with the suspension of April 1552, left unsettled was the central issue of whether the Mass was the 'true sacrifice in the literal sense of the word', of Calvary, though offered in a different, 'unbloody' manner.[60]

The discussion of the Mass and the debate with the Lutherans concerning it were involved with the issue of justification. Luther emphasised the Crucifixion as the perfect and unrepeatable saving work of Christ, by which alone our justification was accomplished, and 'It is quite certain that Christ cannot be sacrificed over and above the one single time he sacrificed himself'. Indeed, to propose to renew that action was even to suggest that it had failed to achieve its original redemptive purpose, a blasphemy, 'the greatest and most terrible abomination', 'the worst of all the papal idolatries'. The Mass conceived in that way was a spurious 'good work' through which man vainly hoped to achieve his own justification. To Luther, the rite was properly an act of gratitude for and commemoration of that unique sacrifice, a *Begencknisz*, a memorial for daily observance by all Christians. This view was countered in the Council at Bologna in 1547 in the proposed denunciation as heresy of the belief that the Mass 'is not a sacrifice, nor an offering for sins, but only a commemoration'. The difference might be expressed in terms of an opposition of tenses of the verb. Luther saw Christ's redemption in the past perfect tense, an historic action to be recalled. In contrast, it had already been put to the Council in 1547 that the Mass *is* a sacrifice, a 'representation of the passion and not simply a commemoration of it', and the present tense was used for the way that in the Mass Christ 'offers his body and his blood under the forms of bread and wine to God the father'.[61]

As the Council moved towards its conclusions on the Mass in September 1562, personal attacks on leading Protestants formed a background to propositions that the sacrifice played an ongoing part in securing redemption, that it was 'truly propitiatory' and those present at it '*obtain mercy and find grace in seasonable aid*. For, appeased by this sacrifice, the Lord grants the grace and gift or penitence and pardons even the gravest crimes and sins'. The Mass was not a repetition of the expiating sacrifice of Calvary but, as was agreed in the twenty-second session, on 17 September 1562, it was identical in all aspects save in its *modus operandi* with the sacrifice of the Cross:

> For the victim is one and the same, the same now offering by the ministry of priests who then offered Himself on the cross, the manner alone of offering being different. The fruits of that bloody sacrifice...are received more abundantly through this unbloody one, so far is the latter in any way from derogating from the former.

The Mass, then, was Christ's sacrifice and hence expiatory, but it was not a repetition, taking away from the unique value of Calvary; nor was it a human 'good work'. It was the continuing application and manifestation to the faithful over time of the fruits of Christ's sacrifice. This emergent doctrine of the Mass could secure consensus and encapsulate the 'Catholic consciousness of faith' [Jedin] through its Christocentricity, evident in the statement:

> that His priesthood might not come to an end with His death, at the last supper...that He might leave to His beloved spouse the Church a visible sacrifice...whereby that bloody sacrifice once to be accomplished on the cross might be represented... [He] offered up to God...His own body and blood under the form of bread and wine.

It was the Last Supper in its 'nature...as a sacrifice' [Iserloh] that sealed this perpetuation. Itself 'unbloody', and providing the words of consecration used in the Mass – 'This is My body...This is My blood' – the Last Supper was deemed to be the first Mass, a showing forth of the impending propitiatory sacrifice on Calvary of which every Mass thereafter was a representation. The 'holiest of all things', Mass must not be said or sung in the vernacular and must be attended in a frame of mind 'contrite and penitent, with sincere heart and upright faith'. Its musical accompaniment must be free of all that was 'lascivious or impure' and it must be purified of all 'avarice...bargains'. Finally, the Missal that eventually emerged under Pius V in 1568 reaffirmed the doctrine that the Mass was a sacrifice to, 'avail for salvation...as a sweet saviour, for our salvation...for the...salvation they hope for...to preserve us from eternal damnation'.[62]

Returning to the agenda of reform, the twenty-second session devised further regulations on, *inter alia*, the life and demeanour of the clergy, the quality of candidates for places in cathedral churches, dispensations, wills, appeals, bishops' rights and duties to conduct visitations, and the ownership of ecclesiastical property. Then in the autumn, when the procedures for conferring Holy Orders were being discussed, the issue of episcopal residence arose once more, to divide the Council internally and to set much opinion within it at loggerheads with the papacy. A decision by the legates to try to avert controversy by removing from a motion a statement that bishops were different from priests 'by virtue of divine law' took the protective cap off this explosive topic. The Spanish, led by Pedro Guerrero, Archbishop of Granada, the austere spokesman of the Spanish tradition of reform, had restrained their vehemence on the subject of episcopacy so as to allow the discussion of the Mass to proceed. However, the Spanish bishops' basic position on the obligation of residence by God's command remained fixed in 1562–3, causing particular problems for the pope's agent at the Council, his nephew Carlo Borromeo. Borromeo's negotiations between the autumn of 1562 and the July of 1563 were aimed at preventing the Spanish-inspired episcopalian party from recruiting other nationals and at getting the Catholic sovereigns, above all Emperor Ferdinand, on to the side of the papacy and its view that it needed to staff the Curia with at least some bishops who derived incomes from dioceses by virtue of papal dispensation for non-residence. In October 1562 the papacy's attempt, backed by the Laínez, to relax the absolute requirement of residence had a majority of about seventy-five over fifty-five Council fathers. The arrival in November 1562 of Charles de Guise, Cardinal of Lorraine (1524–74), at the head of a sizeable French delegation, brought the prospect of reinforcements for the episcopalians, for French 'Gallicanism' was traditionally suspicious of the claims of the Holy See over the Church. By December Guise was putting forward the proposition that 'The bishops are appointed by Christ in the Church', an interpretation that would make their residence mandatory, against the view of some papalist theologians that only Peter, deemed to have been the first pope, was directly commissioned by Christ. If the latter were the case, other bishops, deriving their authority by succession from the other Apostles, would in effect be the servants of the heir of Peter.[63]

December 1562 saw the membership of the Council so divided, and the episcopalians and the papacy so polarised, that an innocuous motion put by the legate Gonzaga to the effect that clerics must 'by human and divine law' be answerable to God for the way they carried out their duties, aroused the wrath of the extreme papalists known as *zelanti*, or fanatics. The pope himself was anxious about what some saw as the rise of a new conciliarism, of the kind evident when the Council of Basel launched its attack on Eugenius IV, purporting to depose him in 1439. Trent's deepest crisis came after the 1562 Christmas recess when Guise moved into the leadership of the episcopalian party. In the new year protracted debate over episcopacy by divine right was paralysing the Council's business and holding up a pronouncement on the Sacrament of Matrimony. Intervention by Catholic rulers offered a way out of the impasse. Guise took the dramatic step of travelling to Innsbruck to appeal for Ferdinand's assistance in securing the resumption of the Council's agenda of reform, and the interview did indeed produce a breakthrough in the shape of a delicately phrased letter from the Emperor to the Pope in March 1563 expressing respect for the Holy Father's position but asking him to restrain the *zelanti* and urging the resumption of the Council's reform programme. This pressure from Ferdinand was reinforced by a letter to Pope Pius from Philip II. Rome's opportunity to respond to the Habsburg initiative came with the death early in March of legate Gonzaga, who was swiftly replaced by Giovanni Morone, the finest curial diplomat of the day and well known to Ferdinand from earlier ambassadorial appointments – 'Our good cardinal Morone'.[64]

While the Pope wrote to Philip of Spain, winning him over completely with assurances about the genuineness of Rome's commitment to reform, intense diplomatic efforts were spearheaded by Morone over three weeks in April, assisted by lavish bribery co-ordinated by Borromeo and by further mediation on the part of Germany's leading Jesuit, Canisius, so as to side-step Guise's Innsbruck initiative. Morone's essential task was that of separating Ferdinand from the episcopalian opposition and from Guise, a strategy assisted by the conciliatory offer of the chalice where it was desired in the German lands and by papal support of the Emperor's heartfelt desire to have his son Maximilian (1526–76) formally recognised as his heir. Morone's diplomacy succeeded in isolating Guise, who was now also politically damaged by the murder in 1563 of his brother, François Duke of Guise (b. 1519), leader of the Catholics in the early stages of the French Wars of Religion. Indeed, it was partly the weakness of the Catholic cause in France in the early 1560s that made of Guise, who was a wealthy pluralist, an earnest proponent of reform, though his radical speeches in May advocating the election of bishops by priests tended to remove him from the mainstream of the Council's discussions.[65]

Having gained the German Habsburgs, Morone's next endeavour was to win over or neutralise Guise himself. Important as episcopal residence was to be in the eventual enactment of the reforms so far proposed, Guise probably did his cause no good by exaggerating its value as 'more important than all the rest' of the conciliar issues. His extremist attacks on the curial system once more put him outside the centre of discourse and left him exposed to Morone's silken rebuttals. The French cardinal was rapidly becoming a spent force in Council discussions, though his importance, as aristocrat and senior churchman, in French Catholic life required concessions to him, and he accepted the position of Apostolic Legate to his country. Morone's compromised form of words over episcopal residence – 'It is a divine commandment that bishops shall nourish their flocks' – was close enough to the position that Guise had adopted to conciliate him, for he was committed to reform and to the resumption of the Council's business, not least as a means to ending the agony of religious conflict in France. For almost a year Guise's attachment to the episcopalians had inflated their strength, with the effect of stalling the Council's business. When the twenty-third session opened in July 1563, the Spanish episcopalian party was not reconciled. However, lacking Guise, who had been out-manoeuvred by Morone, and without support from the Habsburgs, they had become a rump in the Council. What Jedin calls the 'great crisis' of Trent had been overcome, largely through Morone's political acumen, but also as a result of his determination to complete the reform legislation. The decree adopted in the twenty-third session in July 1563 acknowledged episcopal 'divine right' principles: 'by divine precept ['*praecepto divino*', by divine command] it is enjoined on all to whom is entrusted the *cura animarum* [the care of souls] to know their sheep'. The practical resolution following on this read 'all who…preside over patriarchal, metropolitan and cathedral churches [including cardinals] are bound to personal residence in their church or diocese, where they are obligated to discharge the office committed to them'. This was to be the norm, though exceptions were to be allowed by papal or other senior episcopal permission, so as to perform state service or for other good cause, but for no more than three months in any one year. Workable legislation on episcopal residence, the prerequisite of the Tridentine reforms, had been secured.[66]

Discussion could now proceed on the topic of the priesthood. This in fact formed the bulk of the business of the twenty-third session, fifteen out of the eighteen reform canons of that session being devoted to the subject. These included the examination of testimonials for candidates for the priesthood, minimum age requirements, procedures for conferring ordination, episcopal approval of confessors, and assignment of priests to churches. Starting with the insistence that ordination must always be conferred by the bishop of the diocese in which an ordinand was to serve, emphasis was placed on the authority of the bishop over priests, for bishops belonged to the 'hierarchical order, and have been placed…by the Holy Ghost to rule the Church…they are superior to priests'. The discussion of the status of priests themselves took place against the background of the earlier resolutions on the Mass for which priests must be suitable to 'offer [Christ's] body and blood'. As had been agreed in the fourteenth session in November 1551, the Council was confirmed in its view of them as men apart and 'so to regulate their life and conduct that in dress, behaviour, gait, speech and all other things nothing may appear but what is dignified, moderate and permeated with piety'. Their priesthood was inaugurated in what Constance had already determined, and Trent emphatically affirmed, was one of the seven Sacraments, Holy Orders, 'instilled by Christ the Lord'. This countered Luther's claim, made in the 1520 *Babylonian Captivity of the Church*, that 'of this sacrament the church of Christ knows nothing; it is an invention of the [Roman] church and the pope'. The Council drew a clear line between Luther's 'priesthood of all believers' and the traditional view of a separate sacerdotal *ordo*.[67]

Of all the resolutions on the priesthood none was lengthier and none has been accorded more significance by various commentators, for example Grimm,

Green, Chadwick and O'Donohoe, than Chapter XVIII, 'Directions for Establishing Seminaries for Clerics'. This innovation, it has been said, provided the Church 'with a trained and devoted clergy who deserved much credit for the subsequent gains of Catholicism'. The decree on seminaries was 'the first reform measure of really historical importance that the council had produced', and 'if the Council of Trent had done nothing else for the renewal of the church but initiate the setting up of diocesan seminaries for priests, it would have done a great deal'. The seminary decree 'was to have an incalculable influence over the future history and spiritual efficacy of the Roman Church', and 'Probably the institution of seminaries was more efficacious than any other canon in promoting the chief aim of the Catholic reform – an instructed and pure-hearted priesthood'. 'If the Catholic world has had [since the Reformation] a more learned, a more moral, a more pious clergy...it is wholly due to this decree of Trent'. Nor is recognition of the importance of the seminaries a matter of hindsight awareness only. The Council itself was fully aware of the value of this project, and conferred on bishops unusual powers to raid revenues of chapter, monasteries, hospitals, colleges, confraternities and lay impropriated tithes so as to fund the seminaries. As they were being set up around Europe, a seventeenth-century Jesuit commented that the decree to create them 'would have been enough to compensate for all the trials and difficulties to which the assembly [at Trent] was subjected'.[68]

Certainly the attention to preliminary clerical training that produced the seminaries was a relatively recent development in Catholic thinking, at least as far as general councils of the Church were concerned, though in 826 Pope Eugenius II ruled that in every cathedral a cell should be established 'in which young clerics were to be formed in ecclesiastical discipline'. In 1179 Lateran III decreed that 'in every cathedral church there should be provided a suitable master who shall instruct without charge the clerics of the cathedral church and other poor scholars'. Lateran IV in 1215 confirmed and extended its prede-cessor's decree, but with the same emphasis on providing instruction to priests already ordained. The concept of training after rather than before ordination is also reflected in the legislation of Honorius III (1219) and Boniface VIII (1298), in both cases designed to encourage ordained clerics to study at university. In its earlier thinking on priestly training, in June 1546, Trent echoed the ideas of Lateran IV of an educational provision for ordained priests. However, within the sixteenth century there were experiments in preparatory training which antici-pated Trent's final measures. The reforming bishop of Verona, Gian Matteo Giberti, ran a diocesan college, attended by twenty-five prospective priests, in which a master appointed by the bishop taught Scripture and prayer and the students studied privately. In Germany the educational innovations of Johann Geiler von Kayserberg (1445–1520) were directed at the formation of an elite of future preachers, ecclesiastical administrators and confessors. Loyola was another pioneer in the provision of preparatory training, as in the case of the Jesuits' Roman College (1551) where 'a large number of apostolic workers of our own society will be educated, with their studies directed solely at the...end of the common good…a nursery of ministers of the Apostolic See for the service of the holy Church and the good of souls'. This whole approach to training priests for their ministry prior to their ordination represents a key stage in the professionalisation of the priesthood as an avocation like others, requiring career preparation. Trent's decree setting up seminaries should be seen as the co-ordination of all the various efforts so far traced to school the Catholic priesthood in advance of ordination for their work. That said, it should be realised that the Council did not make attendance compulsory and the provision of seminaries was a slow process, as we shall see in Chapter 6.[69]

When the Council, following a vacation, resumed its proceedings in November 1563, it moved towards the completion of its conclusions on the Sacraments, taking up Matrimony, which had already, in 1547, been enumerated amongst the seven, as had earlier been affirmed by the Council of Basel, Christ's union with the Church being its warrant. Both Councils cited the authority of St Paul (in Ephes., 5: 32) for calling it '*sacramentum*', for that was how Paul's Greek translated into the Latin of the Vulgate, though both the Authorised Version and the modern Catholic 'Jerusalem' English translation use the word 'mystery'. Like the *English Book of Common Prayer* which called marriage 'an honourable estate, instituted of God in the time of man's innocency', Trent held marriage in high esteem, though it did not, as the Prayer Book did, instance Christ's endorsement of it in the Marriage Feast of Cana. It also denied that marriage was superior to chastity under vows and it upheld clerical celibacy. Though the Council's language tended to be male-oriented – 'Christians' were not to have several *wives* [*uxores*] – the Chapter, VIII, 'Concubinage is severely punished' provided protection for women, as did Chapter VII seeking to restrain bigamous vagrants, along with the ruling in Chapter VI invalidating marriages enforced on women in abduction (though, being freed, a woman might choose to wed her abductor). The Council was seriously divided over the recognition of secret marriages, though the ruling that emerged provided some scope for their validation. The canon long known as *Tametsi* from its opening words '*Tametsi dubitandum*' – '*While there is no doubt*' (that secret marriages are valid) – left intact 'clandestine marriages made with the free consent of the contracting parties', even without parental approval. Here the Council aimed to guard ecclesiastical control of matrimony against the dictation of families, and also against overlords and representatives of the state – as it did in Chapter IX, headed 'Temporal lords or magistrates shall not attempt anything contrary to the freedom of marriage'. Marriage according to the Council was in fact, not a 'secular affair' [Jedin] of the state but a Sacrament of the Church, ideally to be prefaced by the reception of two other Sacraments, Penance and Holy Communion. Trent's rulings on marriage, often hurried over in commentaries, represent some of its finest work, showing respect for human freedom, especially that of women and young people, and infused with shrewd pastoral awareness of human nature.[70]

When the Council returned to the area of reform, a grand sweep of renewal was to emerge in two sessions, guided by Morone. The draft comprised forty-seven chapters, making up what Jedin calls 'the great reform text', enrolled in two sessions on 11 November (twenty-fourth session) and a further twenty-six on 3 and 4 December (twenty-fifth session). These resolutions, which were the outcome of demands for thorough-going reform that had become increasingly strident during the months when the Council was hamstrung by the dispute over episcopacy, encountered opposition from some cardinals, as well as privileged religious orders and cathedral chapters. The first instalment of this final efflorescence of renewal took in: procedures for the election of bishops; the pope's appointment of cardinals from a larger number of nations; the restoration of provincial councils; the frugal manner of conducting episcopal visitations; the responsibility (also covered in session five, in June 1546) of bishops to preach, especially on Scripture and the Sacraments; the duty of parish priests to deliver sermons, with provisions for episcopal approval of preachers; the pope's criminal jurisdiction over bishops; the need for religious instruction of the laity in the vernacular languages; arrangements for public penitence and the provision of specialist confessors; the reduction of exemptions from bishops' supervision; and the qualifications, quality and duties of cathedral canons. The diocese was the focus of legislation to cover vacancies occurring between episcopal appointments; the jurisdiction of bishops was protected from intervention by papal legates and nuncios. The diocese apart, a special centre of attention in this instalment of reform legislation was to make the priesthood of the Catholic Church the basic nucleus of the Catholic Church, the parish and its priesthood, 'worthy and competent'. The norm of one parish per priest was firmly restated, with provisions for confiscation of supernumerary holdings of benefices by priests. Poor parishes could be fused and might be spared extra taxes; parish boundaries should be clearly drawn, and profiteering from parish incomes was condemned. The treatment of the parish priesthood as a profession was furthered by what Jedin calls 'a competitive method of selecting priests', and by the open advertisement of posts whereby 'those who wish to be examined [for a parish] may be summoned by a public notice', to be interviewed by the bishop and his expert assessors. Professionalisation was also evident in the requirement of adequate financial rewards.[71]

The resumption of the disciplinary reform decrees in the twenty-fifth session early in December was coloured by the sobriety appropriate to the penitential season of Advent and included provision for the exemplary 'perpetual sermon of modest furniture and a frugal table' in the homes of bishops. These calls for simplicity of life were, however, resented by Cardinal Alessandro Farnese (1520–89), a lavish builder and spectacular pluralist, with incomes from dozens of parishes in Italy and Portugal and from two monasteries. Farnese, however, was yesterday's man in terms of his High Renaissance lifestyle financed by the 'ungodly covetousness' of pluralism condemned in Chapter XVII of the decrees. Although personal simplicity of manner of life was expected of bishops, the 'honour which is in keeping with their dignity' of office was upheld by giving them precedence in processions and in choir. Their jurisdiction was extended through the further restriction of exemptions. Bishops (along with superiors of religious orders) were empowered to investigate and tidy up proliferations of endowed Masses. The role of the bishop as the principal agent of excommunication (which had been scandalously over-used in the pre-Reformation period to exact financial demands) was restated and the Church's autonomy in this area was protected from the state. Episcopal councils were envisaged as the executive arms of all the Council's legislation.[72]

The elimination of inheritance of benefices had been the goal of Church reformers since the time of Gregory VII and legislation of the Second Lateran Council in 1139. Trent's twenty-fifth session deemed 'odious' and forbade the succession of priests' sons to their fathers' cures. The administration of hospitals, pilgrims' hostels and nursing homes was regulated, along with patronage in presentation to benefices, while respecting the 'legitimate rights' of property-owners. All tithes due to the clergy were to be paid in full and parish churches were to receive their proper proportions of funeral dues. The strictest penalties, graded through fines, suspensions, deprivations and even executions, were prescribed for the 'filth of impurity and unclean cohabitation' on the part of clerics, targeting bishops as well as priests. An ambitious project to extend the renewal of the clergy to what Jedin calls the 'reform of the princes' – warning rulers off interfering with ecclesiastical fiscal and legal rights – ran into objections from the French members, with their national sense of the political overlordship of the Church by the crown. However, it was to become increasingly apparent that the success of the reforms passed by the Council would be dependent on their support by Catholic rulers, as in Philip II's territories, where in 1564 the king commanded the reception of the decrees – as long as they did not run counter to his rights. In the event, the Council in the twenty-fifth session passed what Jedin describes as a 'harmless admonition' in which, tactfully enough, 'The Rights of the Church are recommended to the Princes for Observance and Protection' (rulers were, though, threatened with excommunication if they permitted duelling). The celebration in the concluding sessions of 'the memory of the Emperor Charles V' (not always a friend of the Council) along with compliments to 'the most serene Emperor Ferdinand, ever august, orthodox and peaceful' and to 'the most serene kings, who have promoted and protected this universal council...earthly kings, the preservers of the right faith' suggest the Council fathers' recognition of the need, which was to be all the greater in the years to come, for the support of rulers for the Catholic recovery.[73]

A number of rulings in the twenty-fifth, final session tended to obscure the distinction between 'reform' and 'doctrine', though they did renew the Council's earlier tendency to highlight differences between Catholicism and Protestantism, as was the case with the assertion of the utility of fasts and abstinence in food, so as to 'mortify the flesh' and 'increase piety'. This amounted to a practical expression of the Church's claim that meritorious practices availed for salvation and also opposed the demand for Christian freedom evoked especially by the Swiss reformer Zwingli in defying the Lenten fast in Zürich in 1522. Reassertion of the value of 'intercession and invocation of the saints' led naturally into encouragement of the 'religious celebration of festival days'.[74]

Perhaps somewhat belatedly, since they had been the ostensible cause of the Lutheran Reformation, the Council in this session tackled what Luther had termed 'lies and deceits', indulgences, affirming that the 'power of granting indulgences was conferred by Christ on the Church'. Nevertheless, while maintaining the doctrine of indulgences, the Council took up the criticism by Erasmus and his school of the corruption and credulity involved in their sale (Tetzel's Indulgence was retailed at the standard price of three marks), banned all trading in them and directed bishops in their forthcoming synods to investigate abuses in this area and report back to the pope. On the closely related issue of the doctrine of Purgatory, the Council confirmed its rulings in the sixth session of January 1547, as well as the decree of the Council of Florence, to the effect that such a state existed. Bishops were to ensure that the teaching of the subject be 'sound', but, perhaps betokening some pruning of what had become a luxuriant sub-cult within late medieval Catholicism, the decree advised the avoidance in 'popular instructions to uneducated people' of the 'more difficult and subtle' implications of the doctrine.[75]

In the immense burst of reforming legislation in the twenty-fifth session, the religious orders were dealt with in twenty-two chapters, 'Concerning Regulars and Nuns'. The Council accepted the well-ordered religious life at its traditional high valuation – 'how great a splendor and usefulness accrues to the Church of God from monasteries properly regulated' – and it took up the insistence of the late medieval Observant movements within the religious orders that they realign their practice with their rules, including vows of poverty, fixity of place for monks and enclosure for nuns. Particular rulings for nuns provided for examination of the freedom of choice of prospective entrants, for the convents had been abused as receptacles for the unmarried daughters of the upper classes, regardless of their own choice. The impulse to subject the orders to diocesan control remained evident, for instance in their being obliged to observe diocesan feasts; restrictions were placed on the holding of titular abbacies in the *commendam* system.[76]

The twenty-fifth session brought the Council of Trent's business to a close. It was the longest ecumenical council in the Church's history, stretched over three decades and long mooted before its actual convening. Its savage workload had taken the lives of two legates, Gonzaga and Seripando, in March 1563, but the task of implementing its decrees lay in the future. Pius IV's serious illness at the end of November lent weight to Morone's call, against those who wished the Council to be prolonged so as to deal with abuses in the Curia, for a closure, which would ensure that the Council's status would be clear in the event of the pope's death. A sense of more than relief – 'the most grave prelates wept for joy' – and of achievement was evident in the closing December sessions when the Venetian Bishop Ragazzoni reviewed the Council's work, singling out Morone for credit, and when the Cardinal of Lorraine called on the members to acclaim the holy father, to whom unfinished business – the Index, the Missal and Breviary, the Catechism – was referred. The confirmation of the Council of Trent was enrolled in July 1564. Consolidating the legislation of its late-medieval predecessors, Trent equipped the Church with a solid body of defined doctrine and a code of reform that provided the essential inspiration for the Catholic renewal in early modern Europe.[77]

3 New religious orders

This chapter deals with the establishment of some new regular orders of the Catholic Reformation. We should of course note that the older orders of the Church were reinvigorated in the sixteenth century and that the momentum of the late medieval Observance movements continued. One of the most powerful of the renewals of existing orders was Teresa of Ávila's reform of Spanish Carmelites, from 1562 onwards. Carmelite nuns originated in the fifteenth century, initially inspired by the same spirit of austerity as the male order of friars. A softening of the rule took place over the course of time and, in her earlier years in the Carmelite house in Ávila, Teresa lived under the relaxed rule: 'The convent', writes Po-Chia, 'was a special social space for upper-class women; servants and lay sisters attended to manual work; sisters enjoyed individual rooms furnished by their families; plays, music and dances were performed; and a constant stream of visitors led occasionally to scandal and rumor'. With astonishing energy, determination and indeed, defiance, covering Spain in her itinerant campaign, Teresa set herself the task of restoring the primary rigour of the Carmelite nuns' observance. A vivid expression of the austerity she sought was the abandonment of the comfort of footwear, so that her sisters took the title of the *Discalced* – the shoeless – Carmelites. Her restoration of original discipline in turn ricocheted back on to the male orders of friars, supported by the Franciscan Peter of Alcantara (d. 1562) and the Carmelite mystic John of the Cross (1542–91). By the year of her death, 1582, Teresa had broadcast the Carmelite observant reform, setting up seventeen convents of Discalced Carmelite nuns and fifteen of men. Thus the well-springs of the medieval spirit of asceticism in the religious orders continued to inspire conventual renewal well into the sixteenth century and beyond.[1]

In this chapter, having recognised something of the creative persistence of the continuing renewal of the orders of medieval foundation, we shall be particularly concerned with the reformist innovation of the orders of clerks regular, active units of religious commissioned to concentrate on practical work such as education, poor relief and preaching. Of these clerks regular, far and away the most important were the Jesuits and in this chapter we shall devote very extensive space to them and their founder.

On account of their alleged corruption, the regular orders in the first half of the sixteenth century faced criticism from within the Church as well as from Protestant quarters, and calls were heard to merge them all into a single unit. Decrees of the Council of Trent, for example that concerning wandering monks, reveal an attitude of suspicion towards the regulars and strong pressure to submit them to episcopal control. However, the new regular orders already founded by 1545 proved their worth with their social apostolate amidst the distress of the wars and invasions that afflicted Italy in the first half of the sixteenth century. Their concentration on Italian problems indicates that they arose in the first instance out of a momentum of Catholic reform rather than from a need to counter Protestantism.[2]

Chronologically, the first of the new orders, the Theatines, became a byword for moral strictness. In his aristocratic background the founder, Gaetano di Thiene (1480–1547), typified several of the founders of the new orders. The di Thiene family were eminent in Vicenza in Venetian territory and produced numerous prelates, cardinals and civil servants. Gaetano di Thiene took a degree in canonic and civil law at Padua in 1504 and moved smoothly into a career in ecclesiastical administration, buying a post in the papal chancery, being favoured by Julius II and employed by him in negotiations with Venice. Everything pointed to a lucrative, comfortable career in the Church, until a religious conversion intervened. The di Thiene family's fortunes were badly damaged during the Italian Wars, and Coulson suggests that this crisis turned Gaetano di Thiene towards religious fervour. In 1516 he was ordained priest and joined the Oratorio del Divino Amore, the Oratory of Divine Love, a pious sodality founded in Genoa with the aims of frequent reception of the Sacraments and charitable work. In Rome the Oratory's sixty members included some of the most eminent individuals in the city, working in hospitals, prisons and orphanages and providing a model for similar activities by other religious groups in war-torn Italy's suffering towns and cities. After his ordination di Thiene took up a practice which was to characterise the new orders, saying Mass regularly. He renounced his well-paid ecclesiastical posts but extended his charitable work to co-operate with religious associations in Verona, Vicenza and Venice, attending to the victims of Italy's new plague, syphilis. The piety of di Thiene and his companions was characterised by frequent Holy Communion and veneration of the Blessed Sacrament.[3]

Returning to Rome from his own Venetian territory, di Thiene, along with his new associate Gian Pietro Carafa, who was at that point a bishop, assumed his part in the moral restoration of Rome, which di Thiene labelled 'Babylon' on account of its corruption. Out of the Oratory di Thiene, Carafa, the nobleman Paolo Consiglieri and Bonifacio da Colle, of an old north Italian family, evolved a new religious congregation between June and December 1524, named Theatines after the Latin form of Carafa's southern Italian diocese: his episcopal title was *Theatinus*. Clement VII ratified the congregation in the bull *Exponi nobis*, designating them clerks regular. They prefigured the other new orders of the period in being devoted to the papacy, celebrating their inauguration at the papal altar in St Peter's, in the presence of a papal delegate. The small brotherhood took up the commitment to social work which di Thiene had already adopted, establishing hospitals, but also preaching and providing a focus for the study of Scripture and the liturgy. Consciously elitist and holding up the standards of early Christianity as the model for the Catholic Church to adopt, the group aimed to uphold an example for the purification of the clergy at large, setting norms of holy poverty by holding no property, abstaining even from begging and relying entirely on voluntary charity for their maintenance. The Theatines' separation from the liturgical traditions of the regular orders of the middle ages should not be exaggerated. By normally continuing to recite the Office in choir they resembled medieval monk and friars more than they did the Jesuits, who abandoned choral prayer in favour of active work: the Theatines, writes Jorgensen, 'occupied a middle ground between monasticism and modern clerical practice'.[4]

Di Thiene himself must be regarded as a major architect of the Catholic Reformation, a visionary but also an entirely practical organiser with a strong interest in social welfare. Following his torture by Spanish soldiers in the Sack of Rome in 1527, he regrouped his congregation in Venice. They returned to Rome after di Thiene's death (at which, it was believed, he underwent all the agonies of the Crucifixion) and during the pontificate (1555–9) of their member Carafa as Paul IV. The Theatines' expansion was steady rather than spectacular – there were still only twenty-one of them in 1533 – and they continued to attract noble entrants: Janelle describes them as 'exclusive and aristocratic'; they were also formidably austere. However, while it is true that the Theatines tended to exert their impact through their example and their influence on others, producing bishops and a pope, they also conducted, from their fine town churches, an active mission in urban Italy – in Turin, Genoa, Venice, Milan, Palermo, Messina and Lecce – and subsequently went on to build up a global apostolate, in Peru, Borneo, Sumatra, Georgia, Armenia and Persia. They were invited into Bourbon France by the minister Cardinal Mazarin (1602–61) and into Portugal by John IV (1604–56). Amongst their early emulators were the Somaschi.[5]

The career of the founder of the Somaschi illustrates even more dramatically than that of di Thiene the central role of religious conversion in the lives of founders of new orders of the Catholic Reformation. Girolamo Miani (or Emiliani or Aemiliani) was born the son of a Venetian senator in 1480 and went on to a distinguished career as an army officer, culminating in capture, imprisonment and release (the last, he believed, brought about through the intervention of the Blessed Virgin). He subsequently accepted the post of a town magistrate but, now a follower of the Oratory of Divine Love, he gave up his government position and took on the education of war orphans, gathering both lay and clerical disciples around him and setting up a base of operations at Somascha, between Milan and Bergamo. Early opportunities for the group to pursue its goals of social work came with famine and plague in 1528 when Miani sold his furniture to help the poor and starving. The founding of Miani's 'Society of Servants of the Poor', to give the Somaschi their original title, can be dated to

1531, but full papal approval came only after Miani's death in 1537, in the form of ratification by Paul III in 1541 and confirmation by Paul IV (a friend of Miani) and Pius V. Between 1547 and 1555 the Somaschi were merged with the Theatines but Pius V gave them permission to take religious vows and they were reconstituted as a separate congregation. The Somaschi were heavily concentrated in Italy, whose war-time social problems they had come into existence to address: they opened houses in Venice, Como, and Verona; in Milan, Carlo Borromeo, always a keen supporter of the new orders, especially when these could assist with his reformation of his archdiocese, established them in the San Maiolo church in Pavia. The Somaschi provide us with a clear example of specialisation of functions in the congregations of clerks regular, for while they operated over a considerable range of social work, including running hospitals, orphanages and hostels to rescue prostitutes, they focused heavily on the schooling of poor youths and orphans.[6]

The link between the social misery in Italy in the late 1520s and the emergence of congregations of clerks regular with a social apostolate is evident in the foundation of the Somaschi's coevals, the Barnabites, or Clerks Regular of St Paul, to give them their official title. The principal founder, alongside the two Milanese, Bartolomeo Ferrari (1499–1544) and Giacomo Antonio Morigia (1497–1546), was another representative of an Italian urban elite family, in Cremona in the Duchy of Milan, Antonio Maria Zaccaria (1502–47). Zaccaria showed from boyhood the piety inculcated by his mother. He studied in Cremona, then philosophy at Pavia and subsequently medicine at Padua, where he graduated in 1524 and returned to Cremona to practise medicine. Under the guidance of a Dominican confessor, he abandoned the medical profession and took up theology, studied for holy orders and was ordained, his first Mass reportedly a visionary experience. Zaccaria was another founder of a clerks regular congregation with a pronounced social concern, beginning in Cremona with visits to prisons and hospitals and opening up his house to unfortunates.[7]

In Milan Zaccaria worked with Ferrari and Morigia to form their clerks regular in 1530. The Barnabites aimed at a broad popular appeal, drawing crowds to the spiritual conferences and religious exercises that Zaccaria gave at his home in Milan. As membership numbers increased, canonical institution, by Clement VII, came in 1533; their structures were modelled on those of the Theatines. In addition to the standard vows of poverty, chastity and obedience, the Barnabites took a fourth vow, to accept no office or honour without the permission of the pope. They were thus typical of the clerks regular – and, above all, of the Jesuits – in their attachment to the papacy, but this was twinned with exemptions from episcopal authority, conceded by Paul III in 1535 and 1543. Julius III extended papal favour to the Barnabites by promoting them from a 'congregation' to an 'order'.[8]

The Barnabites thus looked to Rome for encouragement to develop and eventually, in the mid-seventeenth century, moved their general chapter there. However, in their origins and earlier evolution they were inseparably linked with Milan, and with the problems and opportunities presented by that city. Their everyday name was derived from their use of the church of St Barnabas in Milan. Their habit, as adopted by Zaccaria in 1534, was simply the black cassock of Milanese priests. They arose out of what Evennett called the 'pregnant spiritual climate' of Italian cities such as Milan. Morigia and Ferrari were Milanese and Zaccaria came from neighbouring Cremona. The primary task of the group was the moral regeneration of the clergy and people of Milan. They were closely associated with Borromeo in the work of converting the city and archdiocese into the model of the Catholic Reformation on the urban level: Alessandro Sauli (1534–92), the Barnabite 'apostle of Corsica' and later their general, became Borromeo's confessor and Borromeo frequently took retreats at the order's house in Milan. As their cardinal protector, he headed a commission which gave definitive shape to their rule in 1579. Yet the Barnabites did not concentrate all their energies on that one city or diocese. They operated four provinces in Italy and became established in Naples, Asti and Piacenza, as well as Milan and Rome. Despite Paul III's dispensation of them from episcopal control, their members frequently played the roles of bishops' assistants: for example, the reforming archbishop of Bologna, Alfonso Paleotti (in succession to his cousin Gabriele, 1522–97) followed up a report of a visionary's audience with the Virgin, who was said to have recommended the order for use in the archdiocese. The Barnabites retained their Italian focus of operations but spread out to such areas as Hungary, Germany, Austria (favoured by Emperor Ferdinand II, 1578–1637), Bohemia, Malta, France and Savoy, and subsequently to missions in Scandinavia and to China (1718). Henry IV (1553–1610) was their patron in France and they have been credited with the restoration of the southern French province of Béarn, Henry's homeland, from Calvinism to Catholicism. François de Sales (1567–1622) introduced the order into his diocese of Geneva where his successor as bishop was the Barnabite Guérin. This small order contributed over fifty bishops to the Catholic Church, plus a number of cardinals, as well as theological consultants to the Inquisition. In their versatile range of work – preaching, hearing confessions, running missions, visiting hospitals and prisons, the Barnabites included a strong academic vocation arising in the first place from their study of St Paul's Epistles. Out of this grew a profusion of scholarly interests on the part of members – theology, scriptural hermeneutics, Church history, the study of liturgy, archaeology, philosophy, physics and mathematics, architecture, seismology and meteorology. Alongside all that, the Barnabites, noted for what Dickens describes as their 'evangelical open-air meetings in the cities of northern Italy', retained the demotic, dramatic approach of Zaccaria, a leading promoter of the devotional spectacle of the Forty Hours, *Quarant' Ore*. Popularly known as 'the angelic man' and 'God's angel', Zaccaria was a familiar figure in Milan's streets, Milan's version of Rome's Filippo Neri, cross in hand, preaching repentance. His order skilfully developed mastery of symbols and props and cultivated unashamedly histrionic promotional techniques, integrating their homiletic methods to the expectations of popular culture and its love of spectacle and drama: their preachers would hold the cross before their audiences as they preached to them, or they might drag great crosses behind them as they arrived to preach sermons, appearing before their congregations in the halters of condemned criminals and public sinners. A high level of command of theatrical presentation had been achieved.[9]

We should also note the growth of a female Barnabite apostolate. Zaccaria, assisted by the Dominican Fra Battista Carioni da Crema (*c.* 1460–1530), supported the initiative in 1535 of the pious noblewoman Contessa Luigia (or Ludovica or Louisa) Torelli (1499–1569), in association with Virginia Negri (in religion, Paola Angelica Negri, 1508–55) to set up what became known in the confirmation by Paul III in 1545 as the 'Angelicals of St Paul', (or 'Angeliche'). However, the story of the Angelicals confronts us with the acute dilemmas presented by the renewed female conventual life of the Catholic Reformation. Close religious co-operation between male Barnabites and female Angelicals – including spiritual conversations and shared penitential practices – raised the ever-present prospect of 'scandal'. Perhaps even more serious, from the point of view of public relations and the perceptions of ecclesiastical officialdom, the formidable Mother Paola exercised authority over men in holy orders, a disruption of expected gender relations that brought the Inquisition in to investigate in 1536. In the early 1550s Mother Paola was deposed and imprisoned, the male Barnabites and female Angelicals were split and the Angelicals were subjected to conventual seclusion. 'The danger they posed', Po-Chia says, 'lay in the scandal of public female power – a countess parading in penitential clothes in open streets, a divine mother dispensing advice to priests'. Placed under male and episcopal control, their early experiment in unconventionality, radical gender relations, active, free-range female apostolate and female freedom forcibly abandoned, they fell, or were forced, into line with customary expectations of women religious, above all that they be secluded within convents, as the Council of Trent had demanded. A further aspect of their reversion to expected norms was the way that their internal ranking of fully-fledged choir nuns and of manual workers of lesser religious status within the convent exactly paralleled the hierarchical structures of the world and of the social classes from which entrants came from the world beyond the cloister.[10]

Coming in chronological sequence immediately behind the Barnabites, the Jesuits vastly outranked in numbers and overall importance that latter order and, indeed, any of the other new regular formations of the Catholic Reformation. Evennett apologised to his readers for having 'spent too much time in examining the Society of Jesus as the classic example of [the] new, more flexible type of religious community' of this period. We, too, though without apology, in view of the Jesuits' massive contribution – as social workers, educators, missionaries, disputants, confessors, authors and so on – to the process of Catholic recovery in early modern Europe, will devote very extensive space to this new order and a good deal to its founder, Ignatius Loyola, examining the varied influences working upon him.[11]

Don Iñigo López Recalde de Oñaz y de Loyola was born of a noble Basque family – an *hidalgo*, of the minor nobility – at Azpeitia in northern Spain in 1491 and followed his ancestors – seven of whom had fought in one battle against the

Moors in 1321 – in a military career. Indeed, the single most important background influence on Loyola's early development was the centuries-long Spanish military struggle against the Moors, known as the *Reconquista*, the war of reconquest. The pressures of that protracted struggle shaped Loyola and the caste he was born into, instilling into them the ancestral attitudes and values that triumphed in 1492, within a few months of Loyola's birth, with the fall of the last Hispano-Moorish kingdom, Granada, to Catholic arms. Those values were those of endurance, a rigid, intolerant, militant Catholicism, self-sacrifice, loyalty and dour hardihood. Loyola was a man of the Spanish middle ages. The knightly values of the culture that shaped him were set out in a best-seller published in Zaragoza in 1508. This book was a late flowering of chivalric romanticism and heroic knightliness, *Amadis de Gaula*, a work of fiction of whose attitudes Loyola's 'whole mind was full', as he later recalled, for, as 'a man given over to the vanities of the world', with a 'great vain desire to win fame…[,] especially in the exercise of arms', his mind was a prisoner of his reading and his goals were those of honour won through valour. Then in 1521 came, according to Loyola's account in his *Autobiography* (1553–5), a completely unexpected revolution in the life of the Basque *hidalgo*. He was wounded in an engagement against the French at Pamplona in northern Spain. This event and its sequel appeared to him to form the Red Sea of his life, since before it, as he later recalled, he was all that was expected of an *hidalgo* – a little wild, a dandy, a womaniser, 'pretty free in the love of women', as was later said of him. Then, as he recounted, in the painful boredom of convalescence – of recovery not so much from his wounds as from botched surgery on them – he turned to a programme of readings that brushed aside *Amadis de Gaula*. The new reading that supplanted the old consisted of two classics of medieval piety. The *Vita Christi (Life of Christ)* of Ludolph the Carthusian (or Ludolph of Saxony, d. 1378) has been described as 'a history, a commentary borrowed from the Fathers, a series of dogmatic and moral dissertations, and prayers'. It was an enormous late-medieval popular success, especially in the Iberian Peninsula, where it was translated into Castilian, Catalan and Portuguese; it introduced Loyola, writes Brodrick, to the 'profound and tender piety of the late middle ages'. The other piece of devotional literature that apparently dispelled *Amadis de Gaula* from the chambers of Loyola's imagination was a Castilian translation of a work by Jacopo of Voragine, Archbishop of Genoa (d. 1298), *Flos Sanctorum*, popularly known as the *Golden Legend*. In this book Loyola encountered a Christianised chivalry presented through 'the great saints as knights of God, dedicated to the eternal Lord'. Loyola's response to this work was to alter the focus of his emulation from knightly champions, as in *Amadis*, to great saints, especially Francis and Dominic. He recalled autobiographically his new aspirations as a born-again Christian: 'St Dominic did such and such a thing, so I also must do it; St Francis did such and such a thing, so also must I'. Loyola recalled that as a result of his new course of reading he underwent the first phases of a dramatic conversionary process, which he would complete as a mystic and a visionary at the pilgrimage site of Montserrat and the hermitage of Manresa.[12]

We have Loyola's word for it that his experiences following the Pamplona battle divided his life into two sharply contrasted moral panels, the first given over to 'vanities of the world', the second to an awakening to a new life of religion. However, his description of his former self as 'a man given over to vanities', free with women and with 'the things of the flesh', lacks the depth of penitential candour that St Augustine provided in his *Confessions*, where he wrote of:

> the impurity of my life…the unclean corruptions of my soul…a hellish desire to be satisfied…to run wild in many luxuriant pleasures…foggy vapours from my unclean desires…the bubbling up of my youth…the muddy water of lust…unjust desires.

Loyola came to know Augustine's writings well but did not follow the *Confessions* in providing his readers with fuller details about his supposed life of vice along the lines of Augustine's graphic self-disclosures, dark yet with unmistakable meaning. Was Loyola simply ashamed of his youthful vice? Such reticence would hardly be consistent with the conventions of Christian conversionary autobiography based on the creator of the medium, St Paul, with whom Loyola likened himself and who described himself before the Damascus road encounter as 'the chief of sinners' (1 Tim., 1: 15). If Loyola did have a tale to tell of himself as a champion amongst sinners, for his *Autobiography* to have functioned properly as an extended act of contrition, he ought to have made his confession in a fuller and more authentic Augustinian fashion – *if*, that is, he had a major confession to make. It is of course possible that Loyola was restrained from a fuller self-disclosure of a life of gross sin before his religious awakening by the legendary taciturnity of the Basques, redoubled, perhaps, by a soldier's stoical habit of silence. In fact, though, in Loyola's *Autobiography* there is little evidence of such muteness about himself: though reputed to be glad of 'any excuse to stop talking about himself', Loyola was in fact usually a candid, deeply self-aware and self-revealing autobiographer – except, that is, for the meagreness of his information about his supposed life of sin before 1521. Is it, then, possible that the passages in Loyola's *Autobiography* on his career before Pamplona were virtually devoid of details of wickedness because his life was not all that dramatically sinful? May it even have been the case that he was almost always, to a degree at least, a pious and upright youth and young man, with little to tell to the contrary about his sinful adventures before 1521? In other words, it is possible that Loyola was led by the ground rules of conversionary autobiography to sketch himself, in more or less formal, or even perfunctory, terms, as a sinner before what he represented as his transformation. This would have highlighted what O'Malley calls the 'paradigmatic role' of his *Autobiography* as a model for the sea change that all Jesuits must undergo on entry into the Society of Jesus. Such literary effect apart, though, it may be that there was in reality little to tell of a great sinner before what Loyola claimed was his deeply radicalising transformative experience around his thirtieth year.[13]

Of course, it may have been the case, as Evennett wrote, that before 1521

Loyola was in a moral sense 'no better than he should have been'. As a young courtier when he went to seek his fortune in the years following his father's death when he was 14, he may indeed have been no 'enthusiast in religious matters'. He may even have made, at least for a while, a deliberate choice of the 'romantic' courtier's life of 'duels, women and gaming'. It is undeniable that he was arrested for brawling in 1515. However, to set against all that we should also remember – not only if we are to understand the complex dynamics of his conversion but also to grasp how deeply rooted he was in late medieval piety – that Loyola's family were profoundly coloured by that piety, that they named him after a Benedictine saint and that they had available on their bookshelves Castilian translations of devotional works. We should also be aware that young Loyola was, in accordance with his father's wishes, 'a tonsured cleric of the diocese of Pamplona from his early years'; that he was strongly influenced by his devout sister-in-law, Magdalena de Araoz; that at court one of his patrons, the Treasurer General to King Ferdinand the Catholic, Juan Velázquez de Cuéllar, ensured that he received 'the basic formation of a Spanish gentleman and courtier', which, in the traditions of the 'Catholic kings', Ferdinand and Isabella, involved a continuing exposure to religious influences; that the wife of another patron, the duke of Nájera, viceroy of Navarre, was the recipient of the dedication of the *Itinerario de la Cruz* ('Way of the Cross'), attributed to the Catholic kings' Franciscan court poet, Fray Ambrosio Montesino (1448–1512), who translated Ludolph the Carthusian's *Vita Christi*; and that when Loyola served as a court page it was at Arévalo, the centre of the Spanish Franciscan renewal promoted by Cardinal Ximénez de Cisneros and directed by Montesino. In these circumstances, it should not surprise us that Loyola, with a deep Catholic sediment 'at the bottom' of his mind, was already conducting a course of religious reading before he encountered Ludolph in Montesino's version. Montesino's *Itinerario* may well have come his way, as may a devotional work actually published in 1521, by the Carthusian Juan de Padilla (1468–1522), *Los doze triumphos de los doze apóstoles* (*The Twelve Victories of the Twelve Apostles*). Evennett concluded that 'from a spiritual point of view Ignatius could not have been a complete *tabula rasa* when, on his sickbed after Pamplona, the romances gave out and he was fain to turn to Montesino's translation of Ludolph and the lives of the saints'. His life before Pamplona, then, may not have been one of unmitigated immorality but may in fact have formed more of a continuum with his development after the battle. Loyola certainly bore one of the hallmarks of the typical *dévot* in late medieval and early modern Europe – personal attachment to a patron saint, for he 'had devotion to St Peter', on the vigil of whose feast he recovered from a dangerous point of illness arising from his wounds. We should, then, entertain the possibility that the contents of Loyola's convalescent spiritual reading passed though the filter of a mind already prepared, by the impact of other, prior examples of the genre, for the new material that came his way and that his aptitude for a deepening of religious sensibility was shaped by favourable influences in his surroundings and by his own deeply embedded inclinations to piety.[14]

The way Loyola went about his convalescent reading indeed suggests that he was already familiar with this type of literature and that he ingested the contents of Ludolph and Voragine through a mind prepared. Neither of these authors offered light reading and Ludolph's work in particular was a demanding essay in Carthusian spirituality. Loyola studied rather than just read these books, 'over many times…stopped to think about the things he had read' and annotated his study. If, however, he pondered these writings as an *aficionado* of this kind of product might have done, his religious development, which, arguably, had commenced before 1521, still had a good way to run to reach maturity. His mind was still suffused enough by chivalric images to give a gallant, even quixotic, edge to his piety, especially to its Marian features, for 'he imagined what he would do in the service of a certain lady' – Mary. When, following his convalescence, Loyola was physically recovered enough to visit the Marian shrine at Montserrat in Catalonia in spring 1522, he decided, in classic knightly fashion, 'to keep a vigil of arms before the altar of Our Lady of Montserrat for one whole night, neither sitting down nor resting stretched out, but now standing and now kneeling'. He continued to exhibit this romantic chivalric Mariolatry, as if the images of *Amadis de Gaula* were still working on his imagination: when setting off on a planned pilgrimage to Jerusalem early in 1523 he fell into conversation with a Muslim whose ill-advisedly voiced doubts about Mary's virginity induced Loyola to consider the man's murder in order 'to avenge [Mary's] honour'. Loyola's continued attachment to his chivalric fantasies may even have been heightened by Ludolph the Carthusian's use of the knightly image of Christ as a kind of Arthurian captain. The principal effect of Loyola's retention of the values of chivalry was, however, to make him obsessed with self-directed and peerless achievements in his new field, his entrenched competitive desire 'to win fame' now transmuted into a quest for deeds of derring-do in the lists of religious devotion, fortitude and self-punishment, as if, broken in body and no longer able to 'win fame' by feats of arms, he aimed to do it through feats of austerity. The role models of his *machismo* were now no longer Roland and Oliver but Francis and Dominic and 'he was determined to make himself a martyr to his own pleasure. His older brother was astounded and said that he himself would not dare to suffer such pain, but the wounded man endured it with his customary patience'. Loyola extended the 'passion' and 'martyrdom' of his post-operative confinement into his stay in Montserrat and then at nearby Manresa, with his self-starvation, begging and adoption of a discipline reminiscent of the Desert Fathers of the Early Church. Later, as autobiographer, the founder of the Society of Jesus came to see his ultra-ascetic phase retrospectively as a species of self-advertisement, impressing and besieging God through good works of austerity, and he admitted that:

> I seemed…then that holiness was entirely measured by exterior austerity of life and that he who did the most austere penances would be held in the divine estimation for the most holy, which idea made him determined to lead a very harsh life.

Because he was still, prior to a lengthy theological education that took place in the 1520s and 1530s, enmeshed in an attempt to make his own 'satisfaction for his sins' by his extreme austerities, Loyola would remain, for some time, in a mode of wishing to 'imitate the saints' through spectacular penitential disciplines, 'eating nothing but herbs…performing all the disciplines and abstinences which a generous soul…usually wants to do'. Loyola's religious development was slow and gradual rather than sudden. In its early stages an egoistic and self-punitive discipline had not yet made way for the mature realisation of the founder of the Jesuits that useful work for others requires the worker to take reasonable care of himself or herself, for:

> if [the Jesuit] sees that a certain degree of abstinence means that he has neither the bodily strength nor the moderation for his spiritual exercises, he will easily come to estimate what is the right amount to keep up his physical strength.…[In penances] we sometimes go too far, thinking that the body can bear it.

Jesuits going on the missions were 'to take into account their health and strength of body'. This need for reasonable care of oneself was the next lesson that Loyola himself had to learn in the course of his protracted and difficult 'religious education' in the early 1520s.[15]

The next instalment, what Ravier calls the 'Second Stage', in Loyola's religious evolution began in March 1522 and produced extraordinary visionary experiences in a year of retreat in a cave at Manresa, some miles from Montserrat. Loyola's visions recurred throughout his life, but not with the same intensity as during his Manresa period, which must be regarded as his meridian as a seer. His ecstatic perceptions were strongly visual and must have arisen from Ludolph the Carthusian's encouragement to meditants to focus on scenes from the Gospels, a technique used in the meditations of the rosary and developed by Loyola himself, as we shall see, in the *Spiritual Exercises*. In addition, Loyola's ability to 'see' his visions must have been enhanced by the prevalence of sacred images on the holy ground in and around Montserrat. What he tended to see were visions suggested by sacred images and also based on events taking place in his life at Montserrat and Manresa: for example, an apprehension of 'an image of Our Lady with the holy child' occurred during a period within which he both donated money to dress a statue of Mary that was 'poorly adorned' and when he spent a knightly vigil before the statue of Mary at Montserrat. Other manifestations were more disturbing and may have resulted from excessive fasting: apprehensions of a 'very beautiful' wayside crucifix that turned ugly and demonic in appearance and 'the form of a serpent with many things that shone out like eyes'. From the point of view of gaining a name for religious orthodoxy, which Loyola would have to establish if he were to do work for the Church, one series of visions were dangerous since he read into them direct illuminations which might have been officially interpreted, in Spain's nervy attitude to religious deviance in the 1520s, as linked to the 'illuminist' heresy of direct inspiration independent of the Church and Scripture. An impression he had, probably traceable to the eucharistic host in the monstrance – of 'something white from which rays were coming' unfolded to him the mysteries of the creation. A sense, presumably also deriving ultimately from the monstrance, of 'white rays' at the elevation of the host in the Mass gave him a vividly immediate grasp of the real presence of Christ in the Eucharist and he was made aware 'with his understanding…how Jesus Christ our Lord was present therein that most holy sacrament'. His mystic sightings encouraged him to feel independent of the normal routes of instruction based on Scripture that the Church maintained: 'if there were no Scriptures to teach us these matters of faith, he [Loyola] would be resolved to die for them, *only because of what he had seen* [my emphasis]'. Without his realising it, Loyola's reliance on his visions for his religious instruction on such topics as the Eucharist was wafting him dangerously towards the illuminist heresy, of whose tenets he was, not entirely without justification, to be accused during the course of the 1520s. He would need soon to seek out more humdrum channels of religious instruction.[16]

Loyola also underwent extreme depression at Manresa, making him a textbook case of religiously induced psychic crisis, with classic symptoms of deep melancholia, unbearable anxiety over damnation, and suicidal temptations. Like Luther, he experienced acute scruples over meeting the exacting demands of full contrition that were made of the penitent so as to render the Sacrament of Penance effective. Compulsively, he 'made a general confession in writing which lasted three days'. Suicidal tendencies arose and 'often came over him with great force to throw himself into a large hole in his room next to the place where he was praying'. It seems likely that his psyche lost its equilibrium in this way because his diet did. When he began his Manresa experience, he was abstemious, vegetarian and moderate rather than ascetic: 'He did not eat meat or drink wine.…He did not fast on Sundays, and if they gave him a little wine, he drank it'. In this temperate phase, despite being ill-kempt, he was calm and, indeed, 'remained always in nearly the same interior state of great and steady happiness'. However, as scruples came to haunt him and temptations to suicide mounted, he attempted to solve his problems by means of a hunger-strike against the Almighty, exacerbating the problems rather than solving them: 'he would not eat or drink until God took care of him…he persevered the whole week without putting anything into his mouth'. The consequences for a man who had not long before been a patient in a critical condition were delirium, including his hateful vision of the cross, and two near-death experiences. His slow recovery from the deepest points in his dark night was made possible with the assistance of the knowledgeable and sympathetic counsellors available in such a place as Montserrat, and Loyola was painstakingly lifted back to spiritual and psychic recovery by local religious counsellors and a confessor, the Benedictine Chanones.[17]

Loyola's confessor exercised his priestly authority within the Sacrament of Penance of dispensing or withholding absolution so as to impose on his penitent a more balanced regime and to order in particular that, after a week's starvation, 'he break off his abstinence'. (Even so, Loyola disobeyed.) Local devout ladies, who 'out of affection for him, came to watch over him by night', dressed him warmly and he resumed looking after himself, trimming his hair and nails. He also regained psychological stability through adopting the liturgical routines available at Montserrat, the structured order of the Mass and the equally reassuring regularity and punctuality of the monastic Office 'which gave him great consolation'. Another form of patterning, though somewhat obsessive, that gave him comfort was the enumeration of what we might call 'plus points' about himself – five of them, including his devotion to the Trinity. The recovery of his positive visions culminated in a great ecstasy at the River Cardoner when 'spiritual things and matters of faith and learning' were vouchsafed to him, marking his recovery. However, if Manresa exposed dangers of individual self-reliance in spiritual things, Montserrat provided Loyola with human companionship and counsel and the structured liturgical and sacramental provisions of the Church. He was not yet weaned from the self-sufficiency of the knight errant, but he was on the way to discovering the principles of companionable support that would eventually produce the Society of Jesus.[18]

Loyola also continued to benefit from the wide range of spiritual reading that had been produced within the late medieval Church and he added to his study of Ludolph and Voragine, reading Thomas a Kempis's (1380–1471) *Imitation of Christ*. This product of the medieval Netherlands *devotio moderna* became the handbook of lay *dévots* living in the world of work and family. Though it advised the avoidance of 'lustful appetites', it was more concerned with 'spiritual exercises' (the title that Loyola was to give to his own manual of devotion) rather than with asceticism *per se*. Loyola came to love a Kempis's work, 'the pearl of books', 'never wanted to read any other book of devotion', read a chapter a day and divided his days between reading and meditating upon the *Imitation*. Studying spirituality, and having undergone and resolved a profound and disturbed spiritual experience, Loyola began to emerge as a spiritual counsellor, perhaps one of a Montserrat circle of such advisers: 'he busied himself by helping certain souls in spiritual matters who came there looking for him'. His first steps in spiritual writing had their origins during his convalescence when he made a précis of Ludolph and Voragine in a note-book form, 'using red ink for the words of Christ, blue ink for those of Our Lady'. His confessor encouraged him to develop as an author in his own right – 'to write down everything he could remember', the genesis of what became his *Spiritual Exercises*. An additional influence here may have been a manual that the Montserrat Benedictine monks used as a guide for people making spiritual retreats, the *Ejercitatorio* (*The Exercise Book*), by their reforming abbot, García Cisneros, nephew of Cardinal Cisneros.[19]

The vital Montserrat–Manresa experience concluded with his restoration to physical and psychological well-being, Loyola was ready to undertake a planned pilgrimage to Jerusalem, the next phase in the lengthy re-education that he underwent between the beginning of the 1520s and the middle of the 1530s. The purpose of this protracted and arduous expedition, which began early in

1523, was rooted in what was still at this stage a spirituality that Loyola centred on himself: 'his whole aim was to have God alone as his refuge'. The trip to Jerusalem took this hitherto insular Spaniard on a route from Barcelona and Genoa through Rome, Venice and Cyprus, familiarising him with cities of men and women and introducing him to the Italy in which so much of his life as the founder and organiser of a religious order would be lived. Strongly influenced by the Franciscan ideal of holy poverty, he embarked on his sea voyage taking with him only ship's biscuits. On his way to Rome, his vociferous and effective protest against an attempted rape by soldiers recalled the fiery, honourable *caballero* in his make-up, just as the impracticality of his penniless journey bespoke the obstinacy and *quijotería* in his nature. The headstrong bravery of the soldier of his pre-conversion days was also still present, for example, in his rash chastisement of sailors for cursing, for which he risked being marooned by the vexed mariners. In the course of his narrative – an exciting and highly readable one, reminiscent of the account of St Paul's Mediterranean adventures in *Acts* – the matter-of-fact style of his reportage can startle the reader: 'While he was [near Padua] Christ appeared to him'. The edge was taken off the privations of his odyssey, as was to happen at later points in his career, by the generosity and care towards him of fellow-nationals of the Spanish diaspora – a rich compatriot in Venice, another Spaniard in Genoa who fed and housed him and one in the same city who secured him a sea passage, Spanish troops on shipboard who advised him to curb his outspokenness and others in Italy who 'treated him well'. Meanwhile, it may have been a collision between the practical need for money to continue his journey and the Franciscan ideal of total voluntary poverty that produced a further hallucination, a vision of a coin in which 'he saw something round and large as though it were gold' – a dream of a ducat.[20]

A further collision between ideals and practicalities arose after Loyola had arrived in Palestine, for he wanted to be a pilgrim in the Holy Land as Francis had been, whereas the local Franciscan friars, guardians of the holy places, were concerned with the mundane realities of placating the Islamic Turkish occupying power and, indeed, with protecting the lives of pilgrims whose zeal was untempered by considerations of tact or diplomacy. Loyola's ardent desire to live his life as a pilgrim in Jerusalem was firmly quashed by the holy city's Franciscans. A brief pilgrimage-holiday was allowed, taking in the sights and the sites, including what was believed to be the imprint of Christ's foot on Mount Olivet, but his projected stay in the city collapsed in Loyola's resignation and obedience to the friars, whose guardianship of the holy places was exercised 'by authority from the Holy See', to which Loyola always manifested the unquestioning submission that would characterise his Jesuits. Perhaps also we may read into Loyola's account of his stoical acceptance of the Franciscans' veto on his plans a more mature realisation, voiced in his autobiography, that the life he had planned as a pious and impoverished attendant at shrines was not his destiny or 'the Lord's will that he remain in those holy places'. It was, indeed, as if his visit got his fixation with Jerusalem out of his system (though he was to hear the city's call again) and with it much of his project of self-directed piety, for he now began to contemplate the fuller development of a design, already incipient at Manresa, 'to help souls'. He also acquired, perhaps from his adventures and misadventures, a stronger sense of practicality and of ways and means, realising that education was the key to a career of being useful, for which he would need 'to study for some time'. Evennett perceived that his romantic and lyrical period was giving way to more down-to-earth considerations and that 'with his return from Palestine there may be said to end the ecstatic-mystic stage in his religious evolution'.[21]

Loyola's new goal was to become trained for the priesthood, and his realisation of the importance of formal education for that purpose anticipated the priority that Trent, and the Jesuits under his inspiration, would give to it. Up to the point in time at which he chose a mature student's life, it would appear that Loyola was well enough educated by the standards of his class, read Spanish and wrote it with a calligraphy of which he was proud. However, he was, in the technical sense, illiterate, since he had no working knowledge of Latin, the language of the Church and the liturgy, so that he sent himself, for two years, from Lent 1524, to study at a grammar school in Barcelona. Seeing his own Latin classes as a means to an end, Loyola never acquired the passion for the classics characteristic of Renaissance humanism, evinced some suspicion of aestheticism and the cult of literature for its own sake, and insisted that classical studies be directed to the 'greater glory of God'. His secretary Juan Alonso de Polanco set out in 1547 Loyola's essentially utilitarian views on education in the classics and language-learning:

> He is very desirous of having members of the Society [of Jesus] excel in Latin....Languages are undoubtedly helpful in obtaining an understanding of the Scripture....Languages, especially Latin, are very necessary if one wishes to share with others what God has given to him....This learning [of languages] seems to be especially necessary in our Society, both for dealing with men who speak different languages...and to give satisfaction both in preaching and conversation to ordinary people.

There were, however, 'more serious' – religious – matters than Latin, and the sole point of 'these humanistic subjects' was 'the greater service of God and the help of our neighbour'.[22]

Because of the primacy he gave to those higher goals rather than to mundane study, Loyola did not as yet master Latin. In fact, he quickly became, not a successful scholar, but a leading figure in the popular religious life of Barcelona as a spectacular practitioner of piety and charity, attracting disciples. Next, ill-grounded in Latin, at Cardinal Cisneros' university foundation of Alcalá de Henares from March 1526 to June 1527 Loyola applied himself, all in a rush, to the study of the classics of medieval Scholastic theology, attempting to take in Albert of Cologne (1206–80) and Peter Lombard (*c.* 1100–64) and encountering the revival of interest, spearheaded by Domingo de Soto (1494–1560), in the most eminent of the medieval theologians, Thomas Aquinas. Loyola moved on from the recently founded Alcalá to ancient Salamanca (July–September 1527) and it was within this period that he once more drew attention to himself, as a teacher of 'spiritual exercises' and doctrine, as a crowd-puller and as the leader of a group of uniformed companions. Indeed, at Alcalá he was investigated and imprisoned by the Inquisition and in Salamanca was locked up by those watch-dogs of orthodoxy, the Dominicans. The Inquisition had been revived in Castile and Aragon by Ferdinand and Isabella to detect clandestine Jewish beliefs and practices amongst the many Spanish Jews who had been forced or pressured into conversion to Catholicism. An echo of this brief of the Inquisition is heard in the grilling Loyola was given over whether 'he observed the [Jewish] Sabbath' – probably because he favoured observing Saturday as a weekly day in honour of Mary. Vigilant over 'judaising', the Inquisition received a new commission from the 1520s to defend Spain from Lutheranism, from Erasmian compromise and from 'illuminism', of which Loyola was suspected to be an adherent, one of the *allumbrados*, the 'enlightened ones'.[23]

What was illuminism and could Loyola be justly described as of that persua-sion? Illuminism, writes Daniel-Rops, 'sought a more interior, a more spiritual type of Christianity', its 'guiding principles' being 'to create an absolute void in the soul which God would then visit undisturbed, and fill with His light'. Because of its doctrine of 'emptiness', of an unknowing knowledge, illuminism made a particular appeal to those without formal education, such as the visionary Maria de Santo Domingo, a virtual illiterate who had ecstasies lasting for hours and who argued down doctors of theology. In 1526–7 Loyola, making heavy weather with his studies but a man of visions, was closer to the world of Maria de Santo Domingo than he was to that of Albert of Cologne. Of course, any suggestion that he was himself an illuminist has been hotly and loyally denied by Jesuit historians: their founder was 'harassed' by officious doctrinal detectives, 'good but wooden men', and the whole 'inconsequential incident', the 'silly charge', of his investigation was 'fed by irresponsible gossip'. But *was* Loyola's investigation quite so groundless and was he 'perfectly innocent' of the charge? Perhaps not. His visions at Manresa were certainly illuminations, some of them purporting to short-circuit the teaching office of the Church. Later, in Barcelona, what the highly academic Jesuit Laínez called his 'great repugnance to study' drove him back on his visionary resources and illuminations: study was to him 'a matter of grammar and of human things, insipid in comparison with celestial ones'. When Loyola tried to force himself to study, fresh and irresistible illuminations took over his mind. Not surprisingly, the Inquisition took an interest that was, surely, not over-officious in Loyola and his companions who, on the basis of 'illumina-tions', ventured to teach in such sensitive areas as the difference between 'mortal' and 'venial' sins where the Protestants denied the distinction which, however, troubled scrupulous individuals. Indeed, the authorities in Salamanca were surely being notably tolerant when, in effect, they warned off Loyola and his companions with little more than a caution that they were not to give instruction in such fields until they themselves were better instructed – a shrewd response to Loyola's potential as a catechist for the Church. Loyola took the admonition to heart and undertook with new determination the next stage of his education, a fruitful phase which left a deep impact on him, within the famously orderly routines of the University of Paris, the Sorbonne.[24]

In February 1528 an arduous journey brought Loyola to the strictly-run Collège de Montaigu (Erasmus's and Calvin's college) within the Sorbonne, where he enrolled in the Faculty of Arts and, cheated of his money, moved into a poorhouse. In this, his second shot at adult education, he would need to discipline himself in two related ways: to take the syllabus methodically and not, as at Alcalá, chaotically, and to control his visions. Where he had previously resented study as pulling him away from his illuminations – the 'distraction of his studies' – in Paris he was 'resolved to study', so much so that visionary 'things of God' were set aside in favour of 'Aristotle and his logic' and the rest of the curriculum. He also made summer vacation trips to beg for his maintenance from Spanish merchants in Flanders and England.[25]

A real immersion in his studies now took over Loyola as, in Evennett's words, a 'growing scholasticism of action accompanied the studies of scholastic philosophy and theology. A deeper sense of prudence and caution, of the practical, made themselves manifest' – even though a strong element of God's madman remained in place, as when, having touched a plague victim's sores, 'he thrust his hand forcefully into his mouth and moved it about inside, saying, "If I have the plague on my hand, I will also have it in my mouth" '. Nor did his studies stand in the way of his once more building a religious companionship, the tiny nucleus of the Society of Jesus: Loyola's academic seniors, the mystically-inclined Savoyard Pierre Favre (or Le Fèvre, 1506–46, Brodrick's 'first Jesuit') and, a more reluctant convert to Loyola's cause, the brilliant Navarrese Francis Xavier (1506–52). Both were won over by reading the treatise on which Loyola had been working since Manresa, the *Exercises*. To these recruits were added the Spaniards Diego Laínez, Alfonso Salmerón and Nicolás Bobadilla (1509–90) and the Portuguese Simaõ Rodrigues; later additions were the Savoyard Claude Le Jay, the Picard Paschase Broët (*c*. 1500–62) and the Frenchman Jean Codure (1508/9–41).[26]

Amidst the formation of his 'company', the primacy of Loyola's academic goals are clear and his disciplined progress through theology, despite atrocious stomach pains, led to his licentiate in March 1533 and his MA in April 1534. The impact of Paris upon his ongoing development may be divided into general influences and formal education. The informal influences came from the atmosphere of northern Europe's leading city, its cosmopolitanism evident in the spread of nationalities in Loyola's infant company. Paris was the cross-over point between Germanic and Latin Europe: Loyola, for example, was a southern European but his college had been founded by two representatives of the Netherlands *devotio moderna*, Jan Standonck and Jan Mombaer. The acquaintance that Loyola had already made with Netherlands spirituality through his repeated readings of the *Imitation of Christ* cannot have been weakened by his membership of a college that was the Parisian outpost of the Netherlands devotional tradition. Other contemporaneous Parisian strands included the biblical humanism of

Jacques Lefèvre d'E'taples which fed into the genesis of the French Reformation in the years before Calvin's conversion in around 1532. In the year that Loyola took his MA the French capital was shaken by ferocious Protestant poster attacks on the Mass.[27]

The formal aspects of Loyola's training in Paris reflected the Sorbonne's role as the principal academic guardian of the medieval Scholastic tradition of theology. Studying under Dominican masters, Loyola once more, but now much more methodically, approached the leading light of medieval Scholastic teaching, the Dominican Thomas Aquinas, the reading of whose *Summa Theologica* had been restored in the Paris faculty by Pierre Crockhaert and Francisco de Vitoria (1483–1546). Loyola acquired a firm attachment to Aquinas's intellectual system – 'Thomism' – and to the deductive, philosophical Scholastic approach to truth of which Aquinas was the acknowledged master: he preferred Scholastic theology to biblical humanism and language study. Therefore we need to be sceptical about claims that his Paris years, and especially the Sorbonne's theological curriculum, had little effect on Loyola, that he remained, apart from the addition of a couple of diplomas, in essence the untutored visionary of Manresa or that, in Fr Ravier's words, his studies 'neither profoundly modified the "catechism" of Iñigo nor notably enriched his mystical life'. In fact, he was deeply influenced by his studies, not just in medieval Scholasticism but in the study of the early Fathers of the Church ('patristics'); a letter he wrote in 1549, for example, shows his intimate knowledge of the Church fathers Jerome, Augustine, Chrysostom (*c.* 347–407) and others, and of the Scholastics Aquinas, Bonaventure (1221–74) and Cajetan. Further, in the section 'Rules for Thinking with the Church' in his *Spiritual Exercises*, Loyola stressed the obligation:

> to praise…Scholastic doctrine.…[I]t is more proper to the Scholastics, as St Thomas [Aquinas], St Bonaventure, and the Master of the Sentences [Peter Lombard, *c.* 1100–64] etc. to define or explain for our time the things necessary or eternal salvation, and further to impugn all errors and fallacies.

As well as being shaped by Scholasticism, Loyola studied Scripture deeply. Evidence for his enhanced awareness of the Bible can be found by comparing two sets of letters from his years before and at Paris. In the earlier, admittedly brief, missives of the 1520s there are no scriptural references at all, whereas a single page of a letter of 1532 contains six, all from St Paul. Perhaps it was under Paul's influence, as well as that of Augustine, that Loyola moved away from his earlier reliance on his own efforts to win merit and towards an acceptance of the all-sufficiency of divine grace which characterised both Paul and Augustine. A soteriology that leaned as heavily as Augustine's did on grace was linked to a rejection of free will, and the acceptance of predestination that is expressed in what appears to be a late passage of the *Spiritual Exercises*: 'it is very true that none can be saved, unless he be predestined, and without having faith and grace'. It seems clear that the reorientation of Loyola's view of salvation, from what was, in practice, a reliance in the 1520s on his own efforts through austerities and pilgrimage towards a strong realisation of the indispensability of God's saving grace evident in the above passage, which is 'redolent', writes one of his editors, 'of the University of Paris', was indeed a product of a higher education which did in fact 'profoundly modify' Loyola's outlook.[28]

A major shift of priorities in Loyola's mind is also evident in the formation, in the August of the year when he took his MA, 1534, of the Society of Jesus. His goal once more, as in 1523, was Jerusalem, but not now, as then, so as to sanctify Loyola but in order 'to spend their lives in the service of souls'. Loyola laconically recorded the event – 'gathered the companions' – when at Mass in the chapel of St Denis in Montmartre, the priest Favre and five laymen, including Loyola, all intending to go on to the priesthood, were joined in what Brodrick called, 'the laying of the foundation stone of the Society'. Utility was its ethos, for the now more realistically-minded Loyola set down that 'if they were not given permission to remain in Jerusalem, they would return to Rome and present themselves to the vicar of Christ [the pope], so that he could make use of them'.[29]

Meanwhile, an account of what was supposed to be a restful visit to his birth-place in 1535 allows us to assess Loyola's state of development following his graduation. In Azpeitia he showed a capacity for pastoral work, ran a school, suppressed concubinage, campaigned against gambling and introduced the Roman Marian devotion of the Angelus to his Basque village. He also showed political skill in pressuring the local authorities to support his moral crusades. However, he still had to learn human relations, and he affronted his proud family by ostentatiously staying in a hostel rather than in the family home, now his brother's house. The Loyola family again feared losing face in the locality, and 'his brother was very upset and ashamed', when, on his departure, to leave Spain for the projected visit to Jerusalem, Loyola tried to insist on leaving Azpeitia on foot, instead of on horseback, like a proper *caballero*. This time, though, Loyola compromised his own proud humility to make way for the feelings of others and agreed to ride out on a horse: he was beginning to learn tact.[30]

He still had a long way to go along that course, though. While the companions were awaiting clearance for their planned voyage to Jerusalem, shortly after his departure from Spain Loyola, still not in priest's orders (he was ordained in June 1537, with Xavier, Laínez, Salmerón, Rodrigues and Codure), wrote a letter of astonishing impertinence to Gian Pietro Carafa, already joint founder of a religious order and a future pope. The letter offered uninvited and patronising advice on the organisation of Carafa's already established Theatines and on Carafa's lifestyle – 'I am not scandalised or disedified when a person in such a position as yours makes his noble origins or the dignity of his status in life a reason for indulging in…elegance in dress or the furnishing of his apartment'. The missive gave grave offence to the touchy and powerful Carafa, a fierce Neapolitan patriot whose country was occupied by the Spanish: he detested them anyway, even without the gratuitous near-insults offered in the Spaniard Loyola's letter. So this document represented a serious error, because Carafa was emerging as a key reformist within the growing movement for the renewal of the Church promoted by Paul III from 1535 onwards, and the fledgling Jesuits could have used his support. In fact, when Carafa became pope he undertook, writes Brodrick, 'very much to trouble the peace of the nascent Society of Jesus', so the 1536 letter may have had damaging longer term consequences. The fact that it was written, as Brodrick says, 'in perfect innocence' (or, as its author explained, in a manner 'simple and sincere as perfect candour and frankness require') did not lessen the damage it did, for the childlike bluntness that might have been excused in a hermit and visionary needed to be set aside in favour of the greater suavity that Loyola would have to acquire if he were to convert his group of companions into an order of the Church.[31]

In 1537 war between Venice and the Turks sealed off the passage to Jerusalem, a hidden blessing for the evolution of Loyola's companions into a recognised order. Though dispersed, they were held together by performance of the *Spiritual Exercises* and in October 1537 took the name *Compañía de Jesus*, Company of Jesus. Staying behind in Venice, Loyola sent nine brethren to Rome to seek papal approval for the journey to the Holy Land. However, the companions' work was increasingly centred on Italy itself and its appalling social problems after decades as Europe's battlefield. Their tasks, then, were carried out in the peninsula's troubled cities, Venice, Ferrara, Bologna, Siena and Padua, and ranged from hospital work to preaching. It was the perceptive Paul III who remarked that the Jerusalem of their true vocation was Italy. Amidst his own work in urban Italy, including sensationally popular preaching in Vicenza, Loyola's visions returned, two of them directing him to Rome.[32]

It was, he believed, a divine promise given in a vision – 'I shall be propitious to you in Rome' – that directed Loyola and the companions to the place that was to be the centre of the Jesuits' operations, the city of Peter rather than the city of David. In the period when Loyola approached Rome with Laínez and Favre in 1537 the cardinals' report was being prepared which heralded the religious, social and moral renewal of the city, a process in which Loyola and his associates were to play a vital part. Their tasks already included the running of orphanages and of a refuge for former prostitutes. Dramatising the obstacles that he and his companions would have to overcome, with the assistance of divine providence, Loyola recorded 'Then the persecution began', in 1538. This 'persecution' was in fact no more than malicious gossip on the part of an Augustinian, the allegedly crypto-Lutheran content of whose sermons the companions had criticised and who was suppressed by the highest authorities. Far from oppression, the group enjoyed the favour of Rome's elite and were given a 'heartening welcome' in the city. Cardinal Contarini was conducted through the *Spiritual Exercises* and Pope Paul, with whom Loyola had an audience, commissioned the members with important tasks around Italy – monastic reform in Siena, social work in Ischia, missionary and pastoral duties in Parma and Brescia, university teaching in Rome. In November 1538, in what Favre styled the quasi-foundation of the Society of Jesus, the pope accepted the companions' offer of their service placed totally at his disposal.[33]

Loyola himself was acquiring a surer touch in relations with the powerful: in 1538 he wrote in suave tones to Pietro Contarini (1493–1563), nephew of the cardinal, supplicating his assistance against slanderers in Rome. He also prepared for the recognition of his group by soliciting written commendations of the value of their work. Following conferences in the Lent of 1539, in April the companions took the next step in their evolution when they decided to submit themselves for full papal approval, a constitutional ratification of their group identity made all the more necessary by the members' dispersal throughout Italy. Even so, this further step along the road that had been opened at Montmartre in 1534 encountered opposition, on contradictory grounds: that they wanted to be a religious order and the Church already had too many of those, and that they renounced choral prayer and therefore could not be a true religious order. Paul III's resolve to license the new body largely dispelled objections. A paper submitted to the pope in the summer of 1539 was both a petition for recognition and a model of a statute of institution, which Paul in fact incorporated into the bull of 27 September 1540 authorising the establishment of the Society of Jesus, *Regimini Militantis Ecclesiae*. Loyola proceeded to work on the new Society's Constitutions, which were ratified in Julius III's *Exposcit debitum*, further revisions being made up to Loyola's death in 1556. Along with the *Spiritual Exercises*, the Constitutions form the other half of Loyola's 'literary' legacy to the Society of Jesus.[34]

Loyola was approaching 50 when Paul III's bull of approbation was issued and into his fifties – what Ganss calls his 'maturity at Rome' – when he prepared the Constitutions, a model, indeed, of maturity and experience. Immensely long – 275 pages in the Ganss edition – they were based on a wide selection of models: the rules of other orders along with suggestions and modifications from members of the Society working in the field. Written amidst Loyola's recurrent visions, their guiding principle is order, both in their textual arrangement in parts, chapters and numbered clauses, and in what Daniel-Rops called their 'admirable logic and methodical genius'. The Constitutions also convey a powerful sense of legal procedure, and the military absolutism sometimes alleged against the Jesuits is absent. As Evennett wrote, 'How insufficient…it is to regard St Ignatius as simply an ardent Spaniard who brought…a military outlook to his band of followers'. Dickens adds, 'Writers satisfied with the superficial clichés have always exaggerated [the Society's] autocracy and military spirit'. Of course, the abiding military metaphor of this order set up under a papal bull which alluded to the 'Church Militant' was of an armed force, but it was an unusually constitutional army, for its first commander-in-chief, Loyola, made '*praepositus generalis*' – 'superior general' – in 1541, was 'not temperamentally an autocrat', was voted into the position and had to be morally blackmailed into accepting it. (Incidentally, with his limp and record of acute stomach pains, it seems highly unlikely that Loyola would have passed the 'physical' to become a Jesuit or even to have been able to give the correct answer to the question 'whether he has any stomach trouble'.) The constitutional rather than autocratic structures of the Jesuits were underscored by the way that the superior general, guided by a cabinet, operated as 'a monarch whose authority was clearly defined as intended to be exercised in a paternal spirit and in full agreement with the whole body of members'.[35]

As far as the individual Jesuit was concerned, it is true that his hallmark was unquestioning obedience, in Loyola's words, as manipulable as a corpse, as useful as an old man's walking stick; as the Constitutions prescribed, 'All should keep their resolution firm to observe obedience and to distinguish themselves in it'. Indeed, such subjection was the norm in religious orders, but was, of course, assumed voluntarily, in the case of the Jesuits after meticulous testing of a 'deliberate determination' to join the Society. Even within the bounds of voluntarily accepted obedience, the individual Jesuit was given extensive scope for initiative. The close pastoral care of members extended to lapsed Jesuits, whom 'discreet charity' might win back.[36]

Initially, the growth of the Jesuits was held back by a clause inserted in Paul III's bull at the instance of a cardinal who opposed religious orders to the effect that the Society's numbers must be restricted to sixty. Apart from Paul IV, though, popes of the early Catholic Reformation favoured the Jesuits, as Paul III did when in 1543 he lifted the restriction on numbers. Going against the general trend of Catholic reformism, especially at Trent, to subject the religious orders to episcopal control, in 1545 Paul exempted the Jesuits from bishops' authority, allowing them to administer the Sacraments and preach without needing the permission of parish priests or bishops. We may explain this degree of papal indulgence towards the Society in terms of a response to the Jesuits' own emphatic allegiance to the papacy: senior members took a 'fourth vow', of complete obedience to the holy father. This meant that, though the Jesuits had their own superior, the pope was, at it were, their head and was able to deploy them throughout the Catholic and non-Catholic worlds. An early alliance was formed between the Society of Jesus and the Counter-Reformation papacy.[37]

At first the papacy employed the Jesuits in Italy, and above all in Rome, where, in 1541, Paul III made over to the new Society the church of Santa Maria della Strada, reiterating their brief of public preaching, private exhortation, provision of housing for the homeless and education for boys and illiterates. Laínez and Favre were given posts in Rome's university, the Sapienza, in 1537. In 1539 Paul sent Broët to Siena, where he preached to the townspeople and held spiritual retreats for the university students. In Parma, Favre promoted the Sacraments through the medium of the *Spiritual Exercises*. Le Jay used the Sacrament of Penance to reconcile a strife-torn community, as Jesuit missionaries in Europe were to use the Sacraments to bring about social reconciliation in the seventeenth and eighteenth centuries. Another pointer to future areas of Jesuit work, as confessors and counsellors to royal and princely families, was the task that Paul III gave Bobadilla of restoring relations between Ascanio Sforza and his wife Juana of Aragon.[38]

The increase in the Society's numbers was remarkable – from the ten named by Paul in his deed of gift of 1541 to 1,000 at the time of Loyola's death in 1556, 5,000 by the end of the century, rising to over 13,000 in 1613 and 22,000, at the height of their golden age, in 1640. This growth was accompanied by a geographical expansion of their range of operations. In 1541 Salmerón and Broët were sent on a diplomatic mission to rally Irish Catholics against Henry VIII. In the previous year Favre pioneered what was to be a massively effective Jesuit mission to Germany and Le Jay took up a chair in theology at Ingolstadt in Bavaria in 1543. However, had the Jesuits been simply a squadron of academic theologians, they would not have enjoyed the missionary succccesses they did. As with the Dominicans, they combined rigorous academic training with a popular apostolate. For example, Favre, a Paris MA, preached widely and attracted entrants into the Society, in a wide arc from Parma to Cologne, Leuven, Lisbon and Valladolid. His tool was the *Spiritual Exercises*.[39]

Loyola completed the *Spiritual Exercises* in 1548, towards the end of a productive decade of authorship on behalf of the Society. Views of their character as literature differ between those who emphasise their inspirational nature and those who analyse the other literary productions and authorities that may have influenced their composition. In the first camp, Daniel-Rops wrote, 'Literary exegesis gives no account of the unique originality of the *Spiritual Exercises*'. The work came from 'the depths of [Loyola's] soul' and from the 'divine inspiration, the direct working of the Holy Spirit on a human intellect' which the author enjoyed. Bangert also points to 'the action of the Divine Artisan in his creation of this Christian mystic' as the sole explanation for the production. Evennett, however, stressed the literary influences affecting the author of the *Spiritual Exercises* who, though his work is much more than 'a patchwork of earlier writers', yet 'lived in a certain historical setting...he was part and parcel of an age; and...the expression of his perhaps unique spiritual gifts and perceptions and wisdom was necessarily in the mode of his time'. Certainly, the extent to which Loyola as an author was affected by the insights of other writers is evident when we trace the impact of his formal education upon the evolving *Exercises*. The input from the Paris curriculum into the *Spiritual Exercises* was considerable, including, for example, his employment of an image from Augustine of Babylon and Jerusalem. Further, as Rickaby showed, there is a close resemblance between Loyola's 'second method of prayer' in the *Spiritual Exercises* and Augustine's *Ennarationes in Psalmos* (*Commentaries on the Psalms*). Other influences from Loyola's period of higher education include Bonaventure and Bernard: letters, such as one of 1547 containing four separate citations from Bernard, provide confirmation of the impact of that medieval monastic teacher (also esteemed by another Sorbonne student, Calvin) upon him. And, as we have seen, Loyola's 'Rules for Thinking with the Church' within the *Spiritual Exercises* commend the study of the Scholastic foci of Loyola's university education – Aquinas, Bonaventure and Peter Lombard. The inspirational and original features of Loyola's great work are unmistakable, as, however, are also the influences of his university studies, especially of Scholasticism. The outcome of a fusion of vision and Scholastic study, the *Exercises*, as Dickens wrote are 'neither a *pastiche* nor the artless outpourings of an enthusiast'.[40]

Study of the text of the *Spiritual Exercises*, which was, after all, the spiritual drill-book of the most important of the new orders of the Catholic Reformation, is entirely in order – as long as we do not regard the work as a text in the normal sense of the word. For one thing, at one third of the length of the relatively brief *Imitation of Christ*, it is hardly to be considered a book at all, or if it is, then it should be viewed as a manual and an instruction pack, for, as Ravier writes, 'the text of the *Exercises* is but a guide'. That being the case, the person undergoing the *Exercises*, over a four-week period, ought no more to try to 'read' the booklet than he or she would a cookbook or a walker's guide: the *Exercises* were indeed guidance notes and were 'given', ideally on retreats, rather than read. Thus Favre 'gave' them in Parma in 1539, as it was the custom of Loyola – he 'devoted himself to giving the *Exercises*' – and his companions to conduct their clients through them, paying close attention to the varying states of spiritual development of the meditants or retreatants. A trend over time was in the direction of the relaxation of the original ascetic impulse so as to accommodate the varying capacities of individuals.[41]

If the text of the *Exercises* formed only an outline to be filled in by the conductor, that might explain what Daniel-Rops has seen as the aridity of the meditative sections of the work, a 'skeleton', or an 'index', 'devoid of comments'. This was because the director through the *Exercises* was intended to fill in the details, using Loyola's text as a map, but to do so in a vivid and, indeed, visual way. As we saw with his mystical experiences at Manresa, Loyola's imagination was particularly activated by the visual, and he was concerned with creating scenes in the mind's eye of the meditant, stimulated by a skilled guide. In an episode such as the Annunciation, for example, the imagination must be fixed on 'the composition, seeing the place…in particular the house and apartments of our Lady in the city of Nazareth, in the province of Galilee'. Loyola's aim was, as Olin shows, to take his retreatants on an imaginary visual pilgrimage to the Holy Land. The pictorial scenes on which the meditant's imagination should be focused were also exclusively scriptural, as with, to take one example, the *Exercises*' Nativity scene, which is straight out of Luke, 2: 21, while in his excision of pious fables, such as the 'mystical unicorn hunt' featured in medieval reflections on the Rosary, Loyola anticipated the Council of Trent in its ruling on the elimination of legendary and non-scriptural material from sermons.[42]

In some technical features, Loyola's meditative method followed the organising patterns of the Rosary as a meditative prayer: he called his episodes mysteries – 'Los Misterios' – the same term that was used for the passages of the lives of Christ and the Virgin that filled up the Rosary cycle. In its concentration on actuality and the concrete, a precursor of Loyola's system was Dominic of Prussia's 'Life of Christ Rosary'. Indeed, if the meditation passages of the *Exercises* form a kind of Rosary without beads, they also bring to fruition the tendency evident in Dominic of Prussia towards what Dickens calls an 'intensely Christocentric' form of meditation with its roots in the *devotio moderna* and aimed at transforming the individual through the imitation of Christ.[43]

To accommodate the Christocentricity which he derived from Ludolph the Carthusian's *Life of Christ* and from his subsequent familiarity with the *Imitation of*

Christ, in his construction of the meditative frameworks in the *Exercises* Loyola made way, so to speak, for Jesus by lessening emphasis on Mary. He did this by deleting incidents which featured in the Marian Rosary, such as Mary's assumption into heaven and coronation there, and by involving Mary in episodes that were themselves Christocentric: the Annunciation, the Visitation, the Nativity, the Shepherds, the Circumcision, the Adoration of the Magi, the Presentation in the Temple and the Flight into Egypt – scriptural episodes, staying close to gospel sources and with no legendary embroidery. There was even a tendency in the Christocentricity of these meditative sketches to submerge Mary into the background. Her purification receives only a mention, she is no more than a member of an anonymous group 'who carry the Child Jesus to the Temple', and at the Finding in the Temple she is subsumed with Joseph simply into Christ's kin: 'Christ stayed in Jerusalem and his relatives were not aware of it....His parents [*sus Padres*]...found him disputing'. In Loyola's meditative reconstruction of the life of Christ, Mary remains secondary. Above all, in the meditation on the Crucifixion, the prominent role she played in medieval devotional tradition as sharer, through her grief, in the agony of the Passion, was displaced by Loyola in favour of her status as a 'sorrowful mother' *after* the redeeming death of her son alone had been consummated. Nowhere did Loyola diminish Mary, neither in the *Spiritual Exercises* nor in his devotional practice outside of its pages: within the text he entertained the speculation that the Risen Christ appeared first to His mother, and the booklet is full of recitations of the *Ave Maria*. An example of his Marian devotion outside of his book lies in his visit to Mary's shrine at Loreto in Italy prior to seeking papal permission to sail to the Holy Land. Yet, if the meditations of the *Exercises* resemble the Rosary in some respects, and above all in their organisation around a chain of narrative events, their focus is, unlike that of the classic Rosary, not Mary, and insofar as she appears in Loyola's narratives it is on the whole as a passive and secondary rather than active and primary participant. It is highly indicative of Loyola's purpose that a special salutation of the Blessed Virgin – 'A colloquy with our Lady' – is introduced to request her intercession for the meditant 'the better to imitate [Christ]'. The ranking is designed not to downgrade Mary but to highlight Christ, who is given an apotheosis as the captain of His soldiers in a splendid apocalyptic vision of the 'Two Standards'. The centring of Christ is, in turn, intended to concentrate on Him as focus for contrition – *'sentimiento'*, 'grief' – 'because for my sins our Saviour is going to His passion' – and for imitation, climaxing in reflections on the Passion – 'to imitate Him in those things...to consider how all this is suffered for my sins, and what I ought to do and suffer for him'. The meditations of events in the *Spiritual Exercises*, with their heavy, if not exclusive, insistence on Jesus, are incorporated, then, with the meditant's imitation of Christ, and his or her transformation into Christlikeness, – as Dickens puts it, 'transforming the person'.[44]

The *Spiritual Exercises* played an essential part in the training of Jesuits, a process receiving increasing formalisation within the lifetime of Loyola, who adopted a proposal made by Laínez that trainees ('scholastics') should be entered in hostels attached to universities where they were following the set course – as

Loyola had done in Paris. Seven of these hostels had been set up as early as 1544. The next stage was the emergence of designated colleges, both those for the training of Jesuits and the education of youth. In the overseas Jesuit mission already initiated by Francis Xavier in Goa (see pp. 96–8) a college was opened for both indigenous and Portuguese colonist boys. At Gandia in Valencia in Spain the viceroy of Catalonia (and future superior general of the Society), Francisco Borgia (or de Borja, 1510–72) opened a Jesuit training college in 1545. Local families were so impressed by the skill shown in public philosophical debates held in this college that they petitioned for their sons to be admitted alongside trainee Jesuits. Jesuit training colleges arose elsewhere in Spain: in Valencia in 1544, Barcelona and Valladolid in 1545, at Alcalá in 1546 and Salamanca in 1548 and at Burgos in 1550. Italy saw the setting up of Jesuit colleges and schools in Bologna in 1546, Messina in 1548 and Palermo in 1549. [45]

The experiments in Goa and Gandia in teaching beyond the Society's own future trainee priestly membership constituted the most significant Jesuit educational advances of the 1540s, even though such general education was itemised in *Regimini Militantis Ecclesiae* – 'grounding in Christianity boys and unlettered persons....Above all things let them have at heart the instruction of boys and ignorant persons'. In particular, the establishment of the school at Messina, whose conscious purpose was secondary schooling for boys who were envisaged as, for the most part, remaining within the laity, activated what Polanco identified as Loyola's 'strong inclination' 'for the task of educating youth in piety and letters'. The goals and components of the programme were: social education; the classics; the 'Parisian' method; and Christian piety. [46]

Social priorities in Jesuit education are evident in the foundation of the Messina school in 1548, when the inhabitants of the Sicilian city requested Loyola to set up a college to promote 'communal utility' and the welfare of their 'noble city'. Education in Loyola's view was not intended primarily for the sake of the recipient but was, as Ganss writes, 'social and patriotic, for he thought that the lives of citizens in a state would be happy and worthwhile in proportion to the extent to which they were imbued with the Christian spirit'. This was the social philosophy of education in whose spirit Loyola wrote in 1547 to Jesuit students at the Portuguese University of Coimbra, repeatedly urging their care for 'your neighbour', and 'your neighbour's edification'. Especially insofar as it was directed, in Daniel-Rops' phrase, at 'the formation of a social elite', Jesuit education had political as well as social goals, for it was focused on those who would eventually, as Loyola put it, 'play diverse roles...[in] the government of the land and the administration of justice'. The ex-pupils of the Society who, as Cesareo says, 'wielded power and influence' were likely to include some of those magistrates in early modern France and the Spanish Netherlands who used their official positions to put into effect a Tridentine-inspired regime of public morals in the areas they administered. The socio-political thrust of Jesuit schooling dictated the composition of the curriculum, which highlighted the subject of rhetoric, the essentially political art of public persuasion.[47]

The presence of this subject, a prominent feature of ancient Greek and Roman education, also fitted the classical bent of the Jesuit syllabus, for the 'ancient languages', as Daniel-Rops writes, were 'given pride of place in the curriculum'. However, this was a selective classicism, driven by moral considerations, conditioned by the primacy of Christian instruction and focusing on the ancient Roman exemplars of edification (as well as of noble verse and prose), Virgil (70–19 BC) and Cicero (106–43 BC). This concentration on the moral content of the classics was accompanied by recognition of the value of philosophy whose study, and, indeed, the whole range of human learning, Loyola defended by the example of the Church fathers who, in their pursuit of divine truth, 'employed human talents and efforts, learning, eloquence, skill'.[48]

Philosophy and the classics were key features of the 'Parisian system' (*modus et ordo Parisiensis*), 'most useful and exact', whose adoption by Loyola as the pattern for the Jesuit syllabus provides further proof of the impact on him of his time at the Sorbonne. The essential features of the Paris system were the grading of progress in sequence by year, close attention to Latin grammar, development of memory, and written course work. The result in terms of the Jesuit programme, writes Bangert, was 'a distinctly graduated order of studies, a respect for the varying capacity of the students; an insistence on class attendance; an abundance of exercises'. Perhaps the scheme may seem to us a little too packaged – 'tightly organised', as Bangert says. The high ideals were not always realised and the early days of Jesuit education in France in particular were marked by staffing shortages and teachers' ignorance of languages and doctrine. Even so, Jesuit academies throughout Europe – thirty-nine before 1556, nearly 300 by 1607, 669 at the middle of the eighteenth century – provided a standardised high quality of schooling through the monitored progress of students according to age and ability. A number of local programmes arose from various versions of the 'Messina Plan' (1548–51), leading, under the influence of the leading Jesuit educationalist and rector at Messina, Jerónimo Nadal (1507–80), to the standard statement of Jesuit educational aims and methods, the 1599 *Ratio Studiorum* – the '*Study Plan*'. Some of the most positive features of the system were its relative downplaying of corporal punishment in favour of rewards and encouragement and its concern for the health and welfare of students.[49]

The highest of Loyola's educational priorities, the ultimate purpose of schooling, was piety. For example, in his 'Regulations for the Rector of the Roman College', 1551, he laid down that the rector's chief care should be to promote the study of literature for no other ends but the glory of God and the assistance of souls. To further these aims, the Roman College (1551), the beacon and laboratory of Jesuit education, Loyola's pet educational project and staffed by the Society's leading scholars, ran its teaching through a programme of piety – Mass every day, examination of conscience, reception of Penance and Holy Communion weekly. The teaching up to and including university must be suffused with religion and, as the Constitutions prescribed, teachers 'ought to keep alert to touch upon matters helpful for habits of piety and for Christian living' in their courses. The primacy of Christian religion kept the classics in their place and prevented the Jesuit academies from turning into mere grammar schools, for, wrote Loyola 'theology could manage perfectly well with a little less Cicero and Demosthenes'.[50]

The primacy of religion in schooling was also reflected in the Jesuits' use of education for purposes of evangelism. Rome's German College, founded in 1552, was envisaged as the nursing mother for Jesuit missionaries to Germany and northern Europe, 'to open up the eyes of their fellow countrymen to the light of the true faith', the 'means to support the tottering and...collapsed Church in Germany', in Loyola's words. As the sixteenth century progressed and Rome emerged as Catholicism's main seminarian centre for the Church's mission to Europe, the city's Hungarian, Greek and English Colleges for the training of priests destined for those lands were put in the care of the Society. Within Germany, Ingolstadt was the Jesuits' base for missionary recovery by means of education and to it in 1549 were sent outstanding representatives of early Jesuit academic distinction, Alfonso Salmerón and Peter Canisius. In the Holy Roman Empire, by 1650 seventy-six Jesuit colleges and schools were newly established or replaced existing bodies; they played an indispensable role in the German Catholic recovery. The Society was also running sixty-eight educational establishments in France by 1643.[51]

The origins of the Jesuits' mission outside of Europe go back to the earliest days of the Society, perhaps to their interest in the Holy Land in the 1530s. It was in 1538 that the Portuguese principal of the Collège de Sainte Barbe in Paris contacted the companions to discuss with them a possible mission to the Portuguese colonies in the Far East. From 1538 Loyola responded to such overtures with a combination of enthusiasm, and anxiety about over-stretched manpower. In addition, Paul III's resolve to use the group for work in the 'Jerusalem' of urban Italy put a constraint on their ability to undertake missionary work further afield. However, by March 1540 Loyola was in a position to report that, at 'the request of the king of Portugal...[Francis Xavier] with two others are going overseas in the interest of the same king' – John III (1502–57), the early Jesuits' firmest royal supporter.[52]

After Paris Xavier went on to work for the poor, prisoners and the sick in Bologna, where social distress prepared him for the worst colonial Asia had to offer. Once he had set off for the Portuguese colony of Goa in India in 1541, he continued with such work on board his ship, which doubled up as a transport for slaves and convicts. Xavier the missionary has been given a heroic, legendary and miraculous persona, depicted as baptising millions and picking up difficult languages out of thin air. The truth about him is both more ordinary and more remarkable than the myths, for Xavier the teacher was himself taught by his experiences in Asia. Indeed, in the course of his missionary work the attitudes and assumptions of this Basque aristocrat were shaken to the ground. Eventually he rejected, having at first shared, the early form of racism that was implicit in the colonial encounter, and indeed in his Iberian culture, as a legacy of conflict against and repression of Moors and Jews. Eventually, Xavier came to question the very colonial exploitation on which Catholic missionary endeavour relied economically and politically.[53]

Xavier's almost inherited Islamophobia was as deeply entrenched as Loyola's, and it coloured his initial attitude to non-Europeans. When he travelled out along the East African coast, he rejoiced to see on the shoreline 'the cross standing there alone, victorious in the midst of Islam' – planted by the Portuguese: talk of 'Saracens' came naturally to him. The initial narrowness of his cultural horizons made him suspicious of the ancient Nestorian Christians of Asia, whose worship seemed to him formless, as, no doubt it would have done to one seeped in the highly structured Catholic liturgies of the West. For India's mainstream faith, Hinduism, Xavier had no respect, and he secured from Lisbon a ban on 'the superstitions of the infidel in the isle of Goa', authorising house searches for Hindu statues. His religious bigotry spilled over into colour prejudice against the dark-skinned Tamils of southern India, though he was inclined to make honorary Spaniards of the lighter-skinned Japanese, who had a 'king' a 'nobility', a 'duke', who prized 'honour above all else in the world' and were 'a race greatly given to the exercise of reason', 'ingenious and very rational', with 'teachable and reasonable minds', and, therefore, likely to respond better to Catholicism than 'the peoples of India'. Xavier predicted that, led by their 'king' and aristocracy, the Japanese would probably convert within six months of an introduction.[54]

It is less surprising that Xavier, coming as he did from a Spain obsessed with race and 'purity of [non-Jewish] blood' entertained such stereotypes and held such colour and race prejudices than that he overcame their effect. Perhaps it was as a result of his work with Asians, adapting Portuguese pidgin and composing jingles so as to convey his message, that he acquired his fierce protectiveness towards the subject people of the Portuguese empire. He came to refuse to subscribe to the clichés that were used to justify their exploitation – that they were 'outside the law of Jesus Christ....We Christians have no duties towards them'. Eventually he denounced the greed of colonial officials who, he wrote, had coined endless variations on 'that piratical verb rapio [I grab]': it was this thievery, he thundered, that 'left a permanent bruise' on his soul. His letter to the queen of Portugal, imploring her to divert to his catechists her 400 crowns a year profits from the pearl fisheries of Cochin, represents a gentler kind of liberation theology than his harsh denunciations of colonial administrators, but his string of letters to the king in Lisbon protesting, not just against the abuses of the colonial system, but against the heart of the system itself – the routine commercial swindling, the mistreatment of slaves – represent a radical critique of the economic structures upon which the wealth of Portugal and its crown depended so heavily. Indeed, the success of the Catholic mission itself rested on what Loyola called the 'Christian desires and holy purposes' of John III, for it was, as we have seen, in the 'interest of the same king' that Xavier was sent on the mission in the first place, while Loyola issued a reminder of the importance 'for the preservation and increase of the faith in those lands' of the 'rules and regulation which the king...can give from Portugal'. The model of the Catholic missionary – dying heroically in 1552 on the verge of extending his mission into China – Xavier was an early discoverer of the moral contradictions at the heart of Western Christian evangelism within a framework of colonial exploitation.[55]

The decade near the beginning of which Xavier, and in the middle of which Loyola, died was a testing time for the Society. Its enemy Carafa was pope from 1555 to 1559, denouncing Loyola's administration of the Jesuits as a tyranny. The German lands occupied much of Loyola's attention in his last years, including the college which Le Jay planned to open in Vienna and which Loyola saw as the antidote to 'the widespread disease which afflicts Germany'. In 1554 he proposed to Canisius measures to stem the spread of Lutheranism which he believed, accurately, had been encouraged by the propaganda of 'booklets and pamphlets'. The antidote was effective Catholic use of the media and especially the digest of doctrine which he encouraged Canisius to make – the genesis of the latter's *Catechism* (1555), designed for popular use. Loyola was thus the sponsor of the launch of Jesuit journalism aimed at recovering Catholicism's popular appeal in Germany and the Netherlands through such productions as the account of Xavier's adventures disseminated from about 1560 from the Jesuit press in Leuven.[56]

Despite the facts that Loyola and other 'founder-members' of the Society of Jesus were Spanish subjects – as Loyola himself pointed out to Charles V – the Society encountered considerable difficulty in securing a presence in Spain, where their marked allegiance to the papacy raised fears for the autonomy of the Spanish Church under the crown. Something of the earlier suspicions of Loyola's orthodoxy also lingered. As prince and subsequently as king, though, Philip of Spain was a supporter of the Society. A major breakthrough in making the Jesuits more acceptable in Spain came when Francisco Borgia, Duke of Gandia and grandson both of King Ferdinand the Catholic and of Pope Alexander VI, entered the Society following the death of his wife. The well-connected Jesuit – whose promotion to the College of Cardinals, as proposed by his relative Charles V, Loyola strenuously opposed – was a vital asset, within Spain's rank-conscious society, in negotiations on behalf of the Jesuits. Still encountering opposition, the Society in Spain was more firmly established by 1554, when it was grouped into three provinces comprising in all 300 members, about a third of the Jesuits' overall strength at that time.[57]

The growth of the Jesuits in France was impeded by the same kind of political obstacles as in Spain, compounded by the 'Gallican liberties' of the French Church protecting its jurisdictional immunity from Rome: the Sorbonne, and the supreme court, the Parlement of Paris, were the powerful intellectual and legal voices of this Gallicanism, opposing the expansion of Jesuit education, while the bishop of Paris, Eustache du Bellay (1509–65), opposed the Jesuits. Despite his appeals to Charles, Cardinal of Lorraine, against the Sorbonne's allegations that the Jesuits undermined normal ecclesiastical authority, and in spite of the opening of the first college, at Billom, in 1556, the growth of the Jesuits in France was halting within Loyola's lifetime and he did not live to see the foundation of his order's Paris Collège de Clermont in 1562.[58]

From the time that Loyola visited England on one of his student fund-raising trips, the British Isles presented the early Jesuits with considerable potential opportunities. An early link with Ireland was made through the Scot Robert Wauchope (d. 1551), a tutor at the Sorbonne and friend of the companions, appointed by Paul III in 1539 to run the diocese of Armagh, Ireland's primatial see, in order to counter Henry VIII's extension of his break with Rome to that country. In 1540 Wauchope secured from Paul the sending of Broët and Salmerón to Ireland. These Jesuits extended their Irish mission into a British tour, making contacts in Edinburgh. During the remainder of Henry VIII's reign and into the Protestant Reformation under his son Edward VI (reigned 1547–53), there was no further contact between the Society of Jesus and England or the British Isles. The prospects, however, for such a liaison, improved enormously with the accession of Henry VIII's Catholic daughter Mary in 1553, when Loyola wrote to Cardinal Pole to describe his gratitude to God for the opportunity thus presented for the full restoration of England to Catholicism, linking England with Germany as areas to be targeted for Catholic recovery. In contrast with his analysis of the situation in Germany, though, where he partly acknowledged the popular appeal of Lutheranism, in the case of England Loyola saw religious change as having been introduced not by the 'will of the people' but by the 'leaders and princes'. This meant that the alterations that had been imposed by the crown could be readily reversed by 'good governors' in church and state, and as far as Loyola was concerned there were none better for this purpose than Pole, a long-standing ally of the Jesuits, and Mary, backed by the Jesuit supporter, her husband from July 1554, Philip of Spain. Yet Pole stalled against the enthusiasm which Loyola expressed in 1554–5 for an English Jesuit mission, and by the time the Jesuit Pedro de Ribadeneyra (1526–1611) finally gained admission into the kingdom in November 1558 he was in time only to watch the collapse of the Marian Catholic restoration with the deaths of Mary and Pole. Pole's reluctance to encourage the admission of the Jesuits to England requires explanation, for a successful popular Catholic mission conducted by the Society might have shored up the faith to offer resistance to the Elizabethan Protestant settlement in 1559. It is possible that some personal rift spoiled the English Jesuit project – perhaps resentment by Pole at Loyola's earlier removal of Pole's associate Bobadilla from Pole's service. It is also true that Pole favoured the Theatines and the older orders, the Benedictines and Dominicans. Perhaps, though, the real reason for Pole's diffidence over an English Jesuit mission lies in his and Mary's conservative conception of the re-establishment of Catholicism and of the return of what McCoog's calls the 'religious world that had been destroyed by Henry VIII', in what the cardinal and the queen saw as a brief schismatical aberration healed in the formal reconciliation of England with the Holy See at Christmas 1554. The Church thus restored to historic commu-nion with Rome was also an English one, staffed by Englishmen, and very few of these joined the Society of Jesus in its early years. In the context of the xeno-phobia revealed in Wyatt's 1554 rising against Mary's Spanish marriage, Pole was determined to keep the return to Catholicism free not only of the novelty that the Jesuits represented but also, as Loades says, of foreign and particularly of Spanish elements. So the Jesuits, with their zeal, their preaching, publicity and social work, were not on hand to convert the static Marian restoration into a dynamic English Catholic Reformation. When the Jesuits did finally make land-fall in England, from 1580 onwards, they came to minister to what had become a 'recusant' minority in an England whose once well-nigh universal Catholicism was rapidly fading from memory.[59]

On the other extremity of Europe, Poland, to be one of the Jesuits' most fruitful territories in the seventeenth century, but, writes Brodrick, 'semi-heretical' in the mid-sixteenth, won a visit in 1555 from Salmerón who was sardonic about the country and its prospects. But Poland was not high on the list of Loyola's priorities in the 1550s, even though few parts of the globe escaped his attention. Africa attracted him in the shape of Christian Ethiopia and through the potent medieval legend of the Ethiopian Christian king – Prester John. Though Loyola was prepared to allow Ethiopian Christians coming into the Catholic orb to keep 'anything in which they are particularly interested or which they especially value', in fact he envisaged a rapid westernisation of the country's long-established Christianity: Prester John was to be taken through the *Spiritual Exercises, Corpus Christi* processions would be held and the overall incorpo-ration of the 'practices of the Latin Church' would take place. Loyola's enthusiasm for Africa was strong towards the end of his life. By the time of his death in July 1556 he was worn out by incessant work and privations. Perhaps the most significant change in his last months was his reconciliation with Paul IV, who allowed the Jesuit Roman College to award its own degrees and gave the dying Loyola his blessing and a plenary indulgence, a fitting recognition, even from this anti-Jesuit pope, of the deep allegiance of the Society to the papacy. From their launch by Loyola, as we shall see in Chapters 5 and 6, the Jesuits were the strongest single arm of the Catholic missionary offensive in early modern Europe.[60]

The momentum of founding new orders of clerks regular continued beyond the establishment of the Jesuits. The overall trend in these new formations was for them increasingly to dilute the features of religious orders as the middle ages had known them: Filippo Neri's Congregation of the Oratory was an association of individual priests rather than a corporate order with vows. Neri came from a distinguished but impoverished Tuscan family and, as a youth, was a regular visitor to the Florentine Observant Dominican convent of San Marco, Savonarola's institution; thus he exemplifies a personal link between Savonarola's reformism and the Catholic Reformation of the sixteenth century. In 1533 Neri travelled to Naples with the intention of entering his uncle's business, but left Naples and made for Rome, to spend the rest of his life there, playing his indis-pensable part in the Catholic restoration of the Church's capital, which had been acutely damaged physically, spiritually and morally by the horrors of the Sack of 1527. Working as a tutor and adopting a diet of one plain meal a day, Neri merged himself with Rome's identity, praying his way around the city's circuit of catacombs and churches. In 1544 he underwent a pentecostal experience when he felt a ball of fire enter his heart. His adaptation of his mission to the demands of urban popular culture was achieved in large part through his deliberate espousal of carnivalesque comedy and clownishness in his everyday behaviour.[61]

In 1551 Neri was ordained, specialised in preaching, hearing Confessions, and working among the young, and was tempted to go on the mission to China, but was told that his mission field was Rome – as the early Jesuits had been advised that their 'Jerusalem' lay in Italy. As Neri gained disciples, including priests, in 1563–4 fellow Florentines in Rome entrusted to him their church of San Giovanni, which his associates opened as a community under a simple rule, reciting the office through the mornings and preaching, on most days of the week short sermons aimed at the ordinary people of Rome. The group won influential supporters: the first Mass in the early baroque Chiesa Nuova (Santa Maria in Valicella), awarded them as headquarters by Gregory XIII, who approved the Congregation of the Oratory in 1575, was celebrated by Cardinal de' Medici, subsequently pope as Leo XI (1605). Yet the grouping of which Neri was made superior by the pope was a loose kind of clerical society and not an order and did not, as was proposed in 1574, merge with the Barnabites to form an order, for its members took no special views. Indeed, Neri's own aversion from the vows of an order was so intense that he laid it down in the Congregation's Constitutions that even if a majority in the congregation wanted to adopt the vows appropriate to a religious order, a minority opposing such a move would retain the Congregation's property. In 1587 Neri was elected general by the Congregation, the pope ordering him to accept. Relentless austerity weakened Neri before his death in 1595, before which the Oratorian member Cardinal Cesare Baronio (1538–1607) took over its government, in 1593. Paul V (1605–21) confirmed its Constitutions in 1612, making further provision for the costume, diet and prayer of the Congregation.[62]

Though it bore similarities with the Theatines, the Congregation of the Oratory was a new type of organisation of the clergy, a confraternity of priests initially designed by Neri to provide for the religious needs of Rome. Though in Naples the Oratorians took on some of the features of an order, in general they lacked the self-sufficiency of organisation of some of the older corporate regulars. The leading scholar Baronio was typical of the influential station of some Oratorians. Flexibility of organisation was characterised by the absence, on which Neri insisted, of the vows of traditional orders, by the retention by members of their clerical incomes, subject to a kind of subscription arrangement, and by provisions for associate membership by lay people, especially in order to perform works of charity. The government was much more decentralised than was the case in most orders, most houses ruling themselves autonomously, without a chapter general. In each house, though, choral prayer on major feast days was central to the associational life of the members. The elite quality of the Congregation was maintained by exacting scrutiny and lengthy probation of entrants. However, their work was aimed directly at the laity at large, and highlighted the attractiveness of worship, including music of good quality, Giovanni Pierluigi da Palestrina (1525–94) composing many of their *laudi*, or songs of praise. The Oratorians also emphasised public devotions, especially *Quarant' Ore*, and the hearing of Confessions, arranging rotas of Confessors on the vigils of major feasts in preparation for the large-scale reception of Communion. Their approach to the Sacrament of Penance was gentle rather than admonitory. A further key provision for the laity was preaching, adapted to the varying capacities of different audiences. The mature Oratorian homiletic regime provided in each of their churches consisted of four daily thirty-minute sermons – exposition and commentary on Scripture, Church history and lives of the saints. Expanding from Italy (where thirty-five new communities were set up between 1591 and 1650) into Spain and Portugal, Poland, South America, Goa and Ceylon, the Congregation of the Oratory was in the front line of the techniques of promoting and publicising Catholicism and its message that were to be critical to the success of the Catholic counter-offensive in early modern Europe.[63]

The founder of the Congregation of Clerks Regular of the Mother of God, otherwise known as 'Leonardini' or 'Matritani', Giovanni Leonardi (1541–1609) was born of a family of the middle range of society in the Italian city Republic of Lucca in Tuscany in 1541 and at the age of seventeen was sent to study for a career as an apothecary, but, always pious, he abandoned these studies, trained for the priesthood, was ordained, attracted a small number of young men, trainees for the priesthood and keen to assist in Leonardi's work of moral reform and evangelism, and in 1574 set up his congregation, known initially as the Secular Clerics of the Blessed Virgin Mary, established in the Lucca church of Santa Maria della Rosa. As their name indicates, they centred on devotion to Mary, reciting a litany in her honour for an hour daily. Their pastoral mission took in the familiar activist functions of the clerks regular, catechesis, preaching, hearing Confessions, visiting hospitals and aiding the dying, while their Sunday exercises – 'the Exercise of Divine Grace' – were designed to awaken a horror of mortal sins.[64]

As was the case with already established communities of clerks regular, this association benefited considerably from papal patronage, though not from that of the government of Lucca, which turned against Leonardi, who was forced into exile from the Republic for much of his life. However, in 1580 he acquired the church of Santa Maria Cortelandini in the city; the bishop of Lucca was encouraged by Gregory XIII to authorise the group, which was done in 1583 and confirmed by a brief of Clement VIII (1592–1605) in 1595, giving them the status of a congregation of the Church. In 1596 the pope appointed Leonardi as a commissary to reform an order of monks and in 1601 (when the congregation was granted the church of Santa Maria in Portico in Rome) this work of reform of older and contemplative monasticism was renewed. Following Leonardi's death in 1609 Paul V renamed his followers Clerks Regular of the Mother of God and entrusted them with the running of schools. Gregory XV (1621–3), wanting to see them established in various places in Italy, permitted them in 1621 to take the three 'simple' vows, of poverty, chastity and obedience, of regulars. Remaining a small, Italian-based congregation with never more than seven churches in their hands at any one time, – though expanding into Naples (1632), Genoa (1669), and Milan (1709) – the Clerks Regular of the Mother of God were an archetype of the genre we have been studying in this chapter – pastoral, oriented towards devotional provisions for the laity, urban-based, of Italian origin and location, founded by a saintly charismatic, and favoured and directly employed by the papacy. They also typified the liaisons often made between various congregations of clerks regular: Leonardi was a friend of Neri and the Oratorian Baronio became cardinal protector of the congregation. In 1614 they were fused in a union which did not last, with the teaching Piarists of the Pious Schools founded by José de Calasanz (1557–1648).[65]

The same patterns of special devotional focus, urban mission, foundation by a saintly character, papal patronage and of links between sub-divisions of the genus clerks regular, as is evident in the case of the Clerks Regular of the Mother of God, can be seen in the case of the Fathers of the Nail, set up in 1567 by the priest Matteo Guerra in Siena, where the group worshipped in a chapel which preserved as a relic a nail from the Cross. As this association of priests grew, it was granted the church of San Giorgio in Siena, with other favours from Gregory XIII, who confirmed the congregation in 1586. Its members lived in community, with no possessions, following the Constitution which Clement VIII approved in 1596. They were bound to strict obedience to their superior, subordination to whom, according to decrees of Paul V in 1614 and Urban VIII (1623–44) in 1617 only a papal dispensation could remit. The work of the Fathers of the Nail was, again, typical of the new congregations of clerks regular of the sixteenth century – preaching, catechesing children, administering the Sacraments. They and their like contributed vastly to the consolidation of Italy's popular Catholicism in the early modern period.[66]

In Milan, Borromeo used the Barnabites, the Somaschi, the Theatines and the Jesuits to advance the reform of the archdiocese and also initiated a special archidiocesan society of priests and seminarians, bound by a particular vow of episcopal obedience, installing them in 1578 in the Milan church of San Sepolcro and endowing them with revenues from the dissolved Milanese lay religious society, the Humiliati. Indeed, Borromeo seems to have deliberately deployed this congregation, named Oblates of the Blessed Virgin and St Ambrose, as counter-weights to resistance to reform on the part of the Humiliati and of the cathedral canons. He also put them to work – 'bound to him as to their chieftain...completely subject to everything he commanded them' – in such tasks as the direction of colleges, schools and seminaries, diocesan administration throughout his vast territory, serving vacant parishes, conducting retreats and assisting him in implementing the Tridentine programme. Sanctioned in 1578 by Gregory XIII, an enthusiastic sponsor of the new congregations, these priests had a distinctive Milanese identity, as was made plain in the title Borromeo gave them, after Milan's most illustrious archbishop, Ambrose (334/340–397), in whose mould Borromeo himself aimed to operate.[67]

As Borromeo sought to emulate Ambrose, the French priest César de Bus

(1544–1607) aimed to model himself on Borromeo. In 1592 he and his companions assembled as an association in Avignon, whose bishop accepted them for work in his diocese. Confirmed by Clement VIII as the 'Fathers of Christian Doctrine', they were merged with the Somaschi between 1616 and 1647. With their centre of operations in France, where they eventually directed twenty-six colleges in three provinces, they heralded the flourishing of the congregation of the French Oratory (1611) under Cardinal Pierre de Bérulle (1575–1629), a key feature of the distinctive French Catholic Reformation which we shall examine in Chapter 5.[68]

The Roman Fathers of Christian Doctrine were first ratified by Pius V and subsequently received a series of papal approvals. They provided a mix, typical of the clerks regular, of devotional, sacramental and social work – teaching poor children, hearing Confessions, dispensing Holy Communion and providing elaborate public recitations of the Rosary. Another congregation, the 'Clerks Minor', set up in Naples by the Genoese aristocrat Giovanni Agostino Adorno (1551–91), aimed to bring together the ethos of the clerks regular, especially the Theatines, with the Franciscan ideal of holy poverty, a blending of sixteenth-century modernity with thirteenth-century inspiration. They won approval from Sixtus V (1585–90) in 1589 and were subsequently confirmed by Clement VIII and Gregory XIV (1590–1). The Clerks Minor combined teaching with Marian piety. An example of a new foundation devoted to health care were the Poor Infirmarians, or 'Obregonians' established by the ex-soldier Bernardino Obregón (1540–99) and given papal approval in 1567. These spread into Spain, Portugal, Flanders and the Spanish empire, and Obregón ministered to the dying Philip II. Taking the rule of the Third Order of St Francis (with a fourth vow, of carrying out hospital work), they represented, as did the Clerks Minor, the continued appeal in the sixteenth century of the Franciscan vision, which was most fully revived by the Capuchins.[69]

The Capuchins were not a novel congregation of clerks regular but represented 'by far the most successful and the most lasting of the many attempts to return to the letter of the Franciscan rule' – 'outstanding proof of the continuation of the true Franciscan impulse in Italy' (Evennett). Since the thirteenth century, the hard edge of Franciscan holy poverty had been softened by papally approved relaxations accepted by the branch of the order known as Conventuals, though by the early sixteenth century the rigorist Observants were more numerous, and in 1517 Leo X conferred formal recognition on the separate existence of the two branches. The Franciscan Observance had a reservoir of strength and support in the impoverished Marches of eastern Italy, and it was from the diocese of Fermo in that area that a Franciscan of peasant extraction, Matteo da Bascio (1495?–1552), having worked amongst plague victims in 1523, travelled to Rome in 1525 and secured private permission from Clement VII to live as an itinerant evangelist and to wear a beard and hooded habit in imitation of St Francis. He aimed to remain within the Franciscan Observance and, indeed, to persuade the Observant Franciscans at large to accept his restoration of Franciscan simplicity. Yet he faced strong opposition from the mainstream

Franciscan Observance until in 1528 Clement VII's bull *Religionis zelus* set up da Bascio and his associates as hermits, along the lines of the recently reformed Camaldolese order, but following the Rule of St Francis. In 1529 the first chapter general of this new Franciscan branch, consisting of eighteen friars in four houses, was held. Da Bascio was elected vicar-general, though he soon renounced the position in favour of the ex-soldier Ludovico Tenaglia da Fossombrone. New Constitutions defined the order's Franciscan self-disciplinary spirit in considerable detail: houses, designed for contemplation, were to be built of such cheap materials as wattle and daub and were to be located outside of towns, their ownership vested outside the order, with the power of instant eviction given to the vicarious owners. There were to be no modifications of poverty and even begging by these friars was to be used as a last resort, and put at the total discretion of the giver. The hermit mode, though, was only part of the Capuchins' ethos, for they were hermits who preached, and da Bascio had petitioned Pope Clement for permission to undertake this work. Sermons were to be simple, not bookish but scriptural, moral and pious rather than dogmatic, and delivered gratis. Their manifest simplicity of life – they went barefoot – gave the Capuchins a popular appeal in some of Italy's poorest and most neglected rural areas, and on their preaching visits to settlements in the hill country they were acclaimed as the 'hooded men', '*scapuccini*' or 'cappuccini'. Though they recited the Office together in choir, at midnight, private prayer was central to their existence and two hours every day were set aside for it.[70]

Da Bascio has not been accorded the canonisation of some of the sixteenth-century founders of new orders, perhaps because he was not the initiator of a novel experiment, as were di Thiene and Loyola, for example, but rather one who focused a widespread hankering for a full restoration of Franciscan Observance. Nor was da Bascio a dedicated organiser on the lines of Loyola, but a hermit concerned with personal sanctification as much as with evangelism. Yet the 'cappuccini' flourished, absorbing Observant Franciscans in Calabria in 1529, setting up a house in Naples in 1530, along with a Roman station near the church of Santa Maria Maggiore, expanding by 1530 to about 700 members, who were generally won over from the Observants. However, da Bascio's withdrawal left the young order to face a period of some difficulty, featuring rivalry for its leadership, too many rapid changes of headship, opposition from the Observants, who resented the Capuchins' drain on their membership, and Paul III's attempts in 1534, 1535 and 1537 to regulate their growth. The Capuchins' worst crisis of their early years, which was also part of the crisis of the early 1540s for the Italian evangelical movement, came with the conversion to Protestantism in 1542 of their fourth general Bernardino Ochino (1487–1564), a brilliant preacher and member of the evangelical circle of Juan de Valdés. The new order's enemies were thereby given their head and it took the protection of their patron Vittoria Colonna and vigorous pleading at Trent by a leading member, Bernardino d'Asti, to save the life of the order. Survive, though, they did and, as Evennett wrote, in sailing close, in the person of their chief, Ochino, to Protestantism, the order acquired an 'acute sense of the prevalence and power of Protestant ideas which henceforward influenced their whole apostolate'. The leadership was eventually stabilised, and a new recruit, Felice da Cantalice (1515–87), a friend of Borromeo and Neri, rekindled, with his spectacular austerities, the popular affection in Italy for the order that had been endangered by the Ochino affair. Growth in numbers was resumed, to around 2,500 in 1550 and nearly 6,000 in 1587. In 1572 Gregory XIII lifted Paul III's controls on the order's expansion, allowing them to spread beyond Italy. While revised Constitutions of 1552 moderated some of their original austerity, the Capuchins preserved what Dickens calls their 'distinctly democratic' character, and Pius V confirmed the voting rights of the lay brothers within the order. While in their general chapter of 1613 they reaffirmed their Franciscan identity, and especially its simplicity and plainness, and while papal rulings of 1608 and 1627 confirmed their status as authentic Franciscans, in 1619 they were reconstituted as an entirely autonomous order. By the time that definitive Constitutions were issued in 1643 by Urban VIII, the order had grown threefold since 1587 to more than 1,700 members, nearly doubling again, to 3,200, a century later. Between the sixteenth and seventeenth centuries, the Capuchins widened their range to take in nursing. They took care of the sick in Italy and Spain, and in epidemics in Switzerland in 1609 and in Germany in 1611, ran hospitals in the terrible Milan plague of 1630, and dissolved their general chapter in Siena so as to care for the sick in an epidemic in which forty-three of their members died as a result of their care for the sick. In Evennett's words 'second only to the Jesuits in its contri-bution to the Counter-Reformation', the Capuchin order confirms the extent to which Catholic renewal in early modern Europe flowered from medieval roots, in this case that of the Franciscan striving for the 'apostolic life' of preaching and poverty, as reawakened in the Observant movement of the late middle ages.[71]

The sixteenth century witnessed important developments in female religious life: a female branch of Capuchins was established in Naples in 1538. In 1535 in Brescia in northern Italy a group of pious women of middle-class, artisan and commercial backgrounds, growing to twenty-eight in number and made up both of unmarried and married women and of widows, formed a religious society under the patronage of St Ursula and the leadership of a saintly charismatic, Angela Merici (1474–1540). Their initial purpose may have been influenced by the already extant Third Order of St Francis and also by the medieval Low Countries and Rhineland Beguine movement – to retain lay duties, dress and status, but to come together as a sorority for Holy Communion once a month, to lead frugal lives and to carry out social works of charity, including service in hospitals, orphanages and hostels for prostitutes and, especially, teaching religion to girls. Brescia's bishop gave the sisterhood approval and a chaplain in 1536 and it expanded in northern Italy, rising in just four years from twenty-eight to 150 members, living in community or remaining within families. Following Merici's death in 1540, the group, known as Ursulines, won approval from Paul III. In their versatile range of welfare tasks – attending to the poor and the sick, burying the dead, continuing their teaching mission – they resembled clerks regular and are often likened to the Jesuits, on whose organisation theirs was consciously modelled. Their expansion, however, raised issues of control, especially in the light of the restrictive attitude of the Council of Trent to women's religious organisation and its insistence on enclosure in convents. While the group's invaluable social work in teaching and hospital service made it possible to delay the process of seclusion into convents, the steps by which Merici's sisterhood became an order within the Council's kind of definition can also be traced: the adoption of a habit in 1540; affiliation to the Fathers of the Company of Peace, and of a common dwelling apart, by those who wished it, in Milan – a process of conventualisation ratified by the papacy in 1582. In Milan, Borromeo, who set up a squadron of the Congregation in 1566 to teach Christian doctrine to girls, was responsible for a key change in the Ursulines' organisation, subjecting them to local episcopal control. Such alterations may indeed, under the pressure of the 'powerful post-Tridentine resurgence of secular and ecclesiastical authority and of lay and clerical fears about uncloistered communities of women', have 'subverted the [Ursuline] ideal' (Blaisdell) – though the conversion of the Ursulines into a normal conventual congregation seems to have been far from unwelcome to the majority of Milanese members, and the amendments made it possible, by 1584, for 600 sisters, running eighteen schools, to operate in five communities within the Milan archdiocese. The drift towards standard, traditional and Tridentine models of 'safe' enclosed religious communities of women notwithstanding, the Ursulines clung on to some of their distinctive features, not least a social recruitment from middling and lower-middle-class families, reflected in generally modest levels of entry 'dowries' and contrasting this organisation with long-standing patterns of treating convents as refined dumping grounds for the unmarried daughters of European élites.[72]

It was the Borromean Ursuline model that was adopted in France, where women aspiring to the religious life were encouraged in the archdiocese of Avignon to liaise with César de Bus and the teaching congregation, the Fathers of Christian Doctrine. Under this influence, the Milanese Ursuline pattern was introduced in France by 1597, spread rapidly to twenty-nine communities in the south of the country between 1600 and 1610 and went on to become the single most important influence in female education – generally free of charge – in France, with up to 12,000 sisters in 320 institutions spread throughout the kingdom. Even so, the evolution of the Ursulines represented a major alteration of the original vision of Angela Merici, for the sisters reverted to a form of monasticism in which they operated their schools out of their bases in convents where they lived as semi-contemplatives, following the rule of St Augustine. Rapley takes the view that

> it would be a mistake to imagine that the imposition of clausura [enclosure in convents] was a handicap to all Ursulines. For many of them it was, rather, a progression to a more perfect form of life, one fully in tune with the spirit of the Counter-Reformation.[73]

In fact, the case of France illustrates clearly the complex tensions between pressure towards conventual enclosure and the preservation of an active apostolate. It was in teaching girls in a structure in which the Ursulines' pupils came *to* them, in their enclosed convents, that the sisters managed a highly successful adaptation of Tridentine legislation to practical function. The work of my research student Laurence Lux in the Toulouse Ursuline archives indicates the dual focus of the French Ursulines on a combination of the religious life under the vows of poverty, chastity and obedience (along with a fourth vow of perpetual enclosure requested in Toulouse in 1615) with 'the instruction of girls in piety, in the Catholic, Apostolic and Roman Faith, in doctrine, good habits and morals, along with reading, writing and accounts'. In what Lux calls 'the successful compromise' of the French Ursuline regime, the 'yoke of religion in perpetual enclosure and the observance of the rule under the jurisdiction, visitation, supervisory correction and obedience due to the bishop of the diocese', as the records put it, was twinned with the 'formation and education of girls', a task made urgent in the period following the end of the Wars of Religion and the vigorous subsequent French Catholic recovery, especially in what had been an area of heavy Calvinist penetration. While there is clear evidence that Ursuline sisters, or at least a higher echelon amongst them, were recruited from Toulouse's upper bourgeoisie, and especially its Catholic political class of counsellors and *parlementaires*, it is also clear that the order's teaching mission emphasised the systematic production of a future élite of Catholic women, wives and mothers, trained in: 'the method of examining one's conscience, of going to Confession, of receiving holy communion, of hearing Mass, of invoking the Almighty, of reciting the Rosary, of praying and meditating, or reading books of devotion, of avoiding sin and the occasions of sin, or practising virtue and charity, of overseeing and running a household and, in all, of taking up all the duties and responsibilities of a Christian woman'. (They also taught doctrine in Sunday schools to girls of 'all ages and classes'.)

Further, because the Ursulines, in Laurence Lux's words, 'the feminine teaching congregation *par excellence*, growing within the century to an estimated three hundred and twenty communities across the country', took what their documents call 'their principal aim' to be the instruction of girls, they adapted their monastic regime to suit the demands of professional work as teachers: the requirement of the full attendance at all eight daily chantings of the office was relaxed in favour of private recitation and, in a Jesuit-like recognition of the need for effective professional workers to conserve good health, rigorous fasts and other penitential self-punishments were waived. As Lux says:

> The raptures, ecstasies and visions occasioned by extended fasts were the privilege of the contemplative orders, but ran contrary to the aim of educating the young. The traditional religious coarse habit and bare feet were also deemed inappropriate to the classroom; a sister's dress should conform to what was expected from virtuous women, and go no further in asceticism.

Inexorably, and above all as teachers, French Ursulines were taking on the characteristics of a feminine profession, one for which prior training was provided.[74]

Since so much attention is usually given to the formation of Catholic boys, at least as far as the seminaries and the production of priests are concerned, it is worth following Lux's research a little further to unfold the professionalisation of the Ursulines as a teaching congregation revealed in the carefully designed and systematic routines of their pedagogy for girls. The meticulously regimented timetable was unvaried from day to day, starting with an hour's reading, followed by writing, followed by Mass; during the lunch break (the amounts of the residential pupils' *pensions* determined the quality of their lunches), the reading of pious books copied the practice of the regular orders, but the Ursuline establishment was a school, so the readings were followed by interrogations of their contents. There was recreation, followed by further reading and writing lessons and then, climaxing the day, instruction by the head teacher in key prayers and devotions, taught in Latin and French. The *Abrégé du devoir d'une bonne mère de famille et d'une fille à l'endroit de ses parents* taught the duties of girls in their homes and of the Catholic mothers of the future. Rigid control was exercised over the content of reading and the girls, as Laurence Lux writes, were 'instructed not to dance and sing worldly songs, to avoid the company of boys and generally to shrink from all occasions of sin'. The whole programme was intensely devoted to the inculcation of habits of conformity, modesty, tidiness, order, method, industry, practicality and simplicity – an educational system dedicated to the formation of an approved type of French Catholic womanhood.[75]

Aristocratic in composition and contemplative in purpose, the English Augustinian Canonesses Regular of the Lateran, set up in Leuven in 1609, represent part of the regrouping of English female regular life on the Continent in the sixteenth and seventeenth centuries. Their record of a postulant in 1616 recounts how 'the English Jesuitesses and Mrs Mary Ward would very gladly have got her into their company, but she liked not the manner of their life' – for, indeed, the profound seclusion and prayerfulness of Leuven's Augustinians seem light years away from what emerged as the heroic activism of Mary Ward. and her 'Jesuitesses'.[76]

'Mrs' (i.e. 'Mistress') Mary Ward came from a determinedly Catholic 'recusant' gentry family in Yorkshire and grew up within a deeply pious household and amidst an atmosphere of the expectation of suffering, and indeed of martyrdom, for persistent Catholics in a country whose harsh anti-recusant penal laws reflected the situation of a nation the survival of whose government and, indeed, whose very identity were threatened by Catholic Spain under Philip II.[77]

From the time of her sense of a religious vocation at the age of fifteen, Mary Ward was strongly drawn to the monastic life, in the Spanish Netherlands she joined (though subsequently left) the contemplative Poor Clares and was strongly drawn to the Carmelites of the foundation of Teresa of Ávila: 'I practised much prayer, some few fasts, and some austerities....I delighted in reading spiritual books, particularly those which treated of the monastic life'. Her initial scheme of a religious foundation, the *Schola Beatae Mariae* (School of Blessed Mary) of

1612, though it envisaged active work 'to render to the neighbour the services of Christian charity', aimed at perfect enclosed female monasticism: a 'cloister so strictly observed that no access is to be allowed to any extern [outsider] whatsoever'. The monastic life of prayer was to be punctiliously observed:

> All the sisters will rise daily at four in winter and summer, and spend an entire hour of the morning in mental prayer and meditation. All at a fixed hour shall be present at the Sacrifice of the Mass. They shall daily recite piously and devoutly the greater canonical hours or the office of the Blessed Virgin. Twice daily all shall examine their conscience.[78]

Cherishing particularly the spirituality of Ignatius Loyola in the *Spiritual Exercises*, Ward became impelled to emulate the Jesuit's active teaching mission in the world at large, their 'labour *throughout the world* [my emphasis] for the education of youth'. In a decisive severance from the *Schola's* original embedding in monastic tradition, the 1616 Second Plan of the Institute declared: 'In order to attain our end, it is…necessary…to begin and exercise its duties without enclosure…no one is by the Institute obliged to observe strict enclosure, or to wear a determined religious habit, or to perform external penances and austerities'. The clause attempting to free the Institute from episcopal control by putting it directly under papal authority did not endear Ward's congregation to ecclesiastical officialdom, and though for the time being she and her project seemed safe, opposition from the English clergy and, indeed, or especially, the Jesuits, mounted. She enjoyed initial papal encouragement and sponsorship from Catholic rulers in, for example, Bavaria and the Spanish Netherlands, but though in the second half of the 1620s she continued to found outlets in Bavaria, Austria and Hungary, her prestigious schools in Rome were suppressed in 1625, and in 1628 papal nuncios in Catholic countries were ordered to close her branches. Early papal friendship turned to bitter hostility in the harsh language of Urban VIII's Bull of suppression *Pastoralis Romani Pontificis* of 1631, followed by the actual imprisonment, over two months, of the foundress as a 'heretic, schismatic and rebel to Holy Church'. She strove vigorously to clear her name, returned to England in 1637 and died in Yorkshire in 1645. In her later years she conveys to us an impression not of a broken woman but of a project destroyed by little more than unreasoning ecclesiastical anti-feminism and prejudice: typical of charges against her and her colleagues was that: 'They are idle and talkative. They boast of their freedom from enclosure. They do not conform to feminine modesty.'.[79]

Mary Ward's uncloistered female teaching apostolate was in fact eventually vindicated with papal approval in a bull of 1749.

Indeed, even within the repressively anti-feminine atmosphere of early seventeenth-century Catholicism, schemes such as Anne de Xainctonge's (1567–1621) construction of a non-enclosed female teaching institute was approved in 1623. The ventures in devising a professional teaching role for women religious encountered, as we have seen, waves of suspicion and gender prejudice, but they joined the array of new, activist organisations of the Catholic Church in early modern Europe.

4 The papacy and the episcopate of the Catholic Reformation

In Chapter 1 we considered the reforming work of popes up to the time of Trent and in Chapter 2 we looked at the involvement of the papacy with the Council between 1545 and 1563. We shall now examine the part played by popes in the implementation of the Tridentine measures in the second half of the sixteenth century and then turn to review the work of bishops in renewing the religious life of their dioceses, culminating in the activity of Carlo Borromeo at Milan.

Although the papacy continued to direct Catholic renewal well into the seventeenth century and beyond, especially with such popes as Urban VIII and Benedict XIV (1740–58), we shall see that the period from the closure of Trent to the end of the sixteenth century was critical to the rebuilding of the institution's power and prestige in early modern Europe. Pius IV, who had steered the council to a successful conclusion, adopted its measures in the bull *Benedictus Dei* of January 1564. However, as Ranke found, after the dispersal of the Council, this pope's personal commitment to reform lapsed. While he made himself popular with the Romans by executing the corrupt Carafa nephews of Paul IV, Pius IV himself dispensed court patronage in the fashion of the popes of the high Renaissance, had three children and appointed to the College of Cardinals a boy and a young man, both from Italian princely families, both well below the canonical age for appointment – clear departures from the Council's recent directives. With his death in December 1565, the advocates of renewal looked for a restoration of its momentum. When fifty cardinals gathered for the electoral conclave following Pius's death, the Cardinal of Alessandria, Michele Ghislieri (1504–72), was the obvious standard-bearer of reform in the Carafa tradition. Ghislieri was born at Bosco, near Tortona in northern Italy, 'of a poor though noble family' which raised him for the Church. He became a Dominican in 1519, studied theology in Bologna, was ordained in Genoa and taught theology in Pavia for sixteen years. In 1543 Ghislieri made a powerful impact as a reformer at his order's general chapter in Parma and was subsequently prior of various Dominican convents. His association with the Inquisition, which began when it sent him to reconcile disputes in Switzerland, was strengthened when, on the nomination of Cardinal Gian Pietro Carafa, Julius III made him commissary general of the Congregation of the Holy Office. That association with Carafa was consolidated when, following his election as Paul IV, Carafa made him a bishop in 1556 and a cardinal in 1557. Ghislieri's credentials as a Carafa protégé became even more clearly apparent when Paul made him 'perpetual supreme inquisitor', a major advance towards the papacy.[1]

During Pius IV's pontificate, Ghislieri's was the voice of reform. On Pius's death, the late pope's protégés, including Pius's nephew Carlo Borromeo, feared that, since Ghislieri had been a Carafa dependent, if elected he would stage the kind of purge against Pius's family and party that Pius at the beginning of his pontificate had directed against the Carafas. Borromeo was torn. Following a religious conversion after his brother's death, he was an ardent proponent of reform and his support ought to have gone to Ghislieri on those grounds, but he was also head of the family interest of the late pope and had to protect it against any reprisals that might be mounted by the Carafa dependent, Ghislieri. However, Borromeo seems to have discounted all considerations except those of Church renewal in settling on Ghislieri:

> I was determined to consider nothing so much as religion and purity of faith. I was well acquainted with the piety, irreproachable life and devout spirit of the cardinal of Alessandria, afterwards Pius V; I thought none could more fitly administer the Christian commonwealth, and used my best efforts in his favour.

Indeed, having switched his powerful influence in favour of Ghislieri in a protracted conclave, Borromeo gave himself credit for Pius's election: '[I] used my best efforts in his favour'. The modern edition of Butler's *Lives of the Saints* comments that Ghislieri 'was chosen pope, largely through the efforts of St Charles Borromeo, who saw in him the reformer of whom the Church stood in need'. Kelly adds 'the rigorist party led by…Borromeo…achieved the…election of Michele Ghislieri'.[2]

In that analysis Ghislieri's election was secured by a party, under Borromeo's leadership, a reformist coalition, rather than a family faction, a grouping that Ranke termed 'the partizans of a more rigid system in the Church'. This party, which had secured a major election victory, was made up of the spiritual heirs of Paul IV, but it was far from being a Carafa clique, and Ghislieri, in rejecting the papal name of his patron Carafa and choosing that of his predecessor Pius, distanced himself somewhat from the Carafa inheritance. His reform party was powerful both within and beyond the conclave and the Curia, and Philip II, who wrote to Borromeo to thank him for promoting the election, can be said to have been an associate of it: the Spanish ambassador warmly welcomed this result. The new pope Pius resembled his late mentor Paul in many ways, – he was of an authoritarian and violent temperament, associated with repression and the Inquisition, and anti-Jewish. However, the Ghislieri pope was much more than simply a replica of Paul IV and in important ways challenged his old patron's policies. Putting the interests of the beleaguered Church above those of Italy or the papacy as an Italian state, he rejected the policies of Paul which had led to war between the Holy See and Spain and was to choose to work with, rather than against, the grain of Spanish power in Europe. In another way Pius V repudiated the legacy of Paul IV and took up that of Pius IV, a pope of the Council where Paul had kept Trent in suspension. Pius adopted the programme of the Council, completed its postponed work on the Missal, the Breviary and the Catechism and promulgated canon law along Tridentine lines. His assumption of the name Pius, as well as a gesture of conciliation with Borromeo and the group of the late pope, may be read as a signal that he was determined to assume responsibility for the implementation of the Council's work where Pius had left off when he brought it to its conclusion.[3]

Despite the possibility of a degree of wariness between Ghislieri and Borromeo over the legacy of mistrust between the factions of Paul IV and of Pius IV, Pius V and Carlo Borromeo were to construct a common front of reform in the areas of a shared commitment to personal sanctity expressed in austerity and charity; pursuit of urban religious and social renewal in Italy's leading cities of the Catholic Reformation, Rome and Milan; and dedication to the programme of Trent, in the area of diocesan renewal but also in the fields of liturgy.

In contrast with Pius IV's laxity, Pius brought with him to the papacy, as Eugenius IV had in the previous century, the moral style acquired in a strict religious order. Pius made at least two meditations a day on his knees before the Blessed Sacrament, fasted during the whole of Advent as well as Lent, attended to the sick in the hospitals of Rome, washed the feet of the poor, and took lepers in his arms. No more than in the case of Borromeo was this sanctity intended to be private, since a hidden icon is of little use. Pius's holiness was public, exemplary and spectacular and 'The people [of Rome] were led to enthusiasm at the sight of this holy pontiff walking in procession, his head and feet bare...they thought there had never been so pious a pope' – a kind of Filippo Neri within the papal palace. The dramatic monastic conduct of the pope flowed out into the strict regulation of his household. It is true that he appointed a nephew a cardinal, but he gave him no power. He restored the papacy's leadership of the devotional practice of the Church, approving the devotion of the Little Office of Our Lady and resuming the papacy's centrality in the Church's eucharistic worship by giving strong sanction to the rite of *Quarant' Ore*. Pius's regime of sanctity, resembling Borromeo in his personal asceticism and the strict discipline of his entourage, extended its influence into Rome, for whose renewed conversion into a holy city Pius assumed responsibility, as Borromeo did in the case of Milan. Pius expelled prostitutes, banned bullfights and tried to restrict the taverns to use by visitors to the city. However, this potentially unpopular puritanism was matched by social welfare provisions. From the inauguration of his pontificate, when the traditional casual scattering of money broadcast was replaced by planned distribution of alms to the really needy, Pius took in hand the communal needs of Rome, paid during famines for grain imports from France and Sicily to be sold cheaply or given away, encouraged the setting up of interest-free loan banks, *monti di pietà*, and campaigned mercilessly against brigands and hired killers in the city and the Papal States. Pius thus played a vital part in the continuing programme of restoring Rome as the Church's ideal city.[4]

An area of policy in which Borromeo (who took up the archdiocese of Milan in the year of Pius's accession) and Pius were agreed was that of shared determination to enforce the decrees and reforms of Trent. In this resolution Pius issued all Catholic bishops with the approved edition of the decrees of the Council: the Jesuit Canisius distributed this in Germany and within Pius's pontificate the decrees were available in the Spanish and Portuguese colonies in Africa and America. Pius took up the Council's momentum, including insistence on episcopal residence and the regulation of religious orders. He banned monks from nunneries and nuns from monasteries, authorised Borromeo to reform the corrupt Milanese lay order of Humiliati and eventually dissolved this unreformable group. However, Pius V's most influential and enduring applications of Tridentine requirements came in the areas of the Missal, the Breviary and the Catechism, topics which we shall next consider under the heading of the work of his pontificate.[5]

In its consideration of Scripture in 1546–7, the Council had touched on the question of the Missal. Then, in the session in 1562, in discussions of the Mass as a sacrifice, the topic of the Missal was confronted directly. A commission was appointed to list the abuses in the celebration of the Mass highlighted in earlier synods and in the Council of Trent itself, including profusion of saints' cults in the text of the Mass, the inclusion of legendary material, the use of private variants in the rite, the proliferation and abuse of votive celebrations for special intercessions and the luxuriant growth in the linking prayers known as sequences. Distortions had grown more rather than less abundant in the period of the Reformation in confessional borderlands such as Austria where some priests had become accustomed to omit the central consecration in the Mass, the canon. The commission of the Council investigated such matters as the intrusion of spurious pious phrases, and abuses including the simultaneous celebration of private masses during a church's High Mass, as also Masses said without sufficient congregations. However, Trent did not seek absolute uniformity in the rite of the Mass, though it did aim at greater standardisation of ceremonial. The Council's *Decretum de observandis et evitandis in celebratione missae* (*The decree on what to do and what to avoid in the celebration of Mass*) in its fourth and final version on 17 September 1562 focused on the abuses of simony, superstition and the unseemly conduct of the celebration. Masses, it ruled, were to be celebrated in consecrated buildings and the music must be fitting. As for the Missal itself, along with the Breviary, Catechism and Index, work pending should be 'given over to the most holy Roman pontiff...[and] by his judgement and authority be completed and made public'. Pius IV, probably in 1564, set up a commission to implement these requirements and this body was expanded in size by Pius V. Its proceedings are not recorded but its fruit was the revised Roman Missal issued by Pius V in the bull *Quo primum tempore* of July 1570.[6]

This 'Pian' Missal played a large part in the processes of relative standardisation and Romanisation that characterised the Catholic Reformation and which were strongly marked in Pius V, as evident in his revocations of permission for priests of the Latin Church to celebrate Mass in Greek and for Greeks to celebrate their rite in Latin. Indeed, a trend towards amalgamation of local rites into wider standards had already been evident in Scandinavia, the Rhineland, Spain, Portugal, France and Italy. The Pian Missal extended the use of the rite (which was already extensively utilised in the Church at large) of the churches in the city of Rome and specifically 'the use of the Roman curia' to all Catholic churches, cathedrals and monastic houses. Key sections were taken over substantially from the Roman *Ordo Missae* (*Order of Mass*) (1502) drawn up by the papal master of ceremonies, Johannes Burchard. The retention of national and regional varia-tions (and the form used in Pius's own Dominican Order) had to be warranted by an antiquity of at least 200 years, part of a quest for a pristine pure 'form' of the Mass. In the period when revision of the Missal was still under consideration in the Council, Rome sent to Trent a manuscript copy of the 'Sacramentary' of Pope Gregory the Great, for the Missal was to be amended 'according to the custom and rite of the holy fathers' and the Gregorian text had the high prestige of being patristic, ancient and Roman. The Roman form of the liturgy was valued and imposed as a pure one because it was of venerable age, thought to be close to the spirit of the earlier Church and therefore free of abuse and supersti-tion. The large number of saints' days added to the liturgy in the course of the middle ages was reduced to the 150 observances celebrated in Rome by the eleventh century. Yet we should not exaggerate the degree of pruning in the Pian Missal. In particular, the votive Masses for special occasions that had integrated the Mass with social and environmental needs in medieval Europe were respected, in the forms, for example, of Masses for peace, for the avoidance of mortal sickness and of illness in livestock. However, there undoubtedly was a reductive process at work in the composition of Pius V's Missal and much of it had to do with the restoration of a Christocentric theology to the Mass.[7]

Strong Marian intrusions dating from the eleventh century had featured, for example, in the *Gloria*, the hymn of praise of the Trinity, in the medieval English Sarum rite of the Mass, one of those swept away in favour of the Pian form. Some of these phrases might have been viewed as raising Mary too close in status to the Trinity: 'You [Christ] take away the sins of the world. To the glory of Mary....You alone are the holy one, sanctifying Mary. You alone are the most high, crowning Mary'.

If, as Carroll writes, 'one of the most important doctrinal emphases at Trent was a renewed insistence upon the centrality of Christ as compared to the saints and Mary', and if this meant 'a renewed emphasis...upon standard Christocentric ceremonies like the Mass', then, inevitably, the reaffirmation of the Mass as the great Christocentric rite resulted not only in the elimination of much Marian devotion but also of a rich profusion of saints' cults such as were expressed in the English rite in sequences in honour of St Edmund, king and martyr and St Thomas of Canterbury.[8]

It might be argued that, whatever their doctrinal validity, especially in defending Catholicism from Protestant allegations of Catholic Mariolatry and hagiolatry, such excisions in the Missal of Pius V amounted to a loss of liturgical richness and, particularly, of regional and local flavour in the celebration of

Mass. Surely, the cult of national and royal saints, diminished in the new Missal, had added patriotic tones to piety in an age of rising national awareness in late medieval Europe. All in all, in the drive to eliminate 'modern [i.e. medieval] variants' of the Mass, some perfectly legitimate evolutions may have been jettisoned in favour of an inflexible antiquarianism. Indeed, Archdale King argues that the Pian Missal operated from a 'defective historical sense' in the rigid determination it expressed to return at all costs to the earlier, if not the earliest, roots of the Church, failing to take account of arguably valid devotional ornamentations that time had added to the rite.[9]

In fact, though, one criticism of Pius V's Missal might be that it did not go back far enough in its pursuit of the ideals of antiquity, for example to uncover the ancient congregational principles of the Mass and to proceed backwards, as Jungmann says, 'farther and deeper, say in the direction of a restoration of a stronger communion between priest and people'. It was in one of the regional rites allowed to survive on the grounds of their antiquity, the Milanese 'Ambrosian' (the others were the Spanish Mozarabic and those of Trier, Cologne, Liège, Braga and Lyons), that a vital ancient element of a congregational participation, the offertory procession of the laity, bearing the materials for the consecration, endured. However, the overall trend of the Missal of Pius V was in the direction of a unilateral sacerdotal celebration.[10]

Milan clung on to its fragment of a congregational liturgy, but in most places elsewhere, certainly in Italy, the Pian Roman standard prevailed before 1600 and a Venetian variant of the Mass was condemned by the Inquisition in 1596. Philip II encouraged the use of the Pian rite in Spain, though in France the continuing strength of Gallicanism fostered the survival or revival or some regional rites. The encouragement Rome gave to standardisation proceeded with the establishment by Sixus V in 1588 of the Congregation of Rites, to which says King, 'any contemplated change, whether in rite or ceremonial' had to be submitted. Bulls issued by Clement VIII (1604) and Urban VIII (1634) made no substantial change to the Pian Missal. This pope's most central and durable achievement was to leave to the Church his authorised form of its central prayer, whose use was to prevail throughout most of the Catholic world for four centuries. We need only to add that Pius's appointment of a composer of relatively severe liturgical music, Giovanni Pierluigi da Palestrina, as his *maestro di capella* (master of the papal chapel music) made possible the maintenance of the principles of purified and dignified liturgical music enunciated at Trent.[11]

Alongside his concern with the Missal, Pius V authorised the revision of the Breviary, the book containing the 'Office' for the clergy and religious orders, made up of daily prayers, both fixed and variable, and readings. The immediate purpose of this revision, after some decades, since the invention of printing, in which breviaries had been coming off the presses, was that of eliminating errors that had crept into texts in the course of printing. The Pian Breviary also had the same purpose as that of the revised Missal, that of pruning a profusion of saints' days, of deleting bogus legends, but also of restoring Scripture to a prominent position in the variable readings appointed for the Office. The Pian

Breviary was taken up by the Antwerp typographer royal Christophe Plantin (1514–89) who in 1567–8 paid the papal printer Paolo Manuzio (1512–74) for the right to print and distribute the new Breviaries in the Spanish Netherlands and eventually throughout Philip II's domains, producing volumes of superb artistic quality. Pius V's Breviary emphasised Marian piety, with an elaborate observance on 8 December of the feast of the Immaculate Conception. The pope's devotion to Mary was also made evident in his renewal of the Little Office in her honour and in his inclusion in that Office, after the 1571 Christian victory of Lepanto against the Turks, in which the Holy See's fleet had taken part, of the invocation of Mary: 'Help of Christians, pray for us'.[12]

The third commission bequeathed by the Council to the papacy, in Chapter 1 of the twenty-fifth session of December 1563 – a task 'to be given over to the most holy Roman pontiff, that it may by his judgement and authority be completed and made public' – and which Pius V carried out, was the revision of the Catholic Church's teaching manual, the Catechism. This kind of compilation might take the form either of a book aimed directly at the laity, as was Canisius's *Large Catechism* of 1556, or a text for priests to use to explain points of doctrine. Initially, and in some of its earliest proceedings, in April 1546, when a draft decree proposed a Latin and vernacular catechism for children and such adults 'who are in need of milk rather than solid food', Trent envisaged a direct approach to lay people. Subsequently, it was with the doctrine of the Sacraments in mind that the Council, in its decree of session 24, Chapter VII of November 1563, switched its emphasis to a catechetical guide for priests' use:

> That the faithful may approach the sacraments with greater reverence and devotion of mind, the holy council commands all bishops that...they shall...in a manner adapted to the mental ability of those who receive them, explain their efficacy and use, but also they shall see to it that the same is done piously and prudently by every parish priest...in accordance with the form which will be prescribed for each of the sacraments by the holy council in a catechism, which the bishops shall have faithfully translated into the language of the people, by all parish priests.

This stress on catechesis of the Sacraments was fully taken up in the Catechism which eventually emerged under Pius's direction, in which the section on the Sacraments is far and away the longest in the vast compilation, 638 pages in an eighteenth-century edition – the other parts being on the Apostles Creed, the Ten Commandments and the Lord's Prayer.[13]

Of the several titles used for the product that finally appeared under Pius V – the Catechism of the Council, the Catechism for Parish Priests, the Roman Catechism, and the Catechism of Pius V – the first label can certainly be used, for it was the Council that conceived of a 'uniform and comprehensive manual', in place of many national and personal versions, avoiding particular schools of thought or doctrinal emphasis. One detectable influence, though, was that of the

Dominicans who provided seven of the twenty-three-member commission under the direction of a Dominican pope who himself published an edition of the writings of the Dominican theologian Aquinas, whose strong influence is apparent in the large number of references to his writings in the marginalia of the Pian Catechism. The main influence on the commission, however, was its brief to keep 'especially in mind the decrees of the Council of Trent'. The Catechism of Pius V regularly cited the Council as its authority. For example, under the heading of 'Preparation of the Soul', the catechism explains 'The Council of Trent has defined [the matter]', while under 'Why Adultery is Expressly Mentioned', the Catechism recommends 'The pastor...should add the decrees of the Council of Trent'; a particular Sacrament was 'to be numbered among the sacraments of the Church, the council of Trent has established'. The fidelity of the Pian Catechism to the Council is particularly marked in the language of the former, sometimes almost word for word with the Council. In the doctrine of the Mass, for example, the Council laid down:

> And inasmuch as in this divine sacrifice which is celebrated in the mass is contained and immolated in an unbloody manner the same Christ who once offered Himself in a bloody manner on the altar of the cross, the holy council teaches that this is truly propitiatory....For the victim is one and the same.

The Catechism's wording was:

> that the sacrifice of the mass is and ought to be considered one and the same sacrifice as that on the cross, for the victim is one and the same, namely, Christ our Lord, who offered Himself, once only, a bloody sacrifice on the altar of the cross....[T]he mass is...truly a propitiatory Sacrifice.[14]

In its deference to the Council, the Catechism of Pius V was that of Trent: 'The Catechism of the Council'. Nevertheless, we may say that the Pian Catechism was more concerned with the Council than the Council was with the catechism, and Trent's direct interest in the subject was largely lost between 1546 and 1563. Even the Council's initial concept of the catechism, that of an elementary primer for the laity, was set aside, and what emerged under Pius V's hand was a textbook for parish priests to use – what a version published in Paris in 1688 called *Catechismus ad Parochos* – 'The Catechism for Parish Priests'. It was, though, aimed not at *any* parish priest but at the kind of pastor that Trent planned to produce in setting up seminaries – learned enough to follow the Catechism's plentiful references to Scripture, the Fathers, medieval theologians and previous councils, and also to read the Ciceronian Latin in which Borromeo's recruitment of leading classicists for the composition of the work resulted. The Catechism was also a magnificent production in the first Roman folio edition from Manuzio's press in October 1566. A key feature of its 359 pages of text was its wide margins, which were probably designed for annotation by priests for purposes of teaching and preaching. It also comprised a 'copious' index designed for the convenient use of the volume by a busy parish priest. The Catechism was composed specifically for parochial use and followed closely the liturgy of the Mass, to whose readings the contents were adroitly keyed in. The Pian Catechism, then, is a teaching pack for priests to adapt to 'the mental ability of those who receive' the Church's teaching. Addressed to 'the priestly reader' and 'to all pastors of the Catholic Church', it is termed in the 1688 Paris edition, 'Your Catechism, most vigilant shepherds': it is 'The Catechism for Parish Priests'.[15]

It is also both the 'Roman Catechism' and the 'Catechism of Pius V'. The Venetian typographer Paolo Manuzio was brought from his native city to Rome for the production, whose provenance was '*Romae in aedibus populi Romani*' – 'Rome, at the city's public buildings'. Finally, this was, above all, the 'Catechism of Pius V': '*Jussu S. Pii V. Pontifici Maximi editus*' – 'ordered to be published by Pope St Pius V'. Pius both took over and saw through this project, and ensured the orthodoxy of its revision as one of the first tasks of his pontificate by appointing a new editorial commission, and guiding its work of editing into parts and chapters. His personal enthusiasm for the project is unmistakable in his writing about it: 'The Catechism has been brought to a conclusion, and with the help of God will imminently see the light'. He was equally enthusiastic to see it translated into German, Italian, French and Polish. Pius even gave his own authority with a *motu proprio*, a personal brief, to the protection of Manuzio's copyright, with the penalty of excommunication and a fine of 500 gold ducats for unpaid infringement. The Catechism, the encyclopedia of Catholic doctrine for centuries to come, forms the third pillar of Pius's 'editorial' accomplishment.[16]

His achievement in other fields, above all those of diplomacy and international politics, in which he had little experience and little direct knowledge of anything beyond Italy, was less assured, and his excommunication of Queen Elizabeth in the bull *Regnans in Excelsis* of 1570 was ill-timed and a disaster for English Catholics. However, this defining pope of the Catholic Reformation, with his evident sanctity and moral severity, brought the 'restoration of the papacy' to a new high point.

In the conclave following Pius V's death in 1572 there seems to have been an initial attempt to revert to earlier days of the placement of well-off members of Italian noble families in the holy see. A party evidently with that purpose in mind produced support for Cardinal Alessandro Farnese from Cardinals Sforza and Orsini, representatives in the Sacred College of the Milanese and Roman aristocracies respectively. Pastor described 'the powerful Cardinal Alessandro Farnese' as 'the most brilliant member of the Sacred College' but saw him as being checked in his ambitions by Philip II, who had already swung his support in favour of reform at the election of Pius V. However, a new instalment of Pius V's rigour, for example in the person of Borromeo's candidate in the mould of Pius V, the austere Theatine Cardinal Scipione Burali (1511–78), may have been an unwelcome prospect in some quarters. Ordinary Romans, in particular, an observer reported, feared the election of 'a friar or a Theatine', the latter term now being used as a synonym for puritan killjoys. Having privately prevailed on Farnese to stand down, 'in the presence of so many aged and deserving cardinals' and on the curious grounds of preserving 'peace in Italy', Philip's special representative, Antoine Perrenot, Cardinal de Granvelle (1517–86), who was deputed to 'check Farnese in his ambitions', gave his support, as did Farnese himself, to Cardinal Ugo Buoncompagni as a peacemaker, a compromise candidate, and perhaps thought likely to offer a pause after Pius's alleged attempt to turn Rome into a monastery. Neither a saint nor a Spartan, Buoncompagni, 'worldly-minded and fond of display', had an illegitimate son from his younger days and a surname (it means 'good companion') that gave to the Romans, always superstitious about the coincidences of papal nomenclature, messages of good fellowship. However, he was far from being opposed to the resumption of the reform programme and also commended himself to the Spanish interest by some features of his earlier career.[17]

The career in question was that of a safe curial civil servant, diplomat and Roman insider. Ugo Buoncompagni (or Boncompagni), elected to the papacy in 1572 and taking the title of Gregory XIII, was born in 1502 in Bologna where he studied and then taught jurisprudence (to Pole, Hosius and Borromeo, amongst others) before being called to Rome as a jurist under Paul III, serving at Trent in the same capacity. His diplomatic distinctions included a mission to Philip II in the tense period for Hispano–Papal relations under Paul IV and a further visit to Spain to handle the ultra-delicate case of Spain's primate, Archbishop Bartolomé de Carranza (1503–76), imprisoned by the Spanish Inquisition. Buoncompagni's assured progress – he was Pius IV's special representative at Trent and was appointed to the Sacred College in 1565 – made him a strong candidate for the papacy in one conclave or another, and Pius V, on his election, took sardonic pleasure, under a guise of modesty, in having obstructed Buoncompagni's career track: 'My Lord Cardinal, we have occupied your place'.[18]

Perhaps little in Buoncompagni's pre-papal career suggested de Montor's model of the 'noblest religious sentiments'. However, he had been closely identified with the Council and later developed what Janelle called the 'closest personal relations with Borromeo, who brought about in him an actual conversion to the reforming spirit', while Pastor believed that Borromeo had a decisive impact 'upon both the interior and exterior life of Boncompagni', weaning him away from 'the profane influence of the dying Renaissance'. Gregory was a proven administrator and tireless worker and the task that he took up, aided by Borromeo, Burali and Borromeo's aide, Cardinal Tolomeo Galli, the papal secretary of state, was that of the executive implementation of reform, in the spirit of Pius V, resuming the moral, spiritual and architectural restoration of Rome as the foremost model diocese of the Church and as Catholicism's primary pilgrimage centre on a new scale.[19]

An exceptional opportunity to reaffirm Rome's global role fell within Gregory's pontificate with the scheduled Jubilee of 1575, an occasion introduced into the papal calendar in 1300 and from 1450 taking place every twenty-five years. To the preparation for this event of massively intensified pilgrimage with a purpose of acquiring indulgences and pardon for sin, Gregory devoted his formidable administrative skill, preparing for the event from 1573 onwards and neglecting nothing, least of all provisions, prices and rents, as well as precautions to ensure that moral conditions in the city would be edifying. A massive advance promotion exercise was designed to ensure that the Jubilee would be particularly well canvassed within Italy, whence the heaviest waves of pilgrims would be expected to come. The guide-book trade responded enthusiastically, emphasising the special holiness of *Roma Sancta* as a city of churches: indeed the engraver Antoine Lafréry's (or Lafreri, *c.* 1512–77) *Le Sette Chiese di Roma* (*The Seven Churches of Rome*) depicted it as in effect consisting only of churches, with St Peter's (as yet undomed) in the foreground of the city and the Apostle, holding the keys, teaching in front of it. Rome's power to deliver indulgences was celebrated in another work, *Le Sette Chiese Principali di Roma (The Seven Principal Churches of Rome)* and the city's magic as a tourist magnet as well as a heavenly city was advertised in *Le Cose Meravigliose della Alma Città di Roma* (*The Wonderful Things in the Mother City of Rome*). Such books published in Italy had the effect of consolidating Rome's spiritual leadership in the peninsula, but a few years after the Jubilee, targeting the more reserved Anglo-Saxon Catholic reading public, *Roma Sancta* (*Holy Rome*) by the English priest Gregory Martin (d. 1582) prepared his 'cold countrie men' for some embarrassment at the spectacle of Rome's florid piety.[20]

Pilgrims came from all social strata, the most distinguished churchman being Borromeo, whose iconic presence Gregory required in Rome, temporarily transposing to the papal city the Milan archbishop's already evident sanctity: Ambrose deferred to Peter, Milan to Rome, when, before leaving his northern base for the pope's capital on the feast of the Immaculate Conception in 1574, Borromeo upheld the reverence of the tomb of the Apostle Peter. If the 354,400 eucharistic hosts distributed in St Peter's during the Jubilee are anything to go by, as many as 400,000 pilgrims were in Rome that year. Gregory's biographer referred to substantial numbers from Germany and Poland, many from France, even more from Spain and some from Greece, Armenia and the Far East, the last-named cohort revealing the increasing Catholicisation of parts of Asia since Xavier's mission. There were present numbers of professional communicators – preachers – including 600 Augustinians, 300 Capuchins and 800 Franciscan Observants, all having papal audiences. Alongside these, many lay pilgrims were members of confraternities which merged their membership with the Roman ones for the duration of the Jubilee. These pious visitors would certainly be expected, by their fellow confraternity members who had stayed at home, to relate their experiences of the Roman Jubilee. They were likely to bring back souvenirs to illustrate their discourses, especially books, and medallions such as the one showing Pope Gregory inaugurating the Jubilee by opening the Porta Santa in St Peter's, rays sent from God powering his hammer, with the superscription *DOMUS DEI ET PORTA CAELI* (The House of God and the Gate of Heaven). Taking into account the doubtless better-structured reminiscences of preachers, along with confraternity narrations and casual conversations with friends, relatives and neighbours, verbal reportage of the Gregorian Jubilee, on the conservative basis of one speaker addressing an average of twenty auditors, cannot have reached fewer than 8–10 millions, an amazing media distribution of impressions in the early modern Catholic world – even allowing for the fact that disproportionate numbers of pilgrim witnesses came from Italy, where whole villages and towns emptied to go on pilgrimage.[21]

On their return, the pilgrims might have recounted such wonders as the crowded city's escape from plague during the Jubilee year. The city's street-theatre was particularly worthy of recall, producing rich propaganda messages from sacred and ecclesiastical history: pilgrims could witness processions of children dressed as angels, as well as *tableaux vivants* representing Scriptural scenes and characters – St Michael in armour, Adam and Eve, Abraham, Isaac and the Sacrifice (emblem of Calvary and the Mass), and Noah's Ark (symbol of the Church). The themes of the continuity and the triumph of the Church were well to the fore in the representations, the age of the Fathers being captured with figures got up as St Jerome, St Ambrose, St Augustine and St Gregory. Another Gregory, the pope of the hour, was represented atop an invisibly-propelled carriage, accompanied by the figure of prudence, and in a gesture of benediction. His great predecessor and namesake, the reformer Pope Gregory VII (to be canonised at the height of the Catholic Reformation in 1606), was shown in triumph over the impious state in the person of the German Emperor Henry IV (1050–1106), with whom that pope had been locked in conflict. Gregory XIII himself was highlighted, in the processional banner of one parish church, as one in a long chain of popes bearing his name, a tribute to the historical continuity of 'The Catholic Apostolic Roman Church, ruled for many centuries, enlightened and spread by the doctrines and wonderful virtue of twelve Popes who bore the name of Gregory, and now under the thirteenth of that name…happy and triumphant'. At that early stage of the Catholic recovery in Europe, when reverses rather than gains were still the order of the day in the British Isles and the Netherlands, it may have been premature to speak of the *triumph* of the Church – certainly less so than when, at the end of the seventeenth century, Pierre Legros the Younger celebrated the results of a century and a half of Catholic aggression against the Reformation in the sculpture in the Gesù, *The Victory of Faith over Heresy* (1695–9). However, victories of Catholicism achieved so far in the progress of the Catholic Reformation certainly included the consolidation of a Catholic Italy, positively through preaching by the Capuchins, Jesuits and others, more negatively through harsh and effective repression in the Index and by the Inquisition. The shoring up of Italy's Catholic faith was epitomised by the prominent position in a Roman procession of the town of Faenza, once Protestant-influenced (by Ochino), but now once more wholly Catholic. A sense of triumph in victories over Protestantism further afield and of expectation of future gains still to be won in the critical German theatre were conveyed by the leading positions given in the opening of the Jubilee on Christmas Eve 1574 to the pious Jesuit-educated Duke Ernst of Bavaria (1554–1612), future archbishop of Cologne: the Catholic recovery in the German lands would rely heavily on the efforts of his Wittelsbach house. The pope's conferment of the sword and cap, usually presented to kings and emperors, on Prince Karl Friedrich of Cleves, summed up the pope's hopes for a Catholic comeback and the conversion of Protestant princes, especially in the strategically vital Netherlands–Rhineland triangle.[22]

The 1575 Jubilee, whose themes were celebration of the past and confidence in the future, was a soaring success, better attended than any of its predecessors and 'characterised by extraordinary acts of devotion and charity'. In its impact it was, surely, considered worth all the many *scudi* that the normally thrifty pope lavished on it, for example in commissioning special teams of priests to hear pilgrims' Confessions. Focused on his city, the Jubilee also said much about Gregory's European and global horizons: *urbi et orbi*, the inseparable twinning of the city and the world. His policy towards the cardinals and the Sacred College certainly reflected the extra-Italian dimension of his thinking: in September 1574, amidst the preparations for the Jubilee, it was reported that non-Italian cardinals were to be brought to Rome to confer on further reform measures. Appointments to the College were revealing of Gregory's priorities, his care for Catholic recovery in Germany, for instance, expressed in his appointment in 1576 of Andreas of Habsburg, son of the Archduke Ferdinand of Austria (1578–1637), who was active in re-Catholicising his lands. Perhaps because he had been a diplomat, Gregory was more international in his approach than Pius V and put into effect Trent's call for a stronger non-Italian flavour in the College of Cardinals: out of nine appointments in 1578 seven were non-Italians. It seems they were designed to recognise and encourage achievements in areas of particular concern to Gregory, whether those were Catholic revival in France, work in implementing the decrees of the Council in Spain and France or simply notable conversions from Protestantism, as with the French nomination, Bourbon, and the Polish, Radziwiłł, both sons of Protestants: Poland and its Catholic restoration under King Stephen Báthory (reigned 1576–86) were of special interest to Gregory.[23]

If the Jubilee and his cardinalatial appointments reflected Gregory's international interests, his determination to make Rome the Catholic Church's main educational centre showed a design to consolidate the more ephemeral achievement of the events of 1575 in the shape of a permanent seminarian endowment. Gregory's educational patronage was centred on the Jesuits, in whose favour he resurrected the patronage Paul III had shown. The Jesuit educationalist Claudio Acquaviva (1543–1614) became general during his pontificate, in 1580. Encouraged by Canisius, Gregory in effect re-founded Loyola's Collegium Germanicum (1552) with an initial endowment of 10,000 *scudi*, a handsome library provision, and a generous annual maintenance grant. By 1574 the re-established College had already drawn in ninety-four students from the German dioceses, rapidly rising to 130. By 1584 the Germanicum was fused with an earlier Hungarian institute to form the Collegium Germanicum et Hungaricum, with recruitment from the German-, Czech- and Magyar-speaking lands. Switzerland was targeted from the Swiss College, Milan (1579). Gregory's educational interest in the northern countries in which Protestantism had made such impressive strides extended to England. He was the generous sponsor of the English Cardinal William Allen's (1532–94) seminary at Douai (1568) and in 1579 added to that patronage his establishment of the English College, Rome, under Jesuit auspices: he 'ceased not', Jesuit records recalled, 'to heap fresh favours upon it, and to protect and forward its interests by his patronage and authority'. The priests sent into the English mission during Gregory's pontificate from Douai and the English College, Rome, rose from eight in 1575 to 136 in 1583 and played an indispensable part in nourishing the faith of the English Catholic recusant community.[24]

Gregory's construction programme made, in comparison with the gigantic efforts of his successor Sixtus V, a solid rather than sensational contribution to the ongoing redesign of the papal city's building stock, with the aim of restating Rome's position as the 'head and mother' of Catholicism: Freiberg comments that in this area Gregory 'had far grander ideas than ever took shape during his pontificate'. Not surprisingly, a major concern of his architectural work, especially in continuing the schemes of Pius IV, was with equipping Rome to host the 1575 Jubilee, improving access to pilgrim churches, but also affirming the importance of the church of San Giovanni in Laterano as the pope's cathedral in his capacity of bishop of Rome. That basilica's penitential Scala Santa (the 'holy staircase', where pilgrims, on their knees, went over the route of Christ's attributed ascent to Pilate) was a focus of the Sacrament of Penance, itself a principal purpose of the Roman pilgrimage. Gregory also took up the duties expected of him as the chief orchestrator of the Catholic Church's ceremonial life, and especially of the papacy's leadership in the cult of the Blessed Sacrament. The chapel he built within the Lateran in honour of the Blessed Sacrament, a building which was depicted in cheap picture-postcard style prints for pilgrims and which was described as 'certainly one of the richest and most sumptuous [chapels] that can be seen in Rome', encapsulated 'Gregory's veneration for the central mystery of the faith [the Eucharist], a major feature of both his personal piety and public persona'. This surprising pope, who devised a new calendar to accommodate the Church's festal cycle, a political interventionist (for example, in Ireland) who blundered into rejoicing at the terrible massacre of Protestants in France in 1572 but who formally recognised Neri's Oratory in 1575, must have come as a shock to those who had expected a relaxed worldling to occupy the throne of Peter for a few years – for he had not, in Evennett's words, been 'considered in Rome to be one of the extreme reformers'. Yet if Buoncompagni was not an ardent reformer before he became pope, as Gregory XIII he became one. The vignette that perhaps captures most vividly Buoncompagni's own transformation, and with it that of Rome and of the Catholic Church's Italian governing class, is a report of 1576 on the society wedding of the pope's son Giacomo (euphemistically, 'Sr Giacomo Boncompagno of Bologna, closely connected with his holiness'). On that occasion the banqueting, gift-giving, power-dressing, coach-driving and jewel-wearing may have recalled to a very few older memories of the carefree days of Medicean Rome before 1527. On the wedding day, though, Pope Gregory 'went at the same time to the Seven Churches': the pontiff had become Rome's highest-placed penitent and pilgrim.[25]

Gregory XIII's assertion of Rome's world role was echoed by the arrival of Japanese emissaries in the city in the last months of his pontificate, in 1575. He died leaving, according to Pastor, a sizeable treasury surplus of 700,000 *scudi*, and it was entirely in keeping with his favour to the Society of Jesus that a Jesuit delivered his panegyric.[26]

In the conclave that followed, a renewed attempt was made to bring forward the perennial symbol of cardinalatial aristocratic power and wealth, the Cardinal Deacon Alessandro Farnese, 'inflamed and possessed', it was reported, 'by an incredible anxiety to become pope'. The individual who was both the complete opposite of Farnese and in the Mendicant mould of Pius V, the low-born Felice Peretti (1521–90), known as the Cardinal Montalto, achieved a surprising but convincing victory by playing his cards most skilfully in the conclave. On the one hand, he feigned indifference to election (it is said 'He who goes into the conclave a pope comes out a cardinal'):

> Montalto remained apart in his chamber, and did not go into the conclave, pretending to be quite worn out and past human aid. He went out very rarely...and [made] a semblance of being wholly indifferent to what was going forward.

Meanwhile, however, Peretti secured electoral promises from leading cardinals while he cultivated power-brokers in the Sacred College, including Farnese himself, though he did not allow Farnese to know the extent of his ambition and 'did not permit those who were most in need of warning to receive any intimation, nor did [God] suffer either Farnese or his adherents to be awakened'.[27]

The outcome of these stratagems, born, allegedly, of many years of determination to be pope, was a Peretti landslide in the conclave. The gossip that, when the result was announced, Peretti threw away his stage-prop crutches is, unfortunately, without foundation, though it might be interpreted as a further pointer to the accomplished deception with which 'Montalto' had played his cards in the conclave. In fact, unlikely stories had a way of clinging to Peretti and it was perhaps to offset the effect of his disadvantaged background – his father was a gardener 'tilling a little field that belonged to others' – that his life-story was given a miraculous, pseudo-scriptural or even Christlike patina, as with the legend that his father had heard a voice in a dream announcing , 'Rise Peretti, and go seek thy wife, for a son is about to be born to thee, to whom thou shalt give the name of Felix [*Felice* = happy, fortunate], since he is one day to be the greatest of mortals'.[28]

Perhaps because of his under-privileged background, Peretti, who took the title Sixtus in tribute to his predecessor and fellow-Franciscan, Sixtus IV (1471–84), made himself a pope of social justice. At his coronation he renewed

Pius V's suppression of the casual lottery of money-throwing that took place by tradition on those occasions and instead distributed properly organised relief to the poor and the hospitals. He turned down a request for a celebratory banquet for the cardinals on the grounds of 'a pressing scarcity which [exists] in our city today, and the people must have no reason to complain of our want of natural respect in their misery'. In the dearth of the bitter winter of 1585–6 he ordered price control on grain. Reversing harsh anti-Jewish measures put in place by Paul IV and Pius V, he forbade insults and injuries to Jews.[29]

The new pope was an amazing individual, even by the standards of a succession of larger-than-life pontiffs in the second half of the sixteenth century. Massively egoistic but socially insecure, he composed an autobiography full of reminiscences of career successes and of condescension showered on him by the great ('In…1551…three most illustrious cardinals entertained me in Rome.…At the [Franciscan] chapter-general…in 1556 I was elected promoter to masterships'). His egoism apart, his most salient characteristic was his *terribilità*, his frightening air of danger and of a ferocity that was channelled into unrelenting effort but which could explode into extreme measures against criminals. In counterpoint to his terrifying self, he retained the deeply felt piety and simple lifestyle of a model friar, for he had been bred by the Franciscans from the age of nine and had a special devotion to St Francis. To this private piety he added, as pope, punctilious attention to public liturgical ceremonial, especially in his presiding over the pontifical rites of the Blessed Sacrament, when, on Corpus Christi, it was 'his custom to process, bare-headed and on foot, carrying the Host'. His awareness of his capacity to burn himself out – he 'did not think that he would have a long pontificate' – in fact made him work all the more frenetically to accomplish what he could, but his frenzy also resulted in at least one botched endeavour, the edition he authorised of the 'Sistine' Latin Bible whose errors resulted from 'undue haste'.[30]

Pope Sixtus's most complete work, though, was his building programme for Rome, probably planned before his election, as part of his ambitions for his pontificate. The Sistine construction programme was fired by the pope's acceptance of the dream shared by Egidio da Viterbo in the earlier sixteenth century of turning Rome into the new Jerusalem, but Sixtus's design had the special focus of converting the pagan city physically and visually into Christian Rome. As the narrator of one of his most ambitious schemes, Pietro Galesino unfolded it, the goal was:

> That the works of the city, and the images of idolatry, monuments of a vain and false glory, and of an insane superstition preserved too long, and made inveterate by an idle admiration of Roman things of old time, but abhorrent to Christian worship, might be converted to Christian piety.

This did not involve a campaign of destruction or vandalism: just as in an ancient Roman triumph the conqueror's victory was more fully expressed in his exhibition rather than his slaughter of his foes, so the extant legacy of masonry of pagan Rome might be made to serve Sixtus's Christian purpose. This was how he saw its being achieved through the incorporation of imperial Roman statuary into his architectural schema:

> The holy crosses on the summits of the obelisks, and the statues of the principal apostles on the column obliterate the memory of the ancient idolatries. In like manner, the cross placed in the hand of the statue signifying Rome, which stands on the tower of the Capitol, shows that nowadays, Rome, that is the pope, does not use the sword to subjugate the world, as did the infidel Roman Emperors, but the cross to mark the day of salvation to all mankind.

Here is the note of triumphalism that we saw in Gregory XIII's Jubilee, but whereas Gregory's celebration of victory was directed against the Protestant present, Sixtus's was aimed against the pagan past. Sixtus V's aim of making the pagan statues of Rome subserve his Christian goals was perfectly expressed on the occasions when the ancient columns of the emperors Trajan (*c*. 53–117) and Marcus Aurelius (121–80) were newly capped in 1587 with statues of SS Peter and Paul, and when the statue of the goddess Minerva in the Capitoline was left in place, her spear replaced with a cross. Sixtus's insistence on the retention of the name of the Dominican church of Santa Maria sopra Minerva – Our Lady *above* the Temple of Minerva – expressed his vision of Christian conquest of the pagan. However, the clearest expression of his intention to allow what was pagan to survive so as to defer to what was Christian was his bold and massively expensive (38,000 *scudi*) project to re-erect the immense obelisk of the emperor Caligula (12–41) in a position of obeisance in the square before the basilica of St Peter. The workforce of 900 men, sanctified by attendance at Mass and reception of the Sacraments, began their gigantic task on the feast of the Exaltation of the Cross, 1586, for the supremacy of the Christian symbol was what this project involved, and when the obelisk was put in place, its great size now dwarfed by the looming, growing basilica, it was forced to carry a Christian message: 'Christus vincit, Christus regnat, Christus imperat, ab omni malo plebem suam defendit': 'Christ conquers, Christ reigns, Christ rules, and from every evil protects His people'.[31]

Was there a deeper, personal, perhaps even unconscious, motive in Sixtus's transformation of his city from the place of the ruins of the Caesars to the site of the triumph of the Cross? To answer that question it would help to have some understanding of the extent of veneration of the pagan inheritance in Renaissance Rome, of Sixtus's rejection of that cult and of possible reasons for his repudiating it. For the dominant aristocratic côterie in Renaissance Rome aesthetic values had priority and in literature and the fine arts pagan standards reigned supreme: Cardinal Pietro Bembo (1470–1547) warned against reading the Epistles of St Paul because their Greek style was poor; the disinterment of the ancient Roman Laocoön Bronze in 1506 induced something like hysteria in the Rome of the Renaissance. Peretti, though he was not immune to the cult of the classics and included 'some Greek authors' in his library, which consisted largely of the Fathers and theology, came from outside the aristocratic Renaissance circles that had developed the cult of the classics to such a high point. Of lowly background, he hailed from the March of Ancona, to the east of the Apennines, from outside Italy's cultural golden circle of the centre and north between Milan and Rome, its heart Florence where the country's Renaissance civilisation had emerged. Like an earlier papal reformer and outsider, the Dutchman Adrian VI, who had exclaimed when shown the collection of ancient statues assembled by his Renaissance papal predecessors, 'Pooh! – savage baubles' ['*Proh! Idola barbara*'], Sixtus was no aesthete, and detested the Laocoön Bronze. There was much that was deliberately caustic in his attitude of religious superiority over classicism and his dismissal of 'the memory of the ancient idolatries', for, as Pastor wrote, he 'looked upon the monuments of antiquity with quite different eyes from the men of the Renaissance; in their regard he…remembered…that the kingdom of Christ has conquered paganism and made it tributary'. However, his programme of 'christianising the pagan monuments' (Pastor), as well as restoring Rome's ancient Christian architectural legacy (including the venerable Dominican church of Santa Sabina and additions to Santa Maria Maggiore, the 'mother church of Christendom') involved a massive alteration in the city's appearance and lay-out and the rearrangement of the street plan so as to facilitate access for pilgrims. All this was designed to announce that the neo-paganism that had engulfed papal circles in the late fifteenth and earlier sixteenth centuries had been abandoned. Sixtus's completion of the dome of St Peter's in 1590 by his architect Giacomo della Porta (1537–1602) should be seen as the crowning of his plan to round off the final conversion of the city of the Caesars into *Roma Sancta*. The pope, though, was also the heir as well as the supplanter of the Caesars, patron and father of the city and supplier of its needs, including its heavy need for water. In providing his great aqueduct, the twenty-two-mile Acqua Felice – completed in three months, not the three generations that the sceptical Romans predicted – Sixtus conveyed further powerful messages: that he provided water, as the Roman emperors had, for the Roman people, that he dispensed the baptismal symbol of Christianity, the 'religion of water', and that this supply was his personal gift to the Roman people, for the Acqua Felice – the pleasant, the fortunate water – was also that provided by Felice Peretti.[32]

Sixtus V was as intolerant of religious dissidence as he was of the neo-paganism so fashionable in papal circles in the earlier part of the century. Of this former inquisitor, it was, as Pastor wrote 'only to expected that [he] would display the same zeal [as Pius V] in supporting the Inquisition in every way'. Early in his pontificate Sixtus set up branches of the Inquisition in several lesser towns in the Papal States, established a feast for a murdered canonised inquisitor, built a new prison for the Inquisition and restricted appeals from its decisions. Even so, the scope of that body's murderous cruelty was not expanded during his reign, which saw only three executions for heresy within the jurisdiction of the Roman Inquisition. A great *auto da fé* in Rome in 1587, with its well-publicised recantations of dissent, celebrated the orthodox identity of the city.[33]

Time ran out on some of the projects of this hyperactive pontiff: a revision of the Index, which might have been expected from a former member of the Congregation of the Index, was not completed, nor was all the work intended on St Peter's. Sixtus's brief five-year pontificate, extraordinary in its achievements, was also characteristic of the inherent impermanence in the personnel of the sixteenth-century papacy, an institution in which elderly ecclesiastical administrators tended to close their careers with the papacy. The century was exceptionally expensive of popes – seventeen were elected in the period from 1503 to 1592 inclusive, compared, for example, with eleven in that from 1605 to 1691. The reason for the high number of pontificates in the sixteenth century was, of course, their low average duration: four reigns – those of Pius III, 1503, Marcellus II, 1555, Urban VII, 1590, and Innocent IX, 1591, – ended in the year in which they began, and those of Adrian VI , 1522–3, and Gregory XIV, 1590–1, lasted for months rather than years. The longest papal reign of the century from 1503 to 1605 was that of Paul III, which lasted only from 1534 to 1549. There was no long sixteenth-century pontificate along the lines of those of Urban VIII, 1623–44, Clement XI, 1700–21, Pius VI, 1775–99, Pius VII, 1800–23, Pius IX, 1846–78, Leo XIII, 1878–1903, Pius XII, 1939–58 or John Paul II, 1978–. The average length of a pontificate in the period 1503–1605 (taking a reign of less than a twelve-month as lasting a year) was just over six years, and while Philip II ruled in Spain (1556–98) nine popes were elected. The brevity of papal reigns contained obvious potential for instability in a highly personal monarchy and, while within the curial system there were factors making for greater governmental continuity, the Holy See did need to improve its mechanisms of continuous civil service administration so as to bridge the discontinuities of the short papal reigns characteristic of this period. Sixtus V contributed substantially to this greater stabilisation of papal government by leaving the central administration of the Catholic Church with a total of fifteen permanent departments of state, called congregations, as the mechanisms not only for governing Rome and the Papal States under the pope but for financing and co-ordinating the direction of the Catholic Reformation and its missions in Europe and globally.[34]

Despite all he did for his immediate subjects, including the stimulation of industry, the provision of public laundry facilities and the conversion of the Papal States into 'the most secure country in Europe', Sixtus and his severity – he executed a monk and a nun who were lovers – were not popular with all the Romans, and his statue was defaced when it was safe to do it, after his death. Following a programme of public works that might have bankrupted any other small-scale monarchy, he managed to leave a treasury surplus of 3 million gold and 1.5 million silver *scudi* but, in common with other states of this period, he stepped up the disastrous practice of selling salaried state offices, mortgaging the financial future of the state. His conduct of international affairs was generally maladroit and saw no success along the lines of Pius V's involvement in the victory over the Turks at Lepanto. Sixtus was not able to save the Catholic Mary Queen of Scots from her execution by Elizabeth I in 1587 and he left the Holy

See with an unhelpful diplomatic legacy of refusal to recognise the right of succession to the French throne of the Protestant leader Henry of Navarre. For all his shortcomings, though, this pope, in his astonishing and brief reign, was the most effective of the pontiffs of the Catholic Reformation since Paul III.[35]

A series of premature deaths following that of Sixtus V in 1590 confirms the impression of an inherent instability in succession to the papacy. In the conclave of 1590 a kind of law of reaction, in which the style and policies of one sort of pope tended to be set aside in favour of a swing in an opposite direction, may have led to the widely supported election of Giambattista Castagna (1521–90), a well-connected civil and canon lawyer of Roman and Genoese background, an ecclesiastical administrator with a safe and predictable career curve, in the mould of Ugo Buoncompagni. Like most professional Italian ecclesiastical civil servants of his generation and rank, Castagna had done his stint of service at Trent, but little in his career indicated a zealous reformist. He was ordained priest, in 1553, after having been appointed an archbishop. However, Castagna hitched his prospects to Sixtus V's star and became inquisitor general in 1586: the shrewd Peretti had, apparently, predicted his succession by his suave protégé, and following his election Castagna was probably giving notice of his intention to pursue a gentler line than Sixtus by his choice of the papal name, the unusual Urban, not adopted for over 200 years since the election of Urban VI in 1378: one meaning of the Latin *urbanus* is 'pleasant', an adjective that could hardly have been fitted to Sixtus V. An aspect of Sixtus's policy that Urban did not abandon, though, was that of social welfare in Rome, and the provision of bread if not circuses, for he drew up a benefits roster, regulated bread prices by subsidising the bakers and came to the financial aid of the interest-free loan banks, the *monti di pietà*, in the Papal States. There is also every indication that, as a tried administrator, he would have continued Sixtus's measures of reform in the central government of the church, especially in the thorny area of the *Dataria*, a powerful office of complex functions involving petitions, the sale of offices and the issue of bulls. Yet whatever Urban VII's exact intentions and his potential to carry forward the momentum of Sixtus V and his predecessors, he died within a fortnight of election and a new conclave was called for.[36]

In this second 1590 conclave a saint was, eventually, chosen pope. Unlike Sixtus V, Niccolò Sfondrati (1535–91), of a noble Milanese family, came from the inner ring of Italian élites from the great cities of the north and centre that traditionally provided the bulk of the Church's ruling class in the peninsula: Sfondrati was a Vatican insider whose widowed father had been made cardinal by Paul III. He was also, though, a conscientious diocesan bishop, a saintly recluse who was closely associated with the Tridentine programme, admired Loyola, fostered the Jesuits and as pope deferred to Filippo Neri as having a higher stature than his own office. Perhaps this was because he held the papacy in little regard as far as he himself was concerned, and in effect, though elected to it, he rejected it. He was certainly light years away from Peretti's burning human ambition to secure the papacy, but in a painful conclave of over two months, first Cardinal Scipione Gonzaga (1542–93) made plain his disinclination and then the diocesan reformer Gabriele Paleotti failed to secure election, so that the choice fell, with devastating shock, on the 55-year-old Sfondrati. His grief at the election is unmistakable and not to be confused with the bogus dismay of a typical successful *papabile* cardinal: 'God forgive you! What have you done?', he cried out to the cardinals amidst tears, sobs and near-collapse. Despite this inauspicious beginning, a lapse into nepotism, and the continuation of a short-sightedly hostile policy towards Henry of Navarre, the Sfondrati pope, who took the title Gregory XIV, began well enough, with an enlightened policy towards colonised peoples, ordering the payment of compensation to the exploited natives of the Philippines and the abolition of slavery there. However, within a matter of months Gregory XIV was dead, and there is every likelihood that the deep reluctance of this saintly figure to take on the papal office, perhaps exacerbated by the insubordination of his officials, killed him.[37]

Innocent IX (Giovanni Antonio Fachinetti, (1519–91) was, like Gregory XIII, a Bolognese lawyer who had, as had his immediate predecessors, served his time at Trent. He had also done duty as a diocesan bishop but he was in every respect a curialist, and a diplomat who had taken on the burden of papal administration under Gregory XIV and who was made Gregory's successor by a pro-Spanish group in the 1591 conclave, pursuing their goals after his election by continuing the Spanish policy of favouring the ultra-Catholic League over the successor to the French throne, Navarre. Innocent had earlier written as a political theorist against Machiavelli's ideas, but in his foreign policy towards France and Henry of Navarre he could perhaps have used a little Machiavellian realism. The death of the Fachinetti pope after a reign of two months in 1591 brought to a close a period of a year and a quarter in which two papal septuagenarians preceded and followed a younger man who had in effect refused his office by dying in it. In the next conclave a candidate was to be selected from the next generation below that of Castagna and Fachinetti.[38]

The outcome of the conclave following the death of Innocent IX was critical for the balance of outside political, and above all Spanish, influence in the Holy See, with particular reference to the papal recognition of Henry of Navarre, which Philip II wanted to block. The victorious candidate, Ippolito Aldobrandini (1535–1605), of a noble Florentine family traditionally linked to the papal interest, was a professional curialist, lawyer and diplomat whose career had been accelerated by Sixtus V. Indeed, Aldobrandini seems to have occupied the position of the standard bearer of the Sistine inheritance, against an attempt to elect a spokesman for the Spanish bloc. A further consideration swayed the cardinal electors, understandably in view of the fact that they had had to attend four conclaves in so short a period: Aldobrandini's relative youth. As an observer reported,

> The electors had been impelled towards [their] choice, not only by the esteem in which they held Cardinal Aldobrandini, but also from his being only fifty-six years old; for all the cardinals observed that they had had to

deplore the deaths of three pontiffs whose united reigns had occupied only sixteen months.

It must also have strengthened Aldobrandini's claim that, certainly in comparison with Gregory XIV, he actually wanted the papacy, as is clear from his smooth and well-rehearsed posture of diffidence – 'that I may not consent to this election, unless it be for the good of [the] Church' – in contrast with Gregory's hysterical and genuine rejection. In his ambition, Innocent resembled his patron Sixtus V, as he did in his temperament, for although he was described as 'of blameless life, upright intentions', he was also thought vain and, like Sixtus, egoistic and tempestuous:

> Nor does any thing gratify him more than to see himself esteemed, and to know that his reputation, of which he is exceedingly jealous, is respected: and from his very sanguine and choleric disposition, he is very easily exasperated, bustling forth with great vehemence into exaggerations full of heat and bitterness.

Such traits, though, need be no obstacle to the energetic renewal by the new pontiff of the papal programme largely stalled since the death of Sixtus V. Aldobrandini took the name of the previous Florentine pope, Clement VII.[39]

From the commencement of his pontificate in 1592, Clement quickly resumed the drive to establish Rome as the Church's model reformed diocese, patterned on the goals of his long-standing confessor, Filippo Neri, but also given administrative coherence through oversight by a new ministry, the Congregation of the Visitation. The pope's determination to give this body his full support was signalled by the appearance of his own cathedral, San Giovanni in Laterano, at the head of the schedule of its investigative visitations. Clement also took up Gregory XIII's aim of making Rome a priestly educational centre for Catholicism, especially in northern Europe, with the foundation of the Scots College, Rome (1600), while he consolidated the position that Pius V had given the city as the publishing capital of the faith. The edition of the Latin 'Vulgate' Bible in 1598 amended and brought to fruition Sixtus V's hasty work and there were new editions of the Breviary, Missal and other liturgical texts. Clement's formal adoption in 1592 of the veneration of the host in the rite of *Quarant' Ore* confirmed Rome's place as the beating heart of Catholicism's devotional life, focused on papal leadership in the cult of the Eucharist. The dark side of the renewed regeneration under Clement was a revival of the narrowness that had marked the pontificates of Paul IV, Pius V and Sixtus V and which was tragically exemplified with the burning in Rome in 1600 of the dissident thinker Giordano Bruno (b. 1548).[40]

Perhaps because of his origins in Florence, the Italian city-state with the closest historic ties to France, Clement handled Rome's French policy more dextrously than had his predecessors. His absolution of Henry of Navarre, now Henry IV of France, in 1595 paved the way for the dramatic re-Catholicisation of the kingdom over the course of the following century. The Jubilee of 1600, when three million pilgrims – six times the number who attended Gregory XIII's occasion – came to Rome, opened what was to be the crucial century of the Catholic restoration in Europe. The event was given a special French significance, as if to welcome an errant daughter back into the fold. As recalled in a French catechism of about a century later, at the Jubilee 'there appeared a large number of French pilgrims and even heretics, of whom thirty-six repented of their errors at the pope's feet'.[41]

The restoration of the papacy and the reconstruction of Rome as Catholicism's nodal point still had some way to run in the seventeenth century. At the same time, in that century, there is a detectable return to Renaissance styles and preferences in the papacy, a reversion to aristocratic dynasticism, power politics and the promotion of art for art's sake. Po-Chia rightly locates the period of the Counter-Reformation papacy in the second half of the sixteenth century, the period we have covered in this review. Indeed, Clement VIII's pontificate, which lasted until 1605, brought to a close one of the most remarkable half centuries in the history of the institution, the period when the papacy assumed the unchallenged leadership of the Catholic Reformation.

In our study of the rehabilitation of the papacy within the sixteenth century we have devoted attention to its restoration as a bishopric. Rome's emergence in the second half of the sixteenth century as the monstrance of the Catholic renewal was paralleled by the implementation of a set of diocesan renewals, especially in Italy. We shall give particular, but not exclusive, attention to the diocesan reformers Gian Matteo Giberti and Carlo Borromeo.

Giberti has been linked with a group of Catholic reformers generally born in the fifteenth century, and entering the service of the Church under Leo X and Clement VII. As far as diocesan renewal was concerned, this option was not Giberti's first choice of career. Indeed, in the 1520s Giberti, though devout, ascetic and charitable, and also associated with the Roman Oratory of Divine Love, was political adviser to Clement VII, having previously served as his secretary when Clement was Cardinal Giulio de' Medici. Their joint political programme was the anti-Spanish – and therefore pro-French – one of conserving endangered Italian liberty under the leadership of the papacy as a major power in the Italian peninsula. Giberti was Clement VII's leading foreign-policy adviser – 'the pope's heart', as a contemporary styled him – and, in effect, 'chief minister', operating from a position of exceptional executive strength as *Datarius*, in charge of the *Dataria* and handling the vast volume of papal diplomatic correspondence. As Partner says, he fully 'accepted the curial machine for the grant of benefice and favour' it conferred, along with 'the main legal principles of the Roman court', while as a classical scholar he joined in the revival of literary studies under Clement. Cultural pursuits were squeezed into a hectic work schedule, though, for Giberti, as the leading proponent of a pro-French approach in the court of Clement VII had embarked on a foreign policy having Italian, European and, indeed, global implications – a policy driven by his perception of the 'danger to the freedom of Italy and the papacy arising from

the world-wide power of Spain'. To offset that, Giberti promoted the abandonment of papal neutrality and advocated accommodation between Clement VII
and Francis I of France so as to achieve papal leadership of a grand alliance of
Italian states, extending out to take in England, against the super-power
commanded by Charles V. At every juncture of diplomatic negotiation Giberti
was the proponent of an anti-Spanish, anti-Habsburg, pro-French papal policy
for the sake of 'the emancipation of Italy' under the leadership of the Holy See:
there is every evidence that he was a romantic and bellicose Italian patriot.
Having made himself indispensable to Clement, he twice threatened to leave the
papal service unless the pope adhered to the French alliance. His main diplomatic achievement was the 1526 League of Cognac made up of the pope, the
Sforza duke of Milan, Venice and France, and aimed against Charles V.
However, Giberti's anti-Habsburg foreign policy was a high-risk one, as any
policy constructed against a global colossus must be, and the difficulties inherent
in his committing the papacy's resources against Charles V were compounded by
his overestimate of the papacy's strengths and of Francis I's dependability, along
with a fatal underestimation of Charles.[42]

The skein of Giberti's diplomacy began to come apart over the aims of the
League of Cognac, which involved an attack by papal troops against Habsburg-
held Milan, when the French failed to appear in support, casting Giberti into
near-despair by September 1526. Nevertheless, as the Emperor's troops
advanced on Rome towards the end of 1526, Giberti stood alone in advising
Clement against negotiating, even though, as he put it, 'We are on the brink of
ruin'. The real threat to Rome consisted of the mighty army of Germans and
Spaniards, wild, hungry and unpaid, that Charles V had sent into Italy to oppose
the League of Cognac. The Sack of Rome in May 1527 was the war-crime
committed by that force – 'not a conquering army, but...a host of demons
inspired only with avarice, cruelty and lust'. Even so, the presence in Italy of this
marauding multitude, which wreaked such fearful havoc in Rome that it may be
said to have brought the Medicean Renaissance there to an end, would not have
come about had it not been for the foreign policy which Giberti had advocated
in such an emphatic way. Giberti personified the Treaty of Cognac, to which
Charles V had reacted with great anger. He became a hostage for the ransoms
extorted by the soldiers occupying Rome to secure the pope's safety, and Charles
V remained deeply and, on the whole, rightly, suspicious of him as a foe in the
sphere of foreign policy. Giberti's resignation following the Sack of Rome was
his only possible option in the light of the calamity which the policies he
favoured had brought down on thousands of ordinary Romans and on the
papacy's whole position in Europe. The perceptive Cardinal Gasparo Contarini
recorded how Giberti's withdrawal from the Curia to his bishopric (to which
Clement had appointed him in 1524) was necessitated by the compounded
failure of his foreign policy:

> The datary Giberto [*sic*] always retained a larger share than any other
> person of his master's [Clement VII's] confidence; but after the measures

adopted under his administration had resulted in so disastrous an issue, he retired of his own accord, and thenceforth devoted himself to his bishopric of Verona.

The 'datary' was replaced by a pro-Habsburg figure, and Giberti's celebrated Verona reforms, though in no way to be discounted in their importance, were to be activated as a result of the disgrace of a Vatican politician. (Partner adds that a further motive, as with one or two others who 'retired' to their bishoprics at about this time, was a humanist's 'desire for learned leisure' to pursue literature.)[43]

It is important to be aware of the circumstances, and especially of the penitential mode, in which Giberti took up his episcopal duties in Verona. He is too often regarded as a Tridentine diocesan reformer before Trent or as a model for Borromeo, or both, but he was not entirely either of those things, and although his diocesan reforming work was not inconsiderable, in the harshest view he might be described as a discredited diplomat who, in a spirit of remorse, intensified by the trauma of captivity and near-murder by Charles V's mutinous troops, retired from public life to take up what he called the 'fetters' of episcopal ministry. That word was used in a letter of November 1527 to Cardinal Carafa, in which Giberti actually asked permission to take up in person those diocesan duties which the Council of Trent was to assume were a bishop's first and obvious responsibility. Nor, indeed, did Giberti abandon his foreign-policy interests on assuming his duties in Verona, and in March 1529 he was brought back to Rome by a group keen to restore papal anti-Habsburg policies. On that occasion, though, he may have taken on the appearance of a superannuated diplomat brought out of retirement to dust off discredited policies, and his marginalisation must have been confirmed by his total unacceptability to Charles V. On his arrival at Genoa in 1529 in preparation for his imperial coronation by Clement VII, setting the seal on his supremacy in Italy, Charles publicly snubbed the bishop. Giberti remained, though, close to Pope Clement, who was entirely loyal to him, who continued to consult him and use his experience as a diplomat, who nominated him for the College of Cardinals in 1533 and who was deeply consoled at Giberti's visiting him in his last illness. Indeed, we should acknowledge that throughout Clement's pontificate Giberti had used his closeness to the pope as a springboard for the advocacy of reform. In that sense, and though the year 1527–8 obviously represented a right-angled deviation in Giberti's career, there were detectable continuities in his interest in ecclesiastical reform before and after that year.[44]

In particular, the Oratory of Divine Love had been the focus for Giberti's association with Gaetano di Thiene and Carafa, and for this pair's new order of Theatines Giberti provided a house in 1525, an indication of how he used his wealth and influence to promote the cause of religious renovation. As late as 1533 Carafa was still using Giberti's continuing closeness to Clement VII to advance the Theatines. Carafa was Giberti's mentor in the reform of the diocese of Verona which he set in motion from 1528. The diocese was in a parlous state, with non-residence rife, not surprisingly since its previous bishop had been non-resident since his appointment. However, Giberti reversed all that in giving an example by relinquishing those benefices with a cure of souls to which he could not attend in person. His intensified asceticism may be interpreted in terms of personal repentance and severity on himself. Indeed, although Giberti showed affability towards people of all classes in the city and countryside of the diocese, his nature tended towards irritability, and severity and discipline were the hall-marks of his Verona plan, the *Constitutiones Gibertinae*, the system known, aptly, as the *Gibertalis disciplina*, 'Giberti's discipline', a mechanism of admonition whose essential weapon was excommunication. Borromeo was to suggest that in his use of this instrument Giberti was harsh, and was separated from the Milanese reforms by the pastoral spirit of the Council of Trent promulgated in the years between Giberti's laying down (1543) and Borromeo's taking up (1565) the work of diocesan bishops. In short, Borromeo distanced himself from Giberti (the usual form of whose name he apparently could not remember):

> The example of Bishop Giberto is quite near me and I do not doubt that that rare prelate was moved thus [to use excommunication freely] by just cause. But then it had not yet been ruled by the Council which warns us [bishops] to proceed in a reserved fashion and to use the knife of excommunication sparingly.[45]

Giberti in fact used the 'knife of excommunication' in what Pastor termed an 'inexorable' way, alongside an attitude of extreme suspicion of his parish clergy summed up in a diocesan report: 'The priests in this diocese are marked men; all are examined; the unworthy or unsuitable suspended from offices; the gaols are full of *concubinarii* [priests with mistresses]'. Giberti's discipline was also ferocious towards the regular orders, especially those of women, whose convents were visited in what sound like official raids, and against indulgence salesmen. The harsh aspects of his regime may have arisen from the scale of the problems he found in Verona, from the fact that he was working in part-isolation rather than as a member of a collegial Catholic episcopate aiming at agreed goals, and from the absence of seminary provisions to ensure the long-term amelioration of the parish clergy, so that he had to crack down on the human raw material that he inherited. His Roman civil-service background, in which he was used to having his orders obeyed, probably did not help in managing the recalcitrance of the clergy and laity of a provincial diocese in which he may have been regarded as an interloper. It may be a measure of the extremism of his martinet ways that the arch-disciplinarian Carafa had to intermediate between him and the people and priests of the diocese. Borromeo, too, was a disciplinarian and knew that a bishop had sometimes to be 'hard and exacting' on his flock, but, as we have seen, he drew a distinction between his approach and Giberti's. Perhaps he detected some whiff of heresy in Giberti's circle, or perhaps he saw Giberti, in contrast to himself, as one who had, apparently, assumed a bishop's pastoral care as the next best thing to the continuation of a Roman career, but above all

Borromeo realised that though 'discipline' was essential to diocesan reform, it was not synonymous with it.[46]

Even so, the measures adopted by Giberti in the diocese of Verona between 1528 and 1543 cannot be dismissed as merely 'disciplinary', at least not in any negative or purely coercive sense of that word. For though, obviously, he did not have the decrees of Trent to guide him, and though he came into diocesan work from a background of failure in his preferred area of activity, Giberti should be regarded as to a degree pointing towards, though not implementing, the diocesan renewal legislated for by Trent and enacted by Borromeo: 'there is no doubt', Prosperi writes, 'that Borromeo took over no small number' of 'the institutions and instruments of which Giberti had made use' and 'several points of concordance have been pointed out between Gibertine constitutions and Borromean statutes of Councils'. The promotion of the use of the confessional box was one innovation common to both men. Pastorally, Giberti strove to bring about reconciliations between warring individuals and families in Verona with the aim of creating a community 'reformèd, civil, full of good'. He regulated and improved poor relief and provision for the homeless, assisted debtors through the *monti di pietà*, and organised the better-off into a philanthropic sodality, the Society of Charity, to provide money, food, clothing, medical aid, dowries, and health care for the poor and sick. Further, although Giberti was severe against errant priests, he protected the rights and status of his parish clergy. In the fields of liturgy and devotion, Giberti advanced the cult of the Blessed Sacrament through the installation in each church of a box for its reservation, the 'tabernacle', through introducing the ringing of a bell to mark the elevation of the host in the Mass, and by encouraging eucharistic devotions in confraternities of the laity. Giberti preached regularly and ordered the delivery by priests of weekly sermons, in plain language, without literary ornamentation. He brought star preachers into his diocese, sending them to its sermon-starved countryside to provide instruction outside the village churches before Sunday Masses. In all these respects, what Evennett called the 'powerful' and 'persuasive' example of Giberti, 'outstanding' in a group of pre-Trent episcopal reformers which included de Martyribus in Portugal, Fisher in England, Santi in Corsica and de Villanueva in Spain, qualifies him to be considered the most important architect of pre-Tridentine diocesan renewal in the first half of the sixteenth century. In Italy his song of episcopal renewal was taken up, in the north, in Trent, Brescia, Bergamo and Vicenza, in the south, in Naples, Alba and Salerno, and up into France, in Nice, Carpentras and Bayeux. While reform synods were held in the Italian dioceses of Parma and Modena, a series of synodical reforms in the Duchy of Cleves in north-west Germany between the 1530s and the 1560s stressed, as Giberti did, the use of the sermon for elementary catechesis, targeting explanation of the Lord's Prayer, the Creed, the Commandments, Scripture and the real presence of Christ in the Mass.[47]

If Giberti may be regarded as a partly experimental practitioner of diocesan reform during the decades before Trent legislated comprehensively for it, the reforming archbishop of Milan between 1565 and 1584, Carlo Borromeo, is widely viewed as the perfect realisation of the Council's decrees on bishops and their duties. Evennett provided a useful check-list of what the Council required of bishops: residence, frequent preaching, the conduct of annual visitations and synods, oversight of charities, establishment of seminaries, scrutiny of candidates for ordination, discipline and correction of parish priests, staffing and delimitation of parishes, regulation of the regular orders and their preaching, allocation of clerical incomes, implementation of changes in canon law, and giving good examples. The standard lives of Borromeo indicate that he complied fully with that schedule and can be regarded as the embodiment of the Tridentine legislation. As his admirer, the nineteenth-century English Catholic prelate Cardinal Henry Edward Manning (1808–92), wrote:

> The great Council of Trent had laid down the basis of the ecclesiastical reformation of the Church...and in executing its decrees St Charles became the legislator for the Church for future generations. [Borromeo's *Acts of the Church of Milan*] may be called a Commentary on the Council of Trent, and an amplification and development of its decrees.

His entry in a Breviary reads 'He applied himself with great energy to governing his church in accordance with the decrees of the Council of Trent'.[48]

Modern studies too have appreciated Borromeo as Trent in action. Alberigo writes that without the 'pinion' of the 'realization...conclusion [and] acceptance' of the Council of Trent 'the entire episcopal physiognomy of Carlo Borromeo crumbles, dissolves, ceases to exist', and he quotes a remark to the effect that Borromeo was led by 'the spirit and light for the purpose of working, given to bishops and the entire church in celebration of the Council of Trent for the reformation of the church'. Melloni refers to 'Borromeo's loyalty towards the Council of Trent, the enforcement of which he promoted; in this way the whole age of the Council of Trent becomes Borromeo's age'.[49]

Borromeo was indeed the Tridentine ideal of a bishop. A vastly rich career churchman and papal nephew of Pius IV, laden with pensions and other income amounting to an estimated 50,000 *scudi* a year, he had been appointed administrator of Milan and was consecrated its archbishop in 1563, having safeguarded the papal interest at the Council which legislated so profusely on the duties of bishops, and above all their obligation of residence. Pius IV, however, opposed the release to resident episcopal duties for which this capable and trustworthy kinsman petitioned, and for a period Borromeo administered Milan through deputies such as the capable and dedicated Ormanetto who, in 1564, held, on Borromeo's behalf, a synod to issue the decrees of the Council. The discrepancy between those decrees insofar as they concerned episcopal residence and Borromeo's absenteeism was resolved when the new pope, Pius V, released him to take up his duties directly, which he did following his solemn arrival in Milan in September 1565. Thereupon, the Tridentine requirements were fulfilled with amazing vigour and promptness following Borromeo's first provincial council in October to promulgate the Council's measures. The archbishop's visitations, such as those to Swiss valleys which lay within his vast archdiocese in 1567, were models of Tridentine method. There is no doubt that from the beginning of his episcopate Borromeo realised the Tridentine ideal.[50]

Nor, by that time, was there anything particularly remarkable in Borromeo's implementation of the Council decrees and certainly no startling innovation in his recourse to visitations. Pastor's research into the archives of the Sacred Congregation of the Council brought to light, for example, the visitation records of Archbishop Lelio Branacci (1537–99) of Taranto in 1576. The archdiocesan archives in Ravenna contained visitation records (by vicars general) from 1545, 1550 and 1557–9, as well as records of direct episcopal visitations from the years 1567, 1571, 1573 and 1579. Archbishop Christoforo Boncompagni (1537–1603) conducted a minute visitation in that archdiocese in 1579, investigating the religious orders, and a further exacting visitation was made by the vicar general in 1580, examining priests' residence, their administration of the Sacraments and provision of religious teaching. In Ravenna the laity too were examined for their fulfilment of their 'Easter duties' of receiving the Sacraments of Penance and Holy Communion, and public sinners were chastised. Synods, as required by the Council, were held in Ravenna in 1567, 1571, 1580, 1583, 1593, 1599 (diocese) and 1569 and 1582 (province). In terms of the application of the Tridentine ground rules, Ravenna in the second half of the sixteenth century should surely stand comparison with Borromean Milan.[51]

So should the Archdiocese of Bologna under Cardinal Gabriele Paleotti, a member of the Congregation of the Council, the co-ordinator in Bologna of a diocesan administrative team, a pastor holding annual synods, sending out investigating vicars, preaching, catechising, setting up a seminary, attending to the needs of plague victims, incorporating lay religious associations. Yet while Borromeo achieved lasting fame, far beyond his time, country and faith, and speedy canonisation, Paleotti's achievement, though representing a thoroughgoing implementation of the goals of Trent, is known to scholars. Was there, then, a dimension in Borromeo that made him not only the exemplar of Tridentine diocesan reform in Spain, France and Germany, but also revered in lands, notably England, which lay beyond the possibility of implementing Trent: in other words it may be the case that to say that Borromeo put Trent's legislation into effect is to speak the truth – as it is in the case of Paleotti, for instance – but it is not to say enough.[52]

As well as being a supremely efficient executive of the Tridentine decrees, Borromeo achieved a reputation beyond that of other contemporaneous conscientious and effective Tridentine administrators though his realisation of an enduring episcopal ideal to which Trent gave expression in its own time. To find the inspiration for his own fulfilment of ancient diocesan standards, Borromeo deliberately eschewed the models of his own age, such as Giberti, and reached back far beyond Trent into the antiquity of the Church to seek his archetype in his forebear at Milan, Ambrose. He cast himself in an Ambrosian mode, emulating Ambrose in his defence of the rights of the local Church against the state, and appearing in Milan not as a cardinal or a papal proconsul or even as the agent of the Council, but as Milan's bishop and, as Cardinal Baronio wrote, 'a second Ambrose'. He signed, simply as 'bishop', a letter of thanks to a writer on the dignity of the episcopal office, for his great concern was to rehabilitate the status of that office. Ambrose, the model of the Christian pastor, was also the emblem of everything that was distinctive about Milan, including its special rite of the Mass which Borromeo conserved, and whereas the Council in its legislation on bishops may have had in mind some such abstraction as the typical diocese – perhaps one of Italy's multitude of small-scale bishoprics – Milan was not typical but singular, not least in its immensity: it stretched from Genoa to Switzerland, had fifteen suffragan bishops and 3,000 clergy serving over 800,000 people, with 2,000 churches. These particularities meant that the Council's episcopal legislation, extensive as it was, could provide only an outline of work as far as Borromeo's archdiocese was concerned: for example, whereas administratively the Council envisaged a single bishop in a diocese, in Milan Borromeo was the chairman of a large episcopal team. In addition, the length of time – two decades – he spent in post opened up opportunities for Borromeo's developing his ministry which the Council could not fully have considered: for instance the rich popular dimension he gave to his episcopate through his aid to plague victims in 1576 was not written into the Tridentine schedule of bishops' duties. Borromeo was far from respecting everything that was distinctive about Milan, and his battles against the entrenched interests of the once evangelical, but, by Borromeo's time, allegedly corrupt, Humiliati, as well as his clash with the canons of the cathedral, show that he was determined to impose something of a preconceived, indeed a Tridentine, blueprint on the place. However, his ecclesiastical programme amounted to far more than a 'Commentary on the Council of Trent' applied to Milan, and the distinctive regional nature of his reforms are revealed in his *Acta Ecclesiae Mediolanensis* – 'The Proceedings of the *Milanese* Church'. Not surprisingly, the initiative for his canonisation arose from within his diocese.[53]

His canonisation in 1610 in a rite of 'splendor without parallel' indicates the final dimension of Borromeo that gave him a stature greater than that of even the most efficient of other Tridentine administrators: sanctity, recognised by Peter Canisius as early as 1565. This holiness took its rise from a religious conversion prompted by trauma but strengthened by a subsequent experience of religious awakening. As a youth from a noble north Italian family whose modest income was supplemented by ecclesiastical benefices, Borromeo was set on a career of traditional financial exploitation of the Church with an appointment to a local abbacy at the age of twelve. Later, the prospects for his impecunious family rose beyond the dreams of avarice when Borromeo's maternal uncle became pope as Pius IV in 1559, upon which a cornucopia of privileged incomes was poured out on the young churchman – administrator of the Papal States, cardinal deacon, administrator of Milan, legate to Bologna, Romagna and the Marches, Protector of Portugal, of northern Germany and the Catholic parts of Switzerland, and so on. Amidst all this splendour tragedy struck the quiet and studious Carlo Borromeo in the shape of the unexpected death of his elder brother Federigo, an extrovert and dashing character under whose shadow Carlo lived. The severity of the bereavement is unmistakable from his correspondence: 'No human help can be of any comfort under such a terrible blow,' he wrote. 'This event, more than any other, has brought sharply home to me the miseries of this life and the true happiness of eternal glory.' The close connection between this loss and the deepening of his religious experience was traced by Borromeo's agent in the Curia: 'Federico's death occurred as God's arrangement because it taught [Carlo] all the more forcibly to bid farewell to the fleeting affairs of the world'. In fact, now heir apparent of his family's prospects, Carlo Borromeo had to make a decisive choice between the auspicious marriage that his relatives, including his uncle the pope, urged on him and the life of religion, including ordination to the priesthood. His resolution was to serve as Milan's pastor. Borromeo's episcopate was thus the direct outcome of his religious conversion.[54]

Borromeo's grief-induced conversion gave rise to his observing a monastic lifestyle within his archiepiscopal palace and a dramatic adoption of the frugality of the regime that Trent had demanded of bishops. His severance from the simony and nepotism of his earlier years was evident in his renunciation to the Jesuits of the incomes of his titular abbacy. Increasingly Borromeo acquired iconic status in Milan. His escape from a crazed attempt on his life by aggrieved Humiliati lent itself to narration in terms of the miraculous: he was at his prayers in chapel when the would-be assassins' guns were fired, and, *mirabile dictu*, the verse 'Your heart shall not be troubled' was being intoned; his body seemed to ward off the bullets. However, Borromeo's apotheosis as his city's saint in residence came with the plague outbreak of 1576. He had already, in 1572, set up an ambitious famine-relief scheme feeding 3,000. His fortune was likewise put at public disposal in 1576, but this time he was able to use his body, his person, his gestures and his drama to strike up a profound empathy with Milan. It was a cliché of the age that God sent epidemics to chastise communal sins, but Borromeo put a different gloss on that by himself walking in penitential procession, barefoot, with the rope of a condemned prisoner around his neck, carrying in his hand one of the city's relics, a nail that had pinned Christ to the Cross. In this pageant the archbishop was making of himself a suffering servant, a scapegoat and a Christlike expiation for his people's sins, warding off their punishment. The plague abated, and ceased in 1578. Alberigo convincingly hypothesises that Borromeo underwent a second religious conversion at around this time. His *Memoriale* set out the lessons he had learned from the plague outbreak and devotional works for the laity flowed from his pen. The years before his death witnessed his informal canonisation by the Milanese: the Tridentine administrator as bishop and urban saint. In the next chapter we shall see how the Borromean legacy inspired the continuation of episcopal reform into the seventeenth century.[55]

5 The impact of the Catholic Reformation

In this chapter we shall consider the implementation of Catholic reform in Italy, France and the Netherlands in the early modern period. We shall be particularly concerned with the integration of reformed Catholicism with cultures, and especially with popular culture, and also with the question of the adaptation of the reinvigorated Catholicism that had been devised in the course of the sixteenth century (in the forms we have considered in Chapters 2, 3 and 4) to national and regional traditions and identities and to vernacular cultures. A running theme is the relationship between Roman centralisation and standardisation in Catholic practice and a pull in the opposite direction towards adaptation to the requirements, conditions and traditions of particular areas and cultures. We shall also consider reconciliation between popular demands for the continuance of therapeutic and magic-centred religion and the spiritualising, anti-magical trends and opposition to local religion found in Tridentine Catholicity, especially amongst the upper and seminary-trained clergy. The first 'nation' we shall investigate, Italy, was not a nation at all, and for that reason will provide us with information on the way in which the application of Catholic reform took close account of regional varieties in culture and politics.

Italy, above all with Carlo Borromeo in Milan, was the primary laboratory of the Tridentine episcopal renewal. The Borromean model, on the face of it, provided a standardised programme of diocesan reform. However, Milan was itself an idiosyncratic diocese or group of dioceses, with a strong collective sense of its own traditions, not least its liturgical traditions, and of its historic 'Ambrosian' identity. In modelling himself on his Milanese episcopal predecessor, St Ambrose, Borromeo presented himself in the specific identity of a Milanese pastor. He made the *Duomo*, the 'metropolitan church of Milan', dedicated during his archiepiscopate, with its vast array of relics and of altars including St Ambrose's, as much the ritual centre of his episcopate as the popes were making St Peter's the focus of theirs. In adapting the Tridentine programme to the Milanese environment, Borromeo's prestige as the model episcopal reformer implicitly validated local and regional adaptations of Tridentine change. And in sending bishops back to their dioceses, the Council encouraged a reintegration between regional identities and episcopal leadership. Thus, for example, Florence's Archbishop Antonio Altoviti (1521–73) abandoned ecclesiastical politics in Rome and took up the local traditions of Savonarolan piety and of Pierozzi's earlier reforms in his archdiocese. From the time of his official entry into Florence in May 1567, Altoviti made Tridentine reform a regional concern, holding a diocesan visitation, a synod, and a provincial council to co-ordinate the application of the Council's decrees. In Ragusa a bishop who spoke the Slavonic language of the area was chosen. In the vital area of priestly training the individual diocese and its seminary were now the foci of ecclesiastical reform – and often of regional affiliations. In France Gallicanism was the ideology of resistance to Roman centralisation, but in fact in seventeenth-century France the Gallicanism of the bishops certainly did not imply opposition to reform, for they complained that it was the privileges and exemp-tions granted by the Vatican to the religious orders that were impeding the reform of discipline and morals, of Penitential practice and monastic standards, as required by the Council: 'Putting an end to circumvention of episcopal discipline', writes Becker, 'was…the main thrust of the Gallicanism of seventeenth-century [French] bishops'.[1]

Dioceses and episcopal cities, including some of the poorest and most remote in Europe, assumed a renewed importance in the period of the Catholic Reformation, through becoming once more places of episcopal residence, some-times tended by distinguished individuals. Of a leading Genoese family, the Barnabite Alessandro Sauli turned down the archbishopric of his great native city and took up the episcopal care of neglected Corsica. The famous Jesuit theologian, author, Leuven professor and, in 1605, *papàbile*, Roberto Bellarmino (1542–1621) in 1602 took up the poor archdiocese of Capua in Campania and devoted as much attention to it as if it were Milan or Naples. The record of Bellarmino's work in this remote corner charts his meticulous attention to the area's needs, not through suffragans or vicars, but in person, and with special application to its poverty and backward educational provisions. In 1602 Bellarmino delivered discourses in Capua itself on 5, 6,16 and 26 May, 2, 6, 9, 16 and 29 June, 7, 14, 21, 22, 25 and 28 July, 4, 11 and 18 August, was on diocesan visitations for much of September and part of October, was delivering allocutions in Capua on 13, 20, 27–30 October and after diocesan visitations for virtually the whole of November was again teaching and preaching in Capua on 1, 8, 15, 22, 25, 26 and 29 December. In the following November Bellarmino was present in his cathedral as its archbishop on 9, 14, 15, 16, 18, 20, 21, 23, 25, 26 and 29 November: this was what the Tridentine goal of a bishop's residing, working and preaching in his diocese meant in practice and in detail. Episcopal residence sealed a relationship between the bishop and his diocese as a region in which he was an acknowledged leader and it had the potential to raise social, educational and ecclesiastical standards, whether through the disposal of alms, preaching, the administration of Confirmation in the outlying districts and the hamlets of the diocese, or through such details as the replacement at the arch-bishop's expense of wooden eucharistic vessels with silver. In setting up a Jesuit College in Capua in 1611, Bellarmino endowed the city with a secondary and tertiary educational institution and an important library and research centre.

The archbishop, we may say, put his see on the map, raised its profile, brought it prestige and income.[2]

We should not be over-sanguine about the success of episcopal Catholic reform anywhere in early modern Europe, and least of all in the south Italian Kingdom of Naples where Capua lay. Bishops in the south, the *Mezzogiorno*, were often noble sinecurists or Spanish political appointees. The clerical corporate patronal system of the ownership of parishes known as *chiese ricettizie* sheltered priests from episcopal discipline, and the endemic poverty of the south delayed the provision of seminaries in several dioceses of the Terra d'Otranto in Puglia until well into the eighteenth century. Lecce, the second city of the Kingdom of Naples, had none completed until 1709, and five out of the thirteen dioceses of the region had no priests' training institutes even at the end of the eighteenth century. The *Mezzogiorno* was one of those areas of Europe perhaps more suited to missionary treatment by the religious orders than to episcopal governance, Tridentine-style. Even so, in the seventeenth century there is evidence from the South of Italy of successful adaptation by the episcopate to what popular culture demanded of religion, and above all healing. Thus in 1656, when southern Italy was stricken by plague, Giovanni Alfonso Puccinelli, Archbishop of Manfredonia, attempted to stem the contagion by having recourse to a local and traditional saint's cult, that of St Michael the Archangel, in his manifestation as a patron of his area, lodged in his 'grotto-basilica' at Mount Gargano. A record of what transpired, published in 1680, recounted how Michael was invoked as a remedial figure within the local environment who 'miraculously disclosed to the archbishop that the stones of this, his holy basilica, were the authentic remedy to the plague'. The Curia, their members doubtless suffused with Tridentine quasi-rationalism and scepticism over local forms of transformative magic, were not impressed by the reverence for wonder-working stones reportedly commended to the archbishop by the archangel, though the then pope Alexander VII (1655–67) showed some interest. It was Archbishop Puccinelli, however, who, as a pastor attuned to the religious and social needs of his region, had evinced the strongest empathy with what many Europeans (and not just in the rural *Mezzogiorno*, but, as we shall see, in sophisticated cities such as Barcelona) thought: that religion, was, at least in part, for healing and miracles. The archbishop's influence was surely increased rather than decreased by his endorsement of the cult of his neighbour, the 'protector, intercessor and holy helper', Michael.[3]

If the early modern Catholic Church aspired to function as a centrally directed monolith, in point of fact it had few resources to do so, though administrative devices such as the Congregation Propaganda Fide (1622) gave Rome increased global control, at least in the mission field, both in Europe and overseas. However, Trent had reaffirmed the centrality of the diocese as the essential building block of Catholic structures, and the diocese, whether large or small, expressed the devolved rather than centralised nature of the Church. The key role of the diocese reflected a Catholic Church still concerned to function within local area cultures, for example through saints' cults and their celebration through the use of history by means of the medium of relics. It is true that a centripetal momentum in hagiography existed through the Roman Sacred Congregation of Rites, set up in 1588, in the same year that saw the publication of the first volume of the best-selling *Annales Ecclesiastici* by the Church historian and Oratorian, Cesare Baronio. Baronio's work established, contrary to the Lutheran view of a deviation in the Catholic Church away from the Apostolic model, that the Church of his own day was one and the same with the Apostolic institution. In parallel to that, devotion to the relics of that early Church, evidenced in such undertakings as the translation of the bones of supposed martyrs from Sardinia to Piacenza between 1643 and 1647, underwent what Ditchfield calls an 'explosion'. Pious interest in the early Church and its *vestigia* was promoted by Baronio's patron, Filippo Neri, through his passion for the Roman catacombs as testimony both to the continuity of the Church with its apostolic past and also to the focal status of Rome in that story. To that extent, the pursuit of Church history and its revelation in tangible and visible relics formed an exercise in the Romanisation of Catholicism. However, the sanctity of relics of Roman provenance, when they were transferred elsewhere, was domesticated in favour of local churches, as we shall see in the case of relic removals to German cities. Meanwhile, alongside veneration of Roman remains, Italian dioceses fostered their particular ecclesiastical histories through research in the fields of numismatics, archaeology and epigraphy, thereby confirming the convergence of diocesan with regional historical identities. Carlo Borromeo was an enthusiast for this kind of ecclesiastical local history, in which the bishop was responsible for the collection 'together [of] the names, character and pastoral actions of his predecessors'. The exploitation of history so as to authenticate the constitutional claims of regional churches and dioceses, *vis-à-vis* Rome, or against rival claimants to prestige and leadership, is illustrated in the deployment of martyrological archaeology during the rivalry for contest in Sardinia between Sassari, where the archbishop's instructions led to the exhumation in 1614 of three martyrs from Diocletian's (245–313) reign, and Cagliari, where in the same year 'innumerable' (in fact 338) martyrs' skeletons were unearthed, again at the insistance of the city's archbishop. The organised dispersal of these objects to such places as Catalonia and Naples furthered the primatial claims of Cagliari within Sardinia and thereby promoted local urban patriotism. The testimony of history was also critical, writes Ditchfield, 'if a local church was to rescue its cherished cults from the "curial positivism" of the Roman Sacred congregation of Rites'.[4]

Nowhere in Italy was the issue of the autonomy of a regional sub-division of the Church more sensitive than in the case of the Republic of Venice and its relationship with Rome. Venice's well-advertised, if partial, ecclesiastical independence from the Holy See came under threat in the Catholic Reformation period, for the papacy's Congregation of the Holy Office set up in 1542 with a jurisdiction stated in the founding bull of Paul III to extend to 'each and every city, town, territory and place existing in Christendom' operated, in Italy at least, as an arrowhead of papal intervention, invading the ecclesiastical autonomy of states including Venice. Thus the leading propagandist of Venetian Church independence, the Servite friar Paolo Sarpi in his *Sopra l'officio dell'Inquisizione* (*Concerning the Office of the Inquisition*) (1613) exaggerated the independence from Rome of his Republic's Inquisition and, by extension, of its wider Church structures. Venice was sensitive enough about its ecclesiastical self-government for a complete breakdown with the papacy to occur in the interdict of 1606–07, for the Republic practised what Wright calls a 'fully developed form of Erastian control over Church life'. However, the Erastianism (doctrine of state control of the church) in question was not of the secularist form that was to prevail in parts of Europe during the eighteenth-century Enlightenment but rather a kind of Catholic Erastianism, or almost a kind of lay theocracy in which, for example, the highly technical task of investigating heterodoxy was entrusted to the Three Deputies against Heresy, patricians chosen by the state. For Venice operated a degree of separation in Church government from the Holy See because it was seen, not as a godless republic, but as 'a devoutly Catholic state', containing not merely a bishopric but a patriarchate. It was a holy and religious polity whose ruler, the Doge, carried out at San Marco the quasi-priestly functions of the head of a Christian commonwealth. In its Mediterranean provinces, the Republic inherited the Greek traditions of Christian statehood, and civil servants accepted religious honours, in Byzantine fashion. Nevertheless, in those eastern territories Venetian officials, even though the Republic was touchy in regard to Roman suggestions that Church reform was needed in its domains, expressed disgust at the lax, or pre-Tridentine, standards of the Greek clergy, for in the traditions of the Venetian patriciate, from whose ranks came the likes of Contarini and Giberti, the state and its élite took up Catholic reform enthusiastically. Far from being an imposition from outside its territory (which included Giberti's Verona), interest in diocesan renewal reform was an indigenous Venetian trait and, as Logan writes, Venetians 'made a particularly important contribution' to the development of the episcopalism of the Catholic Reformation, with contributions including Contarini's *De officio episcopi libri II* (*Two Books about the Bishop's Role*) (1517).[5]

In the immediate post-Tridentine period the emergent 'doyen of the Venetian episcopate' was Agostino Valier, bishop of Verona from 1565 to 1606. Though closely linked with Carlo Borromeo from their time together in Rome, visiting him and observing his work in Milan, and 'a great…exponent of the Borromean ideal', Valier did not set out simply or slavishly to apply a rigid Milanese reform model to the different situation and traditions of Verona. His adaptation of his episcopal policies to his regional environment can be examined in three areas. First – and in fact just as Borromeo himself did in Milan – Valier cultivated the native traditions and historic ecclesiastical patriotism of the diocese and region, paying special reverence to his predecessors, in the distant past St Zeno (d. *c.* 372), and within his own lifetime, Giberti. Just as Gabriele Paleotti in Bologna saw himself 'as the custodian of a corpus of diocesan legislation handed down by his predecessors', so Valier viewed himself as 'the inheritor of a tradition in the Veronese Church'. Next, Valier modified Borromeo's moral rigour to apply a lighter pastoral discipline than that prevailing in the Milanese pattern. Perhaps because he was sensitive to the fact that he was not himself a Veronese, and might be resented if he aspired to be a moral dictator, Valier exercised *tolerantia* (patience) over his diocesan clergy, his 'angels', as he called them. Third, Valier handled Church–state relations with greater suavity than did the sometimes provocative Borromeo, who challenged Milan's Spanish government: Valier was 'devoted' to the Venetian government of Verona and was sensitive to the Venetian Republic's touchiness with regard to Vatican invasions of its prerogatives. An example arose when he diplomatically arranged to act as a kind of internal visitor alongside a papal nuncio in an Apostolic visitation of the diocese of Verona in 1581. Valier's retention of 'certain reservations about taking Borromeo as a model' sums up his determination to make his episcopal reformation as fully synthesised as possible with local history, regional traditions, territorial identity and political customs.[6]

A further religious field in which the Venetian state of which Verona was a part retained its distinctiveness while accepting Tridentine reform was that of piety. Valier was the author of a manual for devout women in lay as well as religious life, and the Venetian world in which he operated had a vibrant tradition of lay piety, taking evangelical forms in the mid-sixteenth century. Ochino, the most noteworthy of the Italian evangelicals, preached in Venice as late as 1542 and the handbook of the evangelicals, *Il Beneficio di Giesù Christo Crocifisso* was published in the city in 1543. Lay piety was combined with evangelical fervour amongst non-elite as well as patrician elements in Venice: Ochino's sermons and the *Beneficio* were read by 'shopkeepers and artisans'. The dialect poem, *La morte di Giurco e Gnagni* by the jeweller Alessandro Caravia was published in 1550 and reissued in 1603. In it the character Gnagni trusts in good works and austerities for his salvation but Giurco puts his confidence in the evangelical formula, 'of myself I have done no good works; Christ gives Paradise of his grace'. The priest present at Giurco's deathbed confirms, 'by Christ's blood and through nothing else the Christian is justified'. The influences of the *Beneficio* are clearly detectable in *La morte di Giurco e Gnagni*. And indeed the soteriology of grace and faith, of reliance on the 'benefits' of Christ crucified, seems to have been enduring and widely spread in the Republic: Venetian wills expressing individual lay understandings of salvation on the part of a socially quite comprehensive selection of citizens, typically literate bourgeois, present a pervasive evangelical view based on Paul and Augustine, though the emphasis was on the application of the merits of Christ to the believer rather than, specifically, on justification by faith. Examples come from a testator's wish that 'through Jesus Christ, who died for us on the Cross, [God] will know my soul for his', and in a prayer that the Father would not see the penitent's sins but only 'the mirror of Christ'. However, this distinctively Venetian evangelical soteriology was not Protestant, was combined with endowments for Masses and invoked the saints, and belonged integrally, as Logan says, to the 'Catholic tradition' in Venice. It was represented by Sarpi, who opposed the view of the Jesuit theologian, Luis Molina (1535–1600), to the effect that God bestowed salvationary grace to those He foreknew would co-operate with it, an interpretation placing reliance on man's contribution to his salvation. The Venetian tradition for which Sarpi spoke took up a view of the total indispensability of grace and of the Redemption, a line of Catholic thought which we associate particularly with the Venetians Contarini and Cortese and which preserved its Venetian regional distinctiveness well into the Tridentine period. Though Venice was Italy's leading centre for the cultivation of an evangelical soteriology, Catholic emphasis on the value of good works of charity was expressed through the *Scuole grandi*, lay confraternities which provided scope for important religiously inspired civic action on the part of the middle classes excluded from real political power by the Republic's aristocratic governing structures.[7]

One way in which the 'spirit of the Counter-Reformation' could serve the social needs of a given area was through the expression of regional and especially of civic communalism, *pratique unanime*, a community's overwhelmingly or even universally shared religious practice. In Perugia, a middle-sized Papal States bishopric in Umbria in central Italy, the intensification of mass piety under the influence of a succession of Tridentine and – in two cases – eminently saintly bishops from the mid-sixteenth into the early seventeenth centuries, saw the community operating as a civic congregation. Spectacular numbers in attendance at religious rites were the visible expression of *pratique unanime*: 30,000 processed to petition God in 1614 when the vault of the church of San Domenico fell in, a terrible portent in a season of atrocious weather. Renowned visiting preachers, Capuchins and Dominicans, were awaited by vast audiences, and immense crowds went on pilgrimage to the nearby Assisi district or venerated what was believed to be Mary's wedding ring in Perugia cathedral. The confraternities transported huge numbers to the Roman jubilees of 1575 and 1600. It was reported that 60,000 attended the reinterment of a local saint in 1609, and if we accept the estimate of the population of the city and its hinterland as about 64,000 this means that virtually all Perugians attended a particular religious rite that was interwoven with civic and regional patriotism. However, all this regional corporatism, sustained by the revived diocesan structures under the influence of Trent, had its downside. The corporate community imposed conformity and had little room for dissidents and outsiders. In Sicily the Spanish Inquisition was exploited by informants to dispose of their foes. Apart from the fewer than thirty Protestants executed at Palermo between 1542 and 1592, the Inquisition in Sicily pressed down on other dissidents, not just those guilty of obscene blasphemy, a kind of Sicilian art form, but also on colourful freethinkers, such as the 'Catholic Jewish Christian' who worked out lengthy prayers for the Rosary based on the Psalms of David, or the individual who anticipated modern insights by insisting that the Jews had not killed Christ. The tragic fate of the unorthodox Friulian miller, Mennocchio, executed by the Venetian Inquisition in 1585, the possessor of a rich range of deviant views, provides further evidence for the narrowing of belief options in the Italy of the Catholic Reformation. Further intense communalism, especially when centred on local religious symbols of holiness, must have had the effect of limiting people's horizons and fostering a provincial outlook.[8]

Nevertheless, the Tridentine diocese undoubtedly provided a vital focus for religious and communal modes of thought and feeling, the smaller and middle-sized dioceses in particular providing fora for social leadership by resident bishops. The ability of some of these to exercise influence within their dioceses was provided by the personal appearances made on the kind of visitational tours that Bellarmino made in his Capua bishoprics or the ones that a close associate of Carlo Borromeo, Francesco Bossi (or Bossio, d. 1584), bishop of Perugia from 1574, undertook. In Milan Archbishop Federigo Borromeo (1564–1631) conveyed the personal impact of his teaching by a series of allocutions, called *sacri ragionamenti* – 'holy discourses' – applying the Church's doctrine in treatments of the everyday issues of ordinary life. The bishops' power to teach was further facilitated by the rise of literacy and the spread of printing, as bishops such as Perugia's Napoleone Comitoli (bishop from 1591 to 1624) used printed pastoral letters to communicate with the parishes of his diocese. Literate popular piety was stimulated by the printers' productions, for example in Perugia between about 1580 and around 1600, of cheap, sometimes versified and illustrated, religious books and pamphlets on such subjects as the Sacraments, family piety and morals, and a 'happy death'. The rising literacy necessary both to elicit and to respond to this upsurge of printed literature was provided in the Italian dioceses, in particular in the north, by the Schools of Christian Doctrine. First established in Milan in 1536 by Castellino da Castello (1470/80–1566), these voluntary institutions for teaching on Sundays and holy days rapidly spread out in the following decade into Pavia, Venice, Genoa, Verona, Piacenza, Mantua, Parma and so on: Milan acquired about twenty-eight of these schools, teaching 2,000 pupils under the care (in small classes) of 200 teachers. In Bologna by 1577 40 per cent of children were passing through these elementary schools; their teaching methods stressed fun and encouragement, and they raised literacy in northern Italy to probably unprecedented levels. Their emphasis was on the learning of prayers and on practical good conduct and sociable behaviour.[9]

The same practical aims characterised the seminaries that were being set up in Italian dioceses in the period following Trent, adapted to their religious and social needs. The diocese of Novara, Milan's western neighbour and a large, poor, mostly mountainous terrain of 275 parishes, evolved a seminary system from a first foundation in prompt obedience to the Council in 1565, to three institutions by 1593, though these housed only thirty-three students in all and subsisted on slender funds. Another of Borromeo's disciples, Novara's bishop the Barnabite Carlo Bascapè (1550–1615), aimed to increase the diocese's supply of seminaries; he created two new ones, in 1607 and 1609, and prevailed on his own order to open a seminary in the city of Novara. The aim of putting at least the majority of serving priests though seminary, for periods ranging from one to nine years, was achieved: in one group of parishes twenty-five out of thirty-one parish priests were seminary alumni. The teaching they received was practical, and adapted to the situation in this specific diocese: for example, there were few Protestants in that region, so controversial theology to counter them was eschewed in the seminary curricula. While numbers of Novarese priests expanded impressively, tripling between about 1600 and 1750, the production of scholars was not the aim of the seminary scheme, but rather the formation of pastors able to catechise the people and administer the Sacraments, all in what Deutscher calls 'an intelligent, capable manner'. Novara's seminary-trained parish priests were generally conscientious and professional, celebrated Mass regularly, preached sermons based on Scripture and good morals, attended conferences to discuss cases of conscience and pastoral problems, took care of neighbourhood matters in the Sacrament of Penance, where they ordained restitution and reconciliation, and generally did what their bishops told them to. A diocesan seminary system had produced a clergy suitable to the specifics of its situation.[10]

Such priests, established in residence for regular periods of time, could be expected to work most effectively within the relatively well-developed parochial and diocesan structures of the north and centre of Italy. In the south of the peninsula, with its defective parish system, the Tridentine Church adopted a missionary strategy exercised through the religious orders, using techniques that were consciously adapted to the demands, especially for entertainment and theatre, embedded in regional popular culture. The missions both created new strands and expectations in vernacular culture and left durable impressions on it, while being carefully adjusted to its 'consumer' requirements, especially for miracles and cures.

The Jesuits opened their mission to the Terra d'Otranto in poor and remote southern Puglia in the Kingdom of Naples in 1573. The missionary campaign on which they embarked marked the start of a long-term apostolate by religious orders to this part of the *Mezzogiorno*. Vincent de Paul's (*c.* 1580–1660) Fathers of the Mission (otherwise known as Lazarists, or Vincentians) followed, from 1729, and Alfonso Liguori's (1696–1787) Redemptorists arrived in 1732. Though there were differences of approach between the various orders, the common feature of their work arose from the fact that it was not a feature of a permanent diocesan and parochial provision but was of its nature occasional. Therefore, it had to be densely concentrated in its impact, as well as, in Gentilcore's words, being 'simplified and insistent, miraculist and fearful'. Thus the powerful tactics adopted included processions, sermons, and mass Confessions which stressed reconciliation of feuds. The best-known impresario of the techniques outlined was the Jesuit Paolo Segneri, the elder (1624–94), master of the communication of an intensely emotional, imaginative, miraculous, saint-invoking piety. Segneri would make concentrated tours of eight to ten days which were focused on a chosen urban nucleus and its hinterland (the alternative pattern was a route through a string of villages). The hallmark of the Segerian missionary method was the creation of deeply coloured events introduced into the routine lives of townspeople and peasants.[11]

As the content of this kind of evangelism was filtered through assumptions present in existing popular culture, there can be no doubt of the impact of the medium on the senses of people whose lives were, generally, starved of colour and spectacle. In Lecce in 1639, for example, trailer posters were put up on a

Saturday afternoon advertising as a forthcoming attraction the mission to begin the following day. A feeling of mounting anticipation was carefully cultivated as the missioners held a procession with a banner and a crucifix to publicise the assembling of their visitation at the bishop's palace. In this way, and also by the involvement of the mayor, carrying the city banner, and of the local nobility, the forthcoming events were endorsed by local figures of ecclesiastical, social and political power. Regular processions formed the dramatic centre of the mission tour, in which the rector of the city's Jesuit college carried the crucifix, and local clergy the Blessed Sacrament. The area's confraternities came out in force, people attended dressed as penitents, children were instructed, evening prayers and meditations were provided and Confessions were heard throughout the day. Perhaps the most sensational instalment in the whole highly theatricalised routine took place each night, when further, torchlit, processions were made and confraternities, carrying skulls and singing the penitential psalm, the *Miserere*, conducted forays into the red-light district to urge repentance. By the close of the mission on the following Sunday, with High Mass, sermon, a papal blessing and a final procession, this local community had been offered an intensive injection of emotive piety. In this devotional carnival, as with carnival proper, the events obtained much of their effect from the full involvement in them of the area community, conducting its collective occasions, as was customary and natural in the southern Mediterranean, out of doors – though in this case the events were initiated by outsiders.[12]

The Jesuits' cultivation of cathartic theatre involving members of local communities in the dramas being enacted grew, if anything, less inhibited over time. In a Jesuit mission to Squinzano near Lecce in 1646, for example, members of all classes processed barefoot, covered in the ashes of penitence, tied in the ropes and chains of convicted prisoners. A nobleman, assisted by his son who was costumed as a Franciscan, wounded himself with a stone in contrition for his sins; a prostitute played Mary Magdalene, dressed in the sackcloth of remorse; in a village procession the local women wore crowns of thorns and carried babies in the posture of the Madonna. Such carefully choreographed involvement of the laity in the religious dramas that were designed to instruct them seems to have encouraged them to develop their own imitative roles: in 1655 members of one of the missionaries' audiences adopted a familiar preachers' device and conducted a simulated dialogue. The Jesuit missioners were, apparently, turning communities into occasional casts of characters in sacred dramas. The missionaries' highly inventive theatrical techniques could also be mendacious: one Jesuit preacher, when visiting a community, would find out secretly which of its members had died in the recent past and then use his confidential information to powerful effect to call out to these departed by name at the start of his sermon. The Redemptorists tended to be more restrained, though their technique of introducing the character of a deceased neighbour scripted to describe his new residence, hell, and being quizzed about its features in torchlight in a crepuscular church was, surely, no less effective than anything put on in the theatre proper.[13]

In the devotional and penitential routines of the Redemptorists there was a detectable shift of focus in favour of the individual 'devout Christian', for whom powerful meditations on the Passion and on the sorrows (*Dolours*) of Mary were provided. This may have produced a stronger alignment to the spiritual teaching of the Church. However, the Jesuits, by concentrating their presentations on the theatrical, the tangible, the physical and the visible may have ratified the survival or confirmation of a materialist religious culture. There is no doubting the durability of some of the devices imported into vernacular culture by missionary teaching from the late sixteenth century onwards. The use of the *strascino*, for example, a self-degrading performance in which the individual licked the ground in a kneeling procession, survived in the region studied by Gentilcore until the 1950s. The Redemptorists' *abitini di Maria* – 'Mary's little costumes' – are, apparently, still worn today in that area. The overall nature of the complex accommodation reached between missionary teaching and what popular culture expected from religion can be illustrated in the use of the Rosary in the Terra d'Otranto. All the missionising orders taught the use of the Rosary, but in the collective imagination of the region it took on a practical rather than contemplative use in the form of the 'Rosary for those executed by hanging' reported in 1742 and representing an adaptation of a reflective and spiritualising Catholicism to unrelenting practical needs. Likewise, the Sacraments according to the teachings of the Tridentine Church were spiritual therapies, channels of sanctifying grace. In Puglia, however, a famous Confessor had his Confessional turned into a shrine where sick people would have themselves seated to obtain cures and from which splinters were removed for healing purposes. Gentilcore's analysis of forty-one candidacies for canonisation in the Kingdom of Naples between 1588 and 1750 confirms that in that region 'the principal function of saints was to perform miracle cures'. The missionaries' attempts to promote a spiritual Catholicism in the *Mezzogiorno* encountered what Norman Douglas called the 'intense realism of…the religion' of this impoverished zone, but it may be that the missioners' use of the physical to represent the spiritual encouraged the survival of a kind of materialist Christianity.[14]

In its relationship with European vernacular culture the mission, in the widest sense, of the Tridentine Church, whether conducted by bishops and parish priests in stabilised diocesan and parochial frameworks or as a succession of itinerant campaigns by representatives of the religious orders, involved an unvoiced but constantly adjusted negotiation between what the lay recipients of the messages required and what their clerical suppliers sought to convey. Undoubtedly, the institutional Church achieved, certainly in Italy, considerable strides in the presentation of its teaching to a largely receptive laity, making the Catholic Reformation, in Cochrane's words, 'the most universally popular movement in the whole history of Italy'. The large number of, and high rates of membership in, the confraternities in such a diocese as Perugia, including those in which women held office, tends to confirm the thesis Cochrane advanced of a largely popular Tridentine Church. Its teaching on the details of daily and family life, including the purveying of the rulings of the Council on the necessity for freedom in young people's choice of marriage partners and vocations, was broadcast through a string of writings on the Christian family and the Christian upbringing of children. Mothers' responsibilities, particularly for religious nurture, were emphasised, while fathers of families seem to have attended lessons on their duties conducted by parish priests, and in Milan Federigo Borromeo devoted one of his archiepiscopal addresses to parents' care of their children, an allocution published in 1640. To the extent that the Church's accumulated teachings on child nurture were adopted in families, the result in large numbers of early modern Italian households may have been the striking of what Logan calls 'a balance between excessive indulgence and excessive severity'. It seems likely that the Catholic Church in early modern Italy was offering guidance, a great deal of which must have been accepted and put into practice, on the mass behaviour of society in the basic ordering of daily and family life. On the more strictly religious front, the inhabitants of at least one village which came under the ecclesiastical control of Milan and which was missionised by Jesuits and Dominicans seem to have made Catholic Reformation standards, in particular Tridentine and Borromean requirements concerning priests, their own, for they drew up an indenture for their parish priest which committed him to a Tridentine regime of saying Mass, dispensing the Sacraments, holding funerals, making peace, staying in residence and avoiding affairs with women.[15]

The reception of the Catholic Reformation in Italy could not have been as successful as one suggests it was without supportive political factors at work. The well-honed techniques of the Capuchins, applied to counter Protestantism in religiously mixed areas in Piedmont through the glamour of *Quarant' Ore* ceremonies, were assisted by the presence of the nobility and of the ruling house of Savoy which had its own interest in using the Catholic faith to advance its rule over its north Italian duchy. Torre detects a further link between political processes and Catholicisation: and in particular the endowment of Masses, which, in four dioceses in the Asti area within the period 1620 to 1740 seems to have followed patterns of community fiscal indebtedness to the state: by funding the endowment of Masses, tax debtors were practising tax evasion. Protest against taxation in the politics of seventeenth-century urban Italy could also draw moral sustenance from Catholic cults: in Naples from the devotion of the Virgin of the Carmine, protectress of the Neapolitans against harsh Spanish taxes on food, occasioning the Revolt of Masaniello in 1647. Catholic religion in early modern Italy operated as a religious system twinning the sacred and the secular, the spiritual and the social, and coping with the demands of health, community and politics.[16]

In France and francophone Europe, Catholic religious rituals were also deployed during the period of the Catholic Reformation for social and material purposes and for warding off harm. Thus, during a siege of Cambrai in 1649 Our Lady of Grace was invoked to protect 'her' town, the Blessed Sacrament was exposed in all parishes, and when the city was 'miraculously' spared by the besiegers, crowds from all quarters converged on the central place of worship. In the villages of the district virtually all parish churches possessed a statue, chapel or confraternity dedicated to one of the saints customarily addressed against plague. There was, of course, nothing new in this use of the sacred to create the therapeutic, as Galpern shows with particular reference to Champagne in the sixteenth century. The difference, as we move into the age of the French Catholic Reformation, may lie in the stronger emphasis on recourse to international Catholic rather than local cults – the Blessed Sacrament, the Seven Dolours of Mary, and in the invocation of a new hero-saint of Catholic reformism, Carlo Borromeo, who had achieved a pinnacle of sanctity in his actions to counter epidemics in Milan.[17]

Bourbon France emerged as the second front of the Catholic Reformation. The interrelated tasks for Catholicism in that country were threefold. The renewal of a sometimes decadent medieval system, with particular reference to the religious orders, was required; the fuller Catholicisation of the masses, on the levels of the dioceses and parishes as well as through missions to the countryside on the part of the new religious orders, was undertaken; and an intensive Counter-Reformation – the extirpation of what had been, in some regions, a strongly entrenched Calvinist Protestantism – was pursued.

The renewal of the French regular religious life in the seventeenth century may be sub-divided into the reform of the existing orders, and the evolution of new post-medieval foundations, male and female. The growth of the newer orders – including Jesuits, Capuchins, Oratorians, Ursulines, Carmelites and Visitandes – should not distract attention from the renewal of the rich monastic life that medieval France had known. By the seventeenth century the religious quality of the regular life was dulled by its deep involvement in the complex legal and financial vested interests characteristic of Gallican Catholicism, propped up by the Concordat of Bologna accepted by the French crown since 1516: the succession of a long series of abbots from the noble house of Guise, for example, impeded reform in the once exemplary abbey of Cluny. However, under Louis XIII (1601–43), the French crown, along with pious noble houses, and the royal family in the persons of the queen-mother Marie de Medici (1573–1642) and the queen, Anne of Austria (1601–66) sponsored the restoration of conventual life. Though the first minister, Cardinal Richelieu (1585–1642), was not in full sympathy with the reform movement, as its titular abbot – a position that was itself an abuse in Tridentine terms – he had Cluny reformed. Under royal and noble patronage, Paris became a city of religious houses, forty new establishments of the older order being set up there in the period 1600 to 1640: by the time of the Revolution there were 2,858 nuns in the French capital. Of the older orders, the Minims, an austere group dating from the fifteenth century, carried forward the momentum of the late medieval Observant movement into Catholic life in Bourbon France, where they established 150 houses in ten provinces of their order. Famed for their scholarship, their health care and their teaching of the poor, the Minims largely avoided the aristocratically controlled spoils system that continued to mar the French ecclesiastical establishment, though their Third Order won over some pious and highly placed lay people, as well as the devotional writer and bishop of Geneva, François de Sales, and Cardinal Pierre de

Bérulle who also introduced the austere Discalced Carmelites from Spain into France. Bérulle's best-known association with the religious life came in the form of his foundation of the French Congregation of the Oratory, partly on Neri's model, as a mobile and adaptable corps, free of vows and with no predetermined field of action. By 1661 the Oratorians had opened seventy-one houses in France and, effective as they were, for example in missionary work around Paris, the Oratorians came to take part in some of the discord that came to haunt the French Church even in its post-Reformation golden age, in the seventeenth century, for they were associated with the Jansenist theology condemned by Rome (see p. 165–6). A good example of the strides made in the organisation of female religious life in seventeenth-century France, and also of the restrictions placed upon it, is that of the Visitandines, founded by Jeanne-Françoise Frémyot de Chantal (1572–1641), and François de Sales in 1610, originally as a combined contemplative and activist order, though forced to become cloistered. They taught girls and, in the person of the visionary Marguerite Marie Alacoque (1647–90) created one of the most popular devotions of the post-Reformation Church, that of the Sacred Heart of Jesus.[18]

As far as the fuller Catholicisation or re-Catholicisation of the French masses was concerned, the parish and the diocese were the foci of effort, and we shall examine the creation of diocesan seminaries as the indispensable teaching colleges for those countless parish priests whose task it would be to school French people in Tridentine Catholicism. Especially in the early period of the Catholic Reformation, though, some dioceses were treated primarily as if they were mission territory for the religious orders. Cambrai, then lying in the Habsburg Netherlands, underwent an initial period of attempted Catholic reform as early as 1554, when it was targeted by Jesuits, and subsequently, upgraded to an archbishopric in Philip II's 1559 rationalisation of the Netherlands' ecclesiastical structure, it became a laboratory of Tridentine reform under Archbishop François van der Burch (in office, 1615–44), 'one of the great figures of the Catholic Reformation in the Low Countries'. After nine years in his post, the archbishop had consecrated fifty-two churches and 2,849 altars. In four years he gave Holy Communion to about 220,000 people and on some days administered Confirmation for up to ten hours without a break. This Belgian Borromeo also conducted enquiries into priests' ownership of essential texts – the decrees of the Council and of provincial synods, along with catechisms and so on. In 1631 van der Burch issued statutes of special concern to the Catholic lives of the laity, concerning engagements, marriages, the observance of Sundays and feast-days and the orthodoxy of lay faith. The suppression of witchcraft was undertaken, Sunday schools were established, confraternities set up, devotions and pilgrimages flourished, church building continued, alongside artistic innovation and restoration.[19]

The Jesuits also renewed their apostolate in Cambrai from 1595 and 'impressed the Catholic Reformation on this diocese...with an indelible seal', while the Capuchins enjoyed great popular esteem and between 1592 and 1616 opened seven houses in the archdiocese, did heroic work during epidemics, and promoted the devotion of *Quarant' Ore* to great effect. It was the Jesuits, though, who reported in 1664, with the most shining enthusiasm, on the situation in Cambrai following van der Burch's archiepiscopate, and their own renewed apostolate in the years since 1660, when two Fathers from Namur had set up the Mission of St Francis Xavier to conduct evangelisation in the dioceses of Cambrai, Tournai and Arras:

> Four thousand general Confessions made to the two Fathers, not counting those heard by parish priests; 20,000 or more Holy Communions carefully prepared for; solemn First Communions for children in groups set up every-where; petitionary processions; more than 500 young people of both sexes, most of them married, asking forgiveness from their parents; more than 800 families reconciled; peace restored in 250 homes, invalid marriages dissolved or regularised; all lawsuits under way given up on the same day in one partic-ular town; confraternities set up for the observance of the Christian life.[20]

Yet despite all the efforts of van der Burch, the Capuchins and the Jesuits, when in 1696–7, following the absorption of the archdiocese into France as a result of Louis XIV's conquest, Archbishop François de Salignac de la Mothe-Fénelon (1651–1715) took over, he had, apparently, to start from scratch, for a century and more of haphazard and discontinuous efforts (grossly interrupted by war) had left a poor state of affairs:

> The clergy are sunk in barbarous ignorance; no study is undertaken in the monasteries any more than among the parish clergy and there is no appetite for learning; neither the religious orders nor the parish priests give any proper example of orderly lives, some are given over to drinking to excess, and the people are poorly instructed as a result of the lack of care and ability on the part of those who are responsible for their spiritual welfare.

Some system of permanence and succession was identified as the prerequisite of a stabilised Catholic Reformation, and to French churchmen by that point in time the key to such a regularised system was the establishment of seminaries, which had not happened in Cambrai: one established at Douai in the area had only a brief spell of success and was burned down in 1637.[21]

So in Cambrai Fénelon introduced what we might term his 'French solution', along the lines on which in France seminaries produced priests 'more sober, more upright, providing a better example'. Set up in Cambrai, seminaries laid 'the foundation of a genuine improvement in the secular clergy'. The seminary, it seems, was the key to a Catholic Reformation that was anything more than ephemeral.[22]

Lebrun argues that in France for a century beginning around 1660 to 1670 the Catholic Reformation took a new and more secure direction – almost, we might say, a second Catholic Reformation. Around that point in time in the second half of the seventeenth century, the towering originators of the first phase of the French Catholic renewal, such as the founder of the Lazarists (designed to train 'an exemplary clergy'), Vincent de Paul, were passing from the scene. 'Now an age of plans was giving way to a period of implementation, the era of mysticism was being superseded by the systematic instruction of souls.' If we take the establishment of the seminaries as a bench-mark for the introduction of the 'instruction', legislation and spirit of Trent, we would see, according to Lebrun, only a halting progress before the middle of the seventeenth century.[23]

Apart from early establishments – in Reims in the first decade of the Wars of Religion, and before the end of the sixteenth century in Pont-à-Mousson in 1579, Avignon in 1586 and Toulouse in 1590 followed by seminaries established in the early seventeenth century in Metz in 1608, Rouen in 1612, Mâcon in 1617, Lyons in 1618, Langres in 1619 and in Nantes in 1626 – the great wave of French seminary foundation tended to come around and after the mid-seventeenth century point. In the Nantes diocese in 1649 Bishop Gabriel de Beauvau negotiated with Jean-Jacques Olier (1608–57), founder of the exemplary Saint-Sulpice seminary in 1641, to introduce a residential college for future priests to train over two or three years in a curriculum made up of spiritual retreats, instruction in liturgy and Gregorian chant, pastoral theology, catechesis, and moral cases of conscience. Nantes' Bishop René Lévesque's seminary scheme followed from 1672. If the seminary was the sheet-anchor of a Catholic Reformation that was dependent, not on spasmodic missions or on outstanding individuals but on a reasonably well-guaranteed succession of qualified and dedicated parish priests, then its arrival in France came late in the period of our topic. Even so, from around that point in time we should expect to see a transformation of the priesthood and, presumably, a measurable impact on the laity, in a stabilisation of the French Catholic Reformation as a consequence of the implementation of Trent's seminary programme.[24]

In the twelve dioceses of the province of Tours, seminaries were established from the 1640s (five), the 1650s (one), the 1660s (three), the 1670s (one) and the 1680s (one). The years 1680–1710 were crucial in establishing seminaries in French dioceses. By around 1760 there were more than 153 of them, sixty run by the Lazarists, thirty-two by the Jesuits, and about twenty by the élite Saint-Sulpiciens. The numerical increase was encouraged by the assumption of responsibility in the 1690s by the leadership of Church and state for encouraging the creation of these vital institutions. In 1696 the new archbishop of Paris, Antoine de Noailles (in office 1695–1729), issued a decree in favour of preparation for holy orders requiring a stay in one of the five seminaries specified for the archdiocese of nine months to prepare for the sub-diaconate, three months in advance of the diaconate and three months leading up to priests' orders. Then, in 1698, Louis XIV commanded 'all the archbishops and bishops of our kingdom immediately to establish seminaries in those dioceses where there are none'. Increasingly, the running of the seminaries was being entrusted to the specialist orders, for example the Lazarists, to run them to a high and uniform standard, emphasising a training, drawn up according to a set formula, that was focused intensively on equipping young men for parochial priestly careers.

In 1728 the bishop of Nantes handed over to the Company of Saints-Sulpice both the diocesan seminary and the training centre that Lévesque had set: the Saint-Sulpiciens increasingly shaped the ruling élite of the Bourbon Catholic Church, providing 200 bishops in the eighteenth century. The contracting-out of the diocesan seminaries to the specialist orders provides an apt instance of co-operation between bishops and the orders in the French Catholic Reformation. Bishops seem to have expected good results from the seminaries run by the orders and their emphasis was on the development of character and personality, which, in the case of the alumni of the Saint-Sulpiciens, has been described by Delumeau as combining 'refinement, a spirit of recollection, austerity of manner and a high degree of learning, both sacred and profane'. Etienne de Champflour, bishop of La Rochelle, who in 1694 entrusted his diocesan seminary to the care of the Jesuits, emphasised the moral formation of character, the inculcation of spirituality and the necessity for compulsory universal basic training of candidates for the priesthood:

> All those who aim at priests' orders spend at least eighteen full months so as to put themselves in a position to receive them, becoming suffused with a priestly spirit, receiving adequate instruction in moral and dogmatic theology and adapting themselves to the demands of the sacred ministry and the guidance of souls....They make every effort to spend their period of study in earnest interior recollection, in ardent attention to spiritual exercises, entire submission and docility towards superiors and administrators...and perfect mildness and charity towards their fellow-students.

On the disciplinary side, to prevent dissipation the seminarians were forbidden, on pain of expulsion, from entering each others' rooms or from dining in town.[25]

What was the likely impact of the seminaries' graduates, as parish priests, on the lives of French parishioners? Miller has conducted a thorough study of the eighteenth-century French seminary course, whose 'principal thrust', he writes:

> was to promote the interiorization of the 'priesthood', to affect the cleric's beliefs and practices, in a way that could bring him to more and more identity with the sacrifice of the suffering Savior, Jesus Christ. This process of 'spirituality', it was believed, required that the young clerics be removed from contact with the world as much as possible in preparation for holy orders.

The correlate of these priests' insulation from lay society was their exposure to clerical companionship, even from an early age. While still a boy, Jean de la Noë-Mesnard, who was to run the Nantes diocesan seminary from 1686, 'sought', his biographer recalled, 'the company of those priests who celebrated Mass with the most fervour. From that point on, God gave him a superb discernment in identifying good priests'. The seminarians were to be immersed without interruption in a proto-priestly atmosphere and there were opportunities for apprentice priesthood even within the seminary period: the original Paris seminary of Saint-Sulpice was responsible for the parish in which it was situated and so provided pre-ordination experience in pastoral care. In 1749 Archbishop de Restignac of Tours introduced a system of oversight by parish priests of seminary students resident, presumably on vacation, in their parishes, where, when called upon, they were to assist the *curés* in the discharge of their duties and keep away from taverns and plays. A 'uniform clerical culture' and priestly *esprit de corps* were being systematically created, 'exemplifying morality and spirituality…but also more closely controlled by the church's hierarchy'. (In the eighteenth century the closeness of the controls may have been strengthened by fear of alien influences from Enlightenment thought.)

Apart from contemplative habits, fostered by pious conferences, Scripture readings and recitations from devotional books, the emphasis in character training was on the development of men of Christlike meekness and mildness, modesty and humility, a pattern, though, transmuted through the classical Stoic values of self-restraint upheld in Bourbon France to produce Lebrun's 'new type of priest' – quiet, reserved, austere, studious, formally polite – emerging from the seminaries more and more from around 1700. They were patterned on Vincent de Paul, himself a realisation of the Tridentine priestly ideal and canonised in 1737. The ideal type was described in works such as *Le bon prêtre* (*The Good Priest*) (1683) by the Breton Jesuit missioner Vincent Huby as 'chaste, temperate, restrained in his behaviour', a man of the study whose library, the bishop of Nîmes prescribed in 1670, should contain at the very least the Bible, the Catechism of Trent, *The Imitation of Christ*, as well as saints' lives, and synodical statutes.[26]

If, once ordained, the model parish priest drank wine, he did so alone, or in company with confrères and certainly not, glass in hand, playing dice in the tavern. If he was forbidden to hunt, that may have been less to avoid his shedding of blood than to keep him away from the lavish eating and drinking and the easy rustic familiarity of those occasions. Above all, the new priest formed by the seminary, dressed in cassock and with short hair, was 'a man of exemplary piety and a pastor meticulously attentive to the duties of his calling'. He said Mass, without special fees, on Sundays, feast-days and, ideally, weekdays, preached, administered the Sacraments (especially Baptism, Penance, and the Last Rites) and provided material as well as spiritual assistance to the poor, the deprived and the sick. He engaged in meditative prayer for at least half an hour a day, along with the recital of his breviary, and made his Confession to a colleague twice a month. He was resident in his parish and had to seek permission – and supply a replacement – for an absence of more than a couple of weeks. He tended to remain in post for long years – more than twenty in the case of nearly half of *curés* serving in the diocese of Le Mans in the eighteenth century. Such was the ideal profile of France's seminary-trained model parish priesthood of the eighteenth century. And it is possible that the process of converting the priesthood

into an order apart, based on the concentrated professional training of the *curés* –
what Delumeau calls 'cutting the priest off from secular life', a process underlined by the steady rise in clerical incomes by the late seventeenth century –
actually *weakened* their impact on large numbers of French people, above all in
the countryside, in the long run and into the eighteenth century. Typically well-
paid, highly trained, celibate professionals of urban background and distanced
by education, culture and lifestyle from most of their parishioners, seminarian
curés were likely to characterise their relations with parishioners in terms of what
Po-Chia calls 'respectful and distrustful distance…and disdain'. The priests' anti-
social seminary education predisposed them to a solitary ethos that conflicted
with French rural communalism. *Curés'* attacks on popular festivals, on local
associations and recreations and their campaigns to close taverns alienated them
from many parishioners. Their real social and didactic impact on wider French
society, and in particular on male and youth cultures, especially in the countryside, suffered accordingly. It is true that Catholic Reformation values found a
response among rural and urban *dévots* and *dévotes* and that many women
responded favourably not just to the devotional life of the Catholic renewal but
also to opportunities for communal action sponsored by the *curés* and to the
values of family responsibility that the parish priests sponsored. Even so, the
planned production of seminary-educated priests as standardised human types,
intended as an effective means of missionising the French countryside for the
Catholic restoration, yet often remote and alien in their attitudes and actions,
proved counter-productive in wide areas of French life.[27]

The question of the influence of the *curés* is related to the even wider one of
the Catholicisation of the French between the sixteenth and eighteenth
centuries. Were the French, and in what sense, say in 1760, and specifically as a
consequence of the labours of the seminarian priesthood, a more Catholic
people than they had been two centuries before, when the Council of Trent ratified the initiation of the momentum of the process we know as the Catholic
Reformation? Had an ancestral syncretism of magical belief and performance
with Christian faith and conduct been replaced by orthodox Catholic doctrine
and practice? Had superstition been eradicated from the minds and behaviour of
the mass of French people by the middle of the eighteenth century and as a
result of a Catholic reform drive?

Certainly the opportunities for people to have access to the rites of the
Catholic Church were, especially in the towns, spectacularly plentiful in Bourbon
France. Durand speaks of an unbroken sequence of religious ceremonies in
seventeenth-century Nantes, a provision demanded by the laity and made available by the profusion of clergy. In 1638 the Nantes church of St Nicholas
provided a High Mass every day of the week, processions and an evening
service. The great feasts, such as the Discovery of the Cross, saw further sung
Masses bestowed by merchants; there were Masses for the deceased and large
numbers of celebrations in chantry chapels. In town and country, the Mass was
indeed at the centre of the cycle of practice. The main parish Mass of Sunday,
ideally sung and generally celebrated at 9 or 10 am (possibly preceded by a dawn

Mass for servants and others) was to be attended by the laity at their own parish church as a matter of religious obligation and, bringing communities together, was something of an occasion to which, especially in dispersed parishes, people converged dressed in Sunday best. There were opportunities for purchases before and after the service, for the exchange of news and gossip and for visits to the tavern (which was supposed to be closed during Mass). If we may assume a widespread high communal attendance at parish Mass, a statistically assessable index of practice, reception of the Sacraments of Penance and Holy Communion at Easter or thereabouts, the ultimate test of Catholic observance, was carefully counted. In the diocese of La Rochelle in 1648 and the rural archdeaconry of Paris in 1672 it was, in effect, total.[28]

If formal attendance at Mass and the Sacraments is to some extent quantifiable – and may indicate, at least in selected regions in Bourbon France, high or even virtually all-inclusive levels of conformity – reconstruction of the quality of religious observance and assessment of the popular understanding of the faith and levels of piety are inherently more elusive. To a large extent, access to the higher reaches of Catholic piety in early modern France was related to literacy and education and thus to social class. The Jesuit preacher, Louis Bourdaloue (1632–1704), drew a distinction in religious observance, not between social classes, but between 'two sorts of persons: the Christians of the present age who walk in the ways of religion, and those who aspire towards, and who indeed elevate themselves to the sublimer routes of perfection'. And it was Bourdaloue (whose lengthy sermons, composed in exquisite *grand-siècle* French, contained learned allusions to the Fathers) who distinguished between formal reception of the Sacraments, and 'receiving them in a holy way, which means that we must receive them with a real conversion of heart'. Yet Bourdaloue's targeted audience was an élite of *dévotes* and *dévots* possessing an intensity of piety and a range of educational and social advantage similar to the audiences of Bishop Jacques-Bénigne Bossuet (1627–1704) whose meditative *élévations* spoke with the abstruse language of the 'heart' that Bourdaloue used, with an additional ecstatic flavour and a hint of erotic metaphor:

> O Jesus, You are He Who must come.
> O Jesus, You come into
> our hearts and You make Your presence felt there by
> an unknowable gentleness, tenderness and power…
> My heart says, *It is so*, amen.

Bossuet was a product of a great French mystical movement of the seventeenth century associated with the founder of the French Oratory, Cardinal Pierre de Bérulle. Himself from the heart of the French establishment and grandson of a chancellor of France, Bérulle emerged in an aristocratic ambience in the Paris salon of Mme Acarie (1566–1618), where guests included the flower of the devout nobility – the Princesse de Longueville, the Marquise de Meignelay and the Marquise de Bréauté. In the provinces, too, piety tended to be associated with rank and education, in Nantes, for example, where the Gondi family, lords of Retz, gave shelter to the young Vincent de Paul and where the wife of Charles de Gondi, Antoinette d'Orléans-Longueville, was a beacon of religious inspiration. Amongst Nantes' mercantile and bourgeois urban elite, the Company (or Confraternity) of the Blessed Sacrament (1629) was favoured and François de Sales's *Introduction à la vie dévote ('An Introduction to a Life of Piety')* (1609) was read. It was the task of de Sales, wrote Cognet, to 'transform monastic devotion into popular devotion' and Daniel-Rops agrees that 'he makes [mysticism] accessible to all, every one of us can assimilate it'. However, the terms 'popular', 'to all' and 'every one', when applied to de Sales's disciples, may need further examination.[29]

De Sales concentrated much of his writing on the Blessed Sacrament and the Eucharist, an intense cult in Bourbon France, focusing abstract contemplation on a visible object, and it is true that teaching of the meaning of the Blessed Sacrament, spread by the confraternity of that name, penetrated relatively deep into seventeenth- and eighteenth-century French society. The Jesuit-educated Voltaire (1694–1778) expressed devotion to it with considerable skill:

> Christ, living victim of our sins
> And living food of His beloved chosen ones,
> Comes down to the altars before their bewildered eyes
> And reveals Himself God, under the form of a bread that is bread no more.

The problem of a devotion to the Eucharist or an understanding of the Mass spread by education and literacy, though, is that as late as the second half of the 1780s, forty-seven per cent of French men were illiterate, while in a group of parishes in the area of La Rochelle at the end of the *ancien régime* twenty per cent of people could not sign their names. Preaching ought to have supplied an oral bridgehead between Catholic thought and popular culture, though when seminary-trained clerical aristocrats tried to talk to peasants the results might be as ludicrous as in the following anecdote featuring the preaching of Cardinal Paul d'Albert de Luynes (1703–88), in the Fontainebleau of Marie Antoinette (1755–93), the cardinal being under the invincible impression that he was, as usual, called upon to rebuke the fashionable vices of courtiers:

> Everything he had prepared had been composed in order to recall high society to the unassuming ways of real Christians. Some hundred of peasants, sitting on their clogs, surrounded by the baskets they had used to carry their vegetables or fruit to market, listened to His Eminence without understanding a single word he addressed to them....[But he was heard] to cry out, in the vehemence of the perfect pastor, 'My dear brethren, why do you bring this luxury with you into the very entrance to the sanctuary? Why do these velvet cushions, these laced and fringed handbags, lie in front of your entry into the Lord's house?

Bourbon France possessed a largely literary and literate Catholic religious culture and, as Roche writes, 'popular culture in Paris was crushed beneath the weight of devotional literature', with titles heavily concerned with the religious demarcation of time – *Journée Chrétienne, Année Chrétienne, Semaine Sainte, Heures. (The Christian Day, The Christian Year, Holy Week, Book of Hours)*. By the eighteenth century Paris had experienced 'a century and a half of literacy dictated by the Counter-Reformation' – in which, in the first four decades of the eighteenth century, one third of published titles in France were on religious subjects. This, though was in an overwhelmingly illiterate society, in which, as late as the 1780s, three-quarters of women could not read. However, the availability of religious literature confronted, on the lower social levels and amongst women, the levels of illiteracy already discussed. The problem of the closed text so created was exacerbated by the continuing high volume of religious works in Latin, taking them out of the reach of those who were literate in the vernacular only, even a liturgical work with a French title, *L'Office de la Semaine saincte (The Divine Worship of Holy Week)* (1627), being entirely in that language. The bilingual *Missal de Paris, latin et français (The Paris Missal, in Latin and French)* (1701) offering vital guidance on the laity's closer involvement with the priest's celebration of the Mass, was, literally, a closed book to all those illiterates.[30]

Insofar, then, as early modern France had a Catholic culture of literacy, one largely driven by élite and middle-class tastes and aptitudes, what success was obtained in conveying the meaning of doctrines which were often recondite to illiterate villagers and townspeople? Sermons and oral catechesis were of course indispensable tools and the rituals of the Church were themselves didactic: Roche writes, 'pictures, singing and music' aided the 'acculturising efforts of the Church'. Pictures were especially important in putting across the Church's message. Catholicism had long been associated with a pictorial religious culture and in a typical denominationally divided urban community in seventeenth-century France, Catholics were sharply distinguished from Huguenots by the former's far greater propensity to own religious paintings. These taught, or reinforced, the Church's doctrines, for example the Sacrament of Penance conveyed through depiction of the penitent Mary Magdalene. However, not only did the ownership of such art works presuppose modest to high levels of, typically bourgeois, affluence, but the full understanding of iconographic representations rested on an educated, in fact a literate, apprehension of Catholicism. We come back, then, to the conquest of illiteracy as a challenge to the Catholic Church's mission in Bourbon France.[31]

Though they were less successful than the Italian Schools of Christian Doctrine, France before 1680 had ventures in elementary education. The *maîtres écrivains* (writing masters) set up in Paris in 1570 spread out to other cities and provided a basic schooling with some Latin. In 1684 a Saint-Sulpice-trained canon of Reims, Jean-Baptiste de la Salle (1651–1719) gave up his comfortable ecclesiastical position and assembled a new institute, the Brothers of the Christian Schools, lay brothers (not priests) with a particular brief of free teaching for the poor, as set out in the papal bull of approval praising de la Salle's 'pity at the sight of the innumerable scandals that spring from ignorance, particularly among those...crushed down by want, or busy with manual labour to gain a livelihood'. From his take-over of a free school in Paris in 1688, his establishment of a teacher-training college in Reims in 1685 and of a Sunday school in Paris in 1699, de la Salle's Institute expanded through France, so that by the time of the Revolution they had 116 establishments and in Paris formed an essential component in the nearly 500 elementary schools linked to the Church operating in Paris alone.[32]

Even so, the Church's mission of teaching doctrine through the inculcation of literacy encountered limits, and, indeed, reverses, to its effectiveness, in part determined by its unwitting provision of reading skills that made it possible to master subversive texts which undermined its own message – the 'popular de-christianising tendency' whose results were evident in France in the Revolution. In fact, well before 1789 the erosion of religious conformity in areas such as Marseilles was accompanying the rise of literacy. However, leaving aside such unsought consequences of its teaching campaign, the Church was still largely failing to school the very poor, especially the rural poor, a major element of Bourbon France's population. Even within the Brothers of the Christian Schools' mission there was a detectable pull away from a poor to a bourgeois apostolate, as the middle classes found the Brothers' practical, vernacular-based curriculum more useful to their requirements than was the high classicism of traditional (and Jesuit) French Catholic teaching. The Institute's boarding schools were particularly attractive to that class, and it seems significant that, as they expanded, the Brothers set up stations in places such as Bordeaux and Toulon, characterised by bourgeois affluence. However, even at the end of the *ancien régime,* much of France still had an underclass of illiterates, and Paris 'an illiterate wage-earning society'. It is revealing of the state of plebeian education in France as a whole that a high proportion of Parisian non-literates were manual low-wage-earners and migrants from the more distant provinces: 50 per cent of Auvergnat immigrant labourers could not read or write. It was in those circumstances that the missions to the French countryside conducted by the religious orders in the eighteenth century must be considered still well adapted to the aptitudes of illiterates. They presented, not a private, contemplative, literate, Salesian, devotional and intellectual, or even entirely Tridentine, Catholicism, but one that remained largely materialist, communal, curative and demonstrative. The faith propagated by the orders, above all the Jesuits, on their missions to the largely unschooled countryside, was visual and spectacular and the teaching was sometimes less an attempt to educate the 'ignorant, superstitious peasantry' into the 'serious reformed Catholicism of the post-Tridentine church' (Pearl) than a multi-layered adaptation to peasant culture as it was, and in its still largely pre-literate state. In Stenay in France in 1759 a Jesuit missionary who seemed to resemble a wandering actor, got the local girls to chant Jesuit hymns and dressed a statue of the Virgin as a lady of fashion, illuminated, in fairground style, with candles. In the Loire Valley, in the previous year, the Jesuits reportedly adopted techniques of display thought to be more suitable to their Paraguayan mission. In Italy, it was reported from France in the same year as the Loire incident, a Jesuit handed out papers of prayers 'of the [Immaculate] Conception, which he gets people to eat in order to be cured': hopeful peasants also tried them on their non-laying chickens. Techniques of adapting religious teaching to peasant culture, devised in the early Catholic Reformation or even in the late medieval missions of the Church to the countryside, still seemed appropriate, and were employed, in the France of the Enlightenment. What is additionally significant, though, is that the alleged excesses of a long-term campaign to bring the gospel into *la France profonde* were reported in the satirical French Jansenist voice of opposition to the Jesuits, the *Nouvelles Ecclésiastiques*, as graphic instances of the meretricious Jesuit approach.[33]

By the time of the bicentenary of the conclusion of Trent, the Jansensist issue had indeed chronically divided the French Catholic Church, whose quarrels sapped its public function, for it spoke with too many conflicting voices, discords which in fact arose out of the tense concords of the Tridentine doctrinal synthesis. In particular, the Council of Trent had declared 'that actual justification...takes its origin from a predisposing grace of God through Jesus Christ...with no existing merits on [the] side [of the justified]'. The Council added, though, that 'those justified [through faith]...are...renewed...by putting to death what is earthly in themselves and yielding themselves as instruments of righteousness for sanctification by observance of the commandments'. Loyola had already shored up an appreciation of the salvific role of good works chosen in the (relative) freedom of the will by emphasising in the *Spiritual Exercises* that 'one must not insist too much on the all-powerful efficacy of grace', and in *Concordia Liberi Arbitrii cum Gratiae Donis* (*The Harmony of Free Will and the Gifts of Grace*) (1588) the Jesuit Luis Molina expanded on that theme. As missionaries, the Jesuits were naturally inclined to play up the role in human salvation of choice, repentance and good works. An alternative voice, though, represented an amplification of Trent's appreciation of the role of grace and justification by faith, as evident in Molina's day in the teachings of the professor of the University of Leuven, Michel de Bay (or Baius, 1513–89). Another Leuven professor, from 1635 Bishop of Ypres, Cornelius Jansen (1585–1638), the results of whose study of the thought of St Augustine were published as *Augustinus* in 1640, emphasised the Augustinian themes of the weakness of the human will to choose good, and the irresistible power of God's 'efficacious' grace poured out on those selected for its reception. With its Augustinian credentials, Jansen's theology could not fail to win over some of the best minds and most ardent spirits in the French Catholic Church, such as Antoine Arnauld (1612–94) and his sister, the abbess of the convent of Port Royal, Marie-Angélique Arnaud (1591–1661). 'Jansenism' became a source of puritan moral renewal in the Church in France and elsewhere, such as the Netherlands, and it pervaded the French Congregation of the Oratory. In the Abbé de St Cyran (1581–1643) Jansenism took on the tone of moral perfectionism in approaching Holy Communion worthily, while in Arnauld's *De la fréquente Communion* ('On Receiving Holy Communion Often' (1643) intense discipline was applied to penitential preparation for Communion.

Blaise Pascal (1623–62) in his *Lettres provinciales* (1656–7) was the brilliant, sardonic anti-Jesuit pamphleteer of the movement.[34]

For all its moral and disciplinary value, Jansenism seemed to its opponents to have its roots in the version of Augustinian theology that had fed the Protestant Reformation – denial of free will, acceptance of predestination, exclusive emphasis on grace: the minister Cardinal Jules Mazarin called it 'reheated Calvinism'. Almost from the time of the publication of *Augustinus*, condemnations flowed from Rome, culminating in Clement XI's (1700–21) bull *Unigenitus* (1713) condemning the work, *Réflexions morales sur le Nouveau Testament* (*Moral Reflections on the New Testament*) (1687–94), of the Jansenist Oratorian Pasquier Quesnel (1634–1719). Nevertheless, partly because of Jansenism's moralising qualities, partly because in many respects it was undeniably Catholic, and partly because the defence of Jansenism went along with maintenance of the autonomy of the Gallican Church, the movement retained great force in Bourbon France and fought back against its Jesuit-led foes. The Fathers were deemed by Pascal and the Jansenist movement to have too easy-going an approach to the conditions of absolution in the Sacrament of Penance, undermining episcopal and parochial discipline, so that the issue of bishops' and parish priests' rights was also caught up in the Jansenist question. The ferocious effectiveness of the Jansenist anti-Jesuit counter-offensive is evident in the 'peevish and intelligent' (Delumeau) *Nouvelles Ecclésiastiques* (1728–1803) but the ecclesiastical civil war between Jansenist and Jesuit partisans also exposed a crippling divisiveness in French Catholicism, which seems eventually to have led to, or encouraged, lay contempt, above all for the Jesuits: in 1758 the *Nouvelles Ecclésiastiques* reported that in Normandy Jesuit missionaries were mocked as foreigners, and there are further signs that the mission to the countryside was breaking down under a weight of lay rejection and anti-clericalism. Arguably, this repudiation was induced by ecclesiastical divisions and encouraged by the continuing Jansenist critique of a Church allegedly dominated by Jesuits, their preaching depicted as meretricious and their Confessional practices ridiculed as a soft option for guilty penitents. Anti-Jesuit criticism certainly received satisfaction in the royal suppression of the Jesuits in France in 1761–4, and a major weapon in the 'mission to the countryside' (as well as a key contribution to secondary and tertiary education) was thereby lost, two centuries after the Society of Jesus had introduced its always controversial evangelism to France.[35]

If the French Church of the late *ancien régime* failed to sing from an agreed sheet of plain chant, a further discordancy arose between traditional world-views and intellectual enlightenment, as some *curés* were being distanced, by their adoption of the rationalist influences rising in eighteenth-century France, from their parishioners' less scientific mindsets. One *curé*, for example, explained the apparent efficacy of his congregants' practice of ringing church bells to dispel storms in terms of the effect of the campanology on ambient air pressure: he was interested in a scientific rationalisation, they wanted a miracle. A popular magicalist attitude long prevailed in both pre- and post-Revolutionary France. In the district of Ganges, north of Montpellier, decades of intense Protestantisation undertaken since the establishment of a Reformed Church in 1560 and including preaching by the *doyen* of European Calvinism following the death of Calvin, Thédore de Bèze (or Beza, 1509–1605), had not eradicated the ancient practices of folk magic. Such techniques were controlled by women, used for curing children and included a strong whiff of animism.[36]

After the end of the sixteenth-century Wars of Religion, with the Edict of Nantes in 1598, the French Catholic Church addressed itself more directly to the Counter-Reformation agenda of the eradication of Protestantism in the kingdom, giving less attention to the elimination of magic from popular mentalities and practice. France became the largest laboratory in early modern Europe for the politically supported replacement by Catholicism of the Protestantism that had been implanted in the sixteenth century. In areas of Valois France, such as Normandy, the Reformation was indeed firmly established. In the south-east of the country, the diocese of Grenoble was saturated with Calvinism and its region, Dauphiné, remained in Huguenot hands until the 1620s. In the south-west, in Guyenne, even before the outbreak of the Wars of Religion, Calvinism reached far down the social scale, ignited iconoclasm and inspired peasant revolt. Its region, Languedoc, had a deeply implanted peasant Calvinism, while amongst provincial cities Lyons provides one example of Protestantism which reached across much of the social scale and was, again, linked with social protest. The southern city of Nîmes had a 75 per cent allegiance to Protestantism and was closely associated with trade.[37]

The techniques adopted to reverse such situations and re-Catholicise France ranged from persuasion and inducements (especially through the *caisses de conversion*, or 'conversion funds') to coercion of varying levels of brutality. The religious orders, including the Minims, the Jesuits and the Recollects, were to the fore in the work of persuasion, though in Nîmes the fact that the orders undertook evangelisation may have taken some of the onus away from a diocesan reinvigoration, and no seminary was introduced until 1667. The link between French Calvinism and opposition to the crown in the Wars of Religion made re-Catholicisation a matter of state, especially after the Huguenot revolt which broke out in 1627 and ended in the Peace of Alais in 1629, imposed by Richelieu and effectively taking away the political guarantees that the Huguenots enjoyed under the Edict of Nantes. The heavily Protestant town of La Rochelle, stronghold of the Huguenot resistance in 1627–8, provides instances of techniques of extremely heavy pressure on individuals and families to turn Catholic: poor relief was made a Catholic parochial responsibility; the charity hospitals were put in the care of the religious orders; the police clamped down on lapses into Protestantism in marriages and the baptism of children; retailing was confessionalised, banning meat sales in Lent and all catering during Mass times; guild membership required Catholic profession; neighbourhoods were secured for public Catholic worship by ordering all householders to clean the streets and decorate their houses in advance of processions of the Blessed Sacrament; and the police court, 'under Catholic control hammered away at la Rochelle's old reformed neighbourhoods, intending to humiliate surviving Protestant notables, to diminish the socio-economic resources of the Calvinist community and to thin the ranks of heretics'. In Guyenne, Huguenot education was suppressed, non-Catholics were barred from public service, ministers were banished, places of Protestant worship destroyed and the daughters of Calvinist families handed over to the Poor Clares to be brought up. The use of billeted soldiers to intimidate families to convert in the notorious *dragonnades* from 1681 culminated in 1685 in the Revocation of the Edict of Nantes, at which point, officially, French Protestantism was no more.[38]

Yet it is hard to know how effective these methods were in inducing real changes of heart among the enforced *nouveaux covertis*, the 'new converts'. In Nîmes, Protestants were victimised after the 1620s and more systematically after 1661, but were still attracting converts until 1680. The dioceses of Nîmes, Alès and Uzès had as many Protestants in 1800 as in 1600. It is indeed possible that enforced Catholicisation damaged the prospects for the Church, or even for Christianity, in Protestantism's French heartlands. In districts of eighteenth-century Provence, the region where there were townships which had been entirely Protestant in the mid-seventeenth century, a widespread aversion to Catholic funereal rites was explained by a reluctance to participate in 'superstition' – an indication, perhaps, that the legacy of deposed Calvinism was popular rationalism. Thus in the midst of its greatest apparent triumph – the extensive destruction of Protestantism in France – the French Counter-Reformation encountered real failure on a wide front in the eighteenth century: inability to eradicate educational barriers to a popular Tridentine Catholicisation ironically lay alongside disparagement of belief as a result of education largely at the hands of the Church; scepticism and irreligion as a result of the French Catholic Church's civil war over Jansenism; and enforced Catholicisation of Protestants resulting in de-Christianisation.[39]

If France under Louis XIV emerged as an intolerant Catholic kingdom with a substantial Calvinist or irreconcilable minority, the United Provinces of the Dutch Republic in the North Netherlands formed a partly tolerant Calvinist-led republic with a significant Catholic element, perhaps settling down at one-third of the total. Study of the situation of that community will enable us to trace some of the realities of post-Reformation Catholic life in Protestant lands in early modern Europe. The religious complexion of the Dutch Republic was established on the basis of tolerance in Clause XIII of the state's founding constitution, the 1579 Union of Utrecht, a provision which arose from a failure to agree on a single religious identity for the seven provinces that broke away from Spanish and Catholic overlordship and which consequently left the individual province and, by extension, each individual, the right to decide on religious preferences. However, Calvinism provided indispensable moral inspiration for the Dutch Revolt, the spearhead of the anti-Spanish revolt in the northern Netherlands in 1572 were the passionately anti-Catholic Sea Beggars and, inevitably, in the course of the struggle of the United Provinces for national survival until 1648, as in England, Catholicism became identified with treason and was subject to persecution: even private worship in teaching was subject to fines, under a state proclamation of 1581. Between the poles of toleration and repression, Dutch Catholicism became established as Europe's most important Romanist minority within a Protestant state.[40]

Catholicism in the late medieval Netherlands throve, fostering lay piety though the Brethren of the Common Life. The tradition of lay, and specifically female, piety, was a mainstay in the survival of north Netherlands Catholicism. So well rooted was the Catholic faith in Holland's exceptionally urbanised civilisation that Amsterdam between 1538 and 1578 had a Catholic-led city government, prepared to enforce the Habsburg Placards against heresy, maintaining the Catholic faith through control of the parishes under the municipal church-warden system, and ensuring the appointment of Catholic preachers. However, because in the 1520s and 1530s Church reform in Amsterdam had implied Protestantism, the strongly pro-Catholic government of the leading Dutch city in the middle decades of the century tended to maintain static and repressive religious conservatism rather than to introduce Tridentine innovation. Yet when Amsterdam changed faith to Calvinism in 1578, the foundations had been laid for a Catholic survival whose characteristic location came to be the seventeenth-century 'secret' chapel of Ons' Lieve Heer Op Solder ('Our Blessed Lord in the Attic').[41]

Numbers of Catholics in the seventeenth-century Dutch Republic, in both town and country, were undoubtedly considerable. In Haarlem, Holland's leading urban Catholic base, it was reported in 1628 that fifty per cent of the population were Romanists and in more Protestant Leiden in 1641 around thirty Mass centres were counted. In the countryside, a swathe of largely Catholic territory ran across the heartland of the Republic, between Utrecht and Leiden. In what is now the Netherlands province of Noord Brabant, where Catholicism had been restored in the Prince of Parma's Spanish reconquest in the 1580s, it proved ineradicable following the territory's conquest by the United Provinces during the Thirty Years' War (1618–48). Even within areas thought to be more solidly Protestant, there were overt Catholic groups, for example in Hoorn in North Holland. Unlike their English co-religionists, who were isolated in a Protestant island, the Dutch Catholics lived alongside some of northern European Catholicism's foremost centres, Cologne, Münster, and, above all, in the showpiece of the northern Catholic Reformation, the Spanish Netherlands. Some consequences of numerical strength, which, in several areas was in actual ascendancy, included ambitious ecclesiastical aspirations on the part of the underground Catholic episcopate, hopes in the breasts of the clergy and laity of full Catholic restoration, and a collective Catholic lay assertiveness or defiance of Protestantism. Administratively, the new bishoprics set up by Philip II were in effect suspended in the territories of the Revolt and in 1592 Clement VIII appointed an administrative vicar apostolic for the provinces. Sasbout Vosmeer, consecrated vicar apostolic in 1602 and in office until 1614, was the chief architect of the new post-Reformation Dutch Catholicism, and his successors as vicars apostolic, Rovenius (1614–51), de la Torre (1651–61), van Neercassel (1663–86) and Codde (1688–1702), encouraged by the relative strength of the

Church over which they presided, were not content with their emergency status as papal deputies and aspired to a restoration of a regularised canonical jurisdiction based on the primatial see of Utrecht. To underline the national identity of the Dutch Catholic community, Vosmeer promoted cults of saints of, or linked to, the Netherlands, including the early missionaries Willibrord (658–739) and Boniface (*c.* 675–754/5), with a confraternity set up in their honour. However, and despite this attempt at reconciliation of Catholicism with national identity, politically the status of Catholics in the Dutch Republic as a large and alienated minority was defined in Gregory XIII's order of 1578 that they abstain from aiding the Dutch rebels against Spain. The Vicars Apostolic looked to the great Catholic powers to bring about a Catholic restoration in the United Provinces – Vosmeer, Rovenius and de la Torre to Spain, van Neercassel and Codde to France. Prophecies popular with the Catholic laity fastened hopes for restoration on various kings. Lay Catholics also expressed their hopes for restoration – their claim to occupy as of right the ecclesiastical territory of the country – by behaving in an assertive and violent fashion towards their Calvinist neighbours, and to the Reformed Church by continuing to use churches converted to Protestant occupancy.[42]

Persecution on a scale not to be underestimated was a major feature of the Dutch Catholics' estranged, unreconciled and often actively defiant stance and identity in the seventeenth-century Netherlands. Van Deursen shows that sympathetic, negligent, or closet-Catholic magistrates acted as barriers to all-out repression, and in Amsterdam, where the addresses of sixty-two small domestic Catholic meeting places were reported to the burgomaster in 1656, records point to the safety of Ons' Lieve Heer Op Solder from mob attack. Spiertz, however, indicates 'an extremely aggressive policy of persecution by the authorities' in the seventeenth century. For example, few of the Jesuits working in Friesland in 1638 escaped persecution. Catholic worship was, after all, legally forbidden in the Dutch Republic, massive fines were imposed on participants in worship and on householders who provided premises for it, and the celebrant might be flogged or banished. The crime of hiding priests also accrued heavy fines or even banishment. Persecution was renewed after the Nine Years' Truce with Spain expired in 1620. In 1685 – when the echo of Calvinist sufferings in France worsened the situation for Catholics in the Netherlands – a Franciscan friar reported that he dare not go out in daylight, but would gather believers together, using a changing succession of buildings for service on Saturday night and Sunday mornings.[43]

The organisational disruption for north Netherlands Catholicism consequent on the Reformation and the targeting of penalties for religious obduracy on priests had the effect of denuding the Dutch Republic of Catholic clergy, while there remained a substantial Catholic lay population minority. The first half of the seventeenth century saw a modest recovery in priestly numbers from a disastrously low point of 215 in 1616. In 1613 Vosmeer set up a college of SS Willibrord and Boniface in Cologne to train priests for the archdiocese of Utrecht (between 1670 and 1683 the college moved to Leuven in the Spanish

Netherlands), and other Netherlands priests were trained in Douai and Rome. However, recovery in priestly numbers was slow, while lay populations were consolidated in such centres as Delft, Haarlem and Utrecht: by 1701 the total of all regulars and seculars in the United Provinces was said to have been 466, just ninety fewer than the clerical population of the French town of Angers in the eighteenth century. Spain, with a (Catholic) population of perhaps eight million, had 100,000 Catholic clerics when the Netherlands, containing an estimated one million Romanists (based on thirty-three per cent of a population total of three million), had 500. Thus, whereas the Netherlands may have had a priest for every 2,000 lay Catholics, the proportion in Spain was one to eighty. Holland, of course, was neither Angers nor Spain, yet it had, as we have seen, large local groups of lay Catholics: in Leiden alone there were 3,000 Catholics, needing the services of priests. To provide for the deficiency between lay demands and clerical supply, as in other European mission fields in hostile political environments, the regular orders came into their own and Jesuit numbers rose from four to eighty by the 1660s. The religious orders applied their own styles of Catholicism: they were generally less strict than secular priests over the conditions of admission to the Eucharist, and were accused by the seculars of laxity, while the Jesuits and Franciscans showed their flexibility in adapting to circumstances by taking a lenient view of marriages contracted by Catholics in the Netherlands Reformed Church. However, the overall result of the shortage of priests in the Netherlands was to hand the everyday direction of the Church to the laity and especially to women. The result was the maintenance of high standards of commitment and behaviour.[44]

The liturgical provisions of post-Reformation Dutch Catholicism were not elaborate but, typically, those of a church under hostile pressure: the lovely Ons' Lieve Heer Op Solder is a plain galleried chapel with limited decoration. The vast number of 1,500 portable altars were consecrated in the period 1625 to 1650 and 1,178 chalices, mostly of tin, were blessed – all in sharp contrast with the splendour of liturgical equipment and performance in the Spanish Netherlands in this period, though the richly worked silver vessels and ornate monstrances now in the Rijksmuseum in Amsterdam may indicate the import, especially in the late seventeenth and eighteenth centuries, of such equipment from Antwerp and other centres in the south. The general impoverishment of liturgical provisions, especially in the earlier seventeenth century, was part and parcel of the same situation of persecution that gave rise to a paucity of priests – a state of affairs to which Vosmeer responded by fostering the laity's role and creating, out of necessity, a kind of diaconate made up of *lectores* who read litanies, prayers and sermons in Dutch and of *directores* who provided protection for religious meetings. Out of the exigencies of repression, then, early modern Dutch Catholicism was anticipating both the modern lay diaconate and vernacular worship. *De Sondaghs-Schole* (or *De Sondaechs-Schoole – The Sunday School*) by the teacher Heyman Jacobsz, offered a prayer-book replacement for all the Masses unavoidably missed as a result of the absence of priests. In Friesland an observer saw some of the effects of a Catholicism left for long periods without priests: a lay person read to congregations on Sundays and feast-days from *De Sondaghs Schole*; the congregation sang hymns and took a collection for the poor. Their simple worship must have looked like that of the Mennonites, Baptists who culti-vated simplicity in all things – so perhaps it is fitting after all that today Amsterdam's Jesuit and Mennonite churches on the Singel Canal are next-door neighbours.[45]

Dutch Catholicism was to a large extent organised by lay people, gathering congregations from groups of villages for Masses, providing maintenance for priests. A further development of this lay structure was the emergence of the *klopjes*, pious celibate women representing an undoubted derivation from the medieval Netherlands female piety of the Beguines (whose tradition survived in Amsterdam, Delft, and in a strong communal form in Haarlem). The Netherlands mission may have had 3,000 *klopjes* by the middle of the seventeenth century, recruited from all social and occupational classes – nobles, bourgeois, artisanal and domestic workers and nurses – who undertook teaching, poor relief and visiting the sick, ensured that premises were available for Mass, for which they assembled congregations, read the lessons during services, and laid on music for worship when it could be had. Out of such key roles of the female laity in the Catholic Church of the Netherlands rose demands for lay involvement in the appointment of priests in the mission. Indeed, Catharina Oly of Haarlem, herself a mirror image of the *klopje* type, recorded the way that, through their indispensable roles, these women led the priests – in the case she described, Jesuits – in running the Church, for 'often when here was something to do in the community, it was done by these maidens; yes, so much so that the [Jesuit] fathers did not regulate them and in external matters they ruled more than the fathers'.[46]

The Netherlands Catholic Church took much of its tone – its high levels of fervour and commitment, its moralism, its highly developed personal religious consciousness and education and its spirituality – from these women. Mysticism was certainly present, especially at the Haarlem community of *dévotes*, where the heritage of medieval Beguine contemplative piety seems to have mingled with the spirituality of Teresa of Ávila. Over the course of time, as Clemens shows, an apocalyptic that initially nourished hopes of full Catholic restoration turned into a kind of personalised eschatology, in which the emphasis in prayer books and manuals of piety in use amongst Dutch Catholics was on the individual's readiness for death and God's judgement, for which the whole of life should be a preparation:

> The Lord presents you with two things
> and leaves the choice to you:
> whether to be eternally with him
> or to live forever in the pains of hell.

The 1667 manual by Abr. van der Matt, *Meditatien tot de heylige communie op alle sondagen des jaers* (*Meditations on Holy Communion for all the Sundays of the Year*) saw the

Eucharist as a safeguard against final judgement and also, incidentally, envisaged, in its title, frequent lay reception. As eschatology moved its site away from the goals of a Catholic restoration intended to resume the Church's lost position within Dutch society at large, Catholics seem to have adopted a more introverted, sectarian view of the superiority of their religion to that of the wider community. Their purity, they believed, was unsullied, as was shown in the 1664 *Weg des hemels* (*Pathway to Heaven*), unlike 'those who do not know [God]'. An increasing sectarianisation tended also to present Catholicism as a family badge inherited from parents for whose fidelity God was to be thanked.[47]

Dutch Catholics were certainly well instructed in their faith, or had every opportunity that could be provided by a society characterised by high literacy rates – seventy per cent amongst males in Amsterdam in 1680 – to become religiously educated. Clemens has consulted twenty catechisms covering the period 1604–1807 – an average of a new catechism every ten years. They were published in the southern Netherlands in Antwerp, Leuven and Brussels, for example, but later in the period, as censorship was lightened, more often within the United Provinces, at Amsterdam. Titles suggested a clear sense of confessional identity – with the labels 'Catholic', 'Roman', or 'Roman-Catholic' – a targeting of youth, a compliance with the Tridentine version and some reliance on Canisius's Catechism. The famous *Mechelschen Catechismus* operates on a high level of doctrinal awareness and is securely anchored in Scripture, with a profusion of citations from both Testaments, as well as liberal references to the fathers of the Church, and even to such an unlikely authority in this sort of compilation as Beza. Authority is also claimed for 'apostolic tradition or handing-down' (traditions that there are four Gospels, that Mary is ever a virgin, that infant Baptism is required, that there are seven Sacraments, that Sunday is the Christian Sabbath, and so forth). Backed by patristic references, there is a strongly realised doctrine of Purgatory ('A place under the earth in which the souls of the faithful are, through fire and other painfulness, purified of all their guilt'): Mass is offered for them. Marian doctrine is set out with equal confidence, including that of the Assumption ('She is with soul and body in heaven'). Amidst extensive treatment of the Sacraments, the absolute doctrine of the real presence is affirmed: 'What is present to us in the holy Sacrament of the Altar? Christ Himself, God and man, with soul and body'. Citing from Trent and the fathers, the value (literally the 'wages') of good works is stressed. The popular *Mechelschen Catechismus*, then, provided a serious digest of Tridentine and early modern Catholic teaching for an embattled Dutch Church.[48]

While, in the provision of catechesis, Dutch Catholics were initially dependent on Belgian resources, Leuven in Brabant came to provide the mainstay of priestly formation for secular clergy in the Dutch Republic. There, at the original well-spring of Jansenism, students learned what Spiertz calls a 'strict Augustinianism', encouraged by the Vicars Apostolic Neercassel and Codde, so as to produce a 'severe church discipline'. Although in the assembling in sermons and the press of an identifiable ideal Dutch national character – clean, frugal, diligent and sober – Catholicism was presented in media propaganda as the opposite of the recommended national typology, in point of fact, with their puritan strictness, Dutch Catholics could on the whole present themselves as men and women of plain lives, neither entirely absorbed in the mainstream culture nor entirely estranged from national values and attitudes. The painter Jan Steen (1626–79), whose widely admired paintings upheld the Dutch bourgeois virtues of prudence, restraint and economy, was a Catholic. '*Klopje* Catholicism', if we may use that term, had more in common with the recommended simplicity, regularity and orderliness of Calvinist Amsterdam than it did with the lordly display of Catholic Venice.[49]

If the Dutch Republic formed a society of minorities, its former partners of the duchy of Burgundy, the ten Spanish-ruled territories that formed the basis of modern Belgium, saw the achievement of a remarkable Catholic religious homogeneity once they were restored to Spanish rule by Parma from the 1580s. Indeed, it was Parma who made plain the intertwining of Catholic and Spanish recovery in the Low Countries, for when he retook Antwerp from the Calvinist rebels against Spain in 1585 he planted Capuchins there, 'received them with all signs of goodwill, promised them his protection'. The Catholic recovery of Antwerp provides, indeed, one of the clearest indicators in our period of the link between the confessional reorientations of regions of Europe and political decisions made on the basis of military force. The Brabant trading metropolis had seen Catholic worship banned in 1581 at the height of rebel success. In the following decades it was to emerge as a northern beacon of the Counter-Reformation. Its Jesuit baroque St Carolus Borromeüskerk (1615–25), with its Rubens ceiling panels, rivalled the city's gothic cathedral for magnificence. The ancestral traditions of Flemish religious art were refashioned in the emergence of a Belgian Catholic baroque, especially with Peter Paul Rubens (1577–1640) and Anthony van Dyck (1599–1641), as well as in the exuberant wood carving that saw Confessional boxes installed in Belgian churches and the baroque statuary that replaced lost works shattered in the Calvinist-inspired iconcoclasm of 1566. The establishment of the Jesuits and the Capuchins throughout the southern provinces mirrored their safe anchorage in Antwerp. Even before the end of the sixteenth century the Society of Jesus had seventeen houses in the southern Netherlands and by 1630 had around 1,700 personnel in the territories, 'relatively more numerous and influential than anywhere [else] in Europe'. The Capuchins' presence rocketed from four in 1583 to almost 1,000 by 1620. These two orders were the arrow-heads of a gigantic relaunch of Belgian Catholicism. There was no reintroduction of Alba's cruel and counter-productive persecution of 1567 to 1573, though censorship and migration to the north stilled dissent. The devout Spanish-appointed rulers from 1598 to 1621, the Archdukes Albert and Isabella, gave a clear lead to the laity in encouraging what clearly became widely popular lay Catholic practice: the Antwerp Marian married men's confraternity tripled in membership to nearly 1,000 by 1664. The Spanish Netherlands had emerged as the model of the Tridentine Reformation in northern Europe, providing, especially for Catholics in the British Isles, enviable glimpses of what a public Catholic establishment meant.[50]

6 The Catholic Reformation and the people

Whereas the public establishment of the Catholic faith in the Spanish Netherlands allowed for magnificence in the celebration of its rites and the importation of baroque religious art and architecture, in England, as in the Dutch Republic, persecution severely restricted opportunities for Catholic liturgical or artistic splendour. In England and Wales, Catholicism under Elizabeth (1558–1603) was equated with treason and associated with attempts, through alliance with Spain, to reverse the nation's Protestant Reformation, fashioned in 1559. The Catholic clerical spokesmen Cardinal William Allen and the Jesuit Robert Persons (or Parsons, 1546–1610) confirmed government suspicions of Catholic loyalty with their advocacy of subversion and Spanish assistance, so as to restore Catholicism. A Catholic-inspired rebellion, the 1569 Revolt of the Northern Earls, directed at replacing Elizabeth with her Catholic cousin Mary Queen of Scots (1542–87), was supported by Pius V's bull of excommunication and dethronement of Elizabeth, *Regnans in Excelsis* (1570). The menacing political implications of a Catholic religious mission to Protestant England became apparent from the 1570s with the arrival in the country of highly motivated Jesuit and seminary-trained priests from the Continent, and Elizabeth's government and parliament responded with such measures as the Act of Persuasions of 1581, making it high treason, punishable by hanging, drawing and quartering, to convert English people to Catholicism or to be so converted. Obdurate lay Catholics (known legally as 'recusants') faced fines of an astronomical £20 per month for absence from Church of England worship, an attempted legislative deterrence of the significant gentry and aristocratic support that accrued to the Catholic cause. A century or so of the most intense penal period can be dated from about 1580, decades in which political crises such as the Spanish Armada of 1588, the 1605 Gunpowder Conspiracy against James I (1567–1625) and the Civil War which broke out in 1642, spasmodically accelerated the rates of persecution, especially of priests, 133 of whom were executed under Elizabeth alone.[1]

Under persecution the English Catholic community reached a demographic platform of about 60,000 in 1680, at around the close of the most bitter period of persecution. The Catholic element very gradually tended to withdraw from political activism and, often led by lay women, cultivated on the whole a quiet, domestic reflective faith, much nourished by spiritual reading. England already had, in such figures as Richard Rolle of Hampole (*c.* 1290–1349), Walter Hilton (d. 1396), Margery Kempe (b. 1364) and Juliana (or Julian) of Norwich (*c.* 1342–*c.* 1413), one of the liveliest traditions in medieval Europe of vernacular spiritual writing, and in the restricted conditions of the penal period religious reading functioned as a supplement to a straitened liturgical life. In the sixteenth century the fame of English Catholic religious literature was maintained by the Leuven professor Thomas Stapleton (1535–98), whose 1300-page *Promptuarium Morale* (*Ethical Guidebook*) was used as a sermon manual by priests in France, Germany, Italy and the Low Countries until well into the eighteenth century. The English Benedictine writer Augustine Baker (1575–1641) advocated the abandonment of secular involvement in favour of the exclusive cultivation of the interior life, while the secular priest Henry Holden's (1597–*c.* 1661) *Analysis of Divine Faith* (1658) provided a Catholicism adapted to a Protestant environment, just as the priest and convert from Nonconformity, John Gother (or Goter, *c.* 1654–1704), whose works 'nourished the piety of the dwindling catholic remnant in its darkest days' (Anstruther), set out an austere pattern of devotion which was diffident towards extravagant rosarian piety or the excessive cult of the saints.[2]

English Catholicism in the seventeenth century, then, was largely nourished by the press, which was, of necessity, for the most part located abroad. The printed production of the period 1558–1640 continued in the years 1641–1700, when a total of 1,333 Catholic-related printed items have been counted, covering England, Wales, Scotland and Ireland. An overall trend, politically, was in the direction of disengagement and acceptance of a Protestant state, while in devotional publications non-denominational Christian themes emerge. The Jesuit English press at their college at St Omer in the Spanish Netherlands produced around 275 works between 1608 and 1759. The orientation of its output changed over time, reflecting, one would argue, a deeper, long-term shift in English Catholics' priorities away from controversy, confrontation and political involvement, and towards contemplation, withdrawal and political recognition by the Protestant-dominated status quo. Indeed, English Jesuit writing had always been concerned with meditation, in the tradition of the *Spiritual Exercises*, and, based upon those, the *Christian Directory* (1582) of Persons, the Jesuit often regarded as the epitome of political militancy, was a best-seller among his co-religionists and, suitably adapted, amongst Protestant readers. Devotional output seems to have taken over the St Omer press in its later years, at the expense of polemical engagements in the public and political arenas, and the production could be said to be targeted to an internal Catholic readership and its spiritual needs. In 1697–9 a major undertaking at St Omer was the published translation, as *The Practice of Christian Perfection*, of a collection of pious writings by a Spanish Jesuit. A further ambitious project was the publication in translation of a devotional work by the Jesuit Bellarmino. It may be that the Jesuits themselves, with their hopes of the kind of political Catholic restoration once associated with Persons finally exploded upon the departure of the pro-

Jesuit Catholic King James II in 1688, had adjusted their sights to the reality of a Catholic community whose profile was becoming devotional rather than militant, largely endorsing the Protestant status quo.[3]

English Catholics obviously looked to the Continent, to Rome and to the presses and seminaries abroad. Female English Catholic life was especially nourished by the convents in Continental Europe. With a predictable preponderance from two leading Catholic counties, Lancashire and Staffordshire, women from recusant families entered convents abroad, as did four members of the Anderton family of Birchley, Lancashire, who went into the Poor Clares at Gravelines, and five Lancashire Blundells who did the same thing, while four Clifton women went into religious houses overseas. These choices were made freely, as Trent required, or as Abbess Sr Mary Caryll said in 1675 'upon a *great* deale of consideration'. Yet despite the orientation of gentry Catholicism towards north-west Europe, the English recusancy of the seventeenth and eighteenth centuries was inexorably becoming adapted to a national culture which itself had become suffused with the outlook of Protestantism. Jansenism had its attraction for some Catholics in England, as well as in Scotland and Ireland. On the whole, the more concentrated on their religion English Catholics were, the more they were probably likely to be looked upon by their neighbours simply as pious Christians. Thus in Chiswick in 1706, Sir Richard Beeling, 'a professed Roman Catholick', had 'the Character amongst us of being a very good man' while others of his religion were described as 'peaceable' and 'harmless'. In the same part of the eighteenth century, perceived threats to Christian morality from 'the general Infidelity...of the Age', as well as the imagined danger to the Church of England from Protestant Dissent, created a sense amongst some Anglicans of a certain solidarity with the Catholics as kindred religious traditionalists. Aveling describes the common ground, occupied in the regions, such as Yorkshire, since the Reformation by the households of godly puritans, pious Anglicans and devout recusants. As Wilson shows, treatises on devotion published in Douai, Antwerp and St Omer were read by Protestants in early seventeenth-century England; Persons, as we have seen, was widely read, as were translations of the Spanish devotional writer Luis de Granada (or Luis de Sarria, 1504–88) and the poet and Anglican churchman John Donne (1572–1631), brought up a Catholic, patterned some of his religious meditations on Loyola's *Spiritual Exercises*.[4]

From the time of the formation of the recusant community under Elizabeth, Catholic marriages, such as the 226 weddings overseen by the priest Nicholas Postgate (*c.* 1598–1679) in his Yorkshire mission between 1631 and 1665, were often accepted in law, despite the difficulties put in their way. A relative decline of the English province of the Society of Jesus after the high noon of its hopes under James II between 1685 and 1688 synchronised with the stabilisation of an incipient episcopal system under four regional Vicars Apostolic, consecrated bishops but answerable direct to Rome. The vicariate apostolic encouraged the emergence of a Tridentine parochial, rather than a missionary, consciousness among groups of secular priests. In parts of England's most Catholic county, Lancashire, a system that was already largely diocesan and parochial in all but name was in place before the end of the seventeenth century. The Lisbon-educated Lancashire priest Edward Booth (1638–1719), was described as 'vicar-general', a diocesan official. It was a Jesuit chaplain in the early eighteenth century who protested at the pursuit by secular priests, in defiance of Tridentine norms, of recreations such as bowling and drinking, pursued by recusant squires. Two or three priests provided, on a stabilised basis, for the needs of Catholics in Great Singleton, Lancashire. Proper registration in a Tridentine-style parochial system was maintained by the 'riding priest' of Westmorland, Thomas Royden (1662–1741) who from 1699 to 1722 assiduously kept his baptismal register, recording a brisk 147 christenings and referring to the parish (*parochia*) as his unit of ministry. Other registers were of deaths (1699–1722), marriages and reconciliations with the Church (possibly associated with mixed marriages). Richard Challoner (1691–1791), Vicar Apostolic of the London District, exercised considerable practical, though still extra-legal, freedom of action to apply the pastoral principles of the Council of Trent, while at the same time consolidating English Catholicism's identity as a denomination in a land of denominations.[5]

Catholic Reformation propaganda held Wales firmly in its sights, aiming at the Principality a steady stream of literature in Welsh, with clear efforts to adjust translated works to the patterns of Welsh culture, so that, for example, the word 'theatre' in a translated French work, *Théâtre du monde – The World's Theatre –* was rendered as a Welsh bardic assembly – a *Gorsedd* – in the translation *Gorsedd y byd – The World's Assembly*, published in Welsh in Paris in 1615. Borromeo's Milan was the place of publication in 1568 of an early work, *Athravaeth Gristonogavl* (*Christian Teaching*) by one of the leaders of the Welsh Catholic Reformation, Morys Clynnog (or Maurice Clenocke, 1528–81), while Borromeo's companion, the canon of Milan Gruffydd Robert (*c.* 1522–*c.* 1610) published in Milan a four-part Welsh grammar (1567–94), perhaps intended for missionary use. Catechesis besides Clynnog's included *Crynnodeb o adysc Cristogaul* (*A compendium of Christian teaching*), published in Paris in 1609, a Welsh version of *Opus catechesticum* (*Catechetical Labour*), published, again in Paris, in 1611, and from an Italian source *Eglurhad helaeth-lawn o'r athrawaeth gristnogawl* (*A Full and Extensive Explanation of Christian Teaching*) (St Omer, 1618). Italian Marian piety was rendered into Welsh, for example in a translation, *Dechreuad a rhyfedhus esmudiad eglwys Fair o Loreto* (*The Origin and Wonderful Transfer of the Shrine of Mary of Loreto*) (Loreto, 1635). All this literary campaign was inspired by a desire to revive a liaison between Catholicism and Welsh speech and culture, and to exploit, though with little success, an image of the Reformation as an English cultural implant.[6]

A simultaneously published account for Scottish Catholics of the house of the Holy Family miraculously removed by flight from the Holy Land to Loreto in Italy appeared in the enchantingly phrased Scots version as *The Wondrous Flittinge of the Kirk of Our B. Lady of Loreto* (Loreto, 1635). While a major effort was made in Scottish Catholic publishing to integrate the faith with national identity, language and tradition, early-modern Scotland provides an example of a Catholicism virtually new-made following the Reformation. The sense of a break with the kingdom's medieval Catholic past was sharpened in 1603 with the death of Archbishop James Beaton of Glasgow, the last personal link with the re-Reformation Scots ecclesiastical system. Thereafter, for decades Scots Catholics were largely looked after by the Jesuits, Benedictines, Dominicans, Franciscans and other orders, and in 1622 the country came under the aegis of the newly established Congregation de Propaganda Fide. Subsequent developments, such as Rome's creation in 1653 of a Scots mission under a Prefect Apostolic, and the later appointment from 1694 of a Vicar Apostolic, served to confirm the institutional dependence of the Scottish Catholic community on the Holy See. However, with the creation in 1731 of a Highland vicariate apostolic, official recognition was given to the strength of the older religion in parts of the Highlands and Islands, such as Canna, Eigg, S Uist and Benbecula, as well as in the Enzie in Banffshire under the noble protection of the Huntly family. The prominence of a Catholicism associated with the Gaelic language in the north and west showed the faith adapting successfully to a still vigorous regional culture and speech. On the other hand, the relative popularity of Jansenism in those parts of southern Scotland where Catholicism had any significant position indicates not only the reliance of the Scottish Catholic faith on French models but also the likelihood that in the Calvinist-dominated kingdom a form of Catholicism whose roots, like those of Calvinism, lay in Augustine's theology, would gain a hold.[7]

Ireland occupied a special position in the complex political patterns under which early modern European Catholicism existed. Its Catholics constituted, not a Romanist majority under a Catholic crown (as in France, Spain and so on), nor a Catholic minority in a Protestant state (as in England, Scotland, the United Provinces) but a Catholic majority under a Protestant state. There is little doubt that by at least the early decades of the seventeenth century, the Catholic preference of the great majority of people who lived in Ireland was regarded as a fixed point of discussion: most of the Irish had stayed Catholic – because they had not become Protestant. By the 1620s, when it was reported that between 6,000 and 7,000 people in one year 'were relapsed to the church of Rome', majority choice of Catholicism – whatever that might have meant in terms of degrees of general alignment to Tridentine norms of belief and practice – was recognised as a fact. During that decade a bishop of the Protestant Church of Ireland endorsed the conclusion that not only had the 'ancient inhabitants' – the so-called 'Old Irish' of Celtic culture and Irish speech – proved resistant to Protestantism, but a key element, long settled on the island, of English stock and speech and traditionally royalists, – 'our English' – had not been won over to the Protestant Reformation. The bishop also reported the setting up of a Catholic episcopate in the 1620s, with a personnel which, as we shall soon see, was closely integrated with local power structures. The Irish towns, where Protestantism might have stood a chance of establishment, were largely not won for the new faith. Even in the capital, where in 1629 eighty Jesuits operated fourteen Mass centres, in 1630 the Church of Ireland Archbishop of Dublin reported large numbers openly attending Mass. By 1635 a Jesuit church, with Confessional boxes, and a railed, stepped, high altar – just like a cathedral – was described. Even the government's attempts to Protestantise Ireland through the Derry plantations in Ulster under James I – where twenty-four Catholic priests ran twenty-nine 'parishes', was influenced by a widely prevailing Catholicism. Yet the Crown in the early modern period was in general ferociously opposed to Irish 'popery' and persecution of the confessional majority was to mount over the course of time, partly because of Catholicism's links with anti-English insurgency, especially in the horrors of the Irish rebellion in 1641. Armed Catholics enlisted for Charles I in the Civil War, from 1642, leading to ferocious reprisals by Oliver Cromwell (1599–1658) in his reassertion of English Protestant rule over Ireland. The reign over Ireland of James II from 1685 to 1688 encouraged the Catholic majority to hope for a full restoration of their faith but the pledge of their support for James led to fresh legal persecution following 1689. By the middle of the eighteenth century, there was widespread Catholic despair over the future of the persecuted faith in the island and in conditions of deprivation and repression a full Tridentinisation of Irish Catholicism to replace a mass of folk beliefs was impeded, some would say until after the mid-nineteenth century famine.[8]

While Tridentine Catholicism in Ireland, as elsewhere in early modern Europe, had to seek accommodations with established popular cultures and cults, organisationally the Catholic Church relied for much of its viability on its interpenetration with local and ancestral power structures of kinship and on the indigenous aristocratic system still respected by the crown. In clerical appointments, though ultimate decisions at the highest levels were made in Rome, generally speaking local interests were decisive. Indeed, it was essential for a candidate for a bishopric to have the backing of local lay élites. In the first half of the seventeenth century Catholic Ireland gained an episcopate modelled on Tridentine and Borromean ideals, but its composition was accommodated to regional power structures. To take a few examples: in Killaloe, Co. Clare, in 1624 a new episcopal appointee had the backing in writing of the dominant O'Briens, in Leighlin in Co. Carlow, Bishop Edmund O'Dempsey received a written undertaking from Terence O'Dempsey, Viscount Clanmalier, that he would receive a yearly stipend from the nobleman, and in Co. Galway, dominated by the Burke earls of Clanricarde, a kinsman, John Bourke, became bishop of Clonfert in 1641 and archbishop of Tuam in 1647. In those decades Ireland's Catholic episcopate became suffused with the goals of Trent but its composition was also intertwined with indigenous structures of power and kinship.[9]

As was the case elsewhere, the Catholic Reformation in Ireland encouraged the production of a literature adapted to the language of the majority of the people. Works in Irish produced on the Continent, especially by Irish Franciscans at St Anthony's, Leuven, included a catechism for the laity by Bonaventure Ó hEoghasa (Bonaventure O'Hosey, OFM, d. 1614), *An teagasc Críosdaidhe* (1611), and liturgical and devotional writings such as the work on philosophy and morals, *Trí bior-ghaoithe an bháis* (*Three Shafts of Death*) (1631) by Geoffrey Keating (Séathrún Céitin, d. 1644). Such works for the clergy (to preach from) and for the literate Irish-speaking laity were based on Continental models but the genre consisted of works of adaptation as well as of simple translation. For example, piety was fostered in Irish writings that derived from the Spanish contemplative school, via the south Netherlands, but they needed to be adapted to the infrequency of the Mass and the Sacraments in what were, after all, more than theoretically penal conditions within Ireland. Again, adaptation to Irish conditions of conflict made the religious material in the Irish language 'highly combative' in tone, as Canny says, and often providing ready-made answers to Protestant polemics. However, the violence of the language of dialectic – for example allegations of Luther's mother's intercourse with Satan, producing a demonic bastard gaelicised as 'Luitéir Mac Lucifer' (Luther son of Lucifer) – derived from the Irish conventions of unrestrained literary invective. Again, attempts were made to integrate the requirements of the Catholic Reformation – even where they were novel, as with the insistence that Confessors be seminary-trained – with Irish antiquity, for instance by invoking 'the old song of penance sung by Saint Patrick'.[10]

Spain provided a greater part of the power behind the Catholic Reformation. At the Council of Trent the Spanish bishops were the spokesmen for morally uncompromising episcopal reform. The Jesuits represented Spain's single most important contribution to the Catholic renewal; the first three generals of the Society, Loyola down to 1558, Laínez from 1558 to 1565, and Borgia from 1565 to 1573, were Spanish, and the second of these played a key role in guiding the theological deliberations of the Council. Of Jewish descent, Laínez came from a social element unique to Iberia – a substantial number of Catholics of Jewish extraction, the progeny of the *conversos*, those forced or persuaded, for reasons of conviction, coercion or advantage, to exchange their Judaism for Christianity. From this same stratum came Spain's greatest Catholic mystic (alongside the Carmelite poet, John of the Cross (Juan de la Cruz), the Carmelite reformer Teresa of Ávila (or Teresa de Jesús). Born in Ávila in Castile, at around twenty years old Teresa de Cepeda y Ahumada entered the Carmelite house of San José in her native city. The convent practised a relaxed form of the Carmelite rule, but it was not until the early 1560s, after years of visionary experience, that Teresa undertook a Carmelite reform at San José. The symbol of the austerity of the reform, which Teresa extended to seventeen female Carmelite houses in Spain, was the *discalced* practice of going shoeless. Teresa was an accomplished organiser of her Carmelite reform and a politician and diplomat accomplished in coping with the anti-feminism present in the Catholic Reformation. She was powered by her meditative and mystical insights, recorded in such works as her autobiography, *El Camino de la Perfección* (*The Way of Perfection*) (1563). Teresa's contemplative aptitudes have been related to the Judaeo-*converso* tradition which prized cultivation of the interior religious life. Williams writes, 'We do not begin to understand [Teresa] as a religious, as a reformer, as a theologian, unless we see her as "displaced person" in the Spain of her day...as a woman and a Jewess [who had] to negotiate her way in an almost wholly suspicious environment'.[11]

Teresa of Ávila trod on the safer side of a line dividing official orthodoxy from heterodoxy. A woman who wore a Carmelite habit and who, like Teresa, took a soubriquet from Jesus, the visionary *beata* Catalina de Jesús came before the tribunal of the Inquisition in Seville in 1623 on charges of spurious ecstasies and illuminist heresy. She recanted and was sentenced to seclusion, in a mounting campaign in Spain in the first half of the seventeenth century to subordinate the independent religious authority of *beatas* to ecclesiastical control. The Inquisition also maintained the role it adopted after its foundation in 1481 of investigating all suspected manifestations of Judaism. Practices maintained by *conversos* with apparent roots in Jewish religious law, such as avoidance of pork and regular bathing, continued to come within the Inquisition's remit as it investigated the alleged outward signs – 'judaising' – of inward Jewish convictions. The 'last great *converso* hunt in the Crown of Castile' (Monter) began in 1558 in the Castilian heartland of Murcia and rounded up men depicted as a fifth column deep within Catholic society – a friar, magistrates, leading citizens. In a series of public burnings of heretics between 1558 and 1568, 603 accused were condemned, over 100 of whom were executed, the most savage wave coming in the first two years of the campaign, when sixty accused 'judaisers' were put to death. Perhaps because 'judaising' was partly associated with reading of Jewish texts, in which women were disadvantaged by lack of education, suspicion did not fall so much on females in these cases. Women's alleged witchcraft, organised in sabbats, or covens, was investigated in Zugurramurdi in Navarre, where six impenitent accused witches were burned in 1610 and larger numbers sentenced. The proximity of this area to the Pyrenees suggests an anxiety on the part of the Inquisition to protect Spain from feared outside 'infection', in this case from France and the Basque country.[12]

Whether or not they were accused of witchcraft, in statistical terms women were disadvantaged in Spanish society in the Catholic Reformation period. In around 1600 the country had 40,600 secular clergy and 25,400 males in the religious orders, but only 25,000 nuns. The disparity of advantage between the genders in access to positions of religious power and prestige is even more marked in the 'saint count' of those canonised within the period. The great ceremony presided over by Gregory XV in 1622 to celebrate five key figures of the first phase of the Catholic Reformation canonised only one woman, Teresa of Ávila. Ahlgren argues that holy women, generally cloistered, had less access to the limelight in which saints were recognised than men did. Further, while religious women had to counter the Inquisition's suspicion of religious inspiration that was charismatic rather than academically supported, women's prayer and reading meetings aroused suspicion as suspected illuminist cells. To an extent, as Teresa posthumously proved by her canonisation, holy females could overcome the disadvantages described, but, as Ahlgren says, they had to play by male rules – as Teresa urged her Carmelite sisters to be 'manly' in their pursuit of holiness. At the same time, the great Carmelite made a shrewd use of obedience as a virtue, including her 'politically astute' protestations of obedience to God, justifying her claims to religious roles unusual for a woman to occupy. Meanwhile, it seems clear that established female saints might be treated, though with due honour, in ways thought suitable to women – given treats, let out of, and returned to, a known home and sometimes even abducted. Thus in a drought in Barcelona in 1651 the local patron, St Madrona, was appealed to, and the people:

> resorted to the usual solution of carrying the body of Saint Madrona to the Cathedral…and as it was close to her feast day it seemed improper that she should be away from her home on that day.…[but] if the glorious saint should provide us with water in abundance she would be returned home on her feast day. The glorious saint heard the prayer of some good soul.

Kidnapped Madrona was returned to her 'home'.

It is also worth noting that when it came to a more serious emergency, plague, Barcelona shifted its search for a patron away from female Madrona and towards a powerful male saint, the Minim founder, Francisco de Paola (1436?–1507).[13]

If pious women in early modern Spain faced an extra barrier in achieving official sainthood, male clerics often fell short, not just of sanctity, but of the basic requirements of the Council of Trent. Despite the supposed progress that had been made in the pre-Tridentine reforms of Cardinal Ximénes de Cisneros, by the 1540s Spanish bishops were complaining of the 'ignorance, illiteracy, crime and immorality' of priests. A special feature, though, and one *not* distinguishing clerics from laymen, was violence by priests, leading some bishops in 1565 and in 1645 to prohibit the carrying of weapons by clerics. As an instance of clerical violence, there was the Toledo priest in 1574 who, dressed in his Mass vestments, left the altar in full view of the whole congregation, insulted a parishioner and struck him repeatedly, ordering him out of the church: he was behaving as a male parishioner might have done in a tavern quarrel. Indeed, the very point that one priest who went out at night armed with sword and buckler was just 'like a lay person' was specifically made by a bishop of Córdoba in 1638. Matters had not improved by the end of the seventeenth century, for in Seville five monks in 1684 took their guns to rustle pigs, forming a robber band of the kind that might have been led by the Valencian friar who in 1693 acted as a brigand chief, robber and murderer. The requirement of the Catholic Reformation of a priesthood qualitatively different from the laity had made no difference to the lives of such individuals.[14]

The completeness of the Spanish Catholic Reformation was also conditioned by the country's ecclesiastical system of royal control of the Church, and especially of its episcopal appointments, and by the crown's power to vet reform legislation. There is no doubting the genuineness of Philip II's commitment to reform, and Cardinal Gaspar de Quiroga, archbishop of Toledo from 1577 to 1594, worked with the king to shape 'the whole course of the Counter-Reformation in Spain'. Philip's enthusiasm for the reform cause encouraged a momentum of renewal that saw the foundation of twenty-three seminaries in the period 1564 to 1610. As required by Trent, and in the immediate aftermath of the Council, the archdioceses of Toledo, Santiago and Granada held synods in 1565, the presence of royal representatives indicating the king's approval for reform proceedings. However, on another vital Tridentine requirement for the reinvigoration of the church – bishops' residence, on which, as we saw, Spanish bishops at Trent insisted so vehemently – the demands of reform could run counter to the Crown's need to recruit its ministers from the episcopate. Residence was patchy even in the Castile of Philip II – by 1579 the diocese of Sigüenza had had no resident bishop for 100 years – and was certainly not improved by Philip's enlistment of six inquisitors general and three presidents of Castile from what ought to have been the resident episcopate. Further, Spain's political crisis of the 1590s forced Philip back into reliance on the families of the higher nobility (*títulos*), whose loyalty was rewarded by the increase in their share of episcopal appointments in Castile, from less than ten per cent in the reformist period of the 1570s and 1580s to twenty-seven per cent between 1586 and 1598. Despite the image of self-seeking often associated with the minister Francisco de Sandoval y Rojas, Duke of Lerma (1553–1625), in power under Philip III (1598–1621) from 1598 to 1618, there was no marked corruption in episcopal appointments, the period of permitted vacancy between promotions was lowered and the use of bishops for non-diocesan tasks was reduced – only two of the five inquisitors general were bishops. Indeed, under Philip IV (1621–65), while the choice of *títulos* for bishoprics was cut drastically, by two-thirds, by the minister Gaspar de Guzmán, Count-Duke of Olivares (1587–1645, in power from 1621 to 1643), in his campaign against unmerited noble privilege, the proportion of state servants made bishops – four out of five presidents of Castile, three Castilian inquisitors general in succession, for example – went up. By this point in time, the mid-seventeenth century – and whether the selection of nobles for bishoprics was in itself a good or a bad thing from the point of view of the quality of the episcopate – sons of the most influential families were not coming into the senior ecclesiastical offices, and the leadership of the Castilian Church was falling increasingly into the hands of members of the religious orders and of lesser noble families. There was, Rawlings claims, an overall deterioration of episcopal quality and talent. Increasingly, under mediocre episcopal direction, the Spanish Church turned in upon itself, losing touch with the world beyond Spain and with new current of ideas within the country.[15]

In Portugal in the period of the Catholic Reformation, Catholic practice strongly supported the affirmation of national identity, threatened as it was by the proximity of the Spanish super-power and endangered by dynastic absorption into the Habsburg empire between 1581 and 1640. Spain and Portugal were, of course, both Catholic but Portugal wore its Catholic faith with a difference, and found in its Catholic distinctiveness some of the moral resources to hold at bay Spain's Iberian imperialism. In Portugal, not only did the retained Braga rite of the Mass contain incidents of great dramatic beauty, for instance in the liturgy of Good Friday, but it also focused on national saints. In particular, the recital of the *Ave Maria* (Hail Mary) at the beginning and the *Salve Regina* ('Hail, holy queen') at the end of the Braga Mass centred on Mary as the nation's patron whose prayers for the country in advance of a victory against Castile in 1385 had then secured Portugal's independence. Thus an entirely orthodox Catholic Marian cult fostered a sense of difference and independence against the powerful neighbour and overlord from 1581. Following Philip II's assumption of the throne of Portugal in that year, Archbishop de Jesus of Braga (in office, 1588–1609) set up a commission charged with assembling material on his diocese's antiquity. It published its findings in 1602, followed in 1637 with a fully documented claim to Braga's ecclesiastical primacy in Iberia, of which its rite was claimed to be an expression. Well before the ultimately successful Portuguese revolt of 1640 – to which the national ecclesiastical establishment lent its full support – the *Portuguese* Catholicism expressed through the Braga rite, and asserted in the claim of Braga's primacy, had become the voice of 'Lusitanian' autonomy and identity. Indeed, the poet Luis de Camões (*c.* 1524–80) rejoiced, in his national epic celebrating Portuguese imperial achievement, *Os Lusiadas* (1572), in the loyal attachment of his countrymen, 'so few and yet so strong', to 'Mother Church'. This loyalty was contrasted with the apostasy of

> the Germans, those conceited cattle
> …Who with the one in Peter's chair did battle
> And now new shepherd and new flock invent

or

> the hard-faced Englishman
> …He fashions a new faith that none has proved.[16]

In Germany and the Habsburg lands Catholic recovery was preeminently initiated as a result of military and political eventualities, especially in the Thirty Years' War when Catholic victories ensured territorial restitutions of the Church, for example in the erstwhile Calvinist Rhineland Upper Palatinate, seized by Bavaria. The Habsburg dynastic lands display the close relationship between re-Catholicisation and the imposition of dynastic political control, if not absolutism. In the early sixteenth century, there were signs that the Lower Austrian capital Vienna was aiming to carve out a constitutional identity on the lines of an independent free city of the *Reich*, staging an anti-Habsburg revolt in 1522. As Protestantism spread in Austria, Vienna's dissidence took on a strong religious cast and it was calculated that, by 1564, eighty per cent of Viennese were Protestants. The Catholic Habsburgs fought back and Emperor Ferdinand I introduced the Jesuits to Austria, while the Catholic preacher Martin Eisengrein (1535–78) delivered a propaganda offensive in St Stephen's Cathedral in Vienna against this strongly entrenched Lutheranism. An eirenic pause followed, with a 'third way' between Reformation and Counter-Reformation under Emperor Maximilian II (reigned 1564–76: 'No sin is more serious than the desire to tyrannize in matters of conscience.'). However, the underlying trend in Austria, facilitated by the link between Protestantism and political opposition, coming especially from the Estates, was in favour of resurgent Catholicism, a prospect that became clearer in the reign of Rudolf II (1576–1612), when the Emperor's attendance at the Viennese Corpus Christi procession in 1578 can be read as signalling the renewed commitment of the Austrian house to the German Catholic restoration. Rudolf also adopted close relations with the Bavaria of the Catholic Wittelsbachs, while his reign was marked by the stridency of a determinedly Catholic 'Spanish' party at the Habsburg courts in Vienna and Prague, and by constitutional checks on the Estates in their demands for freedom of Lutheran worship. Eirenicism was in rapid retreat in the 1580s and 1590s and by the time that the Jesuit former-student Ferdinand II came to the Habsburg throne, fervent 'Counter-Reformation Catholicism with its emphasis on hierarchy and obedience was [seen as] the most appropriate tool to restore order and reclaim lost imperial authority'.[17]

Subsequently, Ferdinand not only imposed Catholicism on his own domains, but, in collaboration with his fellow Jesuit alumnus Maximilian, Duke of Bavaria (1597–1651) worked to rebuild Catholicism in the German lands. The goal of a complete German Catholic restoration was never accomplished in thirty years of war, though the Habsburg victory in the Battle of the White Mountain in 1620 enabled Ferdinand not only to strike heavy blows against the German Protestants of the sixteenth-century Reformation but to destroy the remnant of the once powerful pre-Reformation Hussite movement in Bohemia and to subjugate the country, replacing its nobility with Habsburg dependents. In Austria after the Thirty Years' War the campaign of Catholicisation, especially through missions of the Jesuits, and through undermining the Protestantism of the towns the nobility and the peasantry, continued. The Confraternities of Christian Doctrine, of which a cell was established in Vienna in 1732, carried on the work of indoctrination, fostered by Jesuits such as Ignaz Parhamer (1715–86) who concentrated his attention on areas with non-Catholic pockets of population. The support of the ruling classes for these efforts was made manifest in royal and aristocratic financial contributions to the missions and was seen, for example, in Parhamer's campaign in Salzburg in 1758, when the prince-archbishop and his courtiers, as members of the Confraternity of Christian Doctrine, were in attendance. Saints' cults such as that St John Nepomuk (*c.* 1345–93), who was canonised in 1729 as a hero of the priestly seal of Confession, were sponsored by the dynasty as imperial devotions. The medieval holy woman Blessed Hemma (or Emma) of Gurk (d. *c.* 1045) was promoted as a Habsburg cult in the Austrian provinces and in Croatia. When Austria was at war with Protestant Prussia (1741–8, 1757–63) Catholic rituals were used to solidify loyalty to the Emperor. Pressure was relentlessly applied to Protestants to convert. In the reign of Leopold I (1657–1705) they were forbidden to employ co-religionists as servants or tutors or to hold worship at home. Non-Catholics were held up to ridicule, children were encouraged to act as informers of their parents' Protestant religion, Catholic neighbours preyed on the property of Protestants, migration of Austrian Lutherans to Protestant centres such as Nuremberg increased and 21, 000 Protestants were expelled from the prince-archbishopric of Salzburg in 1731.[18]

Even so, in Austria attempts to use the Catholic faith to further state-building, to shore up loyalty to the ruling family, to create peasant subservience and to integrate an ethnically diverse dynastic empire, may in fact have encouraged repudiation of Catholic propagandising partly out of politically inspired rejection of Habsburg rule, particularly in districts where, in the sixteenth century, Lutheranism had won a popular following. In 1683 a Cistercian was attacked by Lower Austrian Lutheran peasants on the grounds that Habsburg persecution of Protestants in Hungary had caused Turkish aggression. Even so, there was genuine popular Catholic support in much of eighteenth-century Austria, seen in peasant opposition to Joseph II's (1741–90) modernising religious reforms. In Switzerland, meanwhile, the Jesuits, while running missions, for example under the direction of Charles Mailliardoz in 1715–18, concentrated on higher education in the Catholic cantons, providing nearly a dozen colleges and founding sodalities, pious book clubs and charitable agencies, to produce students with an 'awareness of religious duty and of civic responsibility' (Stoye). The Capuchins, who had fifteen convents in Switzerland by the early seventeenth century, conducted a highly effective mission to the common people, both in the remote valleys and in the towns and farming districts.[19]

In other parts of German-speaking Europe Catholic faith and practice became or remained deeply entrenched in the popular imagination over the long period of the Catholic Reformation, often most successfully where the Catholic piety of the post-Reformation period retained continuities with medieval devotions. In particular, where pilgrimage cults were associated with the local and regional environment, where they provided cures, offered recreation, and popularised art and architecture, they ensured a strong following for Catholicism. In Bavaria the remains of catacomb saints were imported into the duchy and then given Bavarian naturalisation by being made the patrons of particular towns. Pilgrimage centres studded the Bavarian terrain with holiness. Always strongly favoured by the undeviatingly Catholic Bavarian Wittelsbachs and promoted by Peter Canisius and Martin Eisengrein, the medieval shrine of Mary at Altötting underwent in the sixteenth and seventeenth centuries a renewal of mass popularity and of effectiveness in producing miracle cures. As the Wittelsbachs showed, in their relative indifference to pilgrimage outside Bavaria and in Duke Albrecht's (reigned 1550–79) promotion of the shrine through his disclosure that Our Lady of Altötting had saved him from drowning, the site was a key feature of *Bavaria Sancta*, 'Holy Bavaria', under its ruling house. Through attracting pilgrims and providing for tourist travel, accommodation, catering and souvenir sales, locations such as Altötting were foci of a sanctified popular culture. A group of ten pilgrimage churches west of Munich, built in the seventeenth and eighteenth centuries and providing a condensed itinerary of piety, had powerful drawing power. The glittering white exterior of the pilgrimage church of Wies (architect: Dominikus Zimmermann, in 1746–54), described by Burrough as 'the finest Rococo church in the world' and set dramatically against a mountain ridge, was, clearly, placed and designed in a way that would draw pilgrims towards it on the last leg of a journey with eager anticipation. The exquisite church of Birnau (Peter Thumb, 1746–58) dominates the north shore of Lake Constance. The interior styles of such churches, though they were often endowed by cultivated aristocrats, were neither academic nor architecturally correct by the pure standards of Palladian classicism: regular geometry was, apparently, spurned, angles giving way to vortices, interior lines were broken, decoration was deliberately profuse and indeed redundant, and colour and light were designed to conspire in creating what Burrough identifies as the guiding purposes of this rococo architecture, 'to excite, thrill and inspire', as well as to tell saints' stories and advertise the Church. The riotousness of the interior at Wies and the *trompe d'oeil* wrought-iron screen at Weingarten (Giacomo Antonio Corbellini, after 1715) are the points at which popular rococo meets kitsch, for this is a mass art form, embroidering the Bavarian countryside. New industrial production, in the form of lithography (1796), had the effect of extending the commercial range of Bavarian popular religious art in the nineteenth century. This inexpensive process brought scenes of recollection (the happy death), representations of intense piety (Christ in chains, from the medieval iconography of the *Schmerzenmann*, the Man of Sorrows), of Catholic Reformation hagiography (St Joseph), and of devout sentimentality (the boy Jesus, the Holy Family) into the iconostasis – the *Herrgottswinkel* – of the pious peasant home. Bavaria provides a German example of the successful fusion of popular culture and Catholic Reformation piety.[20]

Several factors combined to bring about Poland's emergence in the seventeenth century as 'the champion of Catholicism in eastern Europe', culminating in King Jan Sobieski's (1624–96) deliverance of Vienna from Turkish siege in 1683. The critical decades in the process of turning Poland into Catholicism's eastern buttress were the 1560s and 1570s. In this period the single most important individual agent of re-Catholicisation in Poland was Cardinal Stanislaus Hosius, described by Uminski as 'one of the most outstanding figures of European Catholicism in the sixteenth century'. Led by Hosius, a group of bishops began to introduce measures of the Council of Trent, whose decrees were accepted by the Polish crown in 1564 (when Hosius brought in the Jesuits) and by the episcopate at large in 1577. Seminaries were set up, for example in Wilno and Poznań, to train priests both for parishes and for missionary work amongst non-Catholics in Poland. Under kings Sigismund I (or Zygmunt I, 1506–48) and Sigismund Augustus (Zygmunt August, 1548–72), the monarchy still strongly upheld the country's tolerant traditions which allowed its underdeveloped economy to attract foreign skilled workers and entrepreneurs. A change took place in the crown's religious position with the more assertive Catholicism of kings Stephen Báthory and Sigismund (or Zygmunt) III Vasa (1586–1632). With this royal realignment towards the Catholic Church, the nobility who had deserted it began to return to it, most spectacularly in the case of the *voivode* (governor) Mikolaj Krysztov Radziwiłł (1549–1616), formerly the leader of Protestants in Poland and Lithuania, but a convert whose son became a cardinal. Most of the gentry and peasantry had retained a bedrock Catholicism and in the course of the seventeenth century knowledge of the Catholic faith was deepened by missionary work, for example by the Jesuits' promotion of the miracle-working image of the Virgin and Child at Piakary in the diocese of Cracow in southern Poland. The other religious orders pursued specialist functions: the Theatines and Piarists educated boys and the Trinitarians ransomed captives; the Observant Franciscans, known in Poland as Bernardines, vigorously preached Tridentine Catholicism and exercised faculties for absolving persons of heresy. Mob attacks in towns such as Cracow, Wilno and Poznań eroded Protestantism through the destruction of its places of worship: Cracow, for a time a major centre of the Polish Reformation, lost its Protestant church in 1593.[21]

Much of the success of the Polish Catholic Reformation can be related to the increasing fusion between Catholicism and Polish national identity. The religious minorities that had flourished in Poland's sixteenth-century golden age of tolerance – Jews, Orthodox Christians, Moslems, Lutherans, Calvinists and Unitarians – were increasingly linked in Catholic Reformation propaganda with alien identity. At the same time, the Union of Lublin with Lithuania of 1569, in creating a huge and expansionist Polish state, fuelled national pride and led to calls for a religiously uniform Poland. Nostalgia for a Polish golden age looked back to the ancient Sarmatians, a valorous race who were the ancestors, it was believed, of the Polish nobility and gentry. In the course of the country's Catholic Reformation, preachers gave Polish Catholicism a Sarmatian-gentry image. In sermons, Old Testament figures were provided with coats of arms, like Polish squires; Moses became a *hetman*, a tribal leader; the Annunciation was a form of the Polish constitutional device, the *pacta conventa*, though one made between God and mankind; heaven was a chamber of deputies, a celestial Polish *sjem*; in the unlikely event of a Polish noble's going to hell, he would be punished privately, out of sight of the servants. Canonisation, on the other hand, was an ennoblement. Mary was venerated as Queen of Poland, while the religions of non-Poles – the Lutheranism of German 'merchants', the Orthodoxy of the eastern peasants, the Judaism of the landed class's menial stewards – were stigmatised in Polish gentry snobbery and xenophobia. A corollary was that individuals' and families' adoption of Polish naturalisation implied their Catholicisation. As Catholicism came to be associated with Polish, and specifically with noble 'Sarmatian', identity, what became in the seventeenth century the country's dominant Catholic faith was for the most part spared imported religious discord, especially over Jansenism, though the downside of this insulation, claims Tazbir, was isolation and increasing intellectual stagnation in Polish Catholicism. At the same time, the arts and architecture of Catholic religion became Polonised. The baroque, in origin an Italian architecture of stone, was introduced, for example in the great Jesuit pilgrimage church at Swieta Lipka (1687–92), but in Poland's forested landscape the style was adapted to local materials and traditions of building, as in the vernacular masterpieces in Tomaszow Lubelski (1728) or Szalowa (1760) in which local craftsmen created a naturalised Polish baroque or rococo timber architecture for a Polish Catholicism.[22]

Poland's Catholicism was also an arm of the country's expansionism and its sense of its place in the world. Dynastic links with Sweden stimulated Polish encouragement of attempts to reintroduce the Catholic Church there under Sigismund III's father, John III Vasa of Sweden (1537–92), and Jesuits went from Poland to Sweden, from their colleges in Braunsberg and Wilno, in an attempt at a Swedish Catholic Restoration which in the event won little support outside royal circles (Lutheran Scandinavia proved highly resistant to the early modern Catholic counter-offensive). Polish missions also extended to Persia, the East Indies, Japan and China. In those lands, Poles encountered their own facet of the most problematic aspect of religious acculturation in the early modern world, the relationship between Western Catholicism and indigenous cultures.[23]

In Latin America Catholic mission was initially buoyed up by considerable optimism on the part of the missionaries over the receptivity of native peoples to their message. This optimism was itself largely a response to the favourable reactions of American Indians to the missionaries, a welcome, though, based partly on oblique perceptions of what the newcomers' claims amounted to: in the north-west of the viceroyalty of New Spain, for example, the Jesuits were admired for their ability to handle horses. Even so, early collisions, pointing to later difficulties, occurred with medicine men and over conveying the Church's teaching on monogamy. Yet the Indians appeared to the missionaries to be teachable, adapting their habits to the demands of Catholicism, for example by fashioning their *quipus*, knotted strings, so as to keep count of the sins they had to confess. The Franciscans were to the fore in the 'spiritual conquest' of Mexico and when they arrived in 1524 the Indians crowded to hear them preaching and to be baptised. Franciscan apocalyptic hopes rose as the prospect seemed to open up of rebuilding the Apostolic Church in America's apparent *tabula rasa*. Borah calculates that amongst the Pueblo Indians of New Mexico by 1630, fifty Franciscans ministered to up to 50,000 converts in twenty-five missions covering ninety *pueblo* communities. Native American peoples in areas such as the Lima district of Peru were, apparently, becoming Catholic parishioners in the sixteenth and seventeenth centuries. The problem was that the terms on which they did so – theirs – eventually proved unacceptable to their missionary mentors.[24]

Syncretism, the confluence of streams of religious belief and practice to form new syntheses, arose vigorously in Spanish America and arrangements for the co-existence of imported and indigenous religious systems sprung up: in Peru, where native religious leaders retained their authority after the arrival of the missionaries, practices such as the ritual mummification of bodies persisted; a llama's blood might be smeared on the foundations of a building, including a church building, 'to make it strong'; a native god might be petitioned for permission for a worshipper to attend a festival of St Peter. Such accommodations eventually – by 1610 in the Lima district – aroused the ire of missionaries who had come to expect, at least after the expiry of a kind of probationary period of adjustment, the acceptance by native peoples of a 'pure' form of Christianity. Inquisitions were conducted in parishes and were followed by new waves of instruction to form, writes Mills, 'the most systematic attempt ever made in colonial Spanish America to repress Indian religion and uproot its alleged perversions of Catholicism'. The severest phase of 'extirpation' of alleged idolatry and, indeed, reputed demonology, took place in the Lima archiepiscopate of Pedro de Villagómez between 1641 and 1671. A fresh *auto da fé* of native cultic objects – 'idols' – was carried out in 1724 in Chancay in Peru. It may be, though, that in large parts of Latin America the syncretic system was too useful to be abandoned by native peoples, for it made possible the recruitment of saints, figures of great potency from the Christian sacred hierarchy, to supplement the gods who made up the ranks of existing indigenous supernatural power-brokers. Christian saints could be invoked even against harsh parish priests and Spanish governors. The evidence for the continued popularity of the syncretic synthesis in parts of modern South America is readily available, for example in the extant cult of the devil as the god of the underworld by Andean miners who consider themselves to be 'good Christians'.[25]

Needless to say, the Catholic missions could hardly have been established in South America without Iberian political and economic control. Conversely, rejection of such control and acculturation imposed through religious conversion was likely to inspire native anti-colonial revolt, and vice-versa. In the Upper Rio Grande valley, which was centred on the city of Santa Fé and was under the missionary care of the Franciscans, an intensive campaign against the religion and culture of the Pueblo inhabitants was undertaken in the 1670s, perhaps basically because the Spanish colony, cut off most of the time by desert from its source in settled Mexico, felt itself to be under threat of cultural and actual extinction. For whatever underlying reason, the Pueblos' ritual chambers were invaded, altars seized, religious dances forbidden, holy masks and wands broken, the Indian religious leaders gaoled and executed. The result was the Pueblo Revolt of 1681 in which around 380 colonists and twenty-one friars were massacred in a reprisal rebellion whose purpose was the eradication of all Spanish forms and foci of Catholic worship: churches were destroyed, Spanish personal names were forsaken, Indians had themselves ritually de-baptised, the wives wed in Catholic marriages were abandoned. It was, in fact, the counterpart of and response to the Spaniards' own campaign of eradication of Indian religion in the previous decade. Perhaps what had happened, after all, was that the superficiality of the similarities between Indian and Spanish religious cultures had become evident: they were surface resemblances only – for example, a Pueblo birth ceremony using water may have *seemed* like Baptism but was not. Meanwhile, the deeper culture clashes remained, for example over the place of the individual in the community – Western individualism versus Indian collectivism – and over attitudes towards the use of the environment – the exploitation of the colonists versus the ecological respect of the indigenous peoples. Instead of Christianisation proceeding through the routes of Indian language, culture and, indeed, religious values, it was attempted by the Franciscans in New Mexico through hispanicisation, and the result in the revolt of 1681 was Pueblo Indians' rejection both of Spanish culture and of Catholic faith.[26]

The central Roman missionary headquarters office of the Church set up in

1622, Propaganda Fide, was not concerned with the cultural Europeanisation of native peoples, in the way that the Spanish in America attempted hispanic cultural imperialism as well as Christian conversion. Guidance issued to missionaries by Propaganda in 1659 reads:

> Do not regard it as your task, and do not bring any pressure to bear on the peoples, to change their manners, customs, and uses, unless they are evidently contrary to religion and sound morals... [Do not introduce [European values] to them, but only the faith, which does not despise or destroy the manners and customs of any people, always supposing that they are not evil, but rather wishes to see them preserved unharmed....[T]here is no stronger cause for alienation and hate than an attack on local customs. Do not draw invidious contrasts between the customs of the peoples and those of Europe; do your utmost to adapt yourselves to them.

The ambiguities contained in that formula concerning the moral values contained within a cultural system were well brought out in the career of a French Capuchin missionary who arrived in eastern Brazil in 1612, Claude d'Abbeville. Perhaps in an early anticipation of the eighteenth-century European fetish of the 'noble savage', d'Abbeville initially evinced considerable respect for the Tupinamba Indians' ethics and conduct – their cheerful fortitude, common sense, peaceful family life and children's respect for their parents. However, he insisted that they must be introduced to European law and made to 'depart from their evil manner of living'. He instanced cruelty and cannibalism, in rejecting which d'Abbeville was undoubtedly applying the kind of thinking set out by Propaganda in its instruction that what was contrary to Christian 'religion and sound morals' should be shunned. Arguably, though, in his repugnance from what he called 'shameless' nudity, he was transmuting into a moral code his own cultural values, and the detestation of a sexually repressed Western civilisation for nakedness. Though he retained his optimism about the eventual success of the Capuchin mission to Brazil, d'Abbeville increasingly succumbed to stereotypes of a 'demi-brutal' and 'barbarous' indigenous population who lay under the 'devil's tyranny'. His experience suggests that the line that Propaganda was to draw between religion and morality on the one hand and cultural codes on the other was not an entirely tenable one.[27]

The Capuchin overseas mission at its zenith in the seventeenth century epitomised the global outreach of post-Reformation Catholicism, for it took in Venezuela, Trinidad, Spanish Guinea, West Africa, Angola, the Congo, Guadeloupe, Martinique, French Guinea, the Mississippi Valley and Nova Scotia. French missionaries worked in North Africa, Syria, Turkey, Ethiopia, Madagascar, Japan, China, Tibet and Canada. From the beginning, with Jacques Cartier in 1534, Canada had been envisaged as a special mission territory for France, and subsequently the Recollects, from 1615, and the Jesuits, who arrived in 1625 and who sent fifty-four missionaries in the mid-1630s, helped turn a string of trading posts into a colony. Education and the transmission of

French Catholic civilisation were also in the hands of Ursulines, sent from 1639 onwards. However, the French mission to Canada was caught up in a number of tensions and contradictions of which a number of Jesuit martyrs down to 1665 were the pitiable victims of terrible cruelty. Did Canada primarily represent a mission to the Indians, along with their economic reorganisation, as recommended by the Jesuit Lejeune, as settled farmers, or was that vast land viewed first and foremost as an area of settlement for (Catholic) peasants from metropolitan France? How were the rival tribes – the anti-mission Iroquois and the sympathetic Algonquins and Hurons – to be dealt with and what was the relationship between the tribes and the European nations competing for control of Canada? The Protestant English backed the anti-French Iroquois, and the French achieved *some* missionary success in Catholicising the Algonquins and the Hurons. Those successes, though, were limited to about 2,000 converts by 1800. In contrast, the other and much more successful front of the Catholicisation of New France saw the growth of a French-Quebec population originally, of course, immigrant but expanding through extraordinary natural increase – quadrupling in the first half of the eighteenth century – a community whose cultural identity was to be fortified against extinction in anglophone North America by its tenacious Counter-Reformation Catholicism.[28]

The case of Canada shows some of the ways in which European colonisation, and especially rivalry between colonising Western nations, might affect the success or failure of Catholic missionary work. It was one of the curiosities of religion in conditions of colonisation that Catholic missions throve in parts of India controlled by the Protestant British, as in Bombay, where Italian Carmelites were established in 1718 at the behest of the East India Company. A French Capuchin mission was set up in Madras in 1742, also at the Company's invitation, and when the East India Company gained Kerala later in the century a Carmelite mission, with a bishop and two priests, was already in place. Such stations provided for the religious needs of Indian Catholics whose ancestors had been converted before the arrival of the Company, and of Irish Catholic soldiers serving it. In contrast to the dispassionate utilitarianism of the East India Company, Portuguese attitudes within India seem to have been mingled with tense colonialist racism, to the disadvantage of the mission. The Portuguese were reluctant to encourage native vocations and one archbishop of Goa is reputed to have vowed never to ordain a native. That said, a Brahmin Christian convert, Matheus de Castro, who was refused ordination in Goa, travelled overland to Rome in 1625, was there ordained, and was eventually consecrated a bishop and appointed a Vicar Apostolic. It was symptomatic of the friction between the Roman office of Propaganda under the Holy See and Iberian insistence on political control of the imperial missions that Propaganda supported de Castro against the opposition of the Goan Portuguese, who refused to recognise his faculties in the colony. Rome backed de Castro, the Portuguese authorities in Goa opposed him and, following protracted and disedifying conflict, he was the last Indian Catholic bishop until the twentieth century. The Vatican also displayed an enlightened attitude to colonial slavery in the later seventeenth century when in 1686 it issued what Gray calls a 'far reaching condemnation covering a whole range of abuses' of the slave trade. Rome's declaration came about as a result of the agitation, supported by the 'humanitarian concern' of the Capuchin Order, which was conducted by Lourenço da Silva, a Brazilian black leader who arrived in Lisbon in 1681, and in 1682, in Madrid, was made procurator of the Confraternity of Our Lady, Star of the Negroes, one of the sodalities which, in Brazil and Portuguese Africa, played a vital role in the social and religious lives of black Christians. These organisations, that is to say, were foci for Afro-American self-help and self-government. They provided aid for members who were sick or in prison and, with their provision of daily prayer and monthly Penance and Communion, of the Last Rites, obituary commemorations and autonomous chapels and altars in churches, they set up 'a powerful focus for a common [black] identity'. By the later seventeenth century Brazil, as well as metropolitan Portugal, had evolved a large number of such confraternities, providing, Richard Gray says, hope, dignity and self-respect for Afro-Americans and, in such fora as the Bahia (Brazil) Confraternity of Our Lady of the Rosary, a 'recognized mouthpiece for Black rights': it was out of this arena of awareness and solidarity that da Silva travelled to Rome in 1684 and drew the attention of cardinals at Propaganda to the iniquities of the slave trade.[29]

The impression of prejudice that we may take from cases such as that of de Castro needs to be balanced by awareness of the cosmopolitanism of Portuguese missionary education, for example in Goa, where the Jesuit college of St Paul had 110 students as early as 1556. The College educated members of eight Asian language groups, providing them with Latin and Portuguese but also retaining their own tongues, through whose continued use, it was hoped, they might act as missionary conduits to their own peoples. However, the European educational experience in Asia was far from being solely that of one-way European propagation of teaching, for in such societies as India, China and Japan the missionaries and colonists found, and in some cases admired, ancient, complex and advanced civilisations. The Italian Jesuit missionary Roberto de Nobili (1577–1656) retrained himself in south Indian philosophy and literature, adapting himself in dress, appearance and diet to local expectations of what a *sanyassi*, a holy man, was like, but also acquiring knowledge of classical Sanskrit and of south India's Tamil. Attempting to overcome the cultural and caste barriers to Christianisation, de Nobili, who arrived in India in 1605, was by the end of that decade making conversions from amongst the Brahmin caste. Just as he adapted himself to Brahmin ways, so he allowed his converts to retain the signs of their status and their cultural distinctiveness. In numerical terms, though, his eventual results, at least in terms of winning over the all-important highest caste members, may have been fairly paltry – Chadwick gives 178 converts from high caste members between 1607 and 1620 – as well as ephemeral. De Nobili himself tended optimistically to Europeanise the uniqueness of India, conceptually reducing the massive difficulty of his task: in particular, he saw the religiously sanctioned and highly tenacious caste system as if it were little more than a version of the European society of orders or estates. On the other side, his Brahmin converts may responded to his impressive cultural and scholarly Indianisation and seen him as one of the ongoing array of holy men from outside itself whom Hinduism can accommodate without losing its own authenticity. Nobili's relative – and glorious – failure as a missionary further illustrates the bulky cultural impediments in the way of European evangelical endeavours in the period of the Catholic Reformation.[30]

The oriental societies that Europeans most esteemed tended, at least in the long run, to prove most resistant to the allure of Europe's religion, or religions. China held a fascination for Europeans, going back to Marco Polo (1256–1323), if only for its managerial skills. The empire, according to the Portuguese traveller, Mendes Pinto (1510–93) 'was so impressive, so wealthy and thriving', the reason being that it was well supplied with waterways provided by the rulers of what was rightly viewed by Westerners as a highly articulated and closely administered society, in which Christianisation would depend on the benevolence of the ruling class, a cultivated élite imbued with Confucian philosophy. Targeting 'famous nobles and great officers', the Italian Jesuit Matteo Ricci (1552–1610) turned himself into a Confucian philosopher, as de Nobili made himself an Indian holy man, and authored a set of observations on friendship using classical Chinese literary models. He brought Western technology in the shape of clocks, which he repaired, Western memory skills in the form of his 'memory palaces' and a combination of European and Chinese meditative approaches that knitted the Ignatian method with Buddhist techniques. Similarly, and in an another intricate oriental culture, that of Japan, some of Xavier's dream was achieved, creating a Catholicism with a part-Japanese face, so successfully at first that by 1614 the Church had made 300,000 converts. In the event, though, the perception in Japanese anti-Catholic propaganda that Christianisation might mean colonisation helped end Japan's 'Christian century' in a fierce anti-European reaction. A banishment order against foreigners in 1587 was the overture to persecution, with executions of missionaries beginning in 1617 and leading to upwards of 2,000 martyrdoms of Japanese Christians and their missionaries. In another island, on the far side of the world from Japan – but one where persecution of Catholics was also rife in the first half of the seventeenth century – the English Catholic work commemorating Japanese executions in 1622, *The Theater of Iaponia's constancy* was published to provide a moral example from one oppressed community to another. Counter-Reformation Catholicism had become a world faith with a global sense of identity.[31]

7 The Catholic Reformation and the arts

In this final chapter we shall consider the relationship between the Catholic renewal of the sixteenth and seventeenth centuries and the arts used as media for purposes of doctrinal instruction and the raising of religious consciousness. We shall review the art forms of architecture, painting, literature, theatre and music – looking very selectively at a few representative architects, painters, authors and musicians, and we shall consider the question of the baroque as, so to speak, the 'house style' of the Catholic Reformation.

The concept of the baroque, deriving in the first instance from architecture, has been extended to cover all the arts, and even lifestyle or the wider *zeitgeist* of seventeenth-century Europe: what Skrine calls 'baroque culture in its broadest sense', and including, in Friedrich's definition, moral excess and extremism of behaviour. Indeed, excess, distortion and fantasy have often been seen as the essence of baroque building and the characteristics of some of its best-known practitioners: 'dramatic fantasy', for example, is said to have been the hallmark of the architect Francesco Borromini (1599–1667), while the German and Austrian masters of baroque architecture such as Johann Bernhard Fischer von Erlach (1656–1723), the brothers Cosmas Damian Asam (1686–1739) and Egid Quirin Asam (1692–1750) and Balthasar Neumann (1687–1753) are said to have exhibited 'reckless extravagance' (Friedrich). The identification of irregularity as the guiding feature of baroque is, indeed, implicit in the very etymology of the word, which may have been derived from the Portuguese term for a rough-shaped pearl. If baroque represents distortion, though, from what standards is it supposed to have been an aberration? A common view is that baroque means a radical, indeed a revolutionary, departure – Beny and Gunn call Borromini the exponent of a 'revolutionary' art – from the canons of geometric regularity and rational beauty upheld above all in the classicist art of the Renaissance and in its acknowledged masters such as the primary architect of St Peter's, Donato Bramante (1444–1514), and the theorist of neo-classical architecture based on ancient Roman models, Andrea Palladio (1518–80). In the eighteenth century hostile critics of the baroque led by the ardent classicist Johann Joachim Winckelmann (1717–68) employed the term baroque, as Friedrich says, 'to describe works of art and architecture which did not meet the standards they believed to have eternal validity as "classic" forms of beauty'. Further, baroque in its a-rationality has represented in the minds of its critics a flight from reason and indeed from reality itself and a 'highly emotional escape from the miseries of the world' (Cooper). Then, too, while classical architecture has been seen as maintaining the self-evident truth of rational, stable and orderly principles, especially symmetry of design, suspicion hangs over baroque, and above all over baroque architecture, as an art, if not of deception, through techniques such as *trompe d'oeil*, then, as Norman writes, of 'illusion to transport the spectator into a visionary world'. Baroque, then, has been accused of radical departure from the principles of mathematical order associated with the classical architecture of the Renaissance. In other terms, whereas the straight lines of the classical have been seen as representing the veracity of a geometric axiom, baroque, with its kinetics, has been deemed the epitome of subjective and emotional circularity – and of deceit.[1]

If baroque was an innovatory or revolutionary architecture, eschewing the guiding principles of the preceding dominant style, then it might be thought to have abandoned a stylistic canon that was inseparably connected with the dictates of rational regularity, simplicity and severity associated originally with the first-century Roman architect, Marcus Pollio Vitruvius. Palladio was Vitruvius's most influential sixteenth-century disciple in the quest for harmony of form. As iterated by Jacopo Barozzi da Vignola (1507–73) in the *Regole [or Regola] delli cinque ordini d'architettura* (*The Rules of the Five Orders of Architecture*) (1562) Vitruvianism was the application of a geometry in which all proportions were precisely calculated in ratios, for *ratio* means reason, as well as truth and the antithesis of illusion. Geometry was a branch of mathematics, and mathematics were incontestable: according to Aristotle mathematics provided the provable basis of veracity, not of illusion. Above all, the fixed, straight line and the right angle, drawn by the set-square of reason, prevailed in Renaissance classical architecture. They did, for example, in Vignola's designs incorporated in an architectural textbook of which a late eighteenth-century edition carried a frontispiece showing an uncompromisingly severe and geometrical classical arch whose straight verticals and horizontals were capped with a scroll celebrating the partnership of *Matematica* and *Architettura*. In apparent contrast to this Renaissance classical Vitruvian architecture which, Norman says, 'embodied clarity and order' and in which 'the humanist strand was geometry' – with which discipline Renaissance minds were 'in love' – the baroque architecture of the seventeenth century might, from one point of view, be claimed to have espoused riot, circularity and the primacy of effect and emotion over truth and reason, the more so as it grew to maturity and fulfilled its own inner logic. Thus the *Cathedra Petri* (Throne of St Peter) undertaken in 1656 by the master of the Roman baroque Gian Lorenzo Bernini (1598–1680) may appear to be a product of 'stagecraft' (by the 'greatest master of baroque illusionism': Norman) rather than of mathematics. To take another Roman example, Borromini's spire of San Ivo alla Sapienza (1642–60) – said to resemble the twisted horns of a Sicilian goat – seems the epitome of circularity and the antithesis of rational geometry, from the design of the architect who said that the corner – literally the base of geometric building – was 'the enemy of architecture'. Borromini's San Carlo alle Quatro Fontane (Rome, 1638–67) seems likewise to represent the triumph of the anti-geometric, of convex and concave discs in place of 'true' and fixed angles, lines and squares. And as baroque expanded its geographical range within Europe into the eighteenth century, it seemed to fulfil an anti-geometric dynamic within itself. In Turin the creations of the Theatine architect Guarino Guarini (1624–83), such as the church of San Lorenzo (from 1668), celebrate whorls and vortices; as the later baroque flourished in Bohemia, it exhibited, writes Blazicek, 'the intersection of circular shapes', the 'concave curve' 'undulating walls' 'sinuous…flowing, undulating form'. The 'dynamic' pulpit seemingly 'blown into ecstasy', executed by Dominikus Zimmermann (1685–1776) in Die Wies in Bavaria (1746–54) eschews straight lines, and actually appears to defy geometry and indeed gravity. And whereas Vitruvian mathematical architecture proved its rational truth through the axioms of straight lines and fixed angles, baroque, it might be claimed, asserted its emotional power through the dazzlement of circular, fluid and kinetic forms, so that, for example, Bernini's *Cathedra Petri* has been seen as a triumph of a-rational illusionism, a 'theatrical *tableau vivant* before which the devout spectator surrenders, while the agnostic connoisseur turns silently away'.[2]

Perhaps, though, we ought to exercise a little caution in making statements about the non-rational appeal of baroque, about its innovatory or revolutionary departures from Vitruvian-Palladian principles or about its alleged violations of geometry or its anti-rationality. If we stay with our subjects, the arch-rivals Bernini and Borromini, we shall see that they operated to a large extent in the Vitruvian tradition. Borromini is often considered the most baroque – in the sense of the most extravagant – of the seventeenth-century Roman architects, yet in his commission for the Roman Oratory, completed in 1640, for example, although the façade is curvilinear, the architect allowed himself to be constrained into classical restraint by the austere spirit of that 'Congregation of souls so meek that in the matter of ornament they held my hand'. In point of fact, Borromini's whole architecture was one of strict control. For example, underpinning the balletic quality of San Ivo alla Sapienza is a very precise mathematical engineering, and if Borromini was 'revolutionary', it was not because he eschewed geometry or proportion in themselves but because he rejected the specific human-centred geometry of the architectural masters of the Renaissance, including Bramante. Beny and Gunn write:

> The apparently wilful and aimless undulations or meanderings that have disturbed many people who have seen Borromini's buildings are in fact coherent and logical elements in the architect's highly original and brilliantly executed inventions, and there are reputable precedents for all of them.[3]

If Borromini was basically more conventional and, in his massive contribution to the evolution of baroque, less revolutionary than is sometimes assumed, Bernini operated largely within the Vitruvian tradition, to the extent that Carunchio speaks of his classicism, and Thoenes refers to his indebtedness to Palladio and to the genius of Roman classical form in sixteenth-century Rome, Michelangelo. Bernini's high altar for the Barnabite church in Bologna, with its vertical, Corinthian-capped columns and geometrical assemblage, resembles Bramante's *tempietto* (1502) – itself based on the pure, harmonious form of an ancient Roman temple – at San Pietro in Montorio in Rome. The Bologna high altar is in fact a masterpiece of Palladian-Vitruvian classicism, and equally classical in its symmetry, severity and sense of geometry is the chapel of the Palazzo de Propaganda Fide by Bernini (1634), rebuilt by Borromini in 1662. Thus Bernini and Borromini should, along with other accomplished practitioners of baroque architecture, such as the designer of the façade of St Peter's, Carlo Maderna (1556–1629), and Pietro Berrettini da Cortona (1596–1669), be considered as belonging well within the Renaissance-classical legacy and to have been part of an architectural sequence and tradition going back to Bramante's arrival in Rome in 1499. That in turns tells us that the baroque architects of the seventeenth century manifested stylistic evolution rather than revolution, because they were contributing to a long-term project, the restoration and glorification of the papal city of Peter. The summit of that project was the completion of St Peter's begun by Bramante but completed by Bernini in the sense that he put in place the crucial finishing touches, such as the *Cathedra Petri*, that hammered home the message of the meaning of Rome, of its churches and above all of its basilica. As we saw in Chapter 4, the reaffirmation of Rome's role as the Petrine centre of the Catholic world was a protracted and ambitious scheme. Crucial to its success was a unified architectural conception, as continuous in its styling as the project of Rome was itself a unity. Any revolutionary eruption into the classical models of Bramante and Michelangelo of a radically non-classical style would certainly have disrupted the essential sequence of the Roman building project. Bernini's and Borromini's baroque represented, then, a development and an evolution on what had gone before, as with Bernini's colonnade at St Peter's (from 1656), a perfect completion of the conceptions of his predecessors of what the basilica represented – in this case the church of the Apostle embracing the globe.[4]

Much of Bernini's Roman work was indeed concerned with the setting out of a pedagogy about Rome and its papal and Petrine significance, centred on St Peter's. How much this instruction had to do with 'baroque illusion' is what we should next consider. Sometimes viewed as the 'greatest master of baroque illusionism', a conjurer of dazzling prestidigitation, amazing the stupefied beholder with his conquest of self-imposed challenges, Bernini might seem at his most histrionic in the *baldacchino* (1624–33), the sculpted canopy over the high altar in St Peter's believed also to cover the tomb of the Apostle. Surely this work, with its apparent defiance of the classical disciplines, its spiralled columns, circularity, plasticity, dynamic motion and apparent abandonment of regularity, must be regarded as both the 'frontispiece of the baroque' (Kirwin) and a high point of baroque emotionality, deception and 'fantasy'. Yet this is no work of mere decorative virtuosity or of grand illusion, but rather of a carefully thought-out and in fact rather academic set of propositions based on a coherent reading of sacred history. The columns of the *baldacchino* are indeed twisted, in a way that seems totally foreign to the Bramantian classicism that Bernini had adopted in his Bologna Barnabite commission. However, the belief prevailing in Bernini's day was that the twisted pillars in the older Roman basilica of St Peter had come from Solomon's Temple in Jerusalem. Bernini's statement in the bronze of the *baldacchino* is thus that the pope's basilica was the centre of the Church as the temple of the New Covenant. Similarly, the bronze cover of the *baldacchino* is represented as a textile canopy, and if this is 'illusion', then it is a highly didactic form of that art, for a canopy is the covering placed over a living dignitary, in this case Peter who, for Bernini, lives in the person of his successor in office, the pope who sponsored his work, Urban VIII (Maffeo Barberini, pope 1623–44). Likewise, Bernini's *Cathedra Petri* is undeniably emotive and 'theatrical' in its effect but the message of the ensemble is profoundly serious and doctrinal as well as affective, for the spectacular throne in bronze contains an ancient relic believed to be St Peter's wooden chair, and the whole is sustained by four Fathers of the Church, Catholicism's mentors.[5]

Despite all the traditionalism of style we have so far considered, baroque was undeniably a novel mode of architecture. The primary model for the style throughout Europe was the Jesuit church, Il Gesù in Rome, begun in 1568 by Vignola with Cardinal Alessandro Farnese as patron, and continued from 1573 by Vignola's pupil Giacomo della Porta (*c.* 1540–1602) – a church of the new age of the Catholic Reformation, though initially designed by a conservative and classicist architect. Indeed some of the Gesù's features, especially the elimination of columned aisles so as to open up the interior as a huge auditorium for preaching, were novel, in Wittkower's words, not as an outcome of a 'new aesthetic of architecture' but from 'a new concept of the role of the church', one aimed at involving greater frequency of lay attendance at Mass and the Sacraments. Simultaneous Masses were provided for on various altars but there was also a focused concentration of reverence on a high altar, for solemn Masses and also for veneration of the Blessed Sacrament in Benediction and *Quarant' Ore*. In the baroque age the main altar was to be the single most magnetic internal feature of churches, with vision of it maximised by the same openness of space demanded by emphasis on preaching. The drama of the high altar was certainly brought out in Bernini's superb execution in the Barnabites' church in Bologna. Considerable discussion has arisen over the extent to which churches built in the style that emerged in the period of the Catholic Reformation represented a 'Jesuit architecture'. It may be the case, though, that a common stylistic currency, one dictated by considerations of lay use, was evolved for the churches of the orders of clerks regular at large. Orders including the Barnabites, as well as the Theatines and the Oratorians, shared a stress on a mission to the laity and thus on the employment of churches as worshipping halls. Goals common to orders of clerks regular dictated, then, much of the lay-out of the churches of the baroque age. Interior art work was intended to be instructive by means of impact, calling for the force, the movement and the stupendous effect of paintings such as *The Adoration of the Name of Jesus* (1674–9) by Giovanni Battista Gaulli ('Il Baciccio, or 'Baciccia', 1639–1709), placed in the ceiling of the nave of the Gesù. At the same time, the clerks regular focused their missions on towns, and space was often at such a premium that new churches were squeezed into confined quarters, as was, for example, the Barnabites' San Barnaba, substantially the work, from 1561, of Galeazzo Alessi (1512–72), which is fitted into a humdrum terrace in the old centre of Milan and whose façade has a suggestion of a false front. In crowded townscapes the new urban churches of the Catholic Reformation had to establish themselves and advertise their presence as effectively as possible through their architecture. Spectacular façades, perhaps the feature of the baroque that we most immediately associate with the style, could be highly effective in solving this problem of maximising the presence of a church. Thus in 1656, for example, da Cortona added the 'magnificently spectacular' façade and portico of Santa Maria della Pace, which is encountered as a splendid surprise 'in a maze of narrow streets' (Beny and Gunn) in Rome. The grandeur and mass of della Porta's 1575 facade of the Gesù asserted the position of the building in a highly competitive Roman scenery of churches. The architecture of such churches of the Catholic Reformation were designed to express the needs and purposes of orders of clerks regular, including the Jesuits.[6]

The Jesuits certainly propagated the baroque building style, and did so in an entirely utilitarian fashion, conforming to the Society's principle of the subordination of form to purpose, as set out, for example, by the Jesuit poet Gerard Manley Hopkins (1844–89): 'Our Society values…and has contributed to…culture, but only as a means to an end'. The Jesuit purpose of communicating with people might dictate the extensive modification of what has been viewed as the Society's 'house style', the baroque. Thus the Jesuit church of Dillingen (1610–17) in Bavaria (Hans Alberthal/Alberthaler, originally known as Giovanni Albertalli, d. *c.* 1667), a model of Jesuit architecture in German-speaking Catholic lands, falls partly into line with the predominant late medieval gothic German architectural habit and with 'local taste' (Bourke) and tradition. Again, and given that the Jesuits were in the business of teaching and of highlighting their messages through every means at their disposal, we should appreciate that their use of the arts to 'adorn' their churches was inspired by pedagogic and promotional considerations and their urge to publicise the importance of the Society, in part through harnessing the value and power of their founding saints. Such considerations defined the representations of themes in Jesuit art. This was particularly the case with depictions of Ignatius Loyola.[7]

Images of Loyola were strongly promoted in Jesuit churches, as, for example, they were by Rubens in his 1617 *Miracles of St Ignatius* in the Jesuit church of St Carlo Borromeo (St Carolus Borromeüskerk) in Antwerp. For mass distribution, monochrome engravings produced in Brussels in 1609 on the occasion of Loyola's beatification featured key scenes in his career and related his life in popular pictorial form. Loyola's beatification in fact produced a flurry of Jesuit-sponsored art works in commemoration of him, including a scene of his writing the Rules of the Society attributed to the Spanish-born artist Jusepe de Ribera (1588–1656). A depiction of the *Death of Loyola* in the style of the Italian-born Spanish artist Bartolomé Carducho (or Bartolomeo Carducci, *c.* 1560–1608) shows him in the posture of the 'happy death', a genre scene of late medieval origin in which the Christian in his or her last moments is surrounded by relatives. The Loyolan 'family' on this occasion are the founding fathers of the Society of Jesus. A growing trend evident in a selection of renditions of Loyola is that of presenting him as heroic and dramatic. In the porch of the sacristy of the Gesù, a work from the seventeenth century showing Loyola presenting the Jesuit Rule to Paul III centres on the pope, with Loyola in a subordinate kneeling position. However, a painting after the Italian Jesuit artist Andrea Pozzo (1642–1709) showing Loyola commissioning Francis Xavier to go on the missions, has the Jesuit founder in the dominant position, standing, with Xavier submissively half-genuflecting. The trend towards glamorising Loyola may have reached a new level at around the time of his canonisation in 1622. A 1609 *Loyola's Vision of the Trinity* shows a swarthy individual, somewhat coarse-featured. However, in a post-canonisation portrait (1625–6) by Gian-Francesco Barbiero Guercino (1590–1666), Loyola, balding, lightly bearded, fine-featured, has been made handsome. He is partnered by a dashing Francis Xavier but the papal involvement with the Jesuits is not now that of Paul III's condescending to a suppliant Loyola: instead, the latter and Xavier flank, in a posture of parity, one of the greatest of the popes, St Gregory the Great. In this version, the new-minted saints Loyola and Xavier are upgraded by placing them in close association with one of the most venerable saints of the Church. The pictorial enhancement of Loyola upgraded him in an iconography of promotion designed not only to project a powerful image of the saint himself but also to advertise the Society he founded in the most spectacular light possible. The apotheosis of Loyola in his inseparable association with the founding and launching of the Society of Jesus is caught in the silver statue of him by Francisco de Vergara the younger, in the basilica of Loyola. Here a powerful, muscular Loyola, in flowing, jewel-encrusted chasuble and with dominant features and gaze, points to the text he is holding which bears the Jesuit motto, *Ad majorem Dei gloriam* – 'To the greater glory of God'. The magnification of Loyola reached an even higher level with the silver statue (1697) by Pierre Legros the Younger of the saint above his burial altar and grave in the Gesù. Sited so as to place Loyola above the Mass altar and immediately below the Trinity, this representation went as far as it could in putting forward a suggestion that the Jesuit founder was the greatest of saints. Such work, though, with all its hyperbole, is part of a systematic artistic campaign of promotion of the greater glory of the Society of Jesus. While such baroque images incorporated elements of exaggeration, yet this art of hyperbole was conceived with the instructional and promotional functions of publicity in mind.[8]

There remains widespread agreement that the salient features of baroque are violence and brutality, as in the pronounced realism of the Italian Michel Angelo Merisi [or Amerighi] da Caravaggio (1569–1609). Artemesia Gentileschi

(1590–1642) if anything outdid Caravaggio in the unflinching immediacy of her scenes of blood and gore, for instance in her two versions of *Judith Slaying Holofernes* (1612–13, *c*. 1620). If there were, though, a baroque love-affair with the brutal, it also had a didactic purpose. In a work such as Gasparo Celio's (1571–1640) *Christ Carrying the Cross*, there is certainly no shrinking – quite the reverse – from representing the pain of the experience, nor was there any novelty in Western Christian art in bringing to bear a deliberately horrifying realism in Crucifixion scenes, for the depiction of the human agony of the Passion was part of an essential homiletic purpose in iconography. As for renderings of martyrdom, medieval hagiographic art had depicted the widest range of forms of torment in the fullest detail. Some baroque art brought this martyrological realism, as it were, up to date, for example with the frescoes (1583) in the English College, Rome, by Niccolò Circignani (called Il Pomarancio, *c*. 1516–96) featuring with the closest anatomical observation the horrific scenes of the disembowelling of Edmund Campion (b. 1540) and other English martyrs in 1581. If this is to be regarded as a further example of a predilection towards violence in some way typical of baroque, then at least we should bear in mind the utilitarian instructional purpose of this art-work, for it was, wrote Émile Mâle, 'intended to assist the instructors in the tempering of souls, and the images of torture scenes were used as a preparation for martyrdom'. Once more it becomes evident that it was a goal of instruction that set the tone of much of what we think of as being typical of Catholic baroque.[9]

Spanish art of the period of the Catholic Reformation discovered, or rediscovered, the value of simplicity and realism, including the realistic rendition of violence, in religious painting. Religious painting in sixteenth-century Spain had received the impact of two features of Renaissance aesthetics, a cult of the recondite and the celebration of physical beauty. The former tendency can be seen in *Holy Family* (1562–9) by Luis de Morales (known as 'El Divino', 1509–86) which contains arcane allusions and devices such as a basket of eggs (a coded symbol of new life in Christ) and, representing a typical Renaissance classicist amalgam of pagan astrology and Christian doctrine, Christ's horoscope. It was significant of a shifting mood in Spain, and specifically of abandonment of attempts to merge classical-pagan and Christian cultures, that Gerolamo Cardano (1501–76), the original author of the horoscope conceit, was arrested by the Inquisition in Italy soon after Morales's *Holy Family* was completed. A further feature of religious art of the Spanish Renaissance is the glorification of the physical, achieved in part through the deletion of the reality of suffering in favour of the celebration of the human body. The suppression of truth involved in this sort of exercise can be seen, for example, in Pedro Machuca's (1490s–1550) *Deposition* of 1520–5 in which a virtually unmarked Christ is brought down from the Cross: the conception resembles that of the serene and painless Deposition (1507) by Raphael (Rafaello Santi, or Sanzio, 1483–1520), a glorification of physical perfection. As late as 1592 the Italian artist, Pellegrino Tibaldi (called Pellegrino de Pellegrini, 1527–96), was continuing in the vein of celebrating physical athleticism with his pain-free *Martyrdom of St Lawrence*.

However, Morales who painted the recherché *Holy Family* in 1560–70 also carried out an agonised *Pietà* for the Jesuit church in Córdoba. Not only does this work reveal the return to realism in the depiction of the Passion but, deriving perhaps from Flemish influences on Spanish art, it must also reflect an even more immediate Ignatian spirit of meditation through the insistence in Loyola's *Spiritual Exercises* on absolute reality in contemplations of the Gospel narrative. Realism and simplicity were now once more the guiding principles of form and content in Spanish religious art. In the year after Tibaldi's *Martyrdom of St Lawrence*, in which the focus of devotion could be said to be the idealised nude human body, the starkly un-sensuous rendition in 1593 of the death of another saint, St Francis, by Carducho, in a study in Franciscan brown, features clothed figures and exalts holy poverty and simplicity. The devotional emphasis of Trent in its treatment of the arts, along with Catholic and counter-humanist suspicion of the nude, plus the influence of Ignatian meditation – which itself drew on medieval wells – was dictating a major change in the themes and modes of Spanish art before the end of the sixteenth century. Under Philip III the leading minister Lerma gave his favour to the artistic 'reformers' who restored a spirit of simpler piety, directness and realism to Spanish art.[10]

Reflecting the enormous importance of the Mendicant orders – not least as patrons of artists – the Dominican scenes of the protégé of the Ávila convent Pedro Berruguete (1450s–1503/4) had exalted the Order of Preachers, in *The Temptation of St Thomas Aquinas* and *St Dominic Pardons a Heretic*. To set alongside this promotion of Dominican themes, the Franciscans come off poorly in Juan de Flandes's (d. *c.* 1519) *Temptation of Christ* (*c.* 1500) in which the devil is garbed as a Franciscan. Spain, seemingly, was not exempt from the hostility to the traditional religious orders which characterised the age of Erasmus. The Greek adoptive Spaniard, El Greco (Domenico Theotocopouli, 1541–1614), though, manifested an intense respect for the Franciscans. In the *Burial of the Count of Orgaz* (1586–88) it is the two friars present, dressed in simple contrast to the be-ruffed nobles and vested saints, who point out and preach the message of the life and death of the charitable count. The doctrine being drawn out is an anti-Lutheran one, to the effect, as Trent had declared, that the just are saved by their good deeds as well as by faith. Increasingly, too, depictions of Francis himself reflected Tridentine Christocentricity, for Francis was celebrated in Spanish religious art of the Catholic Reformation as Christlike, and as being in close association with Christ. *St Francis Embracing the Crucified Christ* (1620–01), by Francisco de Ribalta (1565–1628), forms an audacious artistic adventure in which Christ lowers an arm from the Cross to clasp Francis. Versions (1656–9, 1657) of the *Stigmatization of St Francis* by Juan Rizi (or Ricci, 1600–81) and by Francisco 'El Mozo' de Herrera (1622–85) honour the moment when Francis's imitation of Christ was perfected.[11]

In Italy, de Maio claims, Naples 'can be regarded as the real capital of the Counter-Reformation…[,] the mirror of its successes, its ambiguities and of its failures'. It was certainly a most religious city, with its thirty canonised saints, eight patron saints, seven miraculous crucifixes, seventeen thorns from the

Crown of Thorns, and its 504 religious houses in 1692. However, if the claim that Naples was the capital of the Counter-Reformation threatens Rome's title, it may at least be possible to consider the southern city as the heart of what de Maio calls the 'rhetorical' Counter-Reformation. Is it possible, for example, that rhetoric, in the sense of evasion of reality, of claims that what is said to be the case *is* the case, is implicit in such a work as Caravaggio's *The Seven Acts of Mercy* (1607) and might this work even be read as presenting an artistic alternative to performing those deeds of charity, in this city where fifty per cent of the population was destitute? Yet Gregori argues that Caravaggio's painting carried out for the Monte della Misericordia which was founded in 1601 specifically for the practical implementation of the Seven Works of Mercy set out in Matt., 25: 35, 36 and elsewhere in Scripture should be read as a clear, and not (as de Maio suggests), 'obscure', mandate to carry out the deeds of mercy – visiting the sick and the imprisoned, feeding and giving drink to the hungry and thirsty, clothing the naked, harbouring strangers, and burying the dead. As Gregori writes, 'The support for the needy demanded by the Church is transformed in [Caravaggio's] painting into a moving participation in tragedy, evoked by the text of Matthew'. If, then, Caravaggio's *Seven Works of Mercy* represents 'rhetoric', it should be seen as a didactic rhetoric in favour of practical action in the direction of the meritorious good works recommended by Trent. Again, it may be possible to see the Naples of the Catholic Reformation as a place of exploitation, of political deference and social conformity, in which the appalling poverty of the many was insulted by the opulence of the city's cathedral, by the elaborate chapel of the city's favourite saint, San Gennaro and by the ornate tabernacles in the Franciscans' churches. From one point of view, the Naples of the Catholic Reformation was a place where 'obedience was the supreme quality' (de Maio), where the Jesuits used the arts and artists for purposes of thought-control and indoctrination in the arts of subordination. On the other hand, we ought at least to be aware that the image of the Virgin of the Carmine, the iconic inspiration for the plebeian anti-state, anti-tax revolt led by the fisherman Masaniello (Tomasso Aniello, 1623–47) in 1647, was one of the city's two Madonnas splendidly rehoused in the 1620s and 1630s: religious images in baroque Naples were capable of fuelling dissidence and revolt as well as 'obedience'.[12]

The same teaching purpose that was to the fore in Catholic baroque religious painting inspired the religious theatre of the Catholic Reformation from the sixteenth century onwards. In fact, this theatre had its roots in the late medieval religious drama that continued to thrive in the earlier sixteenth century in Paris, for example, where the Confraternity of the Passion 'played and acted many fine mysteries for the edification and entertainment of the common people' – though it may have been a changed attitude to the propriety of sacred representation that induced the municipality in 1548 to forbid the Confraternity to enact the Passion or 'any other sacred mysteries'. The medieval roots of the religious theatre which the Jesuits introduced as part of their religious pedagogy are likewise clearly evident from the *perioche*, or plot outline, of a Jesuit play put on at the Jesuit *Gymnasium* (grammar school) in Ingolstadt in Bavaria in 1606. Even the title of this work betrays its essentially medieval character: *Vonn dem Todt oder Todtentanz*, 'All About Death, or the Death Dance', a traditional dramatic representation of the medieval theme of *memento mori*, of the universality of death and of the *danse macabre*. As with most medieval religious theatre, the basic sources of the material are scriptural, rather than classical, in this particular case a text from Isaiah, (40: 6) which, again in entirely medieval theatrical fashion, delivers the message which was to the fore in the morality plays of the middle ages, concerning the certainty of death, regardless of rank: 'All flesh is as grass....In confirmation of this he [Isaiah] finds a skull which answers him saying: "Everyone, great or small, rich or poor, noble or common, must die." '.[13]

Produced in Munich only two years after the Ingolstadt play, a drama by the Jesuit preacher to the court of Maximilian I of Bavaria, Jeremias Drexel (1581–1638), on *Julian the Apostate*, about the Roman Emperor (*c.* 331–63) who abandoned Christianity and reintroduced paganism, has an entirely different feeling from the medievality of *Vonn dem Todt*, for it incorporates the classicism of the Renaissance which the Jesuits utilised for their purposes and which they integrated into their educational programme. *Julian* is based on Roman rather than scriptural history and, in a regularised, classical five-act structure, focuses, as ancient Greek tragedy had, on the central character who gives unity to the action and lends his name to the title of the work. Drexel's *Julian* is in fact presented as a complex and, indeed, almost tragic human being, rather than as a stereotypical figure of vice as in a medieval morality play: Drexel depicts Julian as a learned and virtuous philosopher. Himself a convert from Protestantism, this Jesuit dramatist had every reason to reflect on the theme of change in a person's religious convictions, for conversion of religion was a *leitmotif* of public life and of Jesuit endeavour in Germany in the pre-Thirty Years' War period. Also crucial in the religious make-up of the *Reich*, under the principle of the 1555 Peace of Augsburg summarised as *cujus regio, ejus religio* ('A ruler decides his subjects' religion') was the religious orientation of the prince. Whereas in the Roman Empire of Julian, the emperor's preferences threatened to halt the whole progress of Christianity, in the early-modern Holy Roman Empire of the German Nation the promotion of 'true' religion by regional princes such as the Wittelsbach rulers of Bavaria was vital to the whole success of the Catholic counter-offensive against the Reformation. Classical and medieval history, and especially the issue of religious allegiance under the state, provided the theme of a series of German Catholic dramas of the Catholic Reformation period. England's two saints Thomas – Thomas Becket (1118–70) and Thomas More (1478–1535), both martyred by royal autocrats, were the subjects of such German plays as *S. Thomas Cantuariensis Archiepiscopus & Martyr* (*St Thomas of Canterbury, Archbishop and Martyr*) and *Tragoedia Vom König Henrico II* (*A Tragedy Concerning King Henry II*), both featuring St Thomas Becket, and *Thomas Morus ex Anglie* ('Thomas More of England') in which More's position within the Reformation of the sixteenth century was recalled in extensive historical detail under the thematic caption of the conflict of duties. Classical martyrdom themes fed Jesuit theatre in France, leading eventually to the theatrical masterpiece of the Jesuit pupil Pierre Corneille (1608–84). Janelle comments: 'Corneille may…justifiably be considered as the greatest tragic poet of the Jesuit school, and his *Polyeucte* [1643] as the direct consequence of the Catholic Reformation, and the highest point reached by it in the field of literature'.[14]

In Germany, Drexel's fellow Jesuit Friedrich von Spee (1591–1635) composed poetry in which personal love for Jesus was mingled with themes from nature in works such as *Die Gespons Jesu seufftzet nach jhrem Bräutigam* (*The Bride of Jesus [the Church] Longs for Her Groom*). The note of personal, almost romantic, love for Jesus characteristic of von Spee was captured in the Spanish Netherlands in the *Triumphus Iesu oft Godlücke Lof-Sangen* (*The Triumph of Jesus, or Holy Songs of Praise*) (1633) by an anonymous woman member of the Third Order of St Francis in the Sion cloister in Lier, a town near Antwerp with a tradition of female religious lyricism in Dutch going back to the Beguine Beatrice van Nazareth in the thirteenth century. (There is additional verse material in *Triumphus*, including a 'spiritual pastoral' in the form of a dialogue between a shepherd and a shepherdess, by the Reverend Mother of the Sion cloister, Maria van Etten: the Lier house, 'Sion', is alluded to in the verses of one of the holy poems, one based on a song of the Holy Land). The title of the collection *Triumphus Iesu* is also an allusion to a near-contemporary poem in praise of love, *Triumphus Cupidinis* (*Cupid's Victory*) (1628), by an Antwerp poet, Joan Yselmans (1590–1629). The spiritual lyrics of *Triumphus* are set to well-known popular songs, including ballads of love and fashion, such as *La picarde* (*The Girl from Picardy*) and *Van de nieuw Balette* (*The New Dance*). Reflecting Spanish cultural influences in the southern Netherlands, one of the Jesus poems is set to a popular Spanish tune. However, despite the collection's employment of the devices of popular culture and romance, of 'little songs' and verses to aim its message at youth, the underlying theme was a profoundly spiritual one, aiming, as the title of *Triumphus* says, to banish worldly and trivial verses, by which the *Triumphus Cupidinis* was clearly intended. The message was that religious love was superior to carnal and romantic affection and that the everlasting crown and sceptre of Jesus reigned supreme over the transitory triumphs of the god and goddess and love, Cupid and Venus.[15]

The subtitle of this collection, *Holy (or Godly) Songs of Praise*, *Godlücke Lof-Sangen*, reiterates its central spiritual message, along with its insistence on the meditation of God and Christ. *Godlücke Lof-Sangen* also reflects specific indebtedness to a Jesuit source, the collection (1620) of the Netherlands Jesuit Justus de Harduwijn (1528–1641). The saints feature in the text in the persons, for example, of Augustine as victor over an heretical sect, of Dominic, of the Seven Doctors of the Church, of the Apostle Philip, of Mary Magdalene, of Francis, of St Louis IX as a member of the Third Order of St Francis and of Loyola in two tributes. Naturally, Mary is included, for instance, as 'advocate' and 'fair queen', but the emphasis is on her role *vis-à-vis* Jesus, as in a poem on the Annunciation. Christ, then, is central in this work, as is indicated in the repetition of the device *IHS*, the abbreviation of *Jesus Hominum Salvator*, 'Jesus Saviour of Mankind'. His nativity from a virgin is approached with the kind of simple astonishment at the apparent paradox of the maiden-mother that was recurrent in medieval religious lyrics in Europe:

O Wonderbaer vertoogh! ô wonderbaere Min!
O wonderful sight! O miraculous love
Die sonder eynde is, en noont en had begin,
Quite without beginning or end,
Wi'ns Vader daer was Godt, Wi'ns Moeder was een Maeghet
Whose father was God, whose mother a maiden!

The meditation in *Triumphus Iesu* certainly has its roots in the medieval contemplative tradition and especially in the Netherlands heritage that, through the
Imitation of Christ, had inspired Loyola and through him Jesuit meditative techniques. However, as well as being the product of a long-standing tradition of
piety, *Triumphus* was very much a work of its time, not least in its poignant allusions to the agony of Lier's province, Brabant, amidst plague and hunger, with a
heartfelt cry for peace at that mid-point of the Thirty Years' War. The collection
also had the most direct bearing on the progress of the Counter-Reformation in
the Spanish Netherlands, for it was dedicated to one of the most earnest
promoters of Catholic renewal in the provinces, the bishop of Antwerp, Jan
Malderus (1563–1633), official visitor of the Lier Sion convent. Malderus,
himself a renowned author on Aquinas, on issues of the Confessional, law,
justice, Scripture and synodical regulations, who died in the year of the collec-
tions' publication in Antwerp, must have been aware of the potential utility of
published Dutch-language texts of the sacred songs of *Triumphus Iesu*, which were
probably designed in the first instance for use in the cloister in Lier. However, the
adoption of the lyrics for 'official' ecclesiastical use required some editorial
discussion of their female authorship, which came in the form of a prefatory
explanation that the work, dedicated to Malderus, was not an elevated scriptural
commentary out of the University of Leuven but had its precedents in the use
that Moses had made of the humbler gifts of women to protect the tabernacle of
the Lord.[16]

Whereas the author of *Triumphus Iesu* deployed the 'profane' art of popular
song to propound piety, in Spain theatre – an art form that was sometimes
regarded in Europe as the antithesis of the sacred – was deployed to promote
Catholicism. In the Spain of the 1640s, military disaster at Rocroi (1643), and
the deaths of the queen and the heir to the throne gave rise to a Lenten mood of
national recollection in which the theatres were closed for lengthy periods. It is
against that background that we should consider the career of the dramatist
Pedro Calderón de la Barca Henao y Riano (1600–81). Educated at the Colegio
Imperial of the Jesuits, with his brothers he had led a violent and disorderly life
involving the break-in of a convent. The death of one brother and the murder of
another were followed by his ordination to the priesthood in 1651. As a writer
Calderón turned to resolve a widely sensed contradiction between religion and
priesthood on the one hand and secular literature, especially theatre, on the
other. His Corpus Christi plays, *autos sacramentales*, composed for the city of
Madrid – over seventy of them – present the values of the Spanish Catholic
Reformation and harmonise theatre with piety. It may be true, as Greer writes,

that Calderón has been typecast as 'the dramatist of Catholic orthodoxy', more 'doctrinal and didactic' than his great contemporary Lope de Vega (1562–1635). However, the latter's output included *Rimas sacras (Sacred Verses)* (1614) and *El Isidro* (1599) in honour of Madrid's patron saint, St Isidore, as well as celebrations of Spanish crusading ardour, such as a version of the Italian Torquato Tasso's (1544–95) *Gierusalemme Liberata* (1575), *La Jerusalén conquistada (Jerusalem Conquered)* (1609). With Calderón, though, there is no doubting the specific Jesuit inspiration behind much of his work or the likelihood that 'those close-knit speeches, with elaborate analogies, continued metaphors, conceits, and rhetorical colours…originated in the Jesuits' classrooms and the works he studied there'. Calderón's Jesuit education in the classics gave him the material for *Los encantos de la culpa (The Delights of Sin)* (1649) in which he reinterpreted the Greek legend of Ulysses and Circe, with Ulysses representing mankind and his ship the Church. Specific Jesuit themes in Calderón include a verse romance, on Loyola's experiences at Manresa; the pro-Jesuit *Don Baltasar de Loyola* (1585) concerned a Moorish convert. In an *auto* composed for the feast of Corpus Christi in Toledo, *El mágico prodigioso (The Amazing Wizard)* (1637), Calderón's source was the one that had influenced Loyola's conversion, the *Golden Legend*. Not surprisingly, then, it was a Jesuit who made one of the most favourable of comments on Calderón, his style and the 'sweetness' of his verses as well as the correctness of his theology, all features to be found in *El nuevo palacio del Retiro* (1634). (The title contains a play on words – 'The New Palace of Withdrawal from the World' and 'The New Royal Palace Called 'El Buen Retiro'.) The Jesuit commentator 'viewed this play with great admiration.…It contains well-regulated doctrine'. Focusing on such well-regulated doctrines, *La devoción de la cruz (The Devotion of the Holy Cross)* (1634, 1640) presented, in an intense drama of violence, sex and crime, the Council of Trent's strictures on the necessity for freedom of choice in marriage and the religious life. Freedom in a wider sense, the freedom of the will and its co-operation in opting for virtue – the viewpoint that the Jesuits made their own – is the theme of *La vida es sueño (Life's a Dream)* (1635), with its self-reforming central character Segismundo. Calderón, in Parker's words 'a theological poet', was, in the theatre, the great master of a chief aim of Catholic baroque art and literature, that of instruction through delight.[17]

A distinctive theology of grace and the will suffused a drama by a playwright whom Calderón greatly admired, the Mercedarian friar and artistic disciple of Lope de Vega, Tirso de Molina (Fray Gabriel Téllez, known as El Mercedario, 1571–1648). The subject of sin haunted a play attributed to Tirso, *El Condenado por desconfiado (Damned for Despair)* (*c.* 1624), a work whose composition is said to have been triggered by the author's discovery that a member of his order had turned bandit. The theology of forgiveness in this play is nuanced but leans towards the comforting views of the Jesuit Luis Molina (1535–1601) on the availability of God's forgiveness in accordance with the sinner's willed desire for grace. Indeed, sympathy with Molina's interpretation may have inclined Téllez to adopt part of the name of the theologian. The entry in the *Oxford Companion to Spanish Literature* explains that a 'brilliantly dramatised' Molinist soteriology underpins his play. This doctrine of salvation is conveyed through the sensational use of realism, violence and the depiction of vice by this dramatist who introduced the character of Don Juan to the stage. The central character in *El condenado desconfiado*, who 'lives by gambling, blackmail, contract killings, and the immoral earnings of his mistress', introduces his immorality in a narrative of his malevolence which is intense, high-powered, melodramatic and horrifically gripping in its hasty, excited diction:

> Once, when I was struck
> on some rich man's wife, and I'd gone
> into the house, determined
> to get what I'd wanted from her
> the bitch called out, and her husband
> came into the room. I was mad!
> I took a grip of him
> and lifted him off the ground,
> and once I'd got him like that
> I ran to the open window
> and threw him out, and he died
> where he fell. She began screaming,
> I had my knife; I stabbed her
> five or six times in the breasts.
> Snow white they were, and the blood ran down
> like rubies over the slope,
> and her life ran out with it too.

Divine forgiveness and grace were available to human beings even amidst such stark realisations of evil, but the theological message – which Tirso de Molina claimed was derived from the writings of the Jesuit theologian Bellarmino – was presented with the utmost realism and entertainment value, in precisely the way that baroque religious art taught Catholic doctrine through every resource of diversion that could be summoned.[18]

Instruction through the heightening of effects was also sought by means of deliberate affronts to sensibility through an audacity that was intended to grip the imagination by its power to shock. The Spanish Jesuit writer, Baltasar Gracian (1601–58), for example, imaged the Eucharist as a banquet at which was served 'a Lamb fed with virgin's milk, seasoned with the fire of His love. Oh! what a luxurious dish. Here a heart in love with souls; what a tasty dish!' A boldness of metaphor that ventured up to and beyond the bounds of what a later generation would decree were the limits of taste often characterised baroque literature and forms of artistic expression which included Bernini's representation of the mystical ecstasy of St Teresa as an orgasm. The reason, I suggest, for such artistic boldness in the description of the spiritual through the use of shock tactics by reference to the mundane was a desire to convey the familiar lineaments of Catholicism in novel terms, for teaching purposes.[19]

In the field of music the Council of Trent laid down the clearest canons for composition – restraint, solemnity, the avoidance of secular and romantic motifs. The dominant musical mode in the early sixteenth century in Europe was the complex polyphonic and contrapuntal style of the northern Franco-Flemish school associated with such masters as Josquin des Prés (1440–1521). The characteristics of this school included enormous elaboration of musical complexity, a subordination of the meaning of the words to the aesthetic demands of the music and a free adoption of secular tunes and love songs to furnish tunes for choral Masses. The Mass known as *'L'Homme Armé* (1502) by the greatest composer of polyphony in the Flemish tradition, des Prés, provides a powerful example of the borrowing of music for the Mass from the world of popular song. The Netherlander Orlando di Lasso (Roland de Lassus, *c*. 1532–94) was a composer, on a massive scale, of secular and romantic works as well as of Masses and motets. His Mass known as *Bell'Amfitrit altera* (posthumous, 1610) provides a clear example of the absorption by Church music – even in the Tridentine age – of the worldly themes and the pagan cultural allusions of the Renaissance: 'Bell' Amfitrit', 'Beautiful Amphitrite', was the wife of Poseidon, goddess of the sea (and also the symbol of the maritime Republic of Venice). The di Lasso Mass is a work of intricate complexity, sophistication and ravishing beauty, though with little relationship to the Mass as the Council of Tent had viewed it as being, and it embodies a potentially blasphemous dedication to a pagan goddess.[20]

Catholic reformers detested this kind of music. Savonarola was typical in his criticism that 'figured music does nothing but charm the ear and the senses'. Erasmus took up the theme – 'We have introduced an artificial and theatrical music into the church, a bawling and agitation of various voices' – and he condemned, as Savonarola did, 'the sensuous charm of the ear'. From the time of the reforms of Giberti in Verona worldly music was banned in church and in his Modena diocese Morone legislated against what Savonarola had called 'figured' music. Before the Council of Trent met, then, a body of reformist complaint had built up about the kind of music that had been in vogue for church use in the decades up to the inception of the Catholic Reformation. However, the golden age of polyphony co-existed, especially in Italy, with a strong survival of the pre-polyphonic tradition of 'plain song', 'plain chant' or 'Gregorian chant', an ancient simpler rhythmic mode in which the Office of the Church was sung in monasteries and convents and whose stately pace and apportionment of syllables to notes made for clear hearing of the text. As Sherr writes, 'singing Gregorian chant was the major task of all the singers and composer singers of the Renaissance', and perhaps Italian singers understood only imperfectly the basic techniques of singing 'figured' polyphonic music. Though polyphonic complexity held sway in much of late medieval northern Europe, in Italy the greater simplicity of the older Gregorian form does not seem to have been buried under polyphonic fashion. The revival of religious priorities in the music of the Mass, as demanded by the Council of Trent, can be seen to have had roots in an unbroken Italian musical-liturgical tradition. Particular attention seems to have been given in the Italian attitude to church music to the careful enunciation of the words of the service, as an English visitor to Rome in 1576–8 commented: 'and everie syllable [is sung] so distinctly, so cleare, so commodiously, so fully, that the hearers may perceave all that is done'.[21]

Clarity of enunciation dictated a measured pace, as did the requirement of solemnity. As an Italian bishop wrote in 1549:

> *Kyrie eleison* [a prayer for mercy and forgiveness sung near the beginning of Mass] means 'Lord, have mercy upon us'. The ancient musicians would have expressed this affection of asking the Lord's pardon by using the Mixolydian mode [the mode thought suitable for tragedies] which would have evoked a feeling of contrition in the hearts and souls.

Likewise, audibility and dignity in the musical setting of the Mass were the goals that Trent gave itself: 'All things should be so ordered that the Masses, whether they be celebrated with or without singing, may reach tranquilly into the ears and hearts of those who hear them, when everything is executed clearly and at the right speed'. Tropes should be sung, the Council ordered, 'in a simple clear voice beforehand, so that no one will miss any parts of the eternal reading of the sacred writings'. However, this insistence should be seen as arising out of an emphasis, continuing to concern the Italian school of liturgical music, on religious meaning rather than aesthetic pleasure.[22]

Though a keen student of the Franco-Flemish form of polyphony, the Italian Palestrina carried a heavy debt to plain song and achieved, in his *Missa Papae Marcelli* (*The Requiem Mass for Pope Marcellus*) (1555, published 1567) the sobriety, clarity and grave suitability of tone to occasion which Trent demanded, while at the same time achieving a compromise with polyphony in what Palestrina termed his 'new stylistic approach' (*novo modorum genere*). In 1567, the same year, that Palestrina published the *Missa Papae Marcelli*, his friend Giovanni Animuccia claimed to have achieved a new level of austerity in the musical accompaniment of the Mass – 'to adorn these divine prayers and praise of God as little as possible'. The issue of the decrees of the Council and of the Breviary gave Animuccia standards by which to compose, and the move in the direction of plainer musical settings gained momentum from the powerful backing of Carlo Borromeo: one of the composers of the Tridentine musical style, Vicenzo Ruffo (1508–87) cited the commission:

> which Cardinal Borromeo had formerly imposed on me that in accordance with the decrees of the Council of Trent I was to compose some Masses that should avoid everything of a profane and idle manner in worship....Accordingly...I composed one Mass in this way; so that the number of the syllables and the voices and tones together should be clearly and distinctly understood by the pious listeners.

Nevertheless, the force of the movement in favour of musical austerity in Borromean Lombardy, where Ruffo contributed to the reordering of the music of the Ambrosian rite, should not be exaggerated – though it is true that Borromeo directed a drive against erotic madrigals in Cremona in the Jubilee year, 1575. However, Niccolò Sfondrato (1535–1591), bishop, from 1560, of Cremona – the second city of the province, its musical centre and the birthplace of Claudio Monteverdi (1567–1643) – was committed to a strongly popular form of Catholic Reformation, designed in part to halt the spread of Protestantism in his border diocese. Sfondrato (subsequently pope as Gregory XIV), who attacked the privileges of the cathedral clergy, who developed public schooling, welfare and confraternities and brought in Theatines, Somaschi and Barnabites, could hardly afford to dispense with the extant rich and much-loved musical traditions of the Church as an asset in his campaign to consolidate the orthodoxy of his diocese. Animuccia, one of the new breed of Tridentine composers, sought a reconciliation in which 'the music may disturb the hearing of the text as little as possible, but nevertheless in such a way that it may not be entirely devoid of artifice and may contribute in some degree to the listener's pleasure'. The series of Masses in four, five and six parts by Monteverdi's teacher, Marco Antonio Ingegnero (*c.* 1545–92) represent a new compromise between Tridentine principles and the beautiful legacy of polyphony from the late fifteenth and early sixteenth centuries. This was the musical half-way house that remained in place into the age of Claudio Monteverdi (1567–1643), especially in Rome, where the large choirs needed for the performance of polyphony (*stile antico* or *prima prattica*, both phrases betokening a superseded style) remained available in the early seventeenth century. Monteverdi's own Mass *Il illo tempore* (1610) is set for six voices and deliberately incorporates what a contemporary called 'great seriousness and difficulty', that is to say both liturgical propriety and pleasurable elaboration. His 1610 Mass of the Blessed Virgin Mary has, it is true, strong Gregorian features, but the vespers accompanying it are indebted stylistically to the sixteenth-century Flemish polyphonist Nicholas Gombert (*c.* 1495–1560) and, indeed, introduce a novel operatic method. In such ways, the music, like the other arts of the Catholic Reformation, represented compromise, between an official aesthetic and the need to please a public with its own tastes, formed by the accretions of artistic tradition.[23]

We seem to have ended our survey on an 'upbeat' note of optimism over the Catholic Reformation as a popular or even kindly set of processes. It was far from being entirely that. Whatever revisionisms are conducted over the scale of the Inquisition's cruelties, it was, wherever it extended its reach of operations, an engine of appalling terror. The Counter-Reformation involved a worsened outlook for dissidents and minorities, especially Jews, who were consigned to the ghetto, especially in Italy. The prosecution of Galileo Galilei (1564–1642) epitomised an underlying and lasting Catholic suspicion of scientific research. Large numbers of women accused of witchcraft were executed, particularly in the period from the 1580s to the 1630s and, in Spain especially, women's religious charisms were subjected to intense scrutiny and hostility. Catholic militancy was more than a metaphor, in an age when the papacy rejoiced in the St Bartholomew massacre of the Protestants of France in 1572 and when, in the following century, the Catholic cause in Germany and in Europe at large was upheld through the terrible barbarities of the Thirty Years' War. Above all, in the Czech lands of Bohemia, Catholicisation was the religious accompaniment to political enslavement to Austria. The division of large parts especially of central Europe into reciprocally antagonistic slabs of territory through the processes of 'confessionalisation' left Catholics deeply hostile and suspicious towards other Christians. Through the policing activities of Catholic magistrates and busybody parish priests encouraged by episcopal visitations, much of the rare enjoyment that European peasants took from gruelling lives was proscribed. Indeed, the Counter-Reformation Catholic Church often imposed a puritanism sometimes even more stringent than the Protestant variety, leaving generations of Europeans fearful and guilty over sex, as well as driven by the intense work ethic inculcated by teaching orders such as the Jesuits and the de la Salle Brothers. The majority of modern Europeans, especially in the countries of the European Union, come from backgrounds strongly tinged by the influences of Catholic Reformation Catholicism, and modern Europe, for good or ill, simply cannot be understood without some insight into the processes described in this book.

Notes

1 'Reform in head and members': The medieval background of the Catholic Reformation

1 V. H. H. Green, *Renaissance and Reformation. A Survey of European History between 1450 and 1660*, London, Edward Arnold, 2nd edn, 1964, p. 177; Harold J. Grimm, *The Reformation Era 1500–1650*, New York, Macmillan, London, Collier-Macmillan, revised edn, 1965, p. 366; H. O. Evennett, 'The Counter-Reformation' in Joel Hurstfield (ed.), *The Reformation Crisis*, London, Edward Arnold, 1965, p. 58; see also the discussion in R. P-Chia Hsia, *The World of Catholic Renewal 1540–1770*, New Approaches to European History, Series Editors William Beik *et al.*, Cambridge, Cambridge University Press, 1998, Introduction.

2 Jean Delumeau, *Catholicism between Luther and Voltaire: a new View of the Counter-Reformation*, trans. Jeremy Moiser, London, Burns & Oates, Philadelphia, PA, Westminster Press, 1977, pp. 4–5; John W. O'Malley, 'Reform, Historical Consciousness and Vatican II's Aggiornamento' in O'Malley, *Rome and the Renaissance Studies in Culture and Religion*, London, Variorum Reprints, 1981, p. 580.

3 *Histoire Ecclésiastique. Pour servir de continuer à cette de Monsieur l'Abbé Fleury, tome Vingt-Deuxième. Depuis l'an 1431 jusqu'en 1455*, Paris, Jean Mariette, 1726, p. 204; for constitutional theories of the status of councils of the Church, see J. H. Burns and Thomas M. Izbicki (eds), *Conciliarism and Papalism*, Cambridge Texts in the History of Political Thought, Raymond Geuss and Quentin Skinner (eds), Cambridge, Cambridge University Press, 1997.

4 Norman P. Tanner, SJ, (ed.), *Decrees of the Ecumenical Councils* 2 vols, London, Sheed & Ward, Washington, DC, Georgetown University Press, 1990, vol. II, p. 686; Denys Hay, *The Church in Italy in the Fifteenth Century, The Birkbeck Lectures, 1971*, Cambridge, London, New York, Cambridge University Press, 1977, p. 85.

5 Tanner (ed.), *Decrees of the Ecumenical Councils*, vol. II, p. 743.

6 For the development of Marian doctrine, see Hilda Charlotte Graeff, *Mary. A History of Dogma and Devotion* 2 vols, London and New York, Sheed & Ward, 1963; for Basel on the Immaculate Conception, see Kathleen Ashley and Pamela Sheingorn (eds), *Interpreting Cultural Symbols, Saint Anne in Late Medieval Society*, Athens, GA and London, University of Georgia Press, 1990, intro., pp. 13, 25; *Histoire Ecclésiastique*, vol. 22, pp. 290–1.

7 *Histoire Ecclésiastique*, vol. 22, p. 291; Tanner (ed.), *Decrees of the Ecumenical Councils*, vol. II, p. 667; Ashley and Sheingorn (eds), *Interpreting Cultural Symbols*, p. 47.

8 *Histoire Ecclésiastique*, vol. 22, p. 251; Tanner (ed.) *Decrees of the Ecumenical Councils*, vol. I, p. 527.

9 *Histoire Ecclésiastique*, vol. 22, pp. 116–19; Tanner (ed.), *Decrees of the Ecumenical Councils*, vol. I, pp. 488–92.

10 Delumeau, *Catholicism from Luther to Voltaire*, pp. 197–9, 176; Tanner (ed.), *Decrees of the Ecumenical Councils*, vol. II, p. 737.

11 *Histoire Ecclésiastique*, vol. 25, pp. 131–9; O'Malley, 'Reform, Historical Consciousness, Aggiornamento', pp. 579–80; A. G. Dickens, *The Counter-Reformation*, London, Harcourt, Brace & World, 1969, p. 91; Delumeau, *Catholicism from Luther to Voltaire*, p. 15.

12 Dickens, *The Counter-Reformation*, p. 2; *Histoire Ecclésiastique*, vol. 29, pp. 323, 262; for the *commendam* system, see Hay, *The Church in Italy in the Fifteenth Century*, pp. 74–5.

13 Peter Partner, *The Papal State under Martin V. The administration and government of the temporal power in the early fifteenth century*, London, British School at Rome, 1948, p. 193; Eustace J. Kitts, *Pope John the Twenty Third and Master John Hus of Bohemia*, London, Constable, 1910, pp. 425–6.

14 Hay, *The Church in Italy in the Fifteenth Century*, p. 85; Michael Walsh, *An Illustrated History of the Popes*, London, Marshall Cavendish Editions, 1980, p. 141; Joseph Gill, SJ, *Eugenius IV Pope of Christian Unity*, The Popes through History, Raymond H. Schmandt (ed.), London, Burns & Oates, 1961, pp. 170–1, 184, 186–7, 190 .

15 Gill, *Eugenius IV*, p. 190; *Histoire Ecclésiastique*, vol. 22, pp. 134–5.

16 John W. O'Malley, SJ, 'Giles of Viterbo: A Reformer's Thought on Renaissance Rome' in O'Malley, *Rome in the Renaissance*, pp. 4–11; Jack Freiberg, *The Lateran in 1600. Christian Concord in Counter-Reformation Rome*, Cambridge, New York and Melbourne, Cambridge University Press, 1995, p. 8; Peter Partner, *The Pope's Men. The Papal Civil Service in the Renaissance*, Oxford, Clarendon, 1990, p. 111.

17 Alexis François Artaud de Montor, *The Lives and Times of the Popes*, translated edn, 10 vols, New York; Catholic Publication Society of America, 1911, vol. IV, pp. 141, 151; Miri Rubin, *Corpus Christi. The Eucharist in Late Medieval Culture*, Cambridge, New York and Melbourne, Cambridge University Press, 1991, esp. pp. 176–8; Partner, *The Pope's Men*, p. 112.

18 Partner, *The Pope's Men*, p. 112; Hay, *The Church in Italy in the Fifteenth Century*, p. 86; De Montor, *Lives and Times of the Popes*, vol. IV, p. 151; Peter O'Dwyer, *Mary: A History of Devotion in Ireland*, Dublin, Four Courts Press, 1988, p. 25; Anon., *Histoire des Papes*, Paris, Martin Jouvenal, 1695, p. 298.

19 Hay, *The Church in Italy in the Fifteenth Century*, p. 86; R. J. Mitchell, *The Laurels and the Tiara: Pope Pius II 1458–1464*, London, Harvill Press, 1962, pp. 216–17; *Memoirs of a Renaissance Pope. The Commentaries of Pius II. An Abridgement*, trans. Florence A Gragg, Leona C. Gabel (ed.), London, George Allen & Unwin, 1950, pp. 264–9.

20 Partner, *The Pope's Men*, p. 112; de Montor, *Lives and Times of the Popes*, vol. IV, p. 141; for Burchard's *Commentarii*, see the edition in three volumes, Paris, Ernest Lerou, 1883; Egmont Lee, 'Iacopo Gherardi and the Court of Pope Sixtus IV', *The Catholic Historical Review*, 1979, vol. 65, No. 2, pp. 235–6; see also John W. O'Malley, 'Preaching for the Popes' in Charles Trinkaus and Heiko A. Oberman (eds), *The Pursuit of Holiness in Late Medieval and Renaissance Religion*, Papers from the University of Michigan Conference, Studies in Medieval and Reformation Thought, Heiko Oberman *et al.*, (eds), Leiden, E. J. Brill, 1974, pp. 408–40.

21 Girolamo Savonarola, *Triumphus Crucis Testo Latino e Volgare*, Mario Ferrara (ed.), Edizione Nazionale delle Opere di Girolamo Savonarola Rome, Angelo Belardetti, 1961, p. 526; Michael de la Bedoyere, *The Meddlesome Friar. The Story of the Conflict between Savonarola and Alexander VI*, London, Collins, 1957, p. 159.

22 James Muldoon, 'Papal Responsibility for the Infidel: Another Look at Alexander VI's *Inter Caetera*', *The Catholic Historical Review*, 1978, vol. 69, No. 2, pp. 168–9.

23 ibid., p. 183.

24 Hay, *The Church in Italy in the Fifteenth Century*, pp. 84–5; John C. Olin *The Catholic Reformation: Savonarola to Ignatius Loyola*, New York, Fordhan University Press, 1992, p. 91 and n. 3; John Arthos, 'The Ambiguities of Pope Julius and his Rome' in

Trinkaus and Oberman (eds), *The Pursuit of Holiness*, pp. 478–9; Partner, *The Pope's Men*, p. 112.

25 *Histoire Ecclésiastique*, vol. 25, p. 571; Tanner (ed.), *Decrees of the Ecumenical Councils*, vol. II, pp. 776–84.

26 De Montor, *Lives and Times of the Popes*, vol. V, pp. 3–13; J. N. D. Kelly, *The Oxford Dictionary of the Popes*, Oxford, New York, Oxford University Press, 1986, pp. 258–9.

27 John Coulson (ed.), *The Saints. A Concise Biographical Dictionary*, Bristol, Nicholas Adams, 1958, p. 51; *The Catholic Encyclopedia*, 15 vols, London, Encyclopedia Press, 1913, vol. I, p. 586; Alban Butler, *The Lives of the Fathers, Martyrs and Other Principal Saints* [1756–9], F. C. Husenbeth (ed.), 6 vols, London, Dublin and Belfast, Virtue, n.d., vol. II, p. 141.

28 Butler, *Lives of the Saints*, Husenbeth (ed.), vol. II, p. 141; for Pierozzi's economics, see R. H. Tawney, *Religion and the Rise of Capitalism. A Historical Study*, Harmondsworth, Penguin, 1938, pp. 25, 32, 52–3; for Antonino Pierozzi, see Les Petits Bollandistes, *Vie des Saints de l'Ancien et du Nouveau Testament*, seventh edn, 17 vols, Paris, Bloud et Barral, 1888, vol. 5, p. 438.

29 Cardinal Francis Aidan Gasquet, *Parish Life in Medieval England*, 4th edn, London, Methuen, n.d., pp. 94, 188, 80–3; Tanner (ed.), *Decrees of the Ecumenical Councils*, vol. II, pp. 737–8.

30 A. Daniel Frankfurter, 'The Reformation in the Register: Episcopal Administration of Parishes in Late Medieval England', *The Catholic Historical Review*, 1977, vol. 63, No. 2, pp. 223–4.

31 Richard Lawrence Smith, *John Fisher and Thomas More: Two English Saints*, London, Sheed and Ward, 1935, pp. 6, 38; Philip Hughes (intro.), *Saint John Fisher. The Earliest English Life*, London, Burns Oates and Washbourne, 1935, pp. 31, 65; Tanner, *Decrees of the Ecumenical Councils*, vol. II, pp. 688, 763, 686, 794; T. E. Bridgett, *Life of Blessed John Fisher, Bishop of Rochester, Cardinal of the Holy Roman Church, and Martyr under Henry VIII*, London, Burns & Oates, New York, Catholic Publication Society, 1890, p. 61.

32 Tanner, *Decrees of the Ecumenical Councils*, vol. II, p. 763; Geoffrey Baskerville, *English Monks and the Dissolution of the Monasteries* (1937), paperback edn, London, Jonathan Cape, 1965, pp. 74, 76–7, 90–2, 101–2; Peter Gwyn, *The King's Cardinal. The Rise and Fall of Thomas Wolsey*, London, Pimlico, 1992, pp. 267–8; see also Keith Brown, 'Wolsey and ecclesiastial orders: the case of the Franciscan Observants' in S. J. Gunn and P. G. Lindley (eds), *Cardinal Wolsey. Church, state and art*, Cambridge, New York, Port Chester, Melbourne, Sydney, Cambridge University Press, 1991, pp. 219–238.

33 Eugene F. Rice, Jr, 'The Meaning of "Evangelical"' in Trinkaus and Oberman (eds), *The Pursuit of Holiness*, p. 474; Emile Léonard, *A History of Protestantism*, H. H. Rowley (ed.), trans. Joyce M. H. Reid, 2 vols, London: Nelson, 1965, vol. I, pp. 227–8; *Dictionnaire de Théologie Catholique*, 14 vols, Paris, Librairie Letouzey et Aîné, 1899–1950, vol. 9, p. 144.

34 H. Daniel-Rops, *The Catholic Reformation*, trans. John Warrington, London, J. M. Dent, New York, E. P. Dutton, 1968, pp. 11–12; *The Catholic Encyclopedia*, vol. 15, p. 73; Coulson (ed.), *Lives of the Saints*, pp. 434–5.

35 Adriano Prosperi, 'Clerics and Laymen in the Work of Carlo Borromeo' in John M. Headley and John B. Tomaro (eds), *San Carlo Borromeo Catholic Reform and Ecclesiastical Politics in the Second Half of the Sixteenth Century*, Washington, DC, The Folger Shakespeare Library, London and Toronto, Associated University Presses, 1988, pp. 119–21; Daniel-Rops, *The Catholic Reformation*, p. 14.

36 A. G. Dickens, *Reformation and Society in Sixteenth-Century Europe*, London, Thames & Hudson, 1966, reprinted edn, 1977, p. 189; Henry Brinton, *The Context of the Reformation*, London, Hutchinson Educational, 1968, p. 154; Grimm, *The Reformation Era*, p. 379.

37 Dom David Knowles, *From Pachomius to Ignatius. A Study in the Constitutional History of the Religious Orders. The Sarum Lectures for 1964–5*, Oxford, Clarendon, 1966, p. 46.

38 ibid., pp. 50–1, 62, 63–5; Bede Jarret, OP, *Life of St Dominic 1170–1221*, London, Burns Oates & Washbourne, 1934, pp. 118; Louis Châtellier, *The Religion of the Poor. Rural missions in Europe and the formation of modern Catholicism, c. 1500–1800*, trans. Brian Pearce, Cambridge, Cambridge University Press, Maison des Sciences de l'Homme, 1997, Chapter 1.

39 Châtellier, *The Religion of the Poor*, pp. 10–11, 16; R. Po-Chia Hsia, *Social Discipline in the Reformation Central Europe 1550–1750*, Christianity and Society in the Modern World, General Editors Hugh McLeod and Bob Scribner, London and New York, Routledge, 1989, pp. 48–50; Howard Louthan, *The Quest for Compromise. Peacemakers in Counter-Reformation Vienna*, Cambridge Studies in Early Modern History, Sir John Elliott *et al.*, (eds), Cambridge, Cambridge University Press, 1997, pp. 129–31, 141–2; Meriol Trevor, *Apostle of Rome A Life of Philip Neri 1515–1595*, London, Melbourne, Toronto, Macmillan, 1966, pp. 87, 117.

40 Denys Hay (ed.), *Europe in the Fourteenth and Fifteenth Centuries*, A General History of Europe, London, Longmans, 1966, paperback edn, 1975, p. 317, 318; Iris Origo, *The World of San Bernardino*, London, Reprint Society, 1964, pp. 118–19; Châtellier, *The Religion of the Poor*, pp. 1–15, 60–90.

41 Anne Winston-Allen, *Stories of the Rose. The Making of the Rosary in the Middle Ages*, University Park, PA, The Pennsylvania State University Press, 1997, p. 151; David Herlihy, reviewing Gilles Gerard Meerseman, *Ordo Fraternitatis* in *The Catholic Historical Review*, 1987, vol. 66, No. 4, p. 605; Dickens, *The Counter-Reformation*, p. 20; Marvin B. Becker, 'Aspects of Lay Piety in Early Renaissance Florence' in Trinkaus and Oberman (eds), *The Pursuit of Holiness*, pp. 177–99; Brian Pullan, *Rich and Poor in Renaissance Venice. The Social Institutions of a Catholic State, to 1620*, Oxford, Basil Blackwell, 1971, Intoduction and Part I; Christopher F. Black, *Italian Confraternities in the Sixteenth Century*, Cambridge, New York, Melbourne, Cambridge University Press, 1989.

42 E. L. S. Horsburgh, *Girolamo Savonarola*, London, Methuen, 4th edn, 1909, pp. 199–200; Barry Collett, 'The Civil Servant and Monastic Reform: Richard Fox's translation of the Benedictine Rule for Women, 1517' in Judith Loades (ed.), *Monastic Studies. The Continuity of Tradition*, Bangor, Gwynedd, Headstart History, 1990, p. 222; John O'Malley, 'Preaching for the Popes' in Oberman and Trinkaus (eds), *The Pursuit of Holiness*, p. 423.

43 'A Carthusian Monk', *The History of the Great Chartreuse*, trans. E. Hassid, London, Burns Oates & Washbourne, 1934, pp. 50–1; Dom Lawrence Hendriks, *The London Charterhouse. Its Monks and its Martyrs*, London, Kegan Paul, Trench & Co., 1889, pp. 3–14; Southern, *Western Society and the Church*, p. 355; Winston-Allen, *Stories of the Rose*, pp. 1–2; Michael G. Sargent, 'The transmission by the English Carthusians of some late medieval spiritual writings', *Journal of Ecclesiastical History*, 1976, vol. 27, pp. 225–40: see also J. T. Rhodes, 'Syon Abbey and its religious publications in the sixteenth century', *Journal of Ecclesiastical History*, 1993, vol. 44, pp. 11–25.

44 Hendriks, *London Charterhouse*, pp. 15–17, 55–6; David Mathew and Gervase Mathew, OP, *The Reformation and the Contemplative Life*, London, Sheed and Ward, 1934, pp. 19–20, 56–61.

45 *The Cambridge Modern History*, A. W. Ward *et al.*, (eds) 14 vols, Cambridge, Cambridge University Press, 1902–12, vol. I: *The Renaissance*, p. 434–5; Albert Hyma, *The Christian Renaissance*, 2nd edn, Hamden, CN, Archon, 1965, pp. 82–9; Emile G. Léonard, *A History of Protestantism*, vol. I: *The Reformation*, pp. 33ff.; James Atkinson, *Martin Luther and the Birth of Protestantism*, Harmondsworth, Pelican, 1968, pp. 63, 66, 132–4.

2 The Council of Trent and the Catholic Reformation

1 James Atkinson, *Martin Luther: Prophet of the Church Catholic*, Exeter, Paternoster Press, 1983, pp. 43, 65; Scott H. Hendrix, *Luther and the Papacy Stages in a Reformation Conflict*, Philadelphia, PA, Fortress Press, 1981, pp. 12, 15; for a summary of the doctrinal issues, see, e.g. Euan Cameron, *The European Reformation*, Oxford, Clarendon, 1991, Chapters 6 and 12.

2 For Savonarola, councils and the papacy, Romeo de Maio, *Savonarola e la Curia Romana*, Rome, Edizioni di Storia e Letteratura, 1969, pp. 138–9; Hubert Jedin, *A History of the Council of Trent*, 2 vols, trans. Dom Ernest Graf, OSB, London, Thomas Nelson, 1957, 1961, vol. I: *The Struggle for the Council*, p. 580; for the debate over the role of councils in the Church, see J. H. Burns and Thomas M. Izbicki (eds), *Conciliarism and Papalism*, Cambridge Texts in the History of Political Thought, Raymond Geuss and Quentin Skinner (series eds), Cambridge, Cambridge University Press, 1997.

3 G. P. Blaueu and J. Blaueu, *Histoire du Concile de Trente de Fra Paolo Sarpi*, Amsterdam, 1683, pp. 31–2.

4 Jedin, *History of the Council of Trent*, vol. I, p. 215.

5 ibid., p. 219; Anthony Black, *Council and Commune. The Conciliar Movement and the Council of Basle*, London, Burns & Oates, Sheperdstown, WV, The Patmos Press, 1979, pp. 204–5; Leopold Ranke [*sic*], *The History of the Popes, their Church and State, and Especially of their Conflicts with Protestantism in the Sixteenth and Seventeenth Centuries*, 3 vols, trans. E. Foster, London, Henry G. Bohn, 1856, vol. III: Appendix, p. 141.

6 Jedin, *History of the Council of Trent*, vol. I, pp. 221, and 222, n. 4; Ranke, *The History of the Popes*, vol. III: Appendix, pp. 93–4; *Histoire du Concile de Trente*, p. 29; Cameron, *The European Reformation*, p. 340; *Histoire Ecclésiastique. Pour servir de continuer à cette de Monsieur l'Abbé Fleury*, Paris, Jean Mariette, vol. 25, 1726, pp. 672–3.

7 Barbara McClung Hallman, *Italian Cardinals, Reform, and the Church as Property*, Publications of the UCLA Center for Medieval and Renaissance Studies, Berkeley and Los Angeles, CA, and London, University of California Press, 1985, pp. 148–53; Jedin, *History of the Council of Trent*, vol. I, p. 290; *Histoire Écclésiastique*, vol. 28, pp. 11, 33; Cameron, *The European Reformation*, p. 340; *Histoire du Concile*, pp. 69, 74; Dermot Fenlon, *Heresy and Obedience in Tridentine Italy: Cardinal Pole and the Counter-Reformation*, Cambridge, Cambridge University Press, 1972, pp. 107–14.

8 *Histoire Ecclésiastique*, vol. 28, pp. 36–9. 40–43, 47–92, 170; Jedin, *History of the Council of Trent*, vol. I, pp. 297, 323, 502, 368; H. J. Schroeder, OP, (ed.), *Canons and Decrees of the Council of Trent* (1941), reprinted English text edn, Rockford, IL, Tan Books, 1978, *passim*; Cameron, *The European Reformation*, pp. 290–1, 344–5; *The Catholic Encyclopedia*, 15 vols, London, The Encyclopedia Press, 1912, vol. 13, pp. 324–5. For the background to the Cologne Council and the Archbishop's attempt to head off a repetition in Cologne of the 1535 Anabaptist revolution in Münster, see Ernst Bizer, 'The German Reformation to 1555' in G. R. Elton (ed.), *The New Cambridge Modern History*, vol. II: *The Reformation*, Cambridge, Cambridge University Press, 1962, p. 181.

9 In Colman J. Barry, OSB (ed.), *Readings in Church History*, 2 vols, Westminster, MD, The Newman Press, 1965, vol. II, pp. 96–102.

10 ibid., p. 96.

11 ibid., pp. 96–102.

12 ibid., pp. 96–7, 99, 102; Daniel-Rops, *The Catholic Reformation*, History of the Church of Christ, 5, trans. John Warrington, London, Dent, 1962, p. 100.

13 L. Christiani, *L'Eglise à l'Epoque du Concile de Trente, Histoire de l'Église depuis les Origines jusqu'à nos Jours*, Paris, Boud et Gay, 1948, pp. 33–5; Heinrich Lutz, 'Carlo V e il Concilio di Trento' in Hubert Jedin and Paolo Prodi (eds), *Il Concilio di Trento come crocevia nella politica Europea*, Bologna, Il Mulino, 1977, p. 50; Schroeder (ed.), *Canons and Decrees of Trent*, pp. 1–3; Jedin, *History of the Council of Trent*, vol. I, pp. 321–2,

327–8; *Histoire Ecclésiastique*, vol. 28, pp. 157, 93; *Histoire du Concile*, pp. 79–80; Daniel-Rops, *The Catholic Reformation*, pp. 76–9.

14 *Histoire Ecclésiastique*, vol. 28, p. 248; Jedin, *History of the Council of Trent*, vol. I, pp. 331, 379–91, 419, *The Catholic Encyclopedia*, vol. 10, pp. 575–6; Daniel-Rops, *The Catholic Reformation*, pp. 7–8.

15 Peter Matheson, *Cardinal Contarini at Regensburg*, Oxford, Clarendon, 1972, pp. 176–81 and Chapter 10; Jedin, *A History of the Council of Trent*, vol. I, pp. 390–1, 443–6; Cameron, *The European Reformation*, pp. 344–5.

16 For a summary of the political and diplomatic background, see Roger Lockyer, *Habsburg and Bourbon Europe 1470–1720*, London, Longman, 1974, pp. 227–8.

17 Daniel-Rops, *The Catholic Reformation*, pp. 78–9; Schroeder (ed.), *Canons and Decrees of Trent*, pp. 1, 12–14; Jedin, *A History of the Council of Trent*, vol. II, pp. 29–31.

18 'Decree on the Manner of Living' in Schroeder (ed.), *Canons and Decrees of Trent* pp. 12–14 ; Jedin, *A History of the Council of Trent, vol. II*, p. 27; Schroeder (ed.), *Canons and Decrees of Trent*, pp. 12–14; Pierre Janelle, *The Catholic Reformation*, Milwaukee, WI, Bruce Publishing, London, Collier-Macmillan, 1971, pp. 73–4.

19 ibid., p. 68; A. G. Dickens, *The Counter-Reformation*, London, Harcourt, Brace & World, 1969, p. 109; Jean Delumeau, *Catholicism from Luther to Voltaire*, trans Jeremy Moiser, London, Burns & Oates, 1977, p. 7; Jedin, *A History of the Council of Trent*, vol. II, pp. 40–1.

20 Schroeder (ed.), *Canons and Decrees of Trent*, pp. 15–16; Daniel-Rops, *The Catholic Reformation*, p. 79; Jedin, *A History of the Council of Trent*, vol. II, p. 39; Newman, cited in Bernard Basset, *And Would You Believe It? The Story of the Nicene Creed*, London, Sheed and Ward, 1976, p. 13; Hendrix, *Luther and the Papacy*, pp. 154–6, 81.

21 Schroeder (ed.), *Canons and Decrees of Trent*, pp. 17–20; for Luther's reverence of Scripture, see A. Skevington Wood, *Captive to the Word. Martin Luther: Doctor of Sacred Scripture*, Exeter, Paternoster Press, 1969; for Calvin, T. H. L. Parker, *John Calvin A Biography*, London, J. M. Dent, 1975, p. 75.

22 Schroeder (ed.), *Canons and Decrees of Trent*, p. 17; Jedin, *A History of the Council of Trent*, vol. II, p. 62; Cameron, *The European Reformation*, pp. 136–7; Martin Chemnitz, *Examination of the Council of Trent*, 2 parts, trans. Fred Kramer, St Louis, MO, Concordia Publishing House, 1971, part I, p. 219.

23 Schroeder (ed.), *Canons and Decrees of Trent*, pp. 17–18; Jedin, *A History of the Council of Trent*, vol. II, pp. 56–7; Denys Hay, 'Intellectual Tendencies I: Literature: The Printed Book' in Elton (ed.), *New Cambridge Modern History*, vol. II, pp. 272–3.

24 Schroeder (ed.), *Canons and Decrees of Trent*, pp. 24–8; Jedin, *A History of the Council of Trent*, vol. II, p. 97; L. Leith Spencer, *English Preaching in the Late Middle Ages*, Oxford, Clarendon, 1993, pp. 202–3; W. A. Pantin, *The English Church in the Fourteenth Century*, paperback edn, Notre Dame, CA, 1963, Chapter IX; C. H. Lawrence, *The Friars. The Impact of the Early Mendicant Movement in Western Society*, The Medieval World, General Editor David Bates, London and New York, Longman, 1994, pp. 119–20; Larissa Taylor, *Soldiers of Christ Preaching in Late Medieval and Reformation France*, New York, Oxford, Oxford University Press, 1992.

25 Lawrence, *The Friars*, p. 120; Rosalind B. Brooke, *The Coming of the Friars*, Historical Problems; Studies and Documents, General Editor G. R. Elton, London, George Allen & Unwin, New York, Barnes & Noble Books, 1975, pp. 137–9; Barbara H. Rosenwein and Lester K. Little, 'Social meaning in the monastic and mendicant spiritualities', *Past and Present*, 1974, vol. 63, pp. 4–63; Iris Origo, *The World of San Bernardino*, London, Jonathan Cape, 1963, esp. Chapter VI; Donald Weinstein, *Savonarola and Florence: Prophecy and Patriotism in the Renaissance*, Princeton, NJ, Princeton University Press, 1971, Chapters III, IV, V; Roland H. Bainton, *Here I Stand. A Life of Martin Luther*, New York, Nashville, TN, Abingdon Press, 1950, pp. 78–9; James Atkinson, *The Trial of Luther*, London, B. T. Batsford, 1971, pp. 31–5; *The*

Correspondence of Erasmus. Letters 142 to 297, trans. R. A. B. Mynors and D. F. Thomson, Toronto, and Buffalo, NY, University of Toronto Press, 1975, p. 7; Jedin, *A History of the Council of Trent*, vol. II, pp. 107, 101, 24–7; James O'Donohoe, 'The seminary legislation of the Council of Trent' in *Il Concilio di Trento e la Riforma Tridentina Atti del Convegno Storico Internazionale Trento 2–6 Settembre 1963*, 2 vols, Rome, Freiburg, Basel, Barcelona, Vienna, Herder, 1965, vol. I, p. 159.

26 ibid.

27 Schroeder (ed.), *Canons and Decrees of Trent*, pp. 20–32, 29–46.

28 Erich Przywara, SJ, (ed.), *An Augustine Synthesis*, London, Sheed and Ward, 1936, pp. 315–16.

29 Bard Thompson, *Humanists and Reformers. A History of the Renaissance and Reformation*, Grand Rapids, MI, Cambridge, William B. Eerdmans, 1991, p. 209; for a fourteenth-century view of man's capacity for good that was in some respects even more pessimistic than Augustine's, see Gordon Leff, *Bradwardine and the Pelagians: A Study of His 'De Causa Dei' and its Opponents*, Cambridge, Cambridge University Press, 1957, pp. 116–17: see also Herbert B. Workman, *John Wyclif: A Study of the English Medieval Church* (1926), two vols in one, Camden, CN, Archon Reprints, 1966, Book I, pp. 119–21, 260–1, Book III, pp. 8–10; R. W. Southern, *Western Society and the Church in the Middle Ages*, The Pelican History of the Church, General Editor Owen Chadwick, Harmondsworth, Penguin, 1977, p. 242; Cameron, *The European Reformation*, pp. 42–3, 86–7; Jedin, *A History of the Council of Trent*, vol. II, pp. 258, 181.

30 Gordon Rupp, *The Righteousness of God. Luther Studies*, London, Hodder and Stoughton, 1953, p. 92 and n. 4; J. S. Whale, *The Protestant Tradition. An Essay in Interpretation*, Cambridge, Cambridge University Press, 1955, p. 47; R. Newton Flew and Rupert E. Davies (eds), *The Catholicity of Protestantism: being a Project presented to His Grace the Archbishop of Canterbury by a group of Free Churchmen*, London, Lutterworth Press, 3rd impression, 1951, p. 70; John Dillenberger (ed. and intro.), *Martin Luther. Selections from his Writings*, Garden City, NY, Anchor Books, 1961, pp. 176, 181; *A Commentary on St Paul's Epistle to the Galatians Based on Lectures Delivered by Martin Luther. First Published in 1535*, revised edn, of the 'Middleton' English version, Cambridge and London, James Clarke, 1972, p. 135.

31 Cameron, *The European Reformation*, pp. 84–7, 190; Heiko Augustinus Oberman, *The Harvest of Medieval Theology: Gabriel Biel and Late Medieval Nominalism*, Grand Rapids, MI, William B. Eerdmans, revised edn, 1967, p. 370; Fenlon, *Heresy and Obedience in Tridentine Italy*, Chapter 11; Barry Collett, *Italian Benedictine Scholars and the Reformation. The Congregation of Santa Giustina in Padua*, Oxford Historical Monographs, editors M. G. Brock *et al.*, Oxford, Clarendon, 1985, pp. 96–7, 104–10, Chapter 6; see also Oliver Logan, 'Grace and justification: some Italian views of the sixteenth and early seventeenth centuries', *The Journal of Ecclesiastical History*, 1969, vol. 20, pp. 67–78; for Valdés, see Angel M. Mergal, *Evangelical Catholicism as represented by Juan de Valdés*, in G. H. Williams (ed.), *Spiritual and Anabaptist Writers: Documents Illustrative of the Radical Reformation*, Library of Christian Classics, London, SCM Press, 1957, pp. 297–390; see also Salvatore Caponetto (ed.), *Benedetto da Mantova, Il Beneficio di Christo con le versioni del secolo XVI: documenti e testimonianze*, Chicago, IL, Newbury Library, 1972.

32 Jedin, *A History of the Council of Trent*, vol. II, pp. 180–1, 189–90, 166–316 (esp. 247, 286, 307, 311); Fenlon, *Heresy and Obedience*, Chapter 11; Schroeder (ed.), *Canons and Decrees of Trent*, pp. 29–33, 42: the words in emphasis are Scriptural citations, the profusion of which accompanying the text, and especially the large number of references to Paul, confirm just how 'evangelical' in spirit the Council's rulings on justification are. The influence of Augustine's writings is evident in citations throughout.

33 Schroeder (ed.), *Canons and Decrees of Trent*, pp. 34, 43, 33; Chemnitz, *Examination of the Council of Trent*, Part 1, p. 515; Luther, too, upheld a doctrine of sanctification,

though, as with his theology of justification, it operated from faith: Flew and Davies (eds), *The Catholicity of Protestantism*, pp. 80–1; Jedin, *A History of the Council of Trent*, vol. II, p. 317.

34 ibid., pp. 317–23; Schroeder (ed.), *Canons and Decrees of Trent*, pp. 46–8; Jedin, 'Der Kampf um die bischöffliche Residenzplicht 1562/3' in *Il Concilio di Trento*, pp. 1–25; Delumeau, *Catholicism from Luther to Voltaire*, pp. 16–18.

35 Schroeder, *Canons and Decrees of Trent*, pp. 51, 45, 52.

36 Jedin, *A History of the Council of Trent*, vol. II, Chapter X and pp. 371–2; Norman P. Tanner, SJ (ed.), *Decrees of the Ecumenical Councils*, 2 vols, London, Sheed and Ward, Washington, DC, Georgetown University Press, 1990, vol. I, pp. 541–50; *Luther's Works*, 55 vols, Jaroslav Pelican and Helmut T. Lehmann (eds), St Louis, MO, and Philadelphia, PA, 1960–86, vol. 36: *Word and Sacrament*, vol. II, Abdel Ross Wentz (ed.), p. 91; *Luther's Works*, vol. 37: *Word and Sacrament*, vol. III, Robert H. Fischer (ed.), Philadelphia, PA, Mühlenberg Press, 1961, p. 370; Chemnitz, *Examination of the Council of Trent*, Part 2, pp. 23–44; Grimm, *The Reformation Era*, p. 152.

37 Schroeder (ed.), *Canons and Decrees of Trent*, pp. 55–6.

38 Daniel-Rops, *The Catholic Reformation*, pp. 82–3; Janelle, *The Catholic Reformation*, p. 70; Grimm, *The Reformation Era*, pp. 400–1; Jedin, *A History of the Council of Trent*, vol. II, pp. 419–43.

39 Schroeder (ed.), *Canons and Decrees of Trent*, pp. 73–80; Tanner (ed.), *Decrees of the Ecumenical Councils*, vol. I, pp. 230, 245; St Thomas Aquinas, *On the Truth of the Catholic Faith Summa Contra Gentiles, Book Four: Salvation*, trans and intro. Charles J. O'Neill, Garden City, NY, Image Books, 1957, pp. 257, 266; Anthony Kenny, *Wyclif*, Past Masters, General Editor Keith Thomas, Oxford, New York, Oxford University Press, 1985, p. 87.

40 Owen Chadwick, *The Reformation*, The Pelican History of the Church, General Editor Owen Chadwick, vol. 3, Harmondsworth, Penguin, 1964, pp. 78–80; Cameron, *The European Reformation*, pp. 163–6; Jedin, *A History of the Council of Trent*, vol. II, pp. 431–2.

41 Cameron, *The European Reformation*, p. 66; Chadwick, *The Reformation*, pp. 34–6; Hubert Jedin, *Storia del Concilio di Trento*, Vol. III, Brescia, Morcelliana, 1973, p. 381; Dickens, *The Counter-Reformation*, pp. 117, 115; Grimm, *The Reformation Era*, pp. 370–1; Jared Wicks, SJ, 'Doctrine and Theology' in John W. O'Malley, SJ (ed.), *Catholicism in Early Modern History A Guide to Research*, Volume 2 of Reformation Guides to Research, Ann Arbor, MI, Edwards Brothers, 1988, pp. 234–5; Christiani, *Histoire de l'Eglise*, vol. 17, pp. 122–3; Schroeder (ed.), *Canons and Decrees of Trent*, pp. 75, 79.

42 Jedin, *Il Concilio*, vol. III, Chapter IV; Giuseppe Alberigo, 'The Council of Trent' in O'Malley (ed.), *Catholicism in Early Modern Europe*, p. 215; Frederick C. Church, *The Italian Reformers 1534–1564*, New York, Columbia University Press, 1932, pp. 30–1; Fenlon, *Heresy and Obedience*, p. 48; Elizabeth G. Gleason, *Gasparo Contarini Venice, Rome and Reform*, Berkeley and Los Angeles, CA, Oxford, University of California Press, 1993, p. 239.

43 Schroeder (ed.), *Canons and Decrees of Trent*, pp. 81–7.

44 ibid., p. 91; Tanner (ed.), *Decrees of the Ecumenical Councils*, vol. I, p. 245; William E. Addis and Thomas Arnold, *A Catholic Dictionary Containing Some Account of the Doctrine, Discipline, Rites, Ceremonies, Councils, and Religious Orders of the Catholic Church*, London, Kegan Paul, Trench, Trübner & Co., 1893, p. 699; Aquinas, *On the Truth of the Catholic Faith*, O'Neill (ed.), pp. 249, 277–9, 282; Cameron, *The European Reformation*, pp. 84–5; Thomas N. Tentler, *Sin and Confession on the Eve of the Reformation*, Princeton, NJ, Princeton University Press, 1977, pp. 18–19; Alister E. McGrath, *Reformation Thought: An Introduction*, Oxford, Basil Blackwell, 1988, pp. 72–3; John Bossy, 'The social history of Confession in the age of the Reformation', *Transactions of the Royal Historical*

Society, 1975, fifth series, vol. 25, p. 27; John Dillenberger (ed. and intro.), *Martin Luther Selections from his Writings*, Garden City, NY, Anchor Books, 1961, pp. 317–8.

45 Schroeder (ed.), *Canons and Decrees of Trent*, pp. 99–101; Tanner (ed.), *Decrees of the Ecumenical Councils*, vol. I, p. 541; Dillenberger (ed.), *Martin Luther Selections from his Writings*, pp. 350, 355, 351; Christiani, *L'Eglise à l'Epoque du Concile de Trente*, p. 217; Jedin, *Il Concilio di Trento*, vol. III, p. 468; Paul Althaus, *The Theology of Martin Luther*, trans. Robert C. Schultz, Philadelphia, PA, Fortress Press, 1966, pp. 348–9; Cameron, *The European Reformation*, pp. 159–60.

46 Schroeder (ed.), *Canons and Decrees of Trent*, pp. 105–14; Tanner (ed.), *Decrees of the Ecumenical Councils*, vol. II, pp. 881, vol. I, pp. 212, 243; Alexander Murray, *Reason and Society in the Middle Ages*, Oxford, Clarendon, 1978, pp. 214–17; Timothy Tackett, *Priest and Parish in Eighteenth Century France. A Social and Political Study of the Curés in the Diocese of Dauphiné 1750–1791*, Princeton, NJ, Princeton University Press, 1977, pp. 78, 155; Delumeau, *Catholicism from Luther to Voltaire*, pp. 182–3.

47 Jedin, *Il Concilio di Trento*, vol. III, pp. 479, 487, 498–9; Christiani, *L'Eglise à l'Epoque du Concile e Trente*, p. 134; Schroeder (ed.), *Canons and Decrees of Trent*, pp. 114, 116, 119, 121.

48 ibid., pp. 116, 119, 121; Hubert Jedin, *Crisis and Closure of the Council of Trent. A retrospective view from the Second Vatican Council*, trans. N. D. Smith, London and Melbourne, Sheed and Ward Stagbooks, 1967, p. 13.

49 J. N. D. Kelly, *The Oxford Dictionary of the Popes*, Oxford, New York, Oxford University Press, 1986, p. 263; H. Outram Evennett, *The Cardinal of Guise and the Council of Trent. A Study in the Counter-Reformation*, Cambridge, Cambridge University Press, 1930, p. 43; Jedin, *Crisis and Closure*, pp. 11–12; Jedin, *Il Concilio di Trento*, vol. III, pp. 17–19; Raul de Almeida Rolo, 'L'application de la réforme du Concile de Trente à Braga' in *Il Concilio di Trento Convegno Storico*, vol. II, pp. 558–9.

50 Jedin, *Il Concilio di Trento*, vol. III, pp. 24–5, 28–9; Kelly, *The Oxford Dictionary of the Popes*, pp. 264, 265–6; Daniel-Rops, *The Catholic Reformation*, pp. 85–7; Janelle, *The Catholic Reformation*, p. 66; Jedin, *Crisis and Closure*, p. 9; Grimm, *The Reformation Era*, p. 402; Giuseppe Alberigo, 'Le potestà episcopali nei dibatiti tridentini' in *Il Concilio di Trento Convegno Storico*, vol. II, p. 523.

51 Ranke, *The History of the Popes*, vol. III: Appendix, pp. 161–2; Daniel-Rops, *The Catholic Reformation*, pp. 86–9; Cameron, *The European Reformation*, pp. 395, 373–4; Jedin, *Crisis and Closure*, pp. 14–15; Schroeder (ed.), *Canons and Decrees of Trent*, p. 121.

52 ibid., p. 123; Daniel-Rops, *The Catholic Reformation*, p. 93; Jedin, *Crisis and Closure*, pp. 28, 33.

53 Schroeder, *Canons and Decrees of Trent*, p. 122; Grimm, *The Reformation Era*, p. 404; Daniel-Rops, *The Catholic Reformation*, pp. 92–3. For Philip II's role with regard to the Council, and later its decrees, see Henry Kamen, *Philip of Spain*, New Haven, CN, and London, Yale University Press, 1997, pp. 103–5

54 Jedin, *Crisis and Closure*, pp. 42–5; Daniel-Rops, *The Catholic Reformation*, p. 91; Schroeder (ed.), *Canons and Decrees of Trent*, p. 116.

55 Jedin, 'Der Kampf um die bischöfliche Residenzpflicht', p. 8; *Osservatori Toscani al Concilio di Trento*, Niccolò Rodolico (ed.), Florence, Leo S. Olschki Editore, 1965, p. 203; Jedin, *Crisis and Closure*, pp. 47–8; Schroeder (ed.), *Canons and Decrees of Trent*, p. 131.

56 Jedin, *Crisis and Closure*, pp. 59–61; Howard Kaminsky, *A History of the Hussite Revolution*, Berkeley and Los Angeles, CA, University of California Press, pp. 127–34; Matthew Spinka, trans., *The Letters of John Hus*, Manchester, Manchester University Press, Totowa, NJ, Rowan and Littlefield, 1979, p. 82; Tanner (ed.), *Decrees of the Ecumenical Councils*, vol. I, p. 418.

57 Frederick G. Heymann, *John Zizka and the Hussite Revolution*, New York, Russell & Russell, 1955, pp. 59, 150–3; Tanner (ed.), *Decrees of the Ecumenical Councils*, vol. I,

pp. 54–7; Luther, *On the Holy Sacrament and the Brotherhoods* (1519) in Robert Hendon Fife, *The Revolt of Martin Luther*, New York and London, Columbia University Press, 1957, pp. 461–2; Cameron, *The European Reformation*, pp. 214, 248, 135, 159; Bainton, *Here I Stand*, p. 118; Chadwick, *The Reformation*, pp. 307–8.

58 Schroeder (ed.), *Canons and Decrees of Trent*, pp. 132–5; Jedin, *Crisis and Closure*, pp. 64–5, 61; R. Po-Chia Hsia, *Social Discipline in the Reformation Central Europe 1550–1750*, Christianity in the Modern World, Series Editor Hugh McLeod, London and New York, Routledge, 1989, pp. 39, 40–1; Martin Luther, *Confession Concerning Christ's Supper* (1528), in *Luther's Works*, vol. 37: *Word and Sacrament*, III, Fischer (ed.), p. 312.

59 Schroeder (ed.), *Canons and Decrees of Trent*, p. 134; Philip M. Soergel, *Wondrous in His Saints. Counter-Reformation Propaganda in Bavaria*, Studies on the History of Society and Culture, Victoria E. Bonnell and Lynn Hunt (eds), Berkeley and Los Angeles, CA, London, University of California Press, 1993, pp. 36–8, 81–93; 171–81; R. Po-Chia Hsia, *The Myth of Ritual Murder. Jews and Magic in Reformation Germany*, New Haven, CN, Yale University Press, 1988.

60 Jedin, *Il Concilio di Trento*, vol. III, pp. 479, 487, 498–9; Heiko Augustinus Oberman (ed.), *Forerunners of the Reformation: The Shape of Late Medieval Thought Illustrated by Key Documents*, trans. Paul L. Nyhus, London, Lutterworth, 1967, pp. 256–64; Tanner (ed.), *Decrees of the Ecumenical Councils*, vol. I, p. 54; Christiani, *L'Église à l'Époque du Concile de Trente*, p. 134; Schroeder (ed.), *Canons and Decrees of Trent*, pp. 119–20.

61 Martin Luther, 'Treatise on Good Works' in *Luther's Works*, Vol. 44: *The Christian in Society*, I, James Atkinson (ed.), Philadelphia, PA. Fortress Press, 1955, p. 55; Erwin Iserloh, 'Das tridentinische Messopferdekret in seinem Beziehungen zu der Kontroverstheologie der Zeit' in *Il Concilio di Trento Convegno Storico*, vol. II, pp. 417, 423; Jedin, *Crisis and Closure*, pp. 70–1.

62 Jedin, *Il Concilio di Trento*, vol. IV, tome I (1975), pp. 320–1; Jedin, *Crisis and Closure*, pp. 66–9; Schroeder (ed.), *Canons and Decrees of Trent*, pp. 145–52 (the words in emphasis are from Scripture); Iserloh, 'Das tridentinische Messopferdekret', pp. 430–9; *The Daily Missal and Liturgical Manual. Compiled from the Missale Romanum*, Leeds, Laverty and Sons, 1956, p. 923–43.

63 Schroeder (ed.), *Canons and Decrees of Trent*, pp. 152–9, 149, 103; Jedin, *Crisis and Closure*, pp. 78–87; Ricardo Villoslada, 'Pedro Guerrero represenante de la reforma española' in *Il Concilio di Trento Convegno Storico*, pp. 115–19; Robert Trisco, 'Carlo Borromeo and the Council of Trent: The Question of Reform' in John M. Headley and John B. Tomaro (eds), *San Carlo Borromeo Catholic Reform and Ecclesiastical Politics in the Second Half of the Sixteenth Century*, Washington, DC, The Folger Shakespeare Library, London and Toronto, Associated University Presses, 1988, pp. 52–60. For Guise, Evennett, *The Cardinal of Lorraine and the Council of Trent*, Chapter XI.

64 Jedin, *Crisis and Closure*, pp. 87–102.

65 ibid., pp. 102–8; Trisco, 'Carlo Borromeo and the Council', pp. 56–7; Grimm, *The Reformation Era*, pp. 406–7; Evennett, *The Cardinal of Lorraine*, Chapter XI.

66 Jedin, *Crisis and Closure*, pp. 109–15; Trisco, Cardinal Borromeo and the Council', pp. 60–1; Schroeder (ed.), *Canons and Decrees of Trent*, p. 164; Jedin, 'Der Kampf um die bischöffliche Residenzpflicht', p. 23; Delumeau, *Catholicism from Luther to Voltaire*, pp. 17–18.

67 Schroeder (ed.), *Canons and Decrees of Trent*, pp. 161–3, 164–79; Tanner (ed.), *Decrees of the Ecumenical Councils*, vol. I, p. 541; *Luther's Works*, vol. 36: *Word and Sacrament*, vol. II, Abdel Ross Wentz (ed.), Philadelphia, PA, Fortress Press, 1959, p. 106.

67 Schroeder (ed.), *Canons and Decrees of Trent*, pp. 175–9; Grimm, *The Reformation Era*, p. 408; Jedin, *Crisis and Closure*, pp. 115, 120; V. H. H. Green, *Renaissance and Reformation: A Survey of European History between 1450 and 1660*, London, Edward Arnold, 2nd edn, 1964, p. 189; Chadwick, *The Reformation*, p. 279; O'Donohoe, 'The seminary legislation of the Council of Trent', pp. 157–72.

69 Tanner (ed.), *Decrees of the Ecumenical Councils*, vol. I, pp. 240, 49; Jedin, *Crisis and Closure*, p. 119; O'Donohoe, 'The seminary legislation of the Council of Trent', p. 159, 167–8, 170–1; Francesco C. Cesareo, 'Quest for identity: The ideals of Jesuit education in the sixteenth century' in Christopher Chapple (ed.), *The Jesuit Tradition in Education and Mission: A 450-Year Perspective*, Scranton, PA, University of Scranton Press, London and Toronto, Associated University Presses, 1993, p. 27; Delumeau, *Catholicism between Luther and Voltaire*, pp. 28–9, 32–3.

70 Tanner (ed.), *Decrees of the Ecumenical Councils*, vol. I, p. 550; Schroeder (ed.), *Canons and Decrees of Trent*, pp. 180–90; Jedin, *Crisis and Closure*, pp. 141–5; John Bossy, 'The Counter-Reformation and the people of Catholic Europe', *Past and Present*, 1970, No. 47, pp. 51–70.

71 Schroeder (ed.), *Canons and Decrees of Trent*, pp. 190–213, 217–55; Jedin, *Crisis and Closure*, p. 126.

72 Schroeder (ed.), *Canons and Decrees of Trent*, pp. 232–56; Trisco, 'Carlo Borromeo and the Council', pp. 47–8; Hallman, *Italian Cardinals, Reform and the Church as Property*, pp. 39, 43, 62; Jedin, *Crisis and Closure*, pp. 124–6.

73 Tanner (ed.), *Decrees of the Ecumenical Councils*, vol. I, p. 202; Schroeder (ed.), *Canons and Decrees of Trent*, pp. 239–48, 249–252, 255, 257; Delumeau, *Catholicism from Luther to Voltaire*, pp. 25–6.

74 Schroeder (ed.), *Canons and Decrees of Trent*, pp. 253–4; Jedin, *Crisis and Closure*, pp. 145–7; Cameron, *The European Reformation*, p. 108.

75 Schroeder (ed.), *Canons and Decrees of Trent*, pp. 253–4, 46, 214; James Atkinson, *The Trial of Luther*, London, B. T. Batsford, 1971, pp. 32–3, 105–6; Cameron, *The European Reformation*, p. 67; A. N. Galpern, *The Religion of the People in Sixteenth-Century Champagne*, Cambridge, MA, and London, Harvard University Press, 1976, pp. 17–29

76 Jedin, *Crisis and Closure*, pp. 133–4; Schroeder (ed.), *Canons and Decrees of Trent*, pp. 217–32.

77 Jedin, *Crisis and Closure*, pp. 130–1, 147–58; Schroeder (ed.), *Canons and Decrees of Trent*, pp. 257–8; Dickens, *The Counter-Reformation*, p. 129.

3 New religious orders

1 William E. Addis, *A Catholic Dictionary Containing Some Account of the Doctrine, Discipline, Rites, Ceremonies, Councils, and Religious Orders of the Catholic Church*, London, Virtue & Co., 1928, p. 123; R. Po-Chia Hsia, *The World of Catholic Renewal 1540–1770*, New Approaches to Eurpean History, William Beik *et al.* (eds), Cambridge, Cambridge University Press, 1998, p. 35; Jodi Bilinkoff, 'Teresa of Jesus and Carmelite reform' in Richard L. DeMolen (ed.), *Religious Orders of the Catholic Reformation In Honor of John C. Olin on his Seventy-Fifth Birthday*, New York, Fordham University Press, 1994, pp. 165–86.

2 Pierre Janelle, *The Catholic Reformation*, Milwaukee, WI, Bruce Publishing. London, Collier-Macmillan, 1971, pp. 1, 78–9; H. O. Evennett, *The Spirit of the Counter-Reformation*, John Bossy (ed.), Notre Dame, CA, and London, University of Notre Dame Press, 1968, p. 87.

3 John Coulson (ed.), *The Saints. A Concise Biographical Dictionary*, Bristol, Nicholas Adams, 1958, pp. 100–01; *The Catholic Encyclopedia. An International Work of Reference on the Constitutions, Doctrine, Discipline and History of the Catholic Church*, Charles G. Herbermann *et al.*, (eds) 16 vols, London, Caxton Publishing, New York, Robert Appleton Co., 1907–14, vol. 14, p. 557; Les Petits Bollandistes, *Vies des Saints*, 17 vols, Paris, Bloud et Barral, 188, vol. 9, pp. 378–93; Evennett, *The Spirit of the Counter-Reformation*, pp. 38, 87; Donnani, *et al.* (eds), *Histoire du Clergé Seculier et Regulier*, 4 vols, Amsterdam, Pierre Brunel, 1716, vol. III, pp. 98–103.

4 Coulson (ed.), *Lives of the Saints*, pp. 100–01; *The Catholic Encyclopedia*, vol. 14, pp. 557–9; Keneth J. Jorgensen, SJ, 'The Theatines', in DeMolen (ed.), *Religious Orders of the Catholic Reformation*, p. 19.

5 Coulson (ed.), *The Saints*, pp. 100–1; *The Catholic Encyclopedia*, vol. 14, pp. 557–9; Donald Attwater, *The Penguin Dictionary of the Saints*, Harmondsworth, Penguin, 1973, p. 78; Janelle, *The Catholic Reformation*, pp. 96–7; Jorgensen, 'The Theatines', pp. 14–15, 18.

6 Bonnani *et al.* (eds) *Histoire du Clergé*, vol. III, p. 118; *Histoire Ecclésiastique* [by J. C. Fabre] *pour servir de contination à celle de Monsieur l'Abbé Fleury*, Paris, 1722–38, vol. 27, p. 271; *The Catholic Encyclopedia*, vol. 14, p. 140; AG. Dickens, *The Counter-Reformation*, London, Harcourt, Brace & World, 1969, pp. 70–1; Janelle, *The Catholic Reformation*, pp. 97–8; H. Daniel-Rops, *The Catholic Reformation*, trans. John Warrington, London, J. M. Dent, New York, E. P. Dutton, 1963, p. 23; H. O. Evennett, 'The new orders' in G. R. Elton (ed.), *The New Cambridge Modern History*, vol. II: *The Reformation*, Cambridge, Cambridge University Press, 1968, p. 288.

7 Les Petits Bollandistes, *Vies des Saints*, vol. 15, pp. 464–8; *The Catholic Encyclopedia*, vol. II, pp. 302–5; Richard L. DeMolen, 'The first centenary of the Barnabites (1533–1633)' in DeMolen (ed.), *Religious Orders of the Catholic Reformation*, pp. 59–79.

8 *The Catholic Encyclopedia*, vol. 2, pp. 302–5; Evennett, *The Spirit of the Counter-Reformation*, pp. 16–17; Les Petits Bollandistes, *Vies des Saints*, vol. 15, pp. 465–6; Janelle, *The Catholic Reformation*, p. 98; Bonnani *et al.* (eds), *Histoire du Clergé*, vol. III, pp. 107, 104.

9 Evennett, 'The New Orders', pp. 287–8; *The Catholic Encyclopedia*, vol. 2, p. 302; Bonnani *et al.* (eds), *Histoire du Clergé*, vol. III, p. 104; Dickens, *The Counter-Reformation*, p. 70; Les Petits Bollandistes, *Vies des Saints*, vol. 15, pp. 465–6; Janelle, *The Catholic Reformation*, p. 98; Daniel-Rops, *The Catholic Reformation*, p. 23.

10 Les Petitis Bollandistes, *Vies des Saints*, vol. 15, pp. 466–7; Adriano Prosperi, 'Clerics and laymen in the work of Carlo Borromeo' in John M. Headley and John B. Tomaro (eds), *San Carlo Borromeo Catholic Reform and Ecclesiastical Politics in the Second Half of the Sixteenth Century*, Washington, DC, The Folger Shakespeare Library, London and Toronto, Associated University Presses, 1988, pp. 126–7; Janelle, *The Catholic Reformation*, p. 98; Evennett, 'The new orders', p. 290; DeMolen, 'The Barnabites', pp. 79–82.

11 Evennett, *The Spirit of the Counter-Reformation*, p. 83.

12 Michael Foss, *The Founding of the Jesuits 1540*, London, Hamish Hamilton, 1969, pp. 62, 64; James Brodrick, SJ, *Saint Ignatius Loyola The Pilgrim Years*, London, Burns & Oates, 1956, pp. 31–9, 40, 67; Harvey D. Egan, SJ, *Ignatius Loyola the Mystic*, The Way of the Christian Mystics, General Editor Noel Dermot O'Donoghue, ODC, vol. 5, Wilmington, DE, Michael Glazier, 1987, p. 38; *The Catholic Encyclopedia*, vol. 9, p. 416.

13 *The Autobiography of St Ignatius Loyola With Related Documents*, trans. Joseph F. O'Callaghan, ed. and intro. John C. Olin, New York, Fordham University Press, 1992, pp. 21, 33–55, 24; James Brodrick, SJ, *The Origin of the Jesuits*, London, The Catholic Book Club, 1943, p. 4, n. 2; A. Lynn Martin, *The Jesuit Mind. The Mentality of an Elite in Early Modern France*, Ithaca, NY, and London, Cornell University Press, p. 80; *Letters of St Ignatius Loyola*, selected and edited by William J. Young, SJ, Chicago, IL, Loyola University Press, 1959, pp. 6–7, 45, 72, 148, 183, 184, 193; *The Confessions of St Augustine*, trans. Sir Tobie Matthew, revised Dom Roger Hudleston, London, Collins Fontana, 1960, pp. 56–7; John W. O'Malley, SJ, 'The Society of Jesus' in DeMolen (ed.), *Religious Orders of the Catholic Reformation*, p. 141.

14 Evennett, *The Spirit of the Counter-Reformation*, pp. 56–7; André Ravier, SJ, *Ignatius Loyola and the Founding of the Society of Jesus*, trans. Maura, John and Carson Daly, San Francisco, CA, Ignatian Press, 1980, pp. 394, 396; Brodrick, *The Origin of the Jesuits*, pp. 2–4, 16; William v. Bangert, SJ, *A History of the Society of Jesus*. 2nd edn, St Louis,

MO, The Institute of Jesuit Sources, pp. 3–4; Olin (ed.), *The Autobiography of St Ignatius Loyola*, p. 22; Philip Ward (ed.), *The Oxford Companion to Spanish Literature*, Oxford, Clarendon, 1978, p. 436.

15 Olin (ed.), *The Autobiography of St Ignatius Loyola*, pp. 22–5; Bangert, *History of the Society of Jesus*, p. 6; Brodrick, *The Origin of the Jesuits*, p. 12; Brodrick, *Saint Ignatius Loyola*, pp. 79–80, 82; Foss, *The Founding of the Jesuits*, p. 73; Coulson (ed.), *The Saints*, p. 378; *The Spiritual Exercises of Saint Ignatius. A New Translation*, trans. Thomas Corbishly, SJ, London, Burns & Oates, 1963, pp. 40, 41, 44; Young (ed.), *Letters of Ignatius Loyola*, p. 268.

16 Ravier, *Ignatius of Loyola*, p. 409; Olin (ed.), *The Autobiography of St Ignatius Loyola*, pp. 38, 24, 29, 31–3, 39, 40.

17 ibid., pp. 31, 33–6, 39–41; Evennett, *The Spirit of the Counter-Reformation*, pp. 58–9.

18 Olin (ed.), *The Autobiography of St Ignatius Loyola*, pp. 37–49

19 George F. Maine, trans. and intro., *The Imitation of Christ of Thomas a Kempis*, London and Glasgow, Collins, 1977, pp. 40–1, 79; Olin (ed.), *The Autobiography of St Ignatius Loyola*, pp. 36 and n. 1, 25, 35; Ravier, *Ignatius of Loyola*, pp. 411–12; Evennett, *The Spirit of the Counter-Reformation*, pp. 58–9; Bangert, *History of the Society of Jesus*, p. 10; Brodrick, *The Origin of the Jesuits*, p. 21.

20 ibid., pp. 25–7; John C. Olin, 'The idea of pilgrimage in the experience of Ignatius Loyola', *Church History*, 1979, vol. 48, pp. 387–98; Bangert, *A History of the Society of Jesus*, p. 11; Evennett, *The Spirit of the Counter-Reformation*, p. 60; Ravier, *Ignatius of Loyola*, pp. 415–18, Olin (ed.), *The Autobiography of St Ignatius Loyola*, pp. 41–56.

21 ibid; Evennett, *The Spirit of the Counter-Reformation*, p. 60.

22 Olin (ed.), *The Autobiography of St Ignatius Loyola*, pp. 59–60; Young (ed.), *Letters of St Ignatius of Loyola*, pp. 133–6.

23 Olin (ed.), *The Autobiography of St Ignatius Loyola*, pp. 61–3.

24 Daniel-Rops, *The Catholic Reformation*, pp. 7–8; *The Constitutions of the Society of Jesus*, trans. and intro. George E. Ganss, SJ, St Louis, MO, The Institute of Jesuit Sources, 1970, p. 19; Brodrick, *The Origin of the Jesuits*, pp. 30–1; Bangert, *History of the Society of Jesus*, pp. 12–13; Olin (ed.), *The Autobiography of St Ignatius Loyola*, p. 39.

25 Brodrick, *The Origin of the Jesuits*, pp. 33–7; Ravier, *Ignatius Loyola*, pp. 418–19.

26 Evennett, *The Spirit of the Counter-Reformation*, pp. 61, 62; Olin (ed.), *The Autobiography of St Ignatius Loyola*, pp. 78–9; Brodrick, *The Origin of the Jesuits*, pp. 38–40.

27 Evennett, *The Spirit of the Counter-Reformation*, pp. 38, 61.

28 Olin (ed.), *The Autobiography of St Ignatius Loyola*, p. 80, n. 13; Ganss (ed.), *The Constitutions of the Society of Jesus*, pp. 19–20; Ravier, *Ignatius Loyola*, p. 422; Young (ed.), *Letters of St Ignatius Loyola*, pp. 183–4, 45, 72, 148, 193; Joseph Rickaby, SJ, (ed.), *The Spiritual Exercises of St Ignatius Loyola Spanish and English*, London, Burns & Oates, 1915, pp. 222–5.

29 Olin (ed.), *The Autobiography of St Ignatius Loyola*, pp. 79–81; Brodrick, *The Origin of the Jesuits*, pp. 42–3; Ravier, *Ignatius Loyola*, pp. 422–3.

30 Olin (ed.), *The Autobiography of St Ignatius Loyola*, p. 81.

31 Young (ed.), *Letters of St Ignatius Loyola*, pp. 28–31; Brodrick, *The Origin of the Jesuits*, pp. 62, 29, 49; Evennett, *The Spirit of the Counter-Reformation*, p. 62, n. 1.

32 Olin (ed.), *The Autobiography of St Ignatius Loyola*, pp. 87–9; Bangert, *A History of the Society of Jesus*, pp. 18–19; Daniel-Rops, *The Catholic Reformation*, p. 47.

33 Olin (ed.), *The Autobiography of St Ignatius Loyola*, pp. 91–2; Bangert, *A History of the Society of Jesus*, p. 20.

34 Young (ed.), *Letters of St Ignatius of Loyola*, pp. 36–7; Bangert, *A History of the Society of Jesus*, p. 20–1; Ganss (ed.), *The Constitutions of the Society of Jesus*, pp. 21–2: the version we are considering is the so-called 'B' autograph text of 1550.

35 Daniel-Rops, *The Catholic Reformation*, p. 49, 51–2; Olin (ed.), *The Autobiography of St Ignatius Loyola*, p. 92; Evennett, *The Spirit of the Counter-Reformation*, p. 62; Ganss (ed.),

The Constitutions of the Society of Jesus, p. 89; Bangert, *A History of the Society of Jesus*, p. 22; Owen Chadwick, *The Reformation*, The Pelican History of the Church, General Editor Owen Chadwick, Harmondsworth, Penguin, 1964, p. 260; Dickens, *The Counter-Reformation*, p. 82.

36 Ganss (ed.), *The Constitutions of the Society of Jesus*, pp. 246, 91, 150; Dickens, *The Counter-Reformation*, p. 82.

37 Olin (ed.), *The Autobiography of St Ignatius Loyola*, p. 92; Bangert, *A History of the Society of Jesus*, pp. 21–2; Daniel-Rops, *The Catholic Reformation*, pp. 51, 58.

38 Pietro Tacchi Venturi, SJ, *Storia della Compagnia di Gesù in Italia Narrata col Sussidio di Fonti Inediti*, 2 vols, Rome, 'La Civiltà Cattolica', 1950, vol. I, part 2, pp. 229–33; Bangert, *A History of the Society of Jesus*, pp. 22–3; Louis Châtellier, *The Religion of the Poor. Rural missions in Europe and the formation of modern Catholicism, c. 1500–c. 1800*, trans. Brian Pearce, Cambridge, Cambridge University Press, Maison des Sciences de l'Homme, 1997, pp. 155–8.

39 Daniel-Rops, *The Catholic Reformation*, pp. 58–9; Bangert, *A History of the Society of Jesus*, p. 10.

40 Evennett, *The Spirit of the Counter-Reformation*, pp. 54–6, 51–2; Bangert, *A History of the Society of Jesus*, p. 8; Daniel-Rops, *The Catholic Reformation*, p. 31; Rickaby (ed.), *The Spiritual Exercises*, notes, pp. 219, 222; Young (ed.), *Letters of St Ignatius Loyola*, pp. 126–7; Dickens, *The Counter-Reformation*, p. 78. For further discussion of the textual evolution of the *Exercises*, see Ravier, *Ignatius of Loyola*, pp. 458–60.

41 Ravier, *Ignatius of Loyola*, p. 459–64; Bangert, *A History of the Society of Jesus*, p. 22.

42 Daniel-Rops, *The Catholic Reformation*, p. 33; Rickaby (ed.), *The Spiritual Exercises*, pp. 85, 95; Olin, 'The idea of pilgrimage', p. 394.

43 Anne Winston-Allen, *Stories of the Rose. The Making of the Rosary in the Middle Ages*, University Park, PA, The Pennsylvania State University Press, 1997, pp. 22, 27, 94; Dickens, *The Counter-Reformation*, pp. 77–81.

44 Rickaby (ed.), *The Spiritual Exercises*, pp. 97–100, 104–5, 109–113, 121, 124, 163, 169–75, 177–8, 179–80, 181–5, 112; Ravier, *Ignatius of Loyola*, p. 80; Dickens, *The Counter-Reformation*, pp. 80–1

45 Bangert, *A History of the Society of Jesus*, pp. 26–7; Dickens, *The Counter-Reformation*, pp. 83–4.

46 Bangert, *A History of the Society of Jesus*, pp. 26–7; Francesco C. Cesareo, 'Quest for identity: the ideals of Jesuit education in the sixteenth century' in Christopher Chapple (ed.), *The Jesuit Tradition in Education and Missions: A 450-Year Perspective*, Scranton, PA, University of Scranton Press, London and Toronto, Associated University Presses, 1993, pp. 18–19.

47 Cesareo, 'Quest for identity', pp. 21, 30, 19 (citing Ganss), 20, 26–7; Young (ed.), *Letters of St Ignatius of Loyola*, pp. 120–30; Daniel-Rops, *The Catholic Reformation*, p. 55; Robert Muchembled, 'Lay judges and the acculturation of the masses (France and the southern Low Countries), sixteenth to eighteenth centuries' in Kaspar von Grayerz (ed.), *Religion and Society in Early Modern Europe, 1500–1800*, London, Boston, Sydney, George Allen & Unwin for The German Historical Institute, 1984, pp. 56–65.

48 Bangert, *A History of the Society of Jesus*, p. 27; Daniel-Rops, *The Catholic Reformation*, p. 56; Cesareo, 'Quest for identity', p. 21; Young (ed.), *Letters of St Ignatius of Loyola*, pp. 193–4.

49 Cesareo, 'Quest for identity', pp. 21, 17; Bangert, *A History of the Society of Jesus*, pp. 27–8; Martin, *The Jesuit Mind*, pp. 54, 57, 60; Daniel-Rops, *The Catholic Reformation*, p. 375.

50 Cesareo, 'Quest for identity, pp. 23, 31, n. 34, 25, 17, 29, n. 33; Young (ed.), *Letters of St Ignatius Loyola*, pp. 362, 259, 437–9.

51 Bangert, *History of the Society of Jesus*, pp. 28, 56; Cesareo, 'Quest for identity', p. 27; Janelle, *The Catholic Reformation*, p. 123.

52 Brodrick, *The Origin of the Jesuits*, pp. 81–2; Young (ed.), *Letters of St Ignatius of Loyola*, pp. 35–6, 42.

53 Brodrick, *The Origin of the Jesuits*, pp. 39–40, 55, 61; James Brodrick, *Saint Francis Xavier (1506–1552)*, London, Burns Oates, 1952 (for Xavier and the origin of the Jesuits, see also Georg Schurhammer, SJ, *Francis Xavier His Life, His Times*, Volume I *Europe 1506–1541*, trans. M. Joseph Costelloe, SJ, Rome, The Jesuit Historical Institute, 1973.

54 Jean Delumeau, *Catholicism from Luther to Voltaire: a new view of the Counter-Reformation*, trans. Jeremy Moiser, London, Burns & Oates, Philadelphia, PA, Westminster Press, 1977, pp. 61–2; Brodrick, *The Origin of the Jesuits*, pp. 116, 129–30; Bangert, *A History of the Society of Jesus*, p. 32; Donald Attwater, *The Penguin Dictionary of the Saints*, p. 141; Janelle, *The Catholic Reformation*, pp. 290–2; Dickens, *The Counter-Reformation*, p. 87; Daniel-Rops, *The Catholic Reformation*, p. 287.

55 Brodrick, *The Origin of the Jesuits*, pp. 117, 120–1, 126, n. 1; Attwater, *Lives of the Saints*, p. 141; Brodrick, *Saint Francis Xavier*, Chapters V–XVII; Young (ed.), *Letters of St Ignatius of Loyola*, pp. 298–300: the further development of overseas missions will be considered in Chapter 6.

56 James Brodrick, SJ, *The Progress of the Jesuits (1556–79)*, London, New York, Toronto, Longmans, Green, 1946, p. 28; Young (ed.), *Letters of St Ignatius of Loyola*, pp. 298, 249–52, 345–7; Bangert, *A History of the Society of Jesus*, p. 71; Philip M. Soergel, *Wondrous in His Saints: Counter-Reformation Propaganda in Bavaria*, Studies on the History of Society and Culture, Berkeley and Los Angeles, CA, London, California University Press, 1933, p. 95.

57 Young (ed.), *Letters of St Ignatius of Loyola*, pp. 327, 256, 258; Daniel-Rops, *The Catholic Reformation*, pp. 60–1; Ravier, *Ignatius of Loyola*, pp. 187–8.

58 Daniel-Rops, *The Catholic Reformation*, p. 60; Delumeau, *Catholicism from Luther to Voltaire*, p. 34; Brodrick, *The Progress of the Jesuits*, pp. 32, 33 and Chapter II; Young (ed.), *Letters of St Ignatius of Loyola*, pp. 425–7; Ravier, *Ignatius of Loyola*, p. 190.

59 Thomas M. McCoog, SJ, *English and Welsh Jesuits 1555–1650, part I: A-F*, Catholic Record Society, 1994, vol. 74, pp. 5–13; Olin (ed.), *Letters of St Ignatius of Loyola*, p. 304; Thomas F. Mayer, 'A test of wills: Cardinal Pole, Ignatius Loyola and the Jesuits in England' in Thomas M. McCoog, SJ, *The Reckoned Expense: Edmund Campion and the Early English Jesuits. Essays in celebration of the first centenary of Campion Hall, Oxford (1896–1996)*, Woodbridge, Suffolk, The Boydell Press, pp. 21–37.

60 Brodrick, *The Progress of the Jesuits*, p. 13 and n. 13; Ravier, *Ignatius of Loyola*, pp. 201, 204–5; Young (ed.), *Letters of St Ignatius of Loyola*, pp. 381–90.

61 Alfonso Capelcelatro, *The Life of St Philip Neri Apostle of Rome*, trans. Thomas Alder Pope, 2 vols, New York, Cincinnati, OH, and Chicago, IL, Benziger Bros, 1894, vol. I, pp. 31–2, 389; Donnani *et al.* (eds), *Histoire du Clergé*, vol. III, pp. 136–9; Coulson (ed.) *The Saints*, pp. 377–9; John Patrick Donnelly, SJ, 'The Congregation of the Oratory' in DeMolen (ed.), *Religious Orders of the Catholic Reformation*, pp. 189–93.

62 ibid., pp. 194–5; Donnani *et al.* (eds), *Histoire du Clergé*, vol. III, pp. 136–9; Coulson (ed.), *The Saints*, p. 378; Capelcelatro, *Life of St Philip Neri*, vol. II, p. 408; *The Catholic Encyclopedia*, vol. 11, p. 273.

63 ibid.; Donnani *et al.* (eds), *Histoire du Clergé*, vol. III, pp. 141–2; Donnelly, 'The Congregation of the Oratory', pp. 197–8, 202.

64 *The Catholic Encyclopedia*, vol. 4, pp. 52–3; Bonnani *et al.* (eds), *Histoire du Clergé*, vol. III, pp. 123–4.

65 *The Catholic Encyclopedia*, vol. 4, pp. 52–3; Bonnani *et al.* (eds), *Histoire du Clergé*, vol. III, pp. 123–4; Paul F. Grendler, 'The Piarists of the Pious Schools' in De Molen (ed.), *Religious Orders of the Catholic Reformation*, p. 261.

66 Bonnani *et al.* (eds), *Histoire du Clergé*, vol. III, pp. 120–1.
67 ibid.; Prosperi, 'Cleric and laymen in the work of Borromeo', pp. 115–20; *The Catholic Encyclopedia*, vol. 1, pp. 40–5.
68 Bonnani *et al.* (eds), *Histoire du Clergé*, vol. III, pp. 157–60.
69 ibid., pp. 161–2, 155–6; *The Catholic Encyclopedia*, vol. 11, p. 193.
70 Evennett, *The Spirit of the Counter-Reformation*, p. 27; Evennett, 'The new orders', pp. 278–81; *The Catholic Encyclopedia*, vol. 3, pp. 320–3.
71 ibid., pp. 322–3; Evennett, 'The new orders', pp. 282–5; Elisabeth G. Gleason, 'The Capuchin Order in the sixteenth century' in DeMolen (ed.), *Religious Orders of the Catholic Reformation*, pp. 31–57.
72 Evennett, 'The new orders', pp. 284–5, 289–90; Dickens, *The Counter-Reformation*, p. 71; Charmarie J. Blaisdell, 'Angela Merici and the Ursulines' in DeMolen (ed.), *Religious Orders of the Catholic Reformation*, p. 100; Coulson (ed.), *The Saints*, p. 181; R. Po-Chia Hsia, *The World of Catholic Renewal 1540–1770*, New Approaches to European History, Series Editors William Beik *et al.*, Cambridge, Cambridge University Press, 1998, pp. 35–6
73 Elizabeth Rapley, *The Dévotes: Women and the Church in Seventeenth-Century France*, McGill-Queen's Studies in the History of Religion, Montreal, Kingston, Ont., London, Buffalo, NY, McGill-Queen's University Press, 1990, pp. 28–34, 48–9; Margaret Gorman, RSCJ, 'The influence of Ignatian spirituality on women's teaching orders in the United States' in Chapple (ed.), *The Jesuit Tradition in Education and Mission*, pp. 191–4; Po-Chia Hsia, *The World of Catholic Renewal*, p. 37.
74 I am deeply grateful to Laurence Lux for kind permission to cite research in her Lancaster PhD thesis, in progress.
75 ibid.
76 Dom Adam Hamilton, OSB, *The Chronicle of the English Augustinian Canonesses Regular of the Lateran at St Monica's in Louvain: 1548 to 1625*, Edinburgh and London, Sands & Co., pp. 158–9.
77 Po-Chia Hsia, *The World of Catholic Renewal*, pp. 37–8; M. Emmanuel Orchard, IBVM, *Till God Will. Mary Ward through her writings*, London, Darton, Longman and Todd, 1985, pp. xi–33.
78 ibid., pp. 34–6
79 ibid., pp. 37, 43–5;101–9, 50.

4 The papacy and the episcopate of the Catholic Reformation

1 Leopold von Ranke, *The History of the Popes during the Last Four Centuries*, 3 vols, trans. G. R. Dennis, London, George Bell, 1907, vol. I, pp. 245–6, 268–9; François Arnaud de Montor, *The Lives and Times of the Popes Including the Complete Gallery of the Portraits of the Pontiffs* [1867], 10 vols, New York, The Catholic Publication Society of America, 1911, vol. V, pp. 79–124.
2 Ranke, *History of the Popes*, vol. I, pp. 268–9; Arnaud de Montor, *Lives and Times of the Popes*, vol. V, p. 80–1; Butler's *Lives of the Saints*, Herbert Thurston, SJ and Donald Attwater (eds), 4 vols, London, Burns & Oates, 1956, vol. IV, p. 234; J. N. D. Kelly, *The Oxford Dictionary of the Popes*, Oxford, New York, Oxford University Press, 1986, p. 268.
3 Ranke, *History of the Popes*, vol. I, pp. 268–9; Arnaud de Montor, *Lives and Times of the Popes*, vol. V, p. 81.
4 A. G. Dickens, *The Counter-Reformation*, London, Thames and Hudson, 1968, pp. 120, 125; Butler's *Lives of the Saints*, vol. IV, pp. 234–5; *The Catholic Encyclopedia. An International Work of Reference on the Constitutions, Discipline and History of the Catholic Church*, Charles G. Herbermann *et al.* (eds), 16 vols, London, Caxton, 1907–14, vol. 12, p. 130; *Histoire de la Papauté pendant les XVIe et XVIIe Siècles* quoted in Alfred de

Baudrillart, *The Catholic Church, The Renaissance and Protestantism. Lectures Given at the Catholic Institute of Paris, January to March 1904*, trans. Mrs Philip Gibbs, London, Kegan Paul, Trench, Trübner, 1907, pp. 176–7; Arnaud de Montor, *Lives and Times of the Popes*, vol. V, pp. 91, 82, 93, 120.

5 Thurston and Attwater (eds), *Butler's Lives of the Saints*, vol. II, p. 234; Lewis W. Spitz, *The Renaissance and Reform Movements*, 2 vols, revised edn, St Louis, MO, Concordia Publishing, 1971, vol. I, p. 492; *The Catholic Encyclopedia*, vol. 12, p. 130; Arnaud de Montor, *Lives and Times of the Popes*, vol. V, p. 85; Archdale A. King, *Liturgy of the Roman Church*, London, New York, Toronto, Longmans, Green, 1957, p. 43.

6 Joseph A. Jungmann, SJ, *The Mass of the Roman Rite (Missarum Sollemnia)*, trans. Francis A. Brunner, CSSR, revised Charles K. Riepe, 2 vols in 1, London, Burns & Oates, 1959, pp. 100–1; H. J. Schroeder (ed.), *The Canons and Decrees of the Council of Trent, English Translation* Rockford, IL, TAN Books, 1978, p. 254.

7 Arnaud de Montor, *Lives and Times of the Popes*, vol. V, p. 85; King, *Liturgy of the Roman Church*, p. 42; *Missale Romanum Ex Decreto Sacrosancti Concilii Tridentini Restitum S. Pii V. Pontifici Maximi*, Regensburg, Friedrich Pustet, 1920, pp. vi, 83–5; 102–6, 124; Jungmann, *The Mass of the Roman Rite*, pp. 102–04.

8 J. Wickham Legg (ed.), *The Sarum Missal Edited from Three Early Manuscripts*, Oxford, Clarendon, 1916, p. 7, pp. 484–5, 464–5; Michael P. Carroll, *Madonnas that Maim: Popular Catholicism in Italy since the Fifteenth Century*, Baltimore, MD, and London, The Johns Hopkins University Press, 1992, p. 106.

9 Wigg (ed.), *The Sarum Missal* pp. 490–5; Jungmann, *The Mass of the Roman Rite*, pp. 103–4; King, *Liturgy of the Roman Church*, London, Longmans, Green, 1957, p. 43; John W. O'Malley, SJ, 'Reform, Historical Consciousness and Vatican II's *Aggiornamento*' in O'Malley, *Rome and the Renaissance: Studies in Culture and Religion*, London, Variorum Reprints, 1981, pp. 582–3.

10 Jungmann, *The Mass of the Roman Rite*, pp. 104, 323; *Missale Romanum*, pp. lxxxiv, lxxv, c–cvi.

11 King, *Liturgy of the Roman Church*, pp. 43–4; Les Petits Bollandistes, *Vies des Saints de l'Ancien et du Nouveau Testament*, vol. V, Paris, Bloud et Barral, 1888, p. 350.

12 Arnaud de Montor, *Lives and Times of the Popes*, vol. V, p. 121; Thurston and Attwater (eds) *Butler's Lives of the Saints*, vol. II, p. 234; *Breviarum Romanum ex decreto SS. Concilii Tridentini restitutum, S. Pii V. Pontificis Maximi jussu editum*, Tournai, Desclée, Lefèbvre et Soc., 1884, pp. 687–692; Les Petits Bollandistes, *Vies des Saints*, vol. V, p. 350; Colin Clair, *Christopher Plantin*, London, Cassel, 1960, Chapter 5.

13 Pio Paschini, 'L'edizione del Catechismo sotto S. Pio V' in Paschino, *Cinquecento Romano e Riforma Cattolica Scritti Raccolti in Occasione dell'Ottanesimo Compleanno del Autore*, Rome, Lateranum, 1958, p. 57; John A. McHugh, OP, and Charles J. Callan, OP, trans., *Catechism of the Council of Trent for Parish Priests Issued by the Order of Pope Pius V* [1923], reprinted Rizal, Philippines, Sinag Tala Publishers, 1974, intro. p. xxiii; Schroeder (ed.), *Canons and Decrees of Trent*, pp. 197, 254–5; *Catechismus Romanus Ex Decreto Sacrosancti Concilii Tridentini Jussu S. Pii V. Pontificis Maximi editus*, Rome, Propaganda Fide, 1796. For the long ancestry of medieval and pre-medieval catechisms, see McHugh and Callan (trans.), *Catechism of the Council of Trent*, pp. xi–xviii.

14 ibid., pp. xxiii–xxiv, 247, 433, 322, 258; Schroeder (ed.), *Canons and Decrees of Trent*, pp. 145–6.

15 *Catechismus ad Parochos ex Decreto Concilii Editus*, Paris, Nicholas Pepingue, 1688, p. 3; Paschini, 'L'Edizione del Catechismo sotto S. Pio V', p. 64; *Catechismus Romanus* (Paris, 1796), pp. 15, 333, 16, 299, 95–6, ii.

16 Paschini, 'L'Edizione del Catechismo sotto S. Pio V', pp. 63, 64; McHugh and Callan (trans.), *Catechism of the Council of Trent*, pp. xxv–xxi, xxviii (pp. xxvi–xxxvii for editions and translations).

17　Arnaud de Montor, *Lives and Times of the Popes*, vol. V, pp. 125–6; Ludwig, Freiherr von Pastor, *The History of the Popes from the Close of the Middle Ages*, 39 vols, Ralph Francis Kerr (ed.), London, Kegan Paul, Trench, Trübner, 1930, vol. XIX, p. 12; *The Catholic Encyclopedia*, Vol. 7, p. 2.

18　Arnaud de Montor, *Lives and Times of the Popes*, vol. V, pp. 125–6; *The Catholic Encyclopedia*, vol. 7, pp. 1–2.

19　Arnaud de Montor, *Lives and Times of the Popes*, vol. V, p. 125; Pierre Janelle, *The Catholic Reformation*, Milwaukee, WI, Bruce Publishing, 1963, p. 211; Pastor, *History of the Popes*, vol. XIX, pp. 19–20, 214–15;

20　Pastor, *History of the Popes*. Vol. XIX, pp. 197–8; Jack Freiberg, *The Lateran in 1600: Christian Concord in Counter-Reformation Rome*, Cambridge, Cambridge University Press, 1995, p. 19; Carroll, *Madonnas that Maim*, pp. 15–16.

21　Pastor, *History of the Popes*, vol. XIX, pp. 200, 203–5, 204, n. 1, 3; Freiberg, *The Lateran in 1600*, pp. 16–17.

22　Pastor, *History of the Popes*, vol XIX, pp. 206–7, 202; A. G. Dickens, *The Counter-Reformation*, London, Thames and Hudson, 1968, frontispiece.

23　Freiberg, *The Lateran in 1600*, pp. 16–17; Pastor, *History of the Popes*, vol. XIX, pp. 209–10, 200, 223, 226, 223, 230, 232.

24　Pastor, *History of the Popes*, vol. XIX, p. 234–40, 243–4; Luigi Falcone, 'Incunaboli e cinquecentini di Gregorio XIII', *L'Osservatore Romano*, 24 April 1998: I am grateful to the Rt Rev. Bishop B. C. Foley for bringing this item to my attention and for conversation with him on Gregory XIII's Rome; Henry Foley, SJ, *Records of the English Province of the Society of Jesus. Historic Facts Illustrative of the Labours and Sufferings of its Members in the Sixteenth and Seventeenth Centuries*, 7 vols, London, Burns and Oates, 1877, 75–83, vol. III, pp. 41–8, vol. VI, p. 97.

25　Freiberg, *The Lateran in 1600*, pp. 16, 20, 21; Pastor, *History of the Popes*, vol. XIX, pp. 611–15. 583–4; Evennett, *The Spirit of the Counter-Reformation: The Birkbeck Lectures in Ecclesiastical History*, Cambridge, Cambridge University Press, 1968, p. 119 Ranke, *History of the Popes*, vol. I, pp. 320–1.

26　Pastor, *History of the Popes*, vol. XIX, pp. 166–8.

27　Ranke, *History of the Popes*, vol. III, Appendix, pp. 201–4.

28　ibid., pp. 208, 222, 225; *The Catholic Encyclopedia*, vol. 14, p. 23.

29　Arnaud de Montor, *The Lives and Times of the Popes*, vol. V, pp. 172, 178–9, 201.

30　Ranke, *History of the Popes*, vol. III, Appendix, 213–21; *The Catholic Encyclopedia*, vol. 14, p. 33; Pastor, *History of the Popes*, vol. XXI, pp. 53, 55–6, 58, 59; H. Daniel-Rops, *The Catholic Reformation*, trans. John Warrington, London, J. M. Dent, New York, E .P. Dutton, 1963, p. 329.

31　Pastor, *History of the Popes*, vol. XXII, pp. 202, 243–4, 238–41, vol XXI, dedication; Ranke, *History of the Popes*, vol. III, Appendix, pp. 241, 243, vol. I, pp. 363–3, 364–6.

32　V. H. H. Green, *Renaissance and the Reformation. A Survey of European History between 1450 and 1660*, London, Edward Arnold, second edn, 1964, p. 36; Augustus J. C. Hare, *Walks in Rome*, 2 vols, London, George Allen, 1900, vol. II, pp. 236–7; Pastor, *History of the Popes*, vol. XXI, pp. 28–9, 36, Appendix, pp. 413–14, vol. XXII, p. 239; Daniel-Rops, *The Catholic Reformation*, p. 68; Ranke, *History of the Popes*, vol. I, p. 363; *The Catholic Encyclopedia*, vol. 14, p. 34; Rolof Beny and Peter Gunn, *The Churches of Rome*, London, Weidenfeld and Nicolson, 1981, pp. 133, 247; *The Catholic Encyclopedia*, vol. 14, p. 34; Arnaud de Montor, *The Lives and Times of the Popes*, vol. V, pp. 174–6.

33　Pastor, *History of the Popes*, vol. pp. 192–5.

34　ibid., p. 197; Jean Delumeau, *Catholicism from Luther to Voltaire*, trans. Jeremy Moiser, London, Burns & Oates, Philadelphia, PA, Westminster Press, 1977, p. 30; Janelle, *The Catholic Reformation*, p. 214.

35 Dickens, *The Counter-Reformation*, p. 143; *The Catholic Encyclopedia*, vol. 14, p. 34; Janelle, *The Catholic Reformation*, p. 213; Arnaud de Montor, *The Lives and Times of the Popes*, vol. V, pp. 195, 177.

36 ibid., pp. 209–12; *The Catholic Encyclopedia*, vol. 15, p. 218; Peter Partner, *The Pope's Men: The Papal Civil Service in the Renaissance*, Oxford, Clarendon, 1990, pp. 29–30.

37 R. Po-Chia Hsia, *The World of Catholic Renewal 1540–1770*, New Approaches to European History, Series Editors William Beik *et al.*, Cambridge, Cambridge University Press, 1998, pp. 22–3; *The Catholic Encyclopedia*, vol. 7, p. 4; Arnaud de Montor *The Lives and Times of the Popes*, vol. V, pp. 216–17.

38 ibid; *The Catholic Encyclopedia*, vol. VIII, p. 20.

39 Arnaud de Montor, *The Lives and Times of the Popes*, vol. V, pp. 221–3; Ranke, *History of the Popes*, vol. III, Appendix, pp. 277, 285–6.

40 *The Catholic Encyclopedia*, vol. 4, p. 27; Arnaud de Montor, *The Lives and Times of the Popes*, vol. V, p. 224.

41 *The Catholic Encyclopedia*, vol. 4, p. 27; *Méthode pour apprendre facilement l'Histoire des Papes*, (Paris, 1694), pp. 330–1; there were thirty-six years between the outbreak of the French Wars of Religion in 1562 and the Edict of Nantes (1598) which brought them to a close.

42 Po-Chia Hsia, *The World of Catholic Renewal 1540–1770*, pp. 94–5; Delio Cantimori, 'Italy and the Papacy' in G. R. Elton (ed.), *The New Cambridge Modern History*, vol. II *The Reformation*, Cambridge, Cambridge University Press, 1968, pp. 257–8; Partner, *The Pope's Men*, pp. 44, 77–81, 148, 149.

43 Pastor, *History of the Popes* vol. IX, pp. 244, 254 and n. 2, 277, 274, 284–90, 297, 204, 307–9, 323, 347, 366, 422–26, 433, n. 2, Appendix, p. 508; on the Sack, Mandell Creighton, quoted in V. H. H. Green, *Renaissance and Reformation*, p. 149; Ranke, *The History of the Popes*, vol. III, Appendix, p. 97.

44 Pastor, *History of the Popes*, vol. X, pp. 4 27–8, 44–5, 68, n. 3, 195, 208, 219.

45 ibid., pp. 378, 387, 412, 407–8, n. 2, 428, 429; M. A. Tucker, 'Gian Matteo Giberti, papal politician and Catholic reformer', *The Catholic Historical Review*, 1903, vol. XIX, esp. pp. 439–69; Adriano Prosperi, 'Clerics and laymen in the work of Carlo Borromeo' in John M. Headley and John B. Tomaro (eds), *San Carlo Borromeo. Catholic Reform and Ecclesiastical Politics in the Second Half of the Sixteenth Century*, Washington, DC, The Folger Shakespeare Library, London and Toronto, Associated University Presses, 1988, p. 121.

46 Pastor, *History of the Popes*, vol. X, p. 431, 433–6, 437–9; Prosperi, 'Clerics and Laymen', p. 19.

47 ibid., pp. 210–11; *The Two Gentlemen of Verona*, IV, iv, 157; Pastor, *History of the Popes*, vol. X, pp. 432–4, 439–40; Evennett, *The Spirit of the Counter-Reformation*, p. 9; 'Church Ordinances and Reform Proposals in the United Diocese of Cleves, 1532–33, 1545, 1564' in Colman J. Barry, OSB (ed.), *Readings in Church History*, vol. II *The Reformation and the Absolute States 1517–1789*, Westminster, MD, The Newman Press, 1965, pp. 126–32.

48 Evennett, *Spirit of the Counter-Reformation*, p. 99; for good standard lives of Borromeo, see, e.g. *The Catholic Encyclopedia*, vol. 3, pp. 619–25, Ribadénéira, *les Vies des Saints et Fêtes de Toutes l'Année*, traduction française, L'Abbé É. Darras, Paris, Louis Vives, 1864, pp. 75–100; Les Petits Bollandistes, *Vies des Saints de l'Ancien et du Nouveau Testament*, vol. 13, pp. 178–95; Thurston and Attwater (eds), *Butler's Lives of the Saints*, vol. IV, pp. 255–62; Edward Manning, *The Good Shepherd. A Sermon Preached on the Feast of St Charles, 1860*, London, Burns and Lambert, 1860, pp. 8–9; *The Little Breviary for the use of Both Religious and Layfolk Containing in Simplified Form all the Offices of the Roman Breviary*, Haarlem-Antwerp, J. H. Gottmer, 1957, p. 1663.

49 Giuseppe Alberigo, 'Carlo Borromeo between two models of bishop' in Headley and Tomaro (eds), *San Carlo Borromeo*, pp. 253, 254; Alberto Melloni, 'History, pastorate

and theology: The impact of Carlo Borromeo upon A. G. Roncalli (Pope John XXIII)' in ibid., p. 288.

50 Pio Paschini, 'Mutamenti di spirito nel Cardinale Borromeo' in Paschini, *Cinquecento Romano*, p. 139, n. 8; *The Catholic Encyclopedia*, vol. 3, pp. 620–1; Les Petitis Bollandistes, *Vies des Saints*, vol. 13, p. 181.

51 With great regularity between 1573 and 1585 Gregory XIII also ordered visitations in a long list of Italian dioceses: Pastor, *History of the Popes*, vol. XIX, Appendix, pp. 622–5.

52 Paolo Prodi, 'The application of the Tridentine decrees during the episcopate of Cardinal Gabriele Paleotti (1522–1597)' in Eric Cochrane (ed.), *The Late Italian Renaissance 1525–1630*, Stratum Series, General Editor J. R. Hale, London, Macmillan, 1970, pp. 226–43; *The Catholic Encyclopedia*, vol. 11, p. 419 (for Borromeo's impact on England, transmitted by the Jesuit Edmund Campion: vol. 3, p. 64); *Dictionnaire de Théologie Catholique Contenant l'Exposé des Doctrines de la Théologie Catholique Leurs Preuves et Leur Histoire*, 15 vols, A. Vacant, E. Mangenot and É. Aman (eds) Paris, Librairie Letouzey et Ané, 1932, vol. 11b, p. 1822. For the wider fame of Borromeo's image, see for example, Landor's poem 'To Saint Charles Borromeo On the Massacre [*sic*] at Milan' (*'Saint, beyond all in glory who surround/The throne above!'*), in *The Shorter Works of Walter Savage Landor*, London, George Newnes, 1904, pp. 805–6; for admiration and emulation of Borromeo in Spain, France and Germany, see: A. D. Wright, 'The Borromean ideal and the Spanish Church' in Headley and Tomaro (eds), *San Carlo Borromeo*, pp. 188–209, Marc Venard, 'The influence of Carlo Borromeo on the Church of France' in ibid., pp. 208–27, and John M. Headley, 'Borromean reform in the Empire? *La Strada Rigorosa* of Giovanni Francesco Bonomi' in ibid., pp. 229–47.

53 John B. Tomaro, 'San Carlo Borromeo and the implementation of the Council of Trent' in ibid., pp. 67–94; Thurston and Attwater (eds), *Butler's Lives of the Saints*, vol. IV, p. 262; *The Catholic Encyclopedia*, vol. 3, p. 624.

54 Niels Rasmussen, 'Liturgy and iconography in the canonisation of Carlo Borromeo, 1 November 1610' in Headley and Tomaro (eds), *San Carlo Borromeo*, pp. 275–6; Margaret Yeo, *A Prince of Pastors: St Charles Borromeo*, London, The Catholic Book Club, 1943, pp. vii, 22, 35, 26, 34, 16, 17, 23, 75; Alberigo, 'Borromeo between two models of a bishop', p. 254; Pio Paschini, 'Ultimi mesi della dimora del Borromeo a Roma Sua partenza per Milano' in Paschini, *Cinquecento Romano e Riforma Cattolica*, p. 177; *The Catholic Encyclopedia*, vol. 3, p. 619.

55 Les Petits Bollandistes, *Vies des Saints*, vol. 13, pp. 183–6; Ribadénéira, *Vies des Saints*, vol. 11, p. 87; *The Catholic Encyclopedia*, vol. 3, p. 623; Alberigo, 'Borromeo between two models of bishop', p. 255

5 The impact of the Catholic Reformation

1 Ambrogio Palestra, 'Le visite pastorale del Card. Carlo Borromeo al Duomo e alla Veneranda Fabbrica' in *Il Duomo Cuore e Simbolo di Milano IV Centenario della Dedicazione (1577–1977)*, Archivio Ambrosiano XXXIII, Milan, Centro Ambrosiano di Documentazione e Studi Religiosi, 1977, pp. 160–230; G. Alberigo, 'Altoviti, Antonio', *Dizionario Biografico degli Italiani*, Rome, Istituto della Enciclopedia Italiana, 1960–, vol. 2, p. 572; Eric Cochrane, *Italy 1530–1630*, Julius Kirshner (ed.), Longman History of Italy, General Editor Denys Hay, London and New York, 1988, pp. 185–6. Cochrane (ibid.) also drew attention to the deficiencies in some Italian bishops in the Tridentine period; Michael K. Becker, 'Episcopal unrest: Gallicanism in the 1625 Assembly of the Clergy', *Church History*, 1974, vol. 43, pp. 65–77; A. D. Wright, 'The significance of the Council of Trent', *Journal of Ecclesiastical History*, 1975, vol. 26, pp. 353–62.

2 Cochrane, *Italy 1530–1630*, p. 185; François J. Casta, *Le Diocèse d'Ajaccio*, Histoire des Diocèses de France, J. R. Palanque and B. Plongeron (eds), Paris, Editions

Beauchesne, 1974, p. 94; Antonio Iodice, 'I principi ispiratori della pastorale riformatrice del Bellarmino a Capua' in Gustavo Galeota (ed.), *Roberto Bellarmino Arcivescovo di Capua Teologo e Pastore della Riforma Cattolicia Atti del Convegno Internazionale di Studi Capua 28 settembre–1 ottobre 1988*, 2 vols, Arcidiocesi di Capua Istituto Superiore di Scienze Religiose, 1990: *Teologia, Pastorale*, pp. 316, 320–3; Pasquale Giustiniani, 'Bellarmino, animatore di catechesi' in ibid., pp. 475–87; Filippo Iappelli, 'Il Collegio dei Gesuiti a Capua (1611–1767)' in ibid., pp. 491–514; Antonio Iodice, 'Chronologia dei discorsi pronunciati a Capua dal Bellarmino negli anni 1602–5' in Galeota (ed.), *Roberto Bellarmino: Filosofia, Scienza, Iconografia*, Appendici.

3 David Gentilcore, *From Bishop to Witch: The system of the sacred in early modern Terra d'Otranto*, Manchester and New York, Manchester University Press, 1992, pp. 37–8, 47–8, 105; David Gentilcore, *Healers and Healing in Early Modern Italy*, Social and Cultural Values in Early Modern Europe, Series Editor Paolo L. Rossi, Manchester and New York, Manchester University Press, 1998, Chapter 6; Giovanni de Vita, 'Il Santuario di S. Michele Arcangelo' in Giovanni Battista Bronzini (ed.), *Ex Voto Santuari in Puglia e Il Gargano*, Nuova Serie della Bibliotheca di 'Lares', vol. XLVIII, Bronzini (ed.), Florence, Leo S. Olschki, 1993, p. 137

4 Cochrane, *Italy 1530–1630*, pp. 190–1; Dermot Fenlon, 'Interpretations of Catholic History', *Journal of Ecclesiastical History*, 1982, vol. 33, pp. 261–5; Simon Ditchfield, 'Martyrs on the move: relics as vindicators of local diversity in the Tridentine Church' in Diana Wood (ed.), *Martyrs and Martyrologies: Papers Read at the 1992 Summer Meeting and the 1993 Winter Meeting of the Ecclesiastical History Society, Studies in Church History*, vol. 30, Oxford, Blackwell for the Ecclesiastical History Society, 1993, pp. 283–94: see also Simon Ditchfield, *Liturgy, Sanctity and History in Tridentine Italy: Piero Maria Campi and the Preservation of the Particular*, Cambridge Studies in Italian History and Culture, Giorgio Chittolini *et al* (eds)., Cambridge, Cambridge University Press, 1995.

5 N. S. Davidson, 'Rome and the Venetian Inquisition in the sixteenth century', *Journal of Ecclesiastical History*, 1988, vol. 39, pp. 16–36; Cochrane, *Italy 1530–1630*, pp. 186, 261–2; A. D. Wright, 'The Venetian Mediterranean empire after the Council of Trent' in Diana Wood (ed.), *The Church and Sovereignty c. 590–1918. Essays in Honour of Michael Wilks, Studies in Church History*, Subsidia 9, Oxford, Basil Blackwell for the Ecclesiastical History Society, 1991, pp. 467–77; Oliver Logan, 'The ideal of the bishop and the Venetian patriciate: *c.* 1430–*c.* 1630', *Journal of Ecclesiastical History*, 1978, vol. 29, pp. 415–50.

6 ibid.

7 Cochrane, *Italy 1530–1630*, pp. 192, 262; O. M. T. Logan, 'Grace and justification: some Italian views of the sixteenth and early seventeenth centuries', *Journal of Ecclesiastical History*, 1969, vol. 20, pp. 67–78; P. J. Laven, 'The *Causa Grimani* and its political overtones', *Journal of Religious History*, 1966–7, vol. 4, pp. 184–205. B. S. Pullan, *Rich and Poor in Renaisance Venice. The Social Institutions of a Catholic State, to 1620*, Oxford, Basil Blackwell, 1971, pp. 6–12.

8 Christopher Black, 'Perugia and Post-Tridentine Church Reform', *Journal of Ecclesiastical History*, 1984, vol. 35, p. 429–51; William Monter, *Frontiers of Heresy: The Spanish Inquisition from the Basque Lands to Sicily*, Cambridge, New York and Melbourne, Cambridge University Press, 1990, Chapter 8; Carlo Ginzburg, *The Cheese and the Worms: The Cosmos of a Sixteenth-Century Miller*, trans. John and Anne Tedeschi, London and Henley, Routledge & Kegan Paul, 1980.

9 Black, 'Perugia and Post-Tridentine Church Reform', pp. 429–51; A. Prosperi, 'Bossi, Francesco', *Dizionario Biografico degli Italiani*, vol. 13, pp. 303–05; P. Prodi, 'Borromeo, Federico', ibid., vol. 13, p. 37; Paul F. Grendler, 'The Schools of Christian Doctrine in sixteenth-century Italy', *Church History*, 1984, vol. 53, pp. 319–31.

10 Thomas Deutscher, 'Seminaries and the education of Novarese priests, 1593–1627', *Journal of Ecclesiastical History*, 1981, vol. 32, pp. 303–19; Paolo Prodi, 'Bascapè, Carlo', *Dizionario Biografico degli Italiani*, vol. 7, pp. 55–88; Thomas Deutscher, 'The growth of the secular clergy and the development of educational institutions in the Diocese of Novara (1563–1772)', ibid., 1989, vol. 40, pp. 381–97.

11 David Gentilcore, ' "Adapt yourselves to people's capacities": missionary strategies, methods and impact in the Kingdom of Naples, 1600–1800', *Journal of Ecclesiastical History*, 1994, vol. 45, pp. 269–96.

12 ibid.

13 ibid.

14 ibid.; David Gentilcore, 'Illness in early modern Naples: *Miracolati*, physicians and the Congregation of Rites', *Past and Present*, 1995, No. 148, pp. 117–48; Gentilcore, *From Bishop to Witch*, part II; Norman Douglas, *Old Calabria*, Harmondsworth, Peregrine Books, 1962, p. 74.

15 Cochrane, *Italy 1530–1630*, p. 188; Black, 'Perugia and post-Tridentine Church reform, pp. 429–51; Oliver Logan, 'Counter-Reformation theories of upbringing in Italy' in Diana Wood (ed.), *The Church and Childhood. Papers Read at the 1993 Summer Meeting and the 1994 Winter Meeting of the Ecclesiastical History Society, Studies in Church History*, vol. 31, Oxford, Blackwell for the Ecclesiastical History Society, 1994, pp. 275–84 ; John Bossy, reviewing Alessandro Pastore, *Nella Valtellina nel tardo cinque-cento*, in *Journal of Ecclesiastical History*, 1977, vol. 28, p. 235.

16 Oliver Logan, reviewing Felix Tisserand (ed.), *Les trophées sacrés du missions des Capucins en Savoie à la fin du XVIe et au XVIIe siècle*, in *Journal of Ecclesiastical History*, 1978, vol. 29, pp. 495–6; Angelo Torre, 'Politics cloaked in worship: state, church and local power in Piedmont, 1570–1770', *Past and Present*, 1992, No. 134, pp. 42–92; Peter Burke, 'The Virgin of the Carmine and the Revolt of Masaniello', *Past and Present*, 1983, No. 99, pp. 19–20.

17 Alain Lottin, 'Les temps modernes', in Pierre Pierrard (ed.), *Les Diocèses de Cambrai et de Lille*, Histoire des Diocèses de France, J. R. Pulanque and B. Plongeron (eds), vol. 8, Paris, Éditions Beauchesne, 1978, p. 138.

18 Joseph Bergin, *Cardinal de la Rochefoucauld: Leadership and Reform in the French Church*, New Haven, CT, and London, Yale University Press, 1987, pp. 138–9; J. A. Bergin, 'The crown, the papacy and the reform of the old orders in early seventeenth-century France', *Journal of Ecclesiastical History*, 1982, vol. 33, pp. 234–55; J. Knecht, reviewing Bernard Plongeron, *Le Diocèse de Paris* (1982) in ibid., 1989, vol. 40, pp. 402–3; J. H. M. Salmon, reviewing P. J. S. Whitmore, *The Order of Minims in Seventeenth-Century France*, *Journal of Religious History*, 1969, vol. 5, pp. 274–7; R. Mousnier, 'French institutions and society 1610–61',in J. P. Cooper (ed.), *The New Cambridge Modern History Volume IV: The Decline of Spain and the Thirty Years' War*, Cambridge, Cambridge University Press, 1970, p. 492; H. G. Judge, 'The Congregation of the Oratory in France in the late seventeenth century', *Journal of Ecclesiastical History*, 1961, vol. 12, pp. 46–55; Jean Delumeau, *Catholicism between Luther and Voltaire*, trans. Jeremy Moiser, London, Burns & Oates, Philadelphia, PA, Westminster Press, 1977, pp. 36–7, 190; Elizabeth Rapley, *The Dévotes: Women and the Church in Seventeenth-Century France*, McGill-Queen's Studies in the History of Religion, G.A. Rawlyk (ed.), Montreal and Kingston, London, Buffalo, NY, McGill-Queen's University Press, 1990, pp. 34–41.

19 Louis Châtellier, *The religion of the poor. Rural missions in Europe and the formation of modern Catholicism, c. 1500–c. 1800*, trans. Brian Pearce, Cambridge, New York, Melbourne, Cambridge University Press, Maison des Sciences de l'Homme, 1993, p. 14; Delumeau, *Catholicism between Luther and Voltaire*, pp. 31–2; Lottin, 'Les temps modernes', Part 2, Chapters II, III.

20 Pierrard (ed.), *Les Diocèses de Cambrai et de Lille*, pp. 139–40.

21 ibid., pp. 143–4, 121–2.

22 ibid., pp. 134–6, 139–40, 145.

23 F. Lebrun, 'L'enracinement, 1660–1770' in Lebrun (ed.), *Histoire des Catholiques en France du XVe siècle à nos jours*, Toulouse, Privat, 1980, pp. 147–214; Donald Attwater, *The Penguin Dictionary of Saints*, Harmondsworth, Penguin, 1973, p. 337; William E. Addis and Thomas Arnold (eds), *A Catholic Dictionary Containing Some Account of the Doctrine, Discipline, Rites, Ceremonies, Councils, and Religious Orders of the Catholic Church*, 13th edn, London, Virtue, 1928, p. 515.

24 Maurice Crubellier and Charles Juillard, *Histoire de la Champagne*, Que sais-je?, Paris, Presses Universitaires de France, 1952, p. 51: other early initiatives in Champagne typical of Catholic reformism included the setting up by the Cardinal de Givry in his diocese of Langres of the devotion of the 'Hours of the Cross', the Feast of the Holy Name of Jesus, and Confraternaties of the Blessed Sacrament: ibid; Delumeau, *Catholicism between Luther and Voltaire*, p. 32; Yves Durand, 'Le XVIIe siècle. La Réforme Catholique au Diocèse de Nantes' in Yves Durand (ed.), *Le Diocèse de Nantes*, Histoire des Diocèses de France, vol. 18, B. Plongeron and A.Vauchez (eds), Paris, Beauchesne, 1985, pp. 112–13.

25 Lebrun, 'L'enracinement', pp. 148–52; Durand, 'Le XVIIe siècle', p. 113; Delumeau, *Catholicism between Luther and Voltaire*, pp. 32–4; Philip T. Hoffman, *Church and Community in the Diocese of Lyon 1500–1789*, Yale Historical Publications, Miscellany, 132, New Haven, CT, and London, Yale University Press, 1984, pp. 77–9, 82–3.

26 C. Ronald Miller, *The French seminary in the eighteenth century*, unpublished PhD dissertation, The Catholic University of America, Ann Arbor, MI, 1988, pp. 219–23; Durand, 'Le XVIIe siècle', p. 113; Lebrun, 'L'enracinement', pp. 151, 155–7.

27 Lebrun, 'L'enracinement', pp. 156–8; Delumeau, *Catholicism between Luther and Voltaire*, pp. 188–9; R. Po-Chia Hsia, *The World of Catholic Renewal 1540–1770*, New Approaches to European History, Series Editors William Beik *et al.*, Cambridge, Cambridge Universty Press, 1998, pp. 116–21 Hoffman, *Church and Community*, pp. 140–6.

28 Lebrun, 'L'enracinement', pp. 184–5; Durand, 'Le XVIIe siècle', pp. 117–18; Delumeau, *Catholicism from Luther to Voltaire*, pp. 195–6.

29 'Sermon sur la prière' in *Chefs-d'Oeuvres Oratoires de Bourdaloue*, Paris, Garnier Frères, n.d., p. 199; Bourdaloue, 'Opuscule: Petit nombre des élus' in ibid., p. 519; M. Dreano (ed.), *Bossuet élèvations sur les Mystères ètude Critique avec Introduction, Texte et Variantes*, études de Théologie et d'Histoire de la Spiritualité, XVI, Paris, Librairie Philosophique J. Vrin, 1962, introduction., p. 67; H. Daniel-Rops, *The Catholic Reformation*, trans. John Warrington, London, J. M. Dent, New York, E. P. Dutton, 1963, pp. 366, 385; Durand, 'Le XVIIe siècle', pp. 100–01; Louis Cognet, *Post-Reformation Spirituality*, trans. P. Hepburne Scott, Twentieth Century Encyclopedia of Catholicism, H. Daniel-Rops (ed.) vol. 41, New York Hawthorn Books, 1959, p. 62.

30 Voltaire, *Henriade* (1728) in Wiliam C. Trapnell, *Voltaire and the Eucharist*, Studies on Voltaire and the Eighteenth Century, General Editor Haydn Mason, no. 198, Oxford, The Voltaire Foundation, p. 103; Delumeau, *Catholicism from Luther to Voltaire*, pp. 225, 228; Daniel Roche, *The People of Paris: An Essay on Popular Culture in the 18th Century*, trans. Marie Evans and Gwynne Lewis, Leamington Spa, Warks, Hamburg, New York, Berg, 1987, pp. 205–16; Delumeau, *Catholicism between Luther and Voltaire*, p. 202; Giles Barber, 'Il fallut même réveiller les Suisses: aspects of private religious practice in a public setting in eighteenth-century Versailles' in Nigel Aston (ed.), *Religious Change in Europe 1650–1914 Essays for John McManners*, Oxford, Clarendon, 1997, pp. 89, 82; Lebrun, 'L'enracinement', p. 185.

31 Roche, *The People of Paris*, pp. 216–17; Philip Benedict, 'Towards the comparative study of the popular market for art: the ownership of paintings in seventeenth-century Metz', *Past and Present*, 1985, no. 109, pp. 100–17 .

32 Addis and Arnold, *Catholic Dictionary*, pp. 167–8; Attwater (ed.), *The Penguin Dictionary of Saints*, pp. 200–10; W. J. Battersby, *History of the Institute of the Brothers of the Christian Schools in the Eighteenth Century*, London, Waldegrave, 1960, p. 9; Roche, *The People of Paris*, p. 206.

33 Roche, *The People of Paris*, p. 217; Michelle Vovelle, *Piété Baroque et Déchristianisation en Provence au XVIIIe siècle Les Attitudes devant la Mort d'après les Clauses des Testaments*, Civilisations et Mentalités, Philippe Ariès and Robert Mandrou (eds), Paris, Librairie Plon, 1973, p. 607; Battersby, *The Brothers of the Christian Schools*, Chapter 6; Roche, *The People of Paris*, pp. 204–5; Jonathan L. Pearl, 'French Catholic demonologists and their enemies in the late sixteenth and early seventeenth centuries', *Church History*, 1983, vol. 52, pp. 457–67 ; Châtellier, *The Religion of the Poor*, pp. 207, 208, 227.

34 Norman Tanner (ed.), *Decrees of the Ecumenical Councils'*, 2 vols, London, Sheed & Ward, Washington, DC, Georgetown University Press, 1990, vol. 2, pp. 672–3, 675; H. Daniel-Rops, *The Catholic Reformation*, trans. John Warrington, London, J. M. Dent, New York, E. P. Dutton, 1963, p. 344; Addis and Arnold, *Catholic Dictionary*, pp. 466–9.

35 Addis and Arnold, *Catholic Dictionary*, pp. 479–81; Châtellier, *The Religion of the Poor*, pp. 206–11; Delumeau, *Catholicism from Luther to Voltaire*, pp. 127, 113; Charles R. Bailey, 'The French clergy and the removal of the Jesuits from secondary schools, 1761–1762', *Church History*, 1979, vol. 48, pp. 305–39.

36 Châtellier, *The Religion of the Poor*, pp. 211–16; Stuart Clark, 'French historians and early modern popular culture', *Past and Present*, 1983, no. 100, p. 86; Delumeau, *Catholicism from Luther to Voltaire*, pp. 161–74.

37 J. A. Bergin, reviewing Bernard Bligny (ed.), *Le Diocèse de Grenoble* (1979) and Jacques Lovie (ed.), *Les Diocèses de Chambéry, Tarentaise et Maurienne* (1979), in *Journal of Ecclesiastical History*, 1981, vol. 32, pp. 361–2; Charles Dartigue, *Histoire de la Guyenne*, Que sais-je?, Paris, Presses Universitaires de France, 1950, p. 37; Emmanuel Le Roy Ladurie, *The Peasants of Languedoc*, trans. John Day, George Huppert (ed.), Urbana and Chicago, IL, London, Universty of Illinois Press, 1974, pp. 168–71; Natalie Zemon Davis, *Society and Culture in Early Modern France*, London, Duckworth, 1975, pp. 1–16; John McManners, reviewing Robert Sauzet, *Contre-Réforme et réforme catholique en Bas-Languedoc* (1979), *Journal of Ecclesiastical History*, 1981, vol. 32, pp. 360–1.

38 ibid.; J. H. M Salmon, reviewing P. J. S. Whitmore, *The Order of Minims in Seventeenth-Century France* (1967), in *Journal of Religious History*, 1969, vol. 5, pp. 274–7; Kevin C. Robbins, 'Municipal justice, urban police and the tactics of Counter-Reformation in La Rochelle, 1618–650', *French History*, 1995, vol. 9, pp. 273–93; Dartigue, *Histoire de la Guyenne*, pp. 104–05.

39 Vovelle, *Piété baroque*, pp. 540–1.

40 For the background to the Revolt of the Netherlands and of religion in the early modern Dutch Republic, see, for example Geoffrey Parker, *The Dutch Revolt*, London, Allen Lane, 1972; for the Union of Utrecht, H. H. Bowen, *The Low Countries in Early Modern Times*, London, Harper & Row, 1972, pp. 73–4; A. Th. van Deursen, *Plain Lives in a Golden Age: Popular culture, religion and society in seventeenth-century Holland*, trans. Maarten Ultee, Cambridge, New York, Port Chester, Melbourne, Sydney, Cambridge University Press, 1991, p. 290.

41 Albert Hyma, *The Christian Renaissance*, 2nd edn, Hamden, CN, Archon, 1965; E. F. Jacob, 'Gerard Groote and the beginnings of the "New Devotion" in the Low Countries', *Journal of Ecclesiastical History*, 1952, vol. 3, pp. 40–57; James D. Tracy, 'A Premature Counter-Reformation: The Dirkist government of Amsterdam 1538–1578', *Journal of Religious History*, 1983–4, vol. 13, pp. 150–67; van Deursen, *Plain Lives in a Golden Age*, pp. 283–4, 296.

42 van Deursen, *Plain Lives in a Golden Age*, pp. pp. 286–7, 294, 301; Mathieu G. Spiertz 'Priests and laymen in a minority church: The Roman Catholic Church in the

Northern Netherlands 1592–1686' in W. J. Sheils and Diana Wood (eds), *The Ministry: Clerical and Lay. Papers Read at the 1988 Summer Meeting and the 1989 Winter Meeting of the Ecclesiastical History Society, Studies in Church History*, vol. 26, Oxford, Basil Blackwell for the Ecclesiastical History Society, 1989, pp. 287–301; Th. Clemens, 'The restricted eschaton of the Dutch Roman Catholics in the seventeenth and eighteenth centuries' in Michael Wilks (ed.), *Prophecy and Eschatology. Studies in Church History*, Subsidia 10, Oxford, Blackwell, 1994, pp. 141–50.

43 van Deursen, *Plain Lives in a Golden Age*, pp. 291–4, 296; K. H. D. Haley, *The Dutch in the Seventeenth Century*, London, Thames and Hudson, 1972, pp. 84–99; see also J. L. Price, *Holland and the Dutch in the Seventeenth Century: The Politics of Particularism*, Oxford, Clarendon, 1994, Chapter 6; Spiertz, 'Priests and laymen in a minority church', pp. 287–301.

44 ibid; Delumeau, *Catholicism from Luther to Voltaire*, pp. 38–9; van Deursen, *Plain Lives in a Golden Age*, pp. 286, 294; F. C. Spooner, 'The European economy 1609–50' in J. P. Cooper (ed.), *The New Cambridge Modern History*, vol. IV, pp. 70–1.

45 Mari't Westermann, *The Art of the Dutch Republic 1588–1715*, The Everyman Art Library, London, Calmann and King, 1996, p. 23; Spiertz, 'Priests and laymen in a minority church', pp. 287–301; van Deursen, *Plain Lives in a Golden Age*, pp. 283–4.

46 Spiertz, 'Priests and laymen in a minority church', pp. 287–97; van Deursen, *Plain Lives in a Golden Age*, pp. 284–5.

47 van Deursen, *Plain Lives in a Golden Age*, p. 302; Clemens, 'The restricted eschaton of the Dutch Roman Catholics', pp. 141–50.

48 Geoffrey Parker, *Europe in Crisis 1598–1648*, Fontana History of Europe, General Editor J. H. Plumb, London, Fontana paperbacks, 1979, p. 303; Clemens, 'The restricted eschaton of the Dutch Roman Catholics, pp. 141–50; *Christelyke Onderwyzing of Verklaring en Uitbreiding van den Mechelschen Catechismus*, Antwerp, C. Stichter, 1787, pp. 10, 22, 26, 120–5, 170, 339, 376, 485–9: I am deeply grateful to my friend Edward Vanhoutte (Koninklijk Academie, Gent) for his great kindness in making the Catechism available to me.

49 Spiertz, 'Priests and laymen in a minority church', pp. 287–91; Simon Schama, *The Embarrassment of Riches: An Interpretation of Dutch Culture in the Golden Age*, London, Collins, 1987, p. 201; Peter Burke, 'Venice and Amsterdam in the Seventeenth Century', *Transactions of the Royal Historical Society*, fifth series, 1973, vol. 23, pp. 135–52.

50 Châtellier, *The Religion of the Poor*, pp. 21–2; E. H. Kossmann, 'The Low Countries' in Cooper (ed.), *The New Cambridge Modern History*, vol. IV, pp. 370–1; Guido Marnef, *Antwerp in the Age of the Reformation: Underground Protestantism in a Commercial Metropolis, 1550–1577*, trans. J. C. Grayson, The Johns Hopkins University Studies in Historical and Political Science, Baltimore, MD, and London, The Johns Hopkins University Press, 1996, p. 210.

6 The Catholic Reformation and the people

1 For a survey, see John Bossy, 'The character of Elizabethan Catholicism', *Past and Present*, 1962, No. 21, pp. 39–57.

2 John Bossy, *The English Catholic Community 1570–1850*, London, Darton, Longman & Todd, 1975, pp. 188–9; Michael Richards, 'Thomas Stapleton', *Journal of Ecclesiastical History*, 1967, vol. 18, pp. 187–99; Geoffrey Anstruther, OP, *The Seminary Priests: A Dictionary of the Secular Clergy of England and Wales 1558–1850*, 4 vols, vol. III. 1603–1715, Great Wakering, Essex, Mayhew-McCrimmon, 1976, p. 83.

3 A. F. Allison and D. M. Rogers, *The Contemporary Printed Literature of the English Counter-Reformation between 1558 and 1640*, Aldershot, Hants, Scolar Press, 1989, 1994; Ceri Sullivan reviewing Thomas H. Clancy, SJ, *English Catholic Books 1641–1700: A*

Bibliography, revised edn, in *Notes and Queries*, 1998, NS, Vol. 45, pp. 123–4; Michael J. Walsh, 'The publishing policy of the English College press at St Omer, 1608–1759' in Keith Robbins (ed.), *Religion and Humanism. Papers Read at the Eighteenth Summer Meeting and the Nineteenth Winter Meeting of the Ecclesiastical History Society, Studies in Church History*, vol. 17, Oxford, Basil Blackwell for the Ecclesiastical History Society, 1981, pp. 239–50; see also F. Blom, J. Blom, F. Korsten and G. Scott, *English Catholic Books 1701–1800*, Aldershot, Hants, Scolar Press, 1996: by the eighteenth century works such as Challoner's devotional classics were being distributed throughout an English-reading world, extending from Philadelphia to Preston.

4 Michael James Galgano, *Restoration Recusancy in the North West of England: A Social History, 1658–1673*, Unpublished PhD Thesis, Vanderbilt University, 1971, pp. 195–6; Gordon Huelin, 'Some early eighteenth-century Roman Catholic recusants', *Journal of Ecclesiastical History*, 1956, vol. 7, pp. 61–8; H. Aveling, 'Some aspects of Yorkshire Catholic recusant history' in G. J. Cuming (ed.), *Studies in Church History*, vol. IV *The Province of York*, Leiden, E. J. Brill, 1967, pp. 98–121; Edward M. Wilson, 'Spanish and English religious poetry in the seventeenth century', *Journal of Ecclesiastical History*, 1958, vol. 14, pp. 38–53; Dom Hugh Aveling, OSB, 'The marriages of Catholic recusants, 1559–1642', *Journal of Ecclesiastical History*, 1963, vol. 14, pp. 68–83.

5 J. A. Williams, 'Bishops Giffard and Ellis of the Western Vicariate, 1688–1715', *Journal of Ecclesiasical History*, 1964, vol. 15, pp. 218–28; Galgano, *Restoration Recusancy in the North West of England*, pp. 183–4; Anstruther, *The Seminary Priests*, vol. 3, pp. 19–20; Frank Tyrer, *An Account of the Recusancy of the Blundells of Crosby Family, and the Inhabitants of Little Crosby in Lancashire*, 3 vols, Lancashire Record Office (Preston) typescript, vol. 3, pp. 389–90; Lancashire Record Office, RCLa, acc 6361: 1, 2, 2b, 4, RCFe, 2:1, 4:2, RCEc, 1.

6 *The Dictionary of Welsh Biography Down to 1940*, Oxford, B. H. Blackwell, 1940, pp. 79–80, 857–8; A. F. Allison and D. M. Rogers, *A Catalogue of Catholic Books in English Printed Abroad or Secretly in England 1558–1640*, 2 parts, Biographical Studies, vol. 3, nos. 3, 4, Bognor Regis, The Arundel Press, 1956, part I, 147, 152, 167, 174, part II, p. 268.

7 J. F. McMillan, 'The root of all evil? Money in the Scottish Catholic mission in the eighteenth century' in W. J. Sheils and Diana Wood (eds), *The Church and Wealth. Papers Read at the 1986 Summer Meeting and the 1987 Winter Meeting of the Ecclesiastical History Society, Studies in Church History*, vol. 24, Oxford, Basil Blackwell for the Ecclesiastical History Society, 1987, pp. 267–82; Michael Mullett, *Catholics in Britain and Ireland, 1558–1829, Social History in Perspective*, Jeremy Black (ed.), Basingstoke, Hants., Macmillan, 1998, Chapter 2.

8 Nicholas Canny, 'Why the Reformation failed in Ireland: *une question mal posée*', *Journal of Ecclesiastical History*, 1979, vol. 30, pp. 423–50; K. Bottigheimer, 'The failure of the Reformation in Ireland: *une question bien posée*', *Journal of Ecclesiasical History*, 1985, vol. 36, pp. 196–207; for folk belief, see Raymond Gillespie, *Devoted People: Belief and Religion in Early Modern Ireland*, Social and Cultural Values in Early Modern Europe, Series Editor Paolo L. Rossi, Manchester and New York, Manchester University Press, 1997, esp. Chapter 8.

9 H. F. Kearney, 'Ecclesiasical politics of the Counter-Reformation in Ireland, 1618–1648', *Journal of Ecclesiastical History*, 1960, vol. 11, pp. 202–12.

10 Brian Ó Cuív, 'The Irish language in the early modern period' in T. W. Moody, F. X. Martin and F. J. Byrne, *A New History of Ireland*, 14 vols, Oxford, Clarendon, 1976–84, vol. III: *Early Modern Ireland, 1534–1691*, p. 534, 632; Nicholas Canny, 'The formation of the Irish mind: religion, politics and Gaelic Irish literature 1580–1750', *Past and Present*, 1982, No. 95, pp. 91–116.

11 William E. Addis and Thomas Arnold, *A Catholic Dictionary Containing Some Account of the Doctrine, Discipline, Rites, Ceremonies, Councils and Religious Orders of the Catholic Church,* 13th edn, London, Virtue, 1928, p. 487; James Brodrick, SJ, *The Origin of the Jesuits,* London, The Catholic Book Club, 1943, pp. 219–24; Louis Cognet, *Post-Reformation Spirituality,* trans. P. Hepburne Scott, Twentieth Century Encyclopedia of Catholicism, H. Daniel-Rops (ed.), vol. 41, New York, Hawthorne Books, 1959, pp. 36–51; Rowan Williams, *Teresa of Ávila,* Outstanding Christian Thinker Series, Editor Brian Davies, OP, London, Geoffrey Chapman, 1991, pp. 13–18, 26, 34–8.

12 Mary Elizabeth Perry, 'Beatas and the Inquisition in early modern Seville' in Stephen Haliczer (ed.), *Inquisition and Society in Early Modern Europe,* London and Sydney, Croom Helm, 1987, pp. 147–68; E. William Monter, *Frontiers of Heresy: The Spanish Inquisition from the Basque Lands to Sicily,* Cambridge, Cambridge University Press, 1990, pp. 42–3, 158–61; Gustav Henningsen, *The Witches' Advocate: Basque Witchcraft and the Spanish Inquisition 1609–1614,* Reno, NV, 1980, esp. Chapters 9 and 10.

13 Henry Kamen, 'Clerical violence in a Catholic Society: the Hispanic world' in W. J. Sheils (ed.), *The Church and War. Papers Read at the Twenty-First Summer Meeting and the Twenty-Second Winter Meeting of the Ecclesiastical History Society,* Studies in Church History, vol. 20, Oxford, Basil Blackwell for the Ecclesiastical History Society, 1983, pp. 201–16; Gillian T. W. Ahlgren, 'Negotiating sanctity: holy women in sixteenth-century Spain', *Church History,* 1995, vol. 64, pp. 373–88; Peter Burke, 'How to be a Counter-Reformation Saint' in Kaspar von Greyerz (ed.), *Religion and Society in Early Modern Europe 1500–1800,* London, Routledge, 1984, pp. 45–55; *A Journal of the Plague Year: The Diary of the Barcelona Tanner Miquel Parets,* trans. and ed. James S. Amelang, New York and Oxford, Oxford University Press, 1991, pp. 45–7.

14 Kamen, 'Clerical violence in a Catholic society', pp. 201–16.

15 H. E. Rawlings, 'The secularisation of Castilian episcopal office under the Habsburgs, *c.* 1516–1700', *Journal of Ecclesiastical History,* 1987, vol. 38, pp. 53–67.

16 H. Fulford Williams, 'The diocesan rite of the Archdiocese of Braga', *Journal of Eccesiastical History,* 1953, vol. 4, pp. 123–38; L. C. Taylor (ed.), *Luis de Camões, Epic and Lyric,* trans. Keith Bosley, Aspects of Portugal, Manchester, Carcanet Press in association with the Calouste Gulbenkian Foundation, 1990, pp. 43–4.

17 Howard Louthan, *The Quest for Compromise: Peacemakers in Counter-Reformation Vienna,* Cambridge Studies in Early Modern History, Sir John Elliott *et al.* (eds), Cambridge, New York and Melbourne, Cambridge University Press, 1997, pp. 2–5, 134, 156–7.

18 Parker, *Europe in Crisis,* pp. 53–4; Louis Châtellier, *The Religion of the Poor. Rural missions and the formation of modern Catholicism, c. 1500–c. 1800,* trans. Brian Pearce, Cambridge, Cambridge Univesity Press, Maison des Sciences de l'Homme, 1997, pp. 195–8; Eda Sagarra, *A Social History of Germany 1648–1914,* London, Methuen, 1977, pp. 108–9; Edmund Kern, 'Counter-Reformation sanctity; the Bollandists' *Vita* of Blessed Hemma of Gurk', *Journal of Ecclesiastical History,* 1994, vol. 45, pp. 412–34; W. R. Ward, ' "An Awakened Christianity": The Austrian Protestants and their neighbours in the eighteenth century', *Journal of Ecclesiastical History,* 1989, vol. 40, p. 53–73; David P. Daniel, 'Ecumenicity or orthodoxy: The dilemma of the Protestants in the lands of the Austrian Habsburgs', *Church History,* 1980, vol. 49, pp. 387–400.

19 Sagarra, *A Social History of Germany,* p. 109; Châtellier, *The Religion of the Poor,* pp. 210, 72–3, 68; E. D. Stoye, reviewing Albert Bruckner (ed.), 'Helvetia Sacra, VII', *Journal of Ecclesiastical History,* 1976, vol. 28, pp. 429–30; Jean Delumeau, *Catholicism between Luther and Voltaire,* trans. Jeremy Moiser, London, Burns & Oates, Philadelphia, PA, Westminster Press, 1977, p. 36.

20 Sagarra, *A Social History of Germany,* p. 128; Philip M. Soergel, *Wondrous in His Saints: Counter-Reformation Propaganda in Bavaria,* Studies on the History of Society and Culture, Victoria E. Bonnell and Lynn Hunt (eds), Berkeley and Los Angeles, CA, London, University of California Press, 1993, pp. 267, 158–61, Chapter 4; T. H. B.

Burrough, *South German Baroque: An Introduction Based on a Group of Ten Churches: Obermachtal, Weingarten, Ettal, Steinhausen, Wies, Birnau, Zwiefalten, Ottobeuren, Rott am Inn, Wiblingen*, London, Alec Tiranti, 1956, pp. 9–16, 18–21, 24–5, 26–8, plates 5, 20, 22, 24, 28, 29; Trevor Johnson, 'Holy fabrications: The catacomb saints and the Counter-Reformation in Bavaria', *Journal of Ecclesiastical History*, 1996, vol. 47, pp. 274–97; Helena Waddy Leppovitz, 'The industrialization of popular art in Bavaria', *Past and Present*, 1983, No. 99, pp. 88–122.

21 H. Jablonowski, 'Poland-Lithuania 1609–48' in J. P. Cooper (ed.), *The New Cambridge Modern History*, vol IV, *The Decline of Spain and the Thirty Years' War 1609–48/59*, Cambridge, Cambridge University Press, 1970, Chapter XIX, p. 590; Châtellier, *The Religion of the Poor*, 103–5; J. Uminski, 'The Counter-Reformation in Poland' in W. F. Reddaway *et al.* (eds), *The Cambridge History of Poland from the Origins to Sobieski*, Cambridge, Cambridge University Press, 1950, pp. 398–415; A. Brückner, 'Polish cultural life in the seventeenth century' in ibid., p. 561; Maria Domin-Jactikov (ed.), *Acta Nuntiaturae Polonae*, vol. XXXIV, *Opitius Pallavacini (1680–1688)*, vols II, 1681–5 VII 1681, Rome, Institutum Historicium Polonicum Romae, 1997, pp. 48–9, 261.

22 Euan Cameron, *The European Reformation*, Oxford, Clarendon, 1991, p. 331; Uminski, 'The Counter-Reformation in Poland', p. 403; Janusz Tazbir, 'The Polonisation of Christianity in the sixteenth and seventeenth centuries' in David Loades and Katherine Walsh (eds), *Faith and Identity in Christian Political Experience. Papers Read at the Anglo-Polish Colloquium of the British Sub-Commission of the Commision International d'Histoire Ecclésiastique Comparée 9–13 September 1986*, Studies in Church History, Subsidia 6, Oxford, Basil Blackwell for the Ecclesiastical History Society, 1990, pp. 117–35; Tadeusz Chrzanowski, 'A variety of religious architecture in Poland', ibid., pp. 161–71.

23 Two magisterial works by Oskar Garstein have surveyed Counter-Reformation efforts in Scandinavia: *Rome and the Counter-Reformation in Scandinavia. Jesuit Educational Strategy 1553–1662*, Studies in the History of Christian Thought, 46, Leiden, Brill, 1992, and *Rome and the Counter-Reformation in Scandinavia. The Age of Gustavus Adolphus and Queen Christina of Sweden 1622–1656*, Studies in Christian Thought, 47, Leiden, Brill, 1992; John Bossy, 'Catholicity and nationality in the north European counter-reformation' in Stuart Mews (ed.), *Religion and National Identity. Papers Read at the Nineteenth Summer Meeting and the Twentieth Winter Meeting of the Ecclesiastical History Society, Studies in Church History*, vol. 18, Oxford, Basil Blackwell, 1982, pp. 285–96; Uminski, 'The Counter-Reformation in Poland', p. 414.

24 Fernando Cervantes, 'The devils of Querétario: scepticism and credulity in late seventeenth-century Mexico', *Past and Present*, 1991, no. 130, pp. 51–69; W. R. Borah, 'Latin American 1610–60' in Cooper (ed.), *The New Cambridge Modern History*, vol. IV, Chapter XXIII.

25 Kenneth Mills, 'The limits of religious coercion in mid-colonial Peru', *Past and Present*, 1994, No. 145, pp. 84–121 (see also Inga Clendinnen, 'Disciplining the Indians: Franciscan ideology and missionary violence in sixteenth-century Yucatan', *Past and Present*, 1982, No. 94, pp. 27–48); Tristan Platt, 'Notes on the devil's cult among south Andean miners' in Jim Obelkevich *et al.* (eds), *Disciplines of Faith Studies in Religion, Politics and Patriarchy*, History Workshop Series, General Editor Raphael Samuel, London, New York, Routledge & Kegan Paul, 1987, pp. 245–58.

26 Henry Warner Bowden, 'Spanish mission, cultural conflict and the Pueblo revolt of 1680', *Church History*, 1975, vol. 44, pp. 217–28; Borah, 'Latin America 1610–60', p. 707.

27 Stephen Neill, *A History of Christian Missions*, The Pelican History of the Church: 6, General Editor Owen Chadwick, Harmondsworth, Penguin, 1971, p. 179; Laura Fishman, 'Claude d'Abbeville and the Tupinamba: problems and goals of French

missionary work in early seventeenth-century Brazil', *Church History*, 1989, vol. 58, pp. 20–35.

28 Fishman, 'Claude d'Abbeville', pp. 20–35; Geoffrey Treasure, *Seventeenth-Century France: A Study of Absolutism*, Garden City, NY, Anchor Books, 1967, pp. 116–17; Delumeau, *Catholicism from Luther to Voltaire*, pp. 74–6; Neill, *A History of Christian Missions*, pp. 200–02.

29 Kenneth Ballhatchet, 'The East India Company and Roman Catholic Missionaries', *Journal of Ecclesiastical History*, 1993, vol. 44, pp. 273–88; C. R. Boxer, 'The problem of the native clergy',in G. J. Cuming (ed.), *The Mission of the Church and the Propagation of the Faith. Papers Read at the Seventh Summer Meeting and the Eighth Winter Meeting of the Ecclesiastical History Society, Studies in Church History*, vol. 6, Cambridge, Cambridge University Press, 1970, pp. 85–105; Neill, *A History of Christian Missions*, pp. 180–3; Richard Gray, 'The Papacy and the Atlantic slave trade: Lourenço da Silva, the Capuchins and the decisions of the Holy See', *Past and Present*, 1987, No. 115, pp. 52–68.

30 A. J. R. Russell-Wood, *A World on the Move: The Portuguese in Africa, Asia and America 1415–1808*, Aspects of Portugal, Manchester, Carcanet in association wth the Calouste Gulbenkian Foundation, 1992, pp. 198–9; Delumeau, *Catholicism from Luther to Voltaire*, p. 62; Neill, *A History of Christian Missions*, pp. 183–7 .

31 *The Peregrination of Fernâo Mendes Pinto*, Aspects of Portugal, Manchester, Carcanet in association with the Calouste Gulbenkian Foundation and the Discoveries Commission, Lisbon, 1992, pp. 118–26; Jonathan D. Spence, *The Memory Palace of Matteo Ricci*, London, Boston, MA, Faber and Faber, 1985, p. 230 *passim*; Paul A. Rule, 'Jesuit and Confucian? Chinese Religion in the *Journals* of Matteo Ricci, SJ, 1583–1610', *Journal of Ecclesiastical History*, 1968–9, vol. 5, pp. 105–24; C. R. Boxer, *The Christian Century in Japan 1549–1650*, Berkeley and Los Angeles, CA, 1967, University of California Press, 1967, *passim*; *Deus Destroyed. The Image of Christianity in Early Modern Japan*, Harvard East Asian Monographs, 141, Cambridge, MA, and London, Harvard University Press for Harvard University Council on East Asian Studies, p. 305; Russell-Wood, *A World on the Move*, pp. 200–01; Delumeau, *Catholicism from Luther to Voltaire*, Chapter 4.

7 The Catholic Reformation and the arts

1 Peter N. Skrine, *The Baroque Literature and Culture in Seventeenth-Century Europe*, London, Methuen, 1978, p. 83 *passim*; Carl J. Friedrich, *The Age of the Baroque 1610–1660*, The Rise of Modern Europe, William L. Langer (ed.), New York, Harper & Row, Harper Torchbooks, The University Library, 1962, pp. 38, 68, Chapters 2 and 3; Oldrich J. Blazicek, *Baroque Art in Bohemia*, trans. Slavos Kadecka, Feltham, Middlesex, Paul Hamlyn, 1968, p. 48; Roloff Beny and Peter Gunn, *The Churches of Rome*, London, Weidenfeld and Nicolson, 1981, p. 186; J. P. Cooper, 'General Introduction' in Cooper (ed.), *The New Cambridge Modern History*, vol. IV *The Decline of Spain and the Thirty Years' War*, Cambridge, Cambridge University Press, 1970, p. 9; Edward Norman, *The House of God: Church Architecture, Style and History*, London, Thames and Hudson, 1990, p. 176.

2 Alberto Pratelli (ed. and intro.), *Architettura del Barocco da Vignola Concernente i Cinque Ordini. La 'Regola' del Vignola in una edizione de XVIII secolo*, Bologna, Editrice CLUEB, 1984, pp. xxiv, 14–15, 38–9, 22–3 and frontispiece; Edward Norman, *The House of God*, pp. 76, 217, plates 44–5; Blazicek, *Baroque Art in Bohemia*, p. 48; Beny and Gunn, *The Churches of Rome*, pp. 208, 255; John Bourke, *Baroque Churches of Central Europe*, London, Faber and Faber, 1978, pp. 89–91.

3 Joseph Connors, *Borromini and the Roman Oratory*, New York, The Architectural History Foundation, Cambridge, MA, and London, MIT Press, 1980, p. 3, plate 3; Friedrich, *The Age of the Baroque*, p. 70; Beny and Gunn, *The Churches of Rome*, p. 186.

4 Tancredi Carunchio, 'Ipotesi "barocche"' in Sebastiano Serli, Gianfranco Spagnesi and Mariello Fagiolo (eds), *Gian Lorenzo Bernini e l'architettura europea nel Sei-Settecento*, Rome, Istituto della Enciclopedia Italiana, 1983, p. 35; Christof Thones, 'Bernini architetto tra Palladio e Michelangelo' in ibid., pp. 105–34; Stefano Ray, 'Bernini e la tradizione architettonica del cinquecento romano' in ibid., pp. 13, 17; Klaus Güthlein, 'Bernini architetto e gli Spada: l'altare maggiore et la facciata di San Paolo a Bologna' in ibid., pp. 81–104; Norman, *The House of God*, p. 190; Beny and Gunn, *The Churches of Rome*, pp. 142–3, 145, 139–40, 244–5.

5 W. Chandler Kirwin, 'L'illusionismo del Baldacchino' in Spagnesi and Fagiolo (eds), *Gian Lorenzo Bernini*, pp. 53–80, plates 1, 2, 12; Michael Kitson, 'The age of baroque' in Bernard S. Myers and Trewin Copplestone (eds), *Landmarks of Western Art: Architecture, Painting and Sculpture*, Feltham, Middlesex, Hamlyn Publishing Newnes Books, 1985, pp. 627–8.

6 James S. Ackerman, 'The Gesù in the light of contemporary church design' in Rudolf Wittkower and Irma B. Jaffe (eds), *Baroque Art: The Jesuit Contribution*, New York, Fordham University Press, 1972, pp. 15–28; Wittkower and Jaffe (eds), *Baroque Art*, plates 15c, 14a; Beny and Gunn, *The Churches of Rome*, pp. 192, 267.

7 Wittkower, 'Problems of the theme', in Wittkower and Jaffe (eds), *Baroque Art*, pp. 4–5, 10; Bourke, *Baroque Churches of Central Europe*, pp. 30, 32–3, 119.

8 Wittkower, 'Problems of the theme', p. 10; Karl Rahner, SJ, and Paul Imhof, SJ, *Ignatius of Loyola*, trans. Rosaleen Ockenden, London, Collins, 1979, pp. 48–62, plates, 37, 48, 38, 45, 34, 36; Howard Hibbert, '*Ut picturae sermones*: the first painted baroque decorations in the Gesù' in Wittokower and Jaffe (eds), *Baroque Art*, pp.29–41.

9 Mary D. Garrard, *Artemesia Gentileschi: The Image of the Female Hero in Italian Baroque Art*, Princeton, NJ, Princeton University Press, 1989, plates 4, 8; Wittkower and Jaffe (eds), *Baroque Art*, plate 28; Michael E. Williams, 'Campion and the English Continental seminaries' in Thomas McCoog, SJ, *The Reckoned Expense: Edmund Campion and the Early English Jesuits. Essays in Celebration of the First Centenary of Campion Hall, Oxford (1896–1996)*, Woodbridge, Suffolk, The Boydell Press, 1996, pp. 293–4; Émile Mâle, *Religious Art From the Twelfth to the Eighteenth Century*, London, Routledge & Kegan Paul, 1949, p. 175.

10 Jonathan Brown, *The Golden Age of Painting in Spain*, New Haven and London, Yale University Press, 1991, plates 78, 62, 48, 47, pp. 50, 90–2; Myers and Copplestone (eds), *Landmarks of Western Art*, plate 50; for Cardano see *Dizionario Biografico degli Italiani*, Rome, Istituto della Enciclopedia Italiana, vol. 19, p. 760.

11 Brown, *The Golden Age of Painting in Spain*, pp. 12–14, 80–3, plates 6, 7, 3, 63, 24b, 138, 231.

12 Romeo de Maio, 'The Counter-Reformation and Painting in Naples' in Clovis Whitfield and Jane Martineau (eds), *Painting in Naples 1606–1705: From Caravaggio to Giordano*, London, Royal Academy of Arts in association with Weidenfeld and Nicolson, 1982, pp. 31–5; Mina Gregori, 'Caravaggio and Naples' in ibid., pp. 125–7; Peter Burke, 'The Virgin of the Carmine and the Revolt of Masaniello', *Past and Present*, 1983, No. 99, pp. 3–21.

13 William D. Howarth, *French theatre in the neo-classical era, 1550–1789*, Theatre in Europe: a Documentary History, General Editors Glynne Wickam *et al.*, Cambridge, New York, Melbourne, Cambridge University Press, 1997, pp. 11–12; George W. Brandt, *German and Dutch Theatre, 1600–1848*, Theatre in Europe, Cambridge, New York, Melbourne, Cambridge University Press, 1993, pp. 54–5.

14 Elida Maria Szarota, *Geschichte, Politik und Gesellschaft im Drama des 17 Jahrhunderts*, Bern, Munich, Francke Verlag, 1976, pp. 12–13; Curt von Faber du Fauv, *German Baroque*

Literature: A Catalogue of the Collection in the Yale University Library, New Haven, CT, Yale University Press, 1958, pp. 247ff.; Pierre Janelle, *The Catholic Reformation*, London, Open University Set Book, Bruce Publishing, Milwaukee, Collier-Macmillan, 1971, pp. 155–8.

15 A. Closs and W. F. Maitland (eds), *German Lyrics of the Seventeenth Century*, London, Gerland Duckworth, 1949, pp. 61–5; *Trivmphvs Jesv oft Godlücke Lof-Sangen Verciert met Gheestlijcke Liedekens ende dichten, tot voortganck vande Ionckheyt, recreatie voor de blygeestige: om daer te verdryven alle fabuleuse en lichtveerdighe weireltsche dichten*, Antwerp, Geeraerdt van Wolsschaten, 1633, pp. 12, 17, 19, 25, 26, 33, A3 *passim*: see the edition by Peter Roelens, and Edward Vanhoutte (who most generously made the original available to me), Leuven, Katholieke Universiteit, 1994; Benny de Cupere, *Of Seven Ways of Holy Love: An English Edition of the Middle Dutch Mystical Treatise by Beatrice of Nazareth, With an Historical Discussion*, unpublished MA thesis, University of Lancaster, 1997.

16 *Trivmphus Jesv*, 12, 15, 25, 27, A1-A2 *passim*; Roelens and Vanhoutte (eds), *Trivmphvs Jesv*, intro., pp. 3–6; J. Fr Michaud, *Biographie Universelle Ancienne et Moderne*, 45 vols, Paris, C. Desplaces and M. Michaud, 1854, reprinted Graz, Austria, Akademische Druck-u. Verlagsanstalt, 1968, vol. XXVI, p. 218.

17 Edward M. Wilson, "Calderón", in Edward M.Wilson and Duncan Moir, *The Golden Age of Spanish Drama 1492–1700*, A Literary History of Spain, General Editor R. O. Jones, London, Ernest Benn, New York, Barnes & Noble, 1971, pp. 85–7, 101–3, 110–11, 116; Philip Ward (ed.), *The Oxford Companion to Spanish Literature*, Oxford, Clarendon, 1978, pp. 85–7, 598–9, 353, 154, 263–4; Margret Greer, 'Bodies of power in Calderón: *El nuevo palacio del Retiro* and *El mayor encanto, amor*', in Peter W. Evans (ed.), *Conflicts of Discourse: Spanish Literature in the Golden Age*, Manchester and New York, Manchester University Press, 1990, pp. 145–65; Calderón de la Barca, *La Vida es Sueño y El Alcalde de Zalamea*, ed. Augusto Cortina, Clásicos Castellanos, Madrid, Espase-Calpe, 1964, pp. xxv–xxvi; Phyllis Hartnoll, *A Concise History of the Theatre*, London, Thames and Hudson in association with Book Club Associates, 1968, pp. 95–6.

18 Ward (ed.), *The Oxford Companion to Spanish Literature*, pp. 130, 393, 565; Tirso de Molina, *Damned for Despair*, intro., ed. and trans. Nicholas G. Round, Warminster, Wilts, Aris & Phillips, 1986, pp. xxxviii–xliv, 59–60.

19 Adolphe Coster, 'Baltasar Gracian, 1601–58', *Revue Hispanique*, 1913, pp. 447–8. The same kind of intrepid use of temporal material as an allegorical basis for spiritual descriptions characterised the English Protestant religious writer John Bunyan (1628–1688) whom Dr Skrine considers an artist with baroque affinities (Skrine, *The Baroque*, p. 159): in Part II of *The Pilgrim's Progress* (1684), for example, Bunyan has his character Matthew cured of stomach cramps by the application of the medicine of the flesh and blood of Christ: Michael A. Mullett, *John Bunyan in Context*, Studies in Protestant Nonconformity, editor Alan P. F. Sell, Keele, Keele University Press, 1996, pp. 258–9.

20 e.g., Josquin des Préz, 'Missa "L'Homme Armé"', Stereo Supraphon, Music Antiqua, Prague.

21 Tim Carter, *Music in Late Renaissance and Early Baroque Italy*, London, Batsford, 1992, pp. 13; 303, 103, 102, 104; Janelle, *The Catholic Reformation*, pp. 178–9; Richard Sherr, 'The performance of chant in the Renaissance and its interactions with polyphony' in Thomas Forrest Kelly (ed.), *Plainsong in the Age of Polyphony*, Cambridge Studies in Performance Practice, 2, General Editor Peter Williams, Cambridge, New York, Port Chester, Melbourne, Sydney, 1992, pp. 178, 182, 184–5.

22 Janelle, *The Catholic Reformation*, p. 180; Jerome Roche, *Palestrina*, Oxford Studies of Composers, No. 7, General Editor Colin Mason, London, New York, Toronto, Oxford University Press, 1971, pp. 7, 51; Carter, *Music in Late Renaissance and Baroque Italy*, pp. 105, 106.

23 Paolo Fabbri, *Monteverdi*, trans. Tim Carter, Cambridge, New York and Melbourne, 1994, pp. 9–10, 110–11, 114–15; Carter, *Music in Late Renaissance and Baroque Italy*, pp. 105, 228; Jerome Roche, 'Monteverdi and the prima *prattica*' in Denis Arnold and Nigel Fortune (eds), *The New Monteverdi Companion*, London and Boston, Mass., Faber and Faber, 1985, pp. 159–60.

Index